Social Studies in Elementary Education

John Jarolimek

Social Studies in Elementary Education

EIGHTH EDITION

Macmillan Publishing Company   NEW YORK

Collier Macmillan Publishers   LONDON

Editor: Robert Miller
Production Supervisor: Janice Marie Johnson
Production Manager: Richard C. Fischer
Text Designer: Natasha Sylvester
Cover Designer: Natasha Sylvester
Cover illustration: Istvan Nyari
Illustrations: Vantage Art, Inc.
This book was set in Zapf Book and Helvetica by Progressive Typographers, and
printed and bound by Von Hoffman.
The cover was printed by Von Hoffman.

Macmillan Publishing Company
866 Third Avenue, New York, New York 10022

Collier Macmillan Canada, Inc.

Library of Congress Cataloging-in-Publication Data
Jarolimek, John.
  Social studies in elementary education / John Jarolimek.—8th
ed.
      p.   cm.
  Bibliography: p.
  Includes index.
  1. Social sciences—Study and teaching (Elementary)   I. Title.
LB1584.J3 1990
372.8′3044—dc19   88-35586
ISBN 0-02-360541-3   CIP

Printing: 2 3 4 5 6 7   Year: 0 1 2 3 4 5 6

Preface

As the nation continues its search for quality education for its children and youth, a great deal of reform rhetoric focuses on the need to reorganize and restructure the social studies curriculum. Of course if the curriculum fails to give adequate attention to history, geography, economics, or law-related education, students can hardly be expected to know much about those subjects. Such problems, however, can be easily remedied, but when those subjects *are* included in the curriculum and students are *still* not learning them adequately, we are faced with a different and more complicated set of problems. Now we must look to what the teacher is doing—or is not doing—that is contributing to students' failure to learn. As we sort through the variables that account for a quality social studies program for students, we cannot escape the conclusion that it is the effectiveness of the teacher that is the critical ingredient. Accordingly, this book is designed to help the practitioner build professional knowledge and skills that are known to contribute to quality teaching.

Readers familiar with earlier editions of this book will notice a number of changes in the organization of the eighth edition. This edition begins with an orientation to the social studies curriculum, followed by a discussion of the basic subject matter and related skills, followed by planning and teaching processes. The logic of this arrangement is that one needs to have some sense of the content of the curriculum before getting involved in planning and teaching. For those instructors who prefer the reverse arrangement, they can simply change the order in which they have their students read Parts II and III of the book. This edition ends with a chapter that looks to the future of social studies, with a discussion of some of the persistent problems and challenges that face teachers of social studies now and in the years immediately ahead.

All earlier editions of this book included a chapter on instructional resources for social studies. This edition breaks with that tradition and integrates the treatment of learning and teaching resources in the context of the content throughout the book. Rather than having a separate section on computer use, for example, the reader will find that topic discussed in several places in the book where computer applications are appropriate. Other media are handled similarly.

The content and methods presented in this edition have been updated in terms of current and emerging trends and priorities. The present concern for value, moral, and character education suggested that the addition of a new chapter on that set of topics was warranted. Also, the renewed interest in and emphasis on the teaching of history and geography indicated that the treatment of those subjects should be placed in a new chapter, separate from the remaining social sciences. The middle school, bridging the grades 5 or 6 through 8, is gaining in acceptance, and, therefore, more attention is given to it in this edition. The main thrust of the book is on teaching in a self-contained classroom, which remains the preferred organizational arrangement for the elementary school and, in some modified form, for the middle school as well. Earlier editions of this book have been well received in the field and, in doing the revision, a conscientious effort has been made to preserve those features teachers have found attractive, practical, and useful in planning, teaching, and making sense of social studies.

Learning *about* teaching should never be too far removed from the actual practice of teaching. Thus, the study aids at the ends of chapters focus directly on classroom situations. In nearly all cases, the suggested activities require the reader to apply what is being studied by developing a product that could be useful in an actual classroom setting. Several sample lesson plans are included. The lists of selected references at the ends of chapters have been revised to include relevant current literature, in nearly all cases articles and books published within the past decade.

The author is indebted to a number of individuals and institutions for their cooperation and assistance and wishes to express thanks and appreciation to them: For prepublication reviews and helpful critiques of the manuscript: Professors Harvey A. Allen, University of South Carolina, Columbia, South Carolina; Rosanne Joyner, Missouri Southern State College, Joplin, Missouri; John H. Litcher, Wake Forest University, Winston-Salem, North Carolina; Ann Lockledge, University of North Carolina, Wilmington, North Carolina; and J. David Mohler and Paul Shaker, both of Slippery Rock University, Slippery Rock, Pennsylvania; for assistance with photograph procurement: Jocelyn Eckerman, The University of Texas Institute for Texan Cultures at San Antonio; Pat Flynn, Tacoma School District, Tacoma, Washington; Alberta Sebolt George, Old Sturbridge Village, Sturbridge, Massachusetts; Edna Kellman and Greg Bickel, Seattle Public Schools, Seattle, Washington; Terri Malinowski, Northshore School District, Bothell, Washington; and Sylvia Soholt and Judy Mix, Lake Washington School District, Kirkland, Washington; for the outstanding photography: those photographers whose names appear in the book in the credit line below their work.

The author also wishes to express sincere thanks and appreciation to his wife, Mildred Fleming Jarolimek, for her expert technical assistance in the preparation of the manuscript and in the production of the book.

J.J.

Contents

Part II   Social Studies Content and Content-Related Skills

Part III   Planning and Teaching the Social Studies   267

Part IV   A Look Ahead   421

List of Lesson Plans

I

Orientation to Social Studies Education

1

The Social Studies Curriculum

As this book is being published, we are precisely one decade from the turn of the century. Members of the high school graduating class of the year 2000 are second graders this year. During this decade, the Western Hemisphere nations will celebrate the 500-year anniversary of the first voyage of Columbus into the New World. These events invite speculation about life in the forthcoming century and about the kind of social studies programs that will be needed to equip citizens to live in those memorable years just ahead.

The elementary and middle school teachers of social studies need to have a sense of vision of the future for the children they teach. Users of this text will be teaching a part of the human family that is destined to be in charge of the affairs on this planet during the next six to eight decades. Seated in the classrooms of today's teachers are many children who, as senior citizens, will help this nation celebrate its Tricentennial anniver-

This photograph calls attention to the varied ethnic backgrounds of American schoolchildren today. Moreover, the demographic characteristics of the population of the United States are continuing to change in important ways. During the lifetimes of many of the children in this photograph, the percentage of the minority population of the nation will expand significantly, with a corresponding decrease in the percentage of whites. Even today minority enrollments in the fifteen largest school districts range from 70 to 96 percent. What implications do you see in these demographic trends for social studies education? (Photo by Edna Kellman, Seattle Public Schools.)

sary! This, of course, presumes that there actually will be such an event. Whether or not this nation survives to its Tricentennial and beyond depends in no small measure on how well the forthcoming generations of schoolchildren are instructed in the responsibilities of democratic citizenship. All of this is meant to suggest that teachers of elementary and middle school children have a heavy responsibility for the future of the children they teach and, indeed, for that of the nation.

Research from the behavioral sciences tells us that in large measure human beings *learn* to become who and what they are. One does not inherit the culture through genetic transmission; the culture has to be transmitted through teaching and learning from one generation to the next, or it is lost. It is significant that all human societies make provisions for the young to learn the social and cultural imperatives that characterize that society's particular way of life. In this way, the society perpetuates itself; it provides for social continuity. Through education, the individual becomes acquainted with the mainstream or common culture.

Life in modern societies is so complex and the need for knowledge and skills is so great that the family is simply not able to teach children and youth all that they need to know. Accordingly, schools assume a major responsibility for the transmission to the young of certain knowledge, skills, attitudes, and values that are deemed to be important. The entire school curriculum shares the responsibility for citizenship education, but social studies has historically occupied a unique role in contributing to that process.

A publication of the National Council for the Social Studies defines social studies as an important component of the school curriculum:

> Social studies is a basic subject of the K – 12 curriculum that (1) derives its goals from the nature of citizenship in a democratic society that is closely linked to other nations and peoples of the world; (2) draws its content primarily from history, the social sciences, and, in some respects, from the humanities and science; and (3) is taught in ways that reflect an awareness of the personal, social, and cultural experiences and developmental levels of learners.[1]

The major mission of social studies education is to help children learn about the social world in which they live and how it got that way; to learn to cope with social realities; and to develop the knowledge, attitudes, and skills needed to help shape an enlightened humanity. Social studies focuses specifically on citizenship education, which means learning to participate in group life. The outer edges of that participation for today's child is the global community.

In a democratic society based on individual freedom and citizen participation, citizenship education, and, therefore, social studies education, is directed toward the attainment of two quite different, and sometimes contradictory, ultimate ends. The first has to do with *socialization* and the other with *social criticism*. As a society, we have to depend on individual citizens to "do the right thing" most of the time. Through socialization, citizens internalize values and attitudes that cause them to behave willingly in accordance with prevailing expectations and norms. This is an essential requirement of orderly social life.

But citizenship in a free society also carries with it the obligation to be critical of the system itself, in order that basic rights and freedoms can be

---

[1] National Council for the Social Studies Task Force on Scope and Sequence, "In Search of a Scope and Sequence for Social Studies," *Social Education*, 48 (April 1984), p. 251.

sustained and extended to all citizens. The exercise of social criticism is crucial in a free society, in order to preclude the erosion of rights and civil liberties guaranteed all citizens by the Constitution and to prevent the unnecessary and illegal intrusion of government into the lives of citizens.

There is a fragile balance between teaching for socialization on the one hand and teaching for social criticism on the other. For example, we want citizens to respect the law, but we do not want them to be intimidated by the law or by those who enforce it; we want citizens to support elected officials, but we do not want them to follow blindly the leadership of demagogues. A major dilemma for a democratic society and for citizenship education in such a society is how to socialize children in ways that ensure social tranquility without repressing the necessary dissension that must, on occasion, be unpleasant and not socially acceptable.[2] The elementary and middle school teachers who sow the seeds of citizenship in the hearts and minds of children have a responsibility to keep these two dimensions of social studies education in proper balance.

GOALS FOR THE SOCIAL STUDIES

There are numerous goal statements for social studies education. The National Council for the Social Studies (NCSS) has issued statements that deal with the role of the social studies, as have many school districts and state departments of education. All of the fifty states require the teaching of certain elements of social studies. The following are typical examples of what is expected of social studies education:

Knowledge and Information Goals

Learning about

1. The world, its geography, its people, and their cultures.
2. The history, settlement, growth, and development of the United States.
3. The neighborhood, community, and home state; how people live and work there; how they meet their basic needs of life; how they interact and depend on each other.
4. The legal and political systems of the local community, the state, and the nation.
5. The world of work and an orientation to various careers.
6. Basic human institutions, such as the family.

[2] James P. Shaver, Professor and Associate Dean for Research, College of Education, Utah State University, Logan, Utah, discussed in correspondence with the author.

7. How people use and misuse the earth.
8. The problems and challenges that confront people today in the realm of social living and human relations in the local, state, national, and international arenas.
9. The basic social functions that characterize all societies such as producing, transporting, distributing, and consuming goods and services; providing for education, recreation, and government; protecting and conserving human and natural resources; expressing esthetic and religious drives; communicating with others.

Attitude and Value Goals

1. Knowing the common values of this society as defined in the historical documents of the republic, by laws of the land, by court decisions, and by the religious heritages of this country.
2. Being able to make decisions that involve choices between competing values.
3. Knowing the basic human rights guaranteed to all citizens.
4. Developing a reasoned loyalty to this country.
5. Developing a sense of respect for the ideals, the heritages, and the institutions of this nation.
6. Developing a feeling of kinship toward human beings everywhere.

Skills Goals

SOCIAL SKILLS

1. Living and working together; taking turns; respecting the rights of others; being socially sensitive.
2. Learning self-control and self-direction.
3. Sharing ideas and experiences with others.

STUDY SKILLS AND WORK HABITS

1. Using maps, globes, charts, graphs, and other graphic and pictorial materials.
2. Locating and gathering information from books, the library, and from a variety of other sources and special references.
3. Making reports; speaking before a group; listening when others are reporting; listening to and following directions.
4. Reading social studies materials for a variety of purposes, e.g., to get the main idea; to locate a particular point or fact; to predict outcomes; to detect author bias; to compare and contrast.
5. Organizing information into usable structures such as outlining; mak-

ing charts; making time lines; classifying pictures or data; arranging ideas, events, or facts in a sequence; taking notes; keeping records; and preparing summaries.
6. Conducting an inquiry on a problem of interest.

GROUP WORK SKILLS

1. Working cooperatively on committees and assuming various roles in small groups such as being chairperson, secretary, or group member.
2. Participating in a group discussion; leading a discussion.
3. Participating in group decision making.

INTELLECTUAL SKILLS

1. Defining and identifying problems; relating prior experiences to a present inquiry.
2. Forming and testing hypotheses; drawing conclusions based on information.
3. Analyzing and synthesizing data.
4. Thinking critically; distinguishing between fact and opinion; learning to separate relevant from irrelevant information and to recognize bias in persuasive materials such as advertising, political statements, and propaganda.
5. Sensing cause-and-effect relationships.
6. Comparing and contrasting differing points of view.
7. Recognizing the value components in decision making.

Creative thinking and problem solving are associated with the American ethos, and Americans have taken pride in being stereotyped as creative problem solvers. Accordingly, teaching procedures that are presumed to enhance thinking abilities of students have received a great deal of attention from educators in this century. One of the consistent goals of social studies education has been that of developing in children those attitudes and skills that enable them to be independent thinkers and problem solvers. This means, among other things, that children need to develop a healthy skepticism about things and events in the world. Good problem solvers have a curiosity about what they see going on around them. They develop a questioning attitude. They are adept at figuring out new ways of doing things.

The ultimate outcome of education is, of course, to prepare individuals to make decisions, to make judgments, and to lead lives that are qualitatively superior to those who are uneducated. This involves intellectual processes that we define by the summarizing term "critical thinking." The person who has had the advantage of education should be able to apply appropriate criteria in order to distinguish between what is true and what is not, what is better than something else, what enhances the human condition and what does not, and what is morally uplifting and what is not. These kinds of discriminations in quality are what schools and education are supposed to equip individuals to make. If there were no *qualitative* differences between the lives of persons who went to school and those who did not, society would do away with schools. This is not to suggest that schools are always successful in achieving such goals, only to emphasize that they must continue the effort. When social studies programs identify critical thinking as a goal toward which teachers should encourage children to strive, such programs are contributing to the overall, general goals of education.

Some goals are achieved through the encounters with subject matter whereas others are achieved through the *process* of the study itself. For example, to learn about the history of their country or the geography of the home state or about life in another culture, children must deal with the subject matter appropriate to those topics. On the other hand, to learn the skill of using the encyclopedia, children must be involved in the use of that reference. Similarly, to learn to inquire, they must engage in investigative searches. To learn group-work skills, they must be involved in group-work processes. Soundly based social studies programs build content and process learnings simultaneously. Much of social studies teaching is directed toward the achievement of more than one objective at the same time.

There is good teaching and poor teaching of social studies today, just as there always has been. A social studies program can be no better than the teacher who implements it. Nevertheless, it is possible to look at programs in terms of practices and procedures that have proven to be effective and are recommended by specialists in the field. Several qualities of such programs are summarized in Chart 1.

CHART 1. CHARACTERISTICS OF A GOOD SOCIAL STUDIES PROGRAM

1. The subject matter is drawn from history, geography, and a broad range of social sciences; from the humanities; and from the experiences of children.
2. A global perspective is apparent throughout, with attention to non-Western, non-Christian cultures as well as to those of the West.
3. Many learner-involving activities that call for active learner participation are used.
4. There is use of multiple instructional resources.
5. Application of what is learned is made to out-of-school settings through social participation.
6. Thinking is emphasized as a major concern of social studies; learners are provided many opportunities for creative and critical thinking and for decision making.
7. Pluralism is treated as a social reality at home and abroad, and the contributions of many cultures to humankind are emphasized.
8. A balanced effort is made in developing knowledge, skills, and beliefs and values.

9. Truthful pictures of social reality are provided, as are greater urban focus, more attention to changes due to science and technology, and speculation on the future.
10. Racism, sexism, and racial and sex-role stereotyping are constant concerns of the program.
11. Many options are available to the teacher in terms of various programs, texts, materials, and teaching strategies.

CURRICULUM CONTENT AND SEQUENCE

Although most elementary and middle schools include history and the social science disciplines in their social studies programs, they do not ordinarily conduct separate courses in geography, history, economics,

Social studies experiences can help young children understand and appreciate the various lifeways of the human family through direct contact with artifacts and people from cultures other than their own. Do you think resources needed to provide such experiences are available in most American communities? (Photo by Edna Kellman, Seattle Public Schools.)

political science, or the other social science disciplines. The usual organizational format is one that combines components from more than a single field to form an interdisciplinary study around some topic of interest. Significant subject matter from related disciplines is *infused* in the instructional program. For example, a sixth grade class might study the topic "Crossroads of Three Continents — The Middle East." In such a study, geography would be essential, as would history, economics, and government as well. Doubtless, too, religious concepts would be included because this area of the world was the birthplace of three of the world's major religions.

Most schools are introducing basic concepts from history and the social sciences and related disciplines in the early years of the elementary school although they may not always be labeled as such. When children are studying the local landscape, they are dealing in a simple way with geography. When they learn about the need for rules and laws, they are beginning to understand ideas from political science; and when they study about life in early times, they are having their first brush with history. It is not the purpose of the elementary school to teach the social science disciplines apart from their relevance to social reality. They should be taught in ways that will help children build an understanding of the social and physical world in which they live.

Children learn a great deal about social studies from their life outside of school through travel, television, and contact with adults. This applies not only to informational aspects of social studies but also to skills, values, attitudes, and beliefs. They learn values and skills from their families and from contact with other persons in their social worlds. Consequently, hardly anything encountered in the social studies program will be totally new to all children, perhaps not even to *any* children in some classrooms.

The social studies program should be built on what the child already knows. This means that, in introducing topics or units for study, the teacher will need to explore with the children the extent of their prior experiences with the subject. Social studies programs are then planned to build learnings sequentially year by year as each teacher assumes some responsibility for maintaining continuity in children's learning.

Each year there will be study units and topics that are consistent with the emphasis suggested by the district curriculum for that grade. Ordinarily, topics that are physically close to the child such as the school, family, neighborhood, and community are placed in the primary grades. Topics that are more remote in space and time, such as the home state, the nation, and foreign cultures, appear in the middle and upper grades. It should be noted, however, that newer programs expand the world of the child early and rapidly. For example, even in the primary grades it is not unusual to find children studying family life as it takes place in many parts of the world. Teachers often begin a study by focusing on aspects of a topic that are familiar to the children, such as their own homes, schools, and families; then the study is expanded to include those same institutions in other cultures. The movement from things that are close to those that are far away and back again is common in social studies programs today.

The content and sequence of social studies programs vary from place to place. Nevertheless, some common elements can be found in most elementary and middle school social studies programs.[3] Here are a few:

1. A global perspective is a prevailing theme in many programs. Exposure to the world beyond the immediate environment comes early in most programs and continues throughout the grades, with some apparent emphasis on the non-Western, non-Christian world.
2. Almost everywhere some attention is given to the study of the home state. Often this comes in grade four, but it is also found in grades six and seven.
3. Commonly, grades five and eight deal with the history of the United States.
4. Most programs incorporate aspects of current affairs, holiday observances, and local issues.
5. Many schools include topics of contemporary interest in their curriculum, such as law-related education, the world of work, environmental education, drugs and dangerous substances, energy, or economic education.
6. Most programs reflect an awareness of racism, sexism, and racial and sex-role stereotyping.
7. Greater numbers of schools allow and encourage teachers to explore alternatives and options to the regular program.
8. Research continues to show the strong influence of the textbook on social studies programs.[4]

Curriculum specialists often talk in terms of the "scope and sequence" of a social studies program. The "scope" of the program refers to the substantive content—the subject matter, skills, values, attitudes, and beliefs—that the program is to include. The "sequence" has to do with the order in which the various components are to be presented. In the 1980s there has been a revival of interest in scope and sequence documents at the state and local levels.[5] The National Council for the Social

---

[3] *National Survey Social Studies Education.* Sponsored by The Council of State Social Studies Specialists, an affiliate of the National Council for the Social Studies, (Washington, D.C., 1986).

[4] For a review of research on the extensiveness of textbook use, see John J. Patrick and Sharryl Davis Hawke, "Curriculum Materials," *Social Studies in the 1980s: A Report of Project SPAN,* Chap. 4, Irving Morrissett, ed. (Washington, D.C.: Association for Supervision and Curriculum Development, 1982), pp. 39–50.

[5] Wayne L. Herman, Jr., "Development in Scope and Sequence: A Survey of School Districts," *Social Education,* 52 (September 1988), pp. 385–388.

Studies named a task force to develop a scope and sequence that could be useful to local schools in building their social studies programs. The report of the task force was adopted by the council as a preliminary position statement on scope and sequence. The task force's report suggested the following scope and sequence for the K–12 grades:

RECOMMENDATIONS OF THE NCSS TASK FORCE ON SCOPE AND SEQUENCE

Kindergarten — Awareness of Self in a Social Setting
Grade   1 — The Individual in Primary Social Groups: Understanding School and Family Life
Grade   2 — Meeting Basic Needs in Nearby Social Groups: The Neighborhood
Grade   3 — Sharing Earth-Space with Others: The Community
Grade   4 — Human Life in Varied Environments: The Region
Grade   5 — People of the Americas: The United States and Its Close Neighbors
Grade   6 — People and Cultures: The Eastern Hemisphere
Grade   7 — A Changing World of Many Nations: A Global View
Grade   8 — Building a Strong and Free Nation: The United States
Grade   9 — Systems That Make a Democratic Society Work: Law, Justice, and Economics
Grade 10 — Origins of Major Cultures: A World History
Grade 11 — The Maturing of America: United States History
Grade 12 — One-year course or courses required; selection(s) to be made from the following:

> Issues and Problems of Modern Society
> Introduction to the Social Sciences
> The Arts in Human Societies
> International Area Studies
> Social Science Elective Courses: Anthropology, Economics, Government, Psychology, Sociology
> Supervised Experience in Community Affairs
> Local options[6]

The report also provides three optional programs for grades six through twelve.

The National Council encouraged a continuing dialog among professionals on the subject of scope and sequence throughout the 1980s. It solicited and presented five "alternative" scope and sequence proposals

---

[6] NCSS Task Force, op. cit.

at the annual meeting of the Council in 1986. These were published in *Social Education.*[7]

What follows is a list of *representative examples* of topics and units taught at the grade levels indicated in schools across the nation. The examples should *not* be construed as a model curriculum. What is represented here will not be precisely the same as that found in any particular school program; the teacher will need to consult local curriculum sources to find out what is required.

EXAMPLES OF UNIT TOPICS FOR EACH GRADE LEVEL

Kindergarten Kindergarten programs ordinarily deal with topics that help to familiarize children with their immediate surroundings. The home and school provide the setting for these studies. With some kindergarten children it is possible to include, in a simple way, references to the world beyond the immediate environment.

Learning About Myself
Rules for Safe Living
Learning How My Family Buys Goods and Services
Working Together at School
Continents and the Globe
People Change the Earth

Grade One Grade-one studies are based in the local area, such as the neighborhood, but provision is often made to associate the local area with the larger world. A major criticism of first-grade units in particular and primary units in general has been that they have tended to be too confining and that their content has been thin. Units should provide for easy transition from the near-at-hand to the faraway and back again at frequent intervals — when it is established that the backgrounds of children warrant such movement. Neighborhood and community services can be stressed in this grade.

The Shopping Center
Families at Work
Great Americans
A Japanese Family (comparative study)
Scarcity and Demand
Families: Size and Structure
Families and Their Needs
Dividing the Work

Grade Two The grade-two program provides for frequent and systematic contact with the world beyond the neighborhood. Through the study of transportation, communication, food distribution, and travel, the children begin to learn how their part of the world is connected to other places on earth.

[7] Donald H. Bragaw and others, "Scope and Sequence: Alternatives for Social Studies," *Social Education,* 50 (November–December 1986), pp. 484–542.

Suburban Neighborhoods
Transportation and Communication: Our Links to the World
Rural and Urban Communities
Where and How We Get Our Food
People Work Together in Communities
How Neighborhoods Change

Grade Three The grade-three program often emphasizes the larger community concept: what a community is, types of communities, why some communities grow though others do not, how communities provide for basic needs. Many programs include an outside community for purposes of comparison. Schools are giving a great deal of attention to the large, urban community at this grade level.

Our City's Government
Food for the Community
Keeping Cities up-to-date — Change
Communities at Home and Abroad (comparative cultures study)
Life in Early American Settlements
Why a City Is Where It Is
The Parts of a City
Natural Surroundings and People's Actions

Grade Four In grade four the world as the home of people, showing various geographical features of the earth along with variety in ways of living, is often stressed. These studies help children understand some of the adaptive and innovative qualities of human beings. Home-state studies are popular in grade four; often they are included to meet legislative requirements. Comparative studies are commonly recommended.

Historical Growth and Change of the Home State
The Pacific Northwest (regional study)
Deserts of the World (regions)
Others Who Share Our World (comparative cultures study)
Kenya and Its African Neighbors (comparative study)
India, a Society in Transition (comparative study)
Regions Make a World

Grade Five Almost everywhere the fifth-grade program includes the geography, history, early development, and growth of the United States. The program may focus on the United States alone or on the United States and Canada or on the United States, Canada, and Latin America. The latter option makes the fifth-grade program a heavy one. The fifth-grade emphasis should be coordinated with the eighth and eleventh grades in order to avoid repetitive treatments.

Founding of the New World
The Native Americans
The Making of Our Nation
The War Between the States
An Early American Mining Community
History of the Great Plains
Completion of National Expansion
One Nation; Many Heritages

Grade Six The sixth-grade program may include the study of Latin America and Canada or of cultures of the Eastern Hemisphere. Both of these patterns are in common use. A major limitation of sixth-grade programs is that they attempt to deal with too many topics. Often this results in a smattering of exposures without developing significant depth of understanding. The same criticism applies to the seventh grade. Stronger programs emerge where teachers carefully select a few units that are representative of basic concepts that have wide and broad applicability. For example, a class need not study all the Third World nations in order to gain some understanding of the problems of newly developing countries.

Western Hemisphere Emphasis
Cooperation in the Americas
The Prairie Provinces
Three Inca Countries
The Saint Lawrence Seaway and Its Effect on Canadian Growth
The Organization of American States

Eastern Hemisphere Emphasis
Ancient, Classical, and Medieval Civilizations
The Birthplace of Three Religions
The U.S.S.R. and Eastern Europe in Recent Times
Great Discoveries
The Renaissance and Reformation
Empires and Revolutions
The People's Republic of China

Grade Seven The nature of the seventh-grade program depends on the content of grade six. Either Latin America or culture regions of the Eastern Hemisphere are popular choices for this grade. Some schools are developing exciting programs in anthropology in grade seven. World geography is also included in some districts as are studies of the home state.

Rise of Modern Civilization
Africa: Yesterday, Today, and Tomorrow
The Home State
Challenges of our Times
World Resources: Who Has Them? Who Uses Them?
The Age of Technology—Its Effects on People
Environmental Problems
Principles of Geography
A Look at Tomorrow: The Future

Grade Eight The study of the United States and of the American heritage is widespread in grade eight. The program usually stresses the development of American political institutions and the development of nationality. The approach typically consists of a series of units arranged chronologically. The fifth and eleventh grades also include elements of American history. Defining the emphasis for each of these grades and differentiating appropriately among them in terms of content and approach is necessary in order to avoid unwarranted duplication in the three grades.

Old Nations in the New World
A Free and Independent Nation
A Strong and Expanding Nation
A Divided Nation
Birth of an Industrial Giant
A World Power in the Space Age

SOCIAL STUDIES AND THE COMMON CULTURE

The education of children always assumes that they are being prepared for some kind of social context as adults. Teachers prepare children for adult statuses and roles that are at the present time unknown. The mental images that teachers have of the future are usually an extension of the world of today; that is, we assume that children will need about the same knowledge and skills in the future that the adults of today need. Futurists have repeatedly called attention to the limitations of such assumptions. In a world in which change seems to be the only reliably predictable constant, teachers of social studies are still expected to engender in children a strong attachment to those traditional beliefs and values that have characterized this nation from its beginning — liberty, justice, equality, human dignity.

It is in the social studies that the public purposes of education can be best served. Through social studies, teachers have a major responsibility to help children learn those components of the *common* culture that constitute the social and cultural heritage of this nation. It is these learnings that acquaint citizens with the rituals of our culture and give us a sense of identity as a nation of free people. These ideas have always been important to social studies education but have recently received widespread public attention because of interest in *cultural literacy,* a concept that has been widely discussed in educational circles since the publication of a popular book dealing with that subject.[8]

From an intellectual and philosophical perspective, most teachers can be convinced of the importance of social studies as related to the education of citizens. Many would agree that unless we are able to sustain ourselves as a strong and free people, little else is of much consequence. But there are many demands placed on elementary and middle school teachers today that preempt instructional time. Chief among these is the continued public concern for teaching the basic skills. Thus, in the day-to-day work of the elementary and middle school teacher, it becomes easy to set social studies aside and not give it the attention that specialists tell us it should have.

With the renewed interest in patriotism and civic education that emerged in the 1980s, the challenge to elementary school teachers is to give increased attention to social studies education while, at the same time, not neglect important instruction in the basic skills. Teachers will need to rediscover ways to teach more of the reading, writing, speaking, and listening skills along with some of the art, music, and drama, in connection with social studies. In this way, teachers can use social studies

---

[8] E. D. Hirsch, Jr., *Cultural Literacy: What Every American Needs to Know,* (Boston: Houghton Mifflin Company, 1987).

as the integrating center for the curriculum, and, by their doing so, the other subjects and skills as well as social studies will be well served. The specifics as to how this can be done will be developed in the succeeding chapters.

DISCUSSION QUESTIONS AND SUGGESTED ACTIVITIES

1. Try to recall two or three specific things you learned when you were in the elementary or middle school that would fit in each of the three sets of goals presented in this chapter. Are these things still worth learning by children in school today? Why or why not?

2. Using the list of goals in this chapter, write a one-sentence explanation of the purposes of elementary and middle school social studies.

3. The text stresses the importance of teaching for more than one objective at the same time. In each of the following situations, identify at least one additional objective that could be achieved concurrently.
   a. First grade: Children are learning how the local environment changes in appearance with the seasons.
   b. Third grade: Children are learning how goods and people are moved in and out of their community.
   c. Fifth grade: Children are learning the major geographical features of North America.

4. The education codes of most states stipulate the amount of time that is to be spent on social studies each week. This might be expressed in clock hours per day, per week, days per week or term, or some other standard unit of measure. These minimum time requirements are usually different for primary, intermediate, and upper grades. Check local sources to find out if there are such requirements, and, if so, what they are.

5. Decide when in the day's schedule you would prefer to teach social studies and provide a rationale for your choice.

6. Examine the list of skills on pages 7–8. Which of these skills are also included in other areas of the school curriculum, and which ones fall entirely within the social studies? Suggest ways that social studies and other curriculum areas might be combined for purposes of instruction in skills.

7. Visit the educational materials collection in your campus library, and examine a few social studies curriculum guides from school systems throughout the country. Include the curriculum guides for your state and community. Indicate the extent to which these documents incorporate ideas discussed in this chapter.

8. Study the scope and sequence of a major publishing company's social studies textbook series. To what extent does the program reflect the characteristics identified in Chart 1?

9. What are your views concerning the relative emphasis that should be given to *socialization* as opposed to *social criticism* at the elementary or middle school level? Provide examples of teaching practices that would encourage one or the other of these two thrusts of social studies education.

10. Examine the recommendations of the NCSS Task Force on Scope and Sequence listed on page 13. If you had the responsibility of designing a scope and sequence, which topics would you include that are not on the task force list? Which topics on the task force list would you not include in your scope and sequence? Are there topics you would place in a different grade? Explain.

11. What advantages and limitations are there in a national professional association issuing a position statement on scope and sequence?

12. Become familiar with the magazines *Social Education, Social Studies and the Young Learner, The Social Studies, Instructor, Learning: The Magazine for Creative Teaching,* and *Early Years.* Learn what they have to offer the teacher in the social studies. Locate one or more teaching ideas from these journals, and make plans to apply them in a classroom.

13. Talk to your instructor and/or your supervising teacher about local and state councils for social studies. Arrange to attend one of their meetings.

SELECTED REFERENCES

ATWOOD, VIRGINIA A., ed. *Elementary School Social Studies: Research as a Guide to Practice.* NCSS Bulletin No. 79. Washington, D.C.: National Council for the Social Studies, 1986. Chapter 1.

BRAGAW, DONALD H., AND H. MICHAEL HARTOONIAN. "Social Studies: The Study of People in Society." *Content of the Curriculum,* Ronald S. Brandt, ed. ASCD Yearbook. Alexandria, Virginia: Association for Supervision and Curriculum Development, 1988. Chapter 2.

BUTTS, R. FREEMAN. *The Revival of Civic Learning: A Rationale for Citizenship Education in American Schools.* Bloomington, Indiana: Phi Delta Kappa Educational Foundation, 1980.

CORNBLETH, CATHERINE, ed. *An Invitation to Research in Social Education.* NCSS Bulletin No. 77. Washington, D.C.: National Council for the Social Studies, 1986.

GROSS, RICHARD E., AND THOMAS L. DYNNESON. *What Should We Be Teaching in the Social Studies?* Fastback No. 199. Bloomington, Indiana: Phi Delta Kappa Educational Foundation, 1983. (53 pp.)

HARTOONIAN, H. MICHAEL. "The Social Studies: Foundation for Citizenship in Our Democratic Republic." *The Social Studies*, 76 (January–February 1985), pp. 5–8.

HEPBURN, MARY A., ed. *Democratic Education in Schools and Classrooms*. NCSS Bulletin No. 70. Washington, D.C.: National Council for the Social Studies, 1983.

KALTSOUNIS, THEODORE. *Teaching Social Studies in the Elementary School: The Basics for Citizenship*, 2nd ed. Englewood Cliffs, New Jersey: Prentice-Hall, Inc., 1987. Chapter 3.

LEVY, TEDD, ed., AND WILLIAM M. ALEXANDER, CONRAD F. TOEPFER, JR., MICHAEL G. ALLEN, JOHN H. LOUNSBURY, AND BILL HONIG. "Making a Difference in the Middle." *Social Education*, 52 (February 1988), pp. 104–122. (A special section of six articles on social studies in the middle school.)

MICHAELIS, JOHN U. *Social Studies for Children*, 8th ed. Englewood Cliffs, New Jersey: Prentice-Hall, Inc., 1985. Chapter 1.

National Council for the Social Studies Position Statement. "Essentials of the Social Studies." *Social Education*, 45 (March 1981), pp. 162–164.

———. "Revision of the NCSS Social Studies Curriculum Guidelines" and "How to Use the Guidelines for Social Studies Needs Assessment." *Social Education*, 43 (April 1979), pp. 261–278.

PARKER, WALTER, AND JOHN JAROLIMEK. *Citizenship and the Critical Role of the Social Studies*. NCSS Bulletin No. 72. Published jointly by Washington, D.C.: National Council for the Social Studies, and Boulder, Colorado: ERIC Clearinghouse for Social Studies/Social Science Education, Social Science Education Consortium, 1984.

2

Teaching Content and Content-Related Skills

In this and the succeeding chapter we will examine teaching procedures that are used to achieve the major social studies goals discussed in Chapter 1. Because the subject matter provides the intellectual focus for the study of topics, we address content and content-related skills first. Then, in Chapter 3, strategies used for value, moral, and character education will be presented.

Teaching looks deceptively easy when one observes a master doing it. Everything seems to happen in an unhurried, deliberate way. The transactions between teacher and learners exude a feeling of confidence and assurance. Watching such a teacher, the observer might think, "Anyone could do that!" And, interestingly enough, the more skillful the teacher, the easier the process appears to be. It is only when the beginner attempts to emulate the teaching behavior of the master teacher that the complexity of teaching becomes apparent.

Middle school students from Seattle experience sheep shearing on a firsthand basis at a local fair. The photograph underscores the importance of direct experience in learning the meaning of concepts. These students could not possibly have gained the same level of understanding of concepts related to this process by reading about it in the classroom. What is more, these students will be able to read accounts about it with greater comprehension after having had this direct experience. Good teaching of social studies provides for a balance in both types of learning opportunities. (Photo by Greg Bickel, Seattle Public Schools.)

How one goes about teaching should have something to do with the nature of what is to be learned. For instance, many skills require children to participate actively on a firsthand basis in the process of learning them. Group work skills are of this type; no amount of reading about group work skills or listening to someone explain them will make the learner proficient in their use. On the other hand, if one wants to learn about

European settlements in the New World, reading might be the best way to achieve that objective.

How one goes about teaching should also have something to do with the characteristics of the person doing the learning. A well-presented series of technical, lengthy lectures on the Westward Movement, for example, might be wholly appropriate for a college course in American history. But no matter how well they are presented, such lectures would be inappropriate for fifth-graders studying the same topic; we can do some things with some groups that we cannot do with others.

The techniques and strategies used in teaching social studies, therefore, have to be considered in terms of the goals of the program, the objectives to be achieved, and the maturity of the learners. If we want children to gain information, this can be achieved through reading, viewing, discussing, and other procedures that involve the transmission of information. These are referred to as *expository* teaching strategies. If we want children to develop critical habits of thought, to search for information independently, to be able to form hypotheses and test them, we use *inquiry* teaching strategies. If we want children to learn to work with each other, to plan together, or to apply what they are learning as they are learning it, we would use *activity* teaching strategies. *Demonstration* strategies can be a part of any of the others and would be used to improve the communication process through showing, doing, and telling. What is called discovery learning is a variation of inquiry. Various modes of teaching are discussed in detail in other sources.[1]

Beginning teachers are usually most comfortable starting with an expository strategy. The teaching situation can be controlled sufficiently well to reduce management concerns to a minimum, the objectives can be made specific, the children's study materials can be preselected by the teacher, and the process can be entirely teacher-directed. First encounters with teaching social studies should be short — 20- to 30-minute episodes — and involve teaching a simple concept or skill. This initial teaching experience might be based on the textbook, with heavy reliance on the suggestions presented in the teacher's manual that accompanies the book. After a few experiences of this type, the novice will have gained some confidence in the teaching role, will know how to evaluate responses, and can begin to add variations, such as increased use of visual material, discussion questions, and follow-up activities.

Having achieved a backlog of successful experiences in the expository mode, the teacher might plan a demonstration. Some aspects of map or globe use would serve well for this purpose. Follow-up work to the demonstration might be individualized, by giving children some choice

---

[1] John Jarolimek and Clifford D. Foster, *Teaching and Learning in the Elementary School*, 4th ed. (New York: Macmillan, 1989), pp. 117 – 138.

A teacher can make good use of multimedia and involve students actively in the learning process even in what is basically an expository teaching mode, as is illustrated by this photograph. This type of direct teaching is often effective in achieving objectives that deal with gaining information and knowledge of subject matter. (Photo by John Ringler, Tacoma School District.)

in what they will do. This can be succeeded by a class discussion of the individual follow-up activities.

While doing this type of rather formal teacher-directed expository teaching, the teacher will ask informational questions requiring children to do little more than recall what they have read or observed. The teacher is not concerned with much beyond the literal comprehension of what has been taught. With increased experience and confidence, the teacher should begin asking some questions that require other intellectual operations, such as interpretation, analysis, synthesis, or application. These reflective questions should not be ones that can be answered by recalling factual information but should require children to respond to such queries as "Why?" "How do you know?" "If that happened, how do you explain . . .?" "Can you summarize . . .?" "What conclusion can we come to?" "What other problems does that raise?"

These questions will gradually lead the teacher and the class away from exposition and in the direction of inquiry. In time, children will be raising questions and problems themselves and will speculate about their solutions. These hunches will be converted into hypotheses that result in searches for information, which will necessitate the wide use of resources, individualized assignments, and a variety of interesting learning activities. At this stage the teacher is well on the way to developing professional maturity in the use of teaching techniques and strategies in social studies.

TEACHING CONCEPTS AND GENERALIZATIONS

In everyday parlance, the term *concept* is used to mean *idea*, as when someone says, "My concept of leisure is not the same as yours." In social studies, a concept may also be thought of as an idea expressed as a word, term, or phrase. Social studies concepts often embody an extensive meaning that develops with experience and learning over a period of years. Let us explore in some detail the meaning and implications of concepts for teaching and learning social studies.

The Nature of Concepts

If asked to tell what a village is, most adults would probably say something along this line: "A village consists of a group of persons living in a rural area in a cluster of homes smaller than a city or a town." For most purposes this is an adequate definition to make communication possible. But *village* had a much more elaborate meaning for the Indians of British Columbia, as explained in Margaret Craven's novel *I Heard the Owl Call My Name.* On the boat trip north, the young priest, Mark Brian, recalls what his bishop had told him about the village:

> The Indian knows his village and feels for his village as no white man for his country, his town, or even for his own bit of land. His village is not the strip of land four miles long and three miles wide that is his as long as the sun rises and the moon sets. The myths are the village and the winds and the rains. The river is the village, and the black and white killer whales that herd the fish to the end of the inlet the better to gobble them. The village is the salmon who comes up the river to spawn, the seal who follows the salmon and bits off his head, the bluejay whose name is like the sound he makes—"Kwiss-kwiss." The village is the talking bird, the owl, who calls the name of the man who is going to die, and the silver-tipped grizzly who ambles into the village, and the little white speck that is the mountain goat on Whoop-Szo.

The fifty-foot totem by the church is the village, and the Cedar-man who stands at the bottom holding up the eagle, the wolf and the raven! And a voice said to the great cedar tree in Bond Sound, "Come forth, Tzakamayi and be a man," and he came forth to be the Cedar-man, the first man-god of the people and more powerful than all others.[2]

This is a superb example of a concept because it illustrates so well the richness and depth of meaning that can inhere in a single word label. It also illustrates how vital experience is in developing such meanings. It is doubtful if anyone who did not actually grow up in the village culture of these Indians could understand and appreciate the full meaning of *village* as they conceptualize it. Yet the novelist does very well in conveying the meaning by skillfully building word images for us of things that are familiar because they come out of our own background of experience.

Concepts are sometimes described as abstract categories of meanings. They are abstract because they are removed from specific instances. For example, *island* is the word label for a geographic phenomenon consisting of land completely surrounded by water. Kauai is one specific example of such a set of conditions. There are thousands of other specific examples of the concept *island*. But to know that Kauai is an island (that is, a body of land completely surrounded by water) is not to know very much about that beautiful outcropping of land in the Pacific. To early Hawaiians, Kauai had a meaning closely akin to that of village to the Pacific Northwest Indians described earlier. Concept definitions, therefore, tell us only about those qualities or attributes that a group of examples *has in common.* They do not tell us about the unique features of particular examples.

The human intellect makes use of this system of classifying, categorizing, and organizing the vast amount of specific knowledge with which it deals. Trees having certain attributes are *evergreen;* others having other attributes are *deciduous.* Some groups of animals are known as *mammals;* others, as *reptiles;* and others, as *birds.* A certain form of government is called a *democracy;* another, an *autocracy.* This ability and inclination to classify perceptions of reality into groups having common qualities is what is meant by conceptual thought. Conceptual thought makes it possible to manipulate reality intellectually; that is, one can figure out complex problems "in one's head." This is a distinctly human quality.

Concepts *always* have to do with meanings; words are simply their labels. Animals can be taught to respond to words and some can be taught to speak words. But they can never conceptualize the meanings for

---

[2] From *I Heard the Owl Call My Name,* Copyright © 1973 by Margaret Craven. Reprinted by permission of Doubleday, a division of Bantam, Doubleday, Dell Publishing Group, Inc.

which the word is a referent. Concepts may deal with concrete places, objects, institutions, or events such as these:

mountain	flood	valley
plateau	dairy	ocean
home	island	Chinese
country	famine	harbor
state	community helpers	desert
producer	political party	consumer goods

Concepts may also be more or less abstract ways of thinking, feeling, and behaving, such as these:

adaptation	freedom	responsibility
democracy	justice	cooperation
tolerance	fairness	rights
honesty	liberty	equality
loyalty	interdependence	conflict
culture	free enterprise	legal system

The meanings of these concepts can be developed by description or by definition, providing the descriptions or definitions or both are rooted in the experiences of the learner — that is, in something that is already known. This means that if we are to develop new concepts or extend the meanings of those partially understood, it is critical to link them to prior experience and knowledge.

Social studies material is literally loaded with concepts. The following paragraph was selected from a fifth-grade social studies textbook. The concepts have been italicized here to call attention to them:

> In the *Chicago area* many *foodstuffs* are prepared for *market*. Corn is made into all kinds of *corn products*. Chicago is the *center* for this *industry*. It is also a busy *grain market*. Chicago leads all of our *cities* in the *manufacture* of *farm machinery*. It is also an important *iron and steel center*. Chicago's position on the Great Lakes provides cheap *transportation* for bringing *raw materials* to its *factories*. The *finished products* can also be shipped out cheaply to all parts of the world.[3]

If one tries to simplify this paragraph by substituting alternate words for those that are italicized, one finds that it cannot be done and still convey the same meaning. This example illustrates that concepts carry much of the meaning of social studies.

[3] Allen Y. King, Ida Dennis, and Florence Potter, *The United States and the Other Americas* (New York: Macmillan, 1987), p. 333.

The Nature of Generalizations

Let us return to the village concept cited earlier and ask the question: What can we say about the relationship between the village and the people who live there? Several things could be said, of course, but the following will serve our purpose:

The village embraces the total culture of traditional Pacific Northwest Indians.

This statement expresses a relationship between the concepts *village* and *culture*. Such relationships are called *generalizations* and are expressed as declarative statements. Because generalizations are relationships between two or more concepts, they are summarizing statements that have wide applicability. They can be transferred to many situations. For example, the generalization cited does not apply only to one village but to *all* villages of traditional Pacific Northwest Indians. That is what makes it a generalization. The generalization "All human societies have a culture" has even broader applicability. It would apply to *any* human society anywhere in the world.

Generalizations are similar to concepts in that they, too, help the individual order the physical and social environments. Rather than being represented by a single word or expression, however, generalizations are usually expressed as declarative statements. The following are examples of generalizations often found in social studies. Notice how each expresses a relationship between concepts embedded in the statement.

1. New inventions lead to changes in ways of living.
2. Human beings change (adapt) their living to existing conditions.
3. Peoples of the world are interdependent.
4. Members of families help one another.
5. People influence their environment and are influenced by it.
6. Many people have contributed to our present civilization.
7. Basically, all people are very much alike although they differ in their ways of living because of geographical and historical factors.
8. People live in a continually changing world.
9. Workers in our neighborhood help one another.

Converting Concepts into Thought Forms
Appropriate for Young Learners

Social studies concepts and topics can be studied at various levels of complexity. Kindergartners and first-graders often study the family and family life. Yet a graduate student working on a doctor's degree in sociology or anthropology might take an advanced seminar on the same subject. The United States Supreme Court struggles with the meaning of justice in a complex case, yet children in the elementary school learn about the meaning of "liberty and justice for all." How does a teacher go about setting the complexity of subject matter, concepts, and generalizations and present them in ways that make sense to children? The following are suggested:

1. Define concepts and key ideas in child-oriented terms. For example:

CONCEPT	FOR A YOUNG CHILD THIS MEANS
Justice	Being or playing fair
Laws	Rules
Equality of opportunity	Seeing that everyone gets a turn
Cooperation	Working with others
Responsibility	Doing your part or doing your duty

2. Select subject matter with which children can identify. This does not mean that topics selected for study must in all cases be physically close to them. The usual assumption is that things that are physically close to children will be more familiar than those far away. This is not always the case. Children can study about things far away that are psychologically close to them. On the other hand, things that are physically close may be psychologically remote. The life-styles of families who live across town, for example, may be as unfamiliar to a child as those of people halfway around the world.
3. Develop ideas only to the point where children can apply them to reality. It takes time for children to learn concepts. They acquire a grasp of ideas cumulatively over several years. Do not expect children to learn complex concepts to completion in the early grades. The tendency is to try to teach children more than they want or need to know about a concept or a subject at a particular time.
4. Rely heavily on diagnostic approaches to teaching. Find out how much children already know. This can usually be accomplished through informal class discussions in which children respond to open-ended questions the teacher has prepared in advance. Observe how well they use new terms and concepts naturally and easily. Be aware of the level of interest in what is being studied. Draw on the experiences of children in planning and teaching social studies. Encourage them to talk about what is studied as it relates to their lives.

Concept Development: Three Strategies

In order to have meaning, concepts must be anchored in the experience of an individual. Such experience may be direct or vicarious, real or simulated, but one way or another, new ideas *must* be linked to prior experience. Concepts that are not or that cannot be associated with life experiences will, almost without exception, seem irrelevant to the learners. For this reason, it is not fruitful to attempt to teach complex social studies concepts to children who have impoverished life experiences. This is why real objects, models, illustrations, pictures, field trips, films, and vivid examples are essential to concept learning.

In general, concepts are learned by *citing an example* (Denver is an example of a *city*); by *describing the concept* (a *city* has a high population density); or by *defining the concept* (a *city* is an incorporated municipality whose boundaries and governmental powers are authorized and defined in a charter from the state in which it is located). The teaching strategies used in developing social studies concepts often incorporate all three of these ways of learning concepts.

Strategy One: Listing, Grouping, Labeling.[4] Imagine a primary grade class that has just returned from a field trip to a supermarket. Now back in the classroom, the teacher asks the children to list as many things as they can remember having seen in the supermarket. As they name items, the teacher writes them on the chalkboard — for example, eggs, bread, beans, meat, butter, checkout person, stock clerk, watermelons, candy, store manager, dog food, ice cream, and so on.

After completing the process of listing what they saw, the teacher asks the children to examine their list to see if certain things on the list seem to go together. That is, can these items be put together in groups that have something in common, as, for example, milk, butter, cheese, cream, and yogurt? They catch on to this activity quickly, and soon they are suggesting which items can be placed in the same group. Having placed items that seem to go together in the same group, children are then asked to think of names or labels for these groups. In the foregoing example, a name for that group would probably be "dairy products." The children should develop a name or label for each of the groups.

This listing-grouping-labeling strategy can be used in many ways to teach concepts in social studies. Here are a few additional examples:

1. Suppose a visitor from another country spent a day at our school; what would he or she see?
2. What did you see on the walk through the neighborhood?
3. What are all the ways goods and people can be moved from one place to another?
4. How many things can you list that are manufactured in our city (or state)?

---

[4] The listing-grouping-labeling strategy was developed by the late Hilda Taba and her associates in research related to concept attainment in social studies.

5. What items are sold in a department store?
6. What are things human beings can do that no other creatures can do?
7. What natural resources do we depend on in our everyday life?

This strategy is particularly useful in situations in which learners have made a great number of observations in a short period of time and need to sort out what they experienced into meaningful categories.

In using this strategy with young children, the teacher may have children find examples of the concept in pictures from old magazines. Or the teacher may have a collection of magazine pictures that illustrate examples of the concept and have children group the ones that seem to "go together." Children can then suggest word labels for these groups.

Strategy Two: Experiencing, Hypothesizing, Testing. An intermediate-grade class is studying the concept *advertising*. The teacher begins the study by having the children search for as many different examples of advertising as they can find. This search uncovers newspaper and magazine advertisements, classified ads, radio and television commercials, billboards, signs on transit buses, signs in public buildings, direct mailers, catalogs, and others. These various methods of advertising are discussed in terms of their purpose; the audience to which they are directed; the extent to which they are local, regional, or national; and the nature of the appeal. This leads the class to speculate on the value of advertising. Who benefits from advertising, and how do they benefit? Out of this discussion the children develop the following hypotheses:

1. Advertising helps consumers because it informs them about new products and their prices.
2. Effective advertising tries to create wants for products whether they are needed or not.
3. Local advertising has a more direct effect on sales in local stores than does national advertising.

The children begin searching for information that would support or refute these hypotheses. Much of their information gathering is done outside of school by interviewing consumers, local merchants, and representatives of advertising agencies. This process forces them to explore further such related subconcepts as needs and wants, promotion, audience, client, account, market, layout, impact, theme, and sales appeal. In time, they are able to form some tentative conclusions relating to their hypotheses, but their searches suggest other hypotheses that need exploration. The entire process provides the children with a thorough familiarity with the concept of advertising from several different perspectives.

In one form or another, the procedure just described is frequently used in teaching social studies concepts. What takes place is the following:

1. Learners are provided with extended, direct, firsthand exploratory experiences.
2. Terms and subconcepts related to the main concept are explained, and their meanings are developed as a natural extension of the study.
3. Children discuss ideas relating to the main concept and are encouraged to speculate about explanations of perceived relationships. These speculative statements become hypotheses to be tested.
4. An information search is made to test the hypotheses.
5. Tentative conclusions are drawn, which give rise to other hypotheses, and the search continues.
6. Through extended study and firsthand experiences, the meaning of the main concept is extended and refined.

This strategy is particularly useful in teaching such concepts as *culture, justice, conflict, democracy, equality,* and many others in social studies that do not lend themselves well to easy definition. In fact, there is not even consensus among experts on the exact meaning of many of these concepts. The abstract meanings of such concepts are understood only after extended exposure in many different settings over a long period of time.

Strategy Three: Recognizing Examples and Nonexamples. A sixth-grade class has been studying the development of nations of the Third World. The teacher, Ms. Rush, wants to develop the concept *modernization* and does so in the following way. She writes on the chalkboard:

MODERNIZATION INVOLVES

1. The application of technology to the control of nature's resources.
2. The use of inanimate sources of power and energy.
3. The use of tools to multiply the effects of human energy expended.
4. A high per capita production output.

The teacher then explains the meaning of each of the four attributes by using large pictures. That is, she shows the class specific examples of modernization — situations in which technology is applied to the control of resources, where inanimate power and energy sources are used, where tools multiply human energy, and where the per capita production is high. As children raise questions, these are discussed and issues are clarified. The teacher then provides the class with a series of pictures in which modernization, as defined by the particular attributes, is *not* evident. Again, these are explained and discussed, and questions raised by children are answered.

Having satisfied herself that the children understand the attributes that indicate modernization, the teacher presents the class with another set of pictures, but this time the *children* must identify examples and nonexamples of modernization and tell why or why not each is an example. These pictures are discussed in detail. The teacher then provides the class with back issues of the *National Geographic* and asks them to find picture examples and nonexamples of modernization and to tell why each is or is not an example. Finally, the teacher evaluates the children's ability to understand the concept by having them identify examples and nonexamples from a new set of pictures.

This strategy is less inquiry-oriented than the other two, but it does, nonetheless, present opportunities for search and discovery. In this case, the teacher provided the attributes of the concept in advance rather than having learners define them in the process of study. In summary, the teacher:

1. Identified the label for the concept (modernization).
2. Provided the major attributes (or critical properties) of the concept.
3. Provided examples that illustrated the presence of the attributes.
4. Provided nonexamples in which the attributes were missing.
5. Presented examples and nonexamples and had the children identify the attributes and had them tell why or why not each was an example.
6. Had children find examples and nonexamples on their own.
7. Evaluated their ability to use the attributes in identifying examples and nonexamples.

Many social studies concepts can be developed in this way. This strategy is most useful for those concepts in which there is reasonable agreement among experts on the attributes that define the concept. A few other examples are *island, desert, metropolitan region, industrial park, market, erosion,* and *capital.*

Developing Generalizations

Generalizations are relationships between two or more concepts that are usually expressed as declarative statements. Four different types of generalizations are relevant to social studies education:

1. **A supermarket sells all food products needed by consumers.**

This is a *descriptive* generalization. It could have been a concluding statement made by the children who were using the first strategy described in the prior section on concept development. It describes in summary form the relationship between the supermarket and the food needs of consumers.

2. **Advertising the price of merchandise results in more comparative shopping by consumers.**

This is a *cause-and-effect* generalization. It might have been developed by the class studying advertising in the second strategy described under concept development in the prior section. "If-then" statements are usually generalizations of this type.

3. **Misleading or false advertising takes unfair advantage of consumers and is illegal.**

This generalization is a statement of a *value principle*. It, too, might have evolved in the study of advertising described earlier. Generalizations of this type constitute the guidelines by which individuals govern their actions, and many have been handed down through the ages in the form of proverbs or wise statements for good living.

4. **The capacity of a nation to modernize depends on its natural resource base, the quantity and quality of its labor force, the amount and kinds of capital available to its industry and agriculture, and the institutions, attitudes, values, and habits that determine the effectiveness with which these economic resources are used.**

This generalization is a *universal law* or *principle* and is highly abstract. These generalizations are often used as the organizing frameworks for the social sciences and for social studies curricula. Such a generalization may have been the focus of the study of modernization discussed in the prior section under concept development. The possibility of the children arriving at such a generalization themselves is, indeed, remote, and it is probably inappropriate to expect them to do so.

It should be clear that generalizations are expressed as summarizing statements. That means that they will usually come near the ends of study sequences. For example, in the strategies for concept development described earlier, the children should be involved in stating generalizations that illustrate relationships between concepts. When generalizations are introduced at the beginning of a study sequence, they should be used as hypotheses to be confirmed or rejected in the process of study. This might occur in the following way:

> The teacher says, "Many people believe in the law of supply and demand, which states, 'Scarcity of goods results in higher prices whereas an oversupply of goods drives prices down.' How might we go about finding out whether or not this is true of the things we and our families buy on an everyday basis?"

At this point the search begins in order to test the validity of the generalization the teacher has provided as a working hypothesis.

Generalizations, like concepts, have to be developed out of the experiences of children. It is essential that they understand the concepts in the generalizations in order to grasp the meaning of the relationship being expressed. For this reason, it is not appropriate for learners simply to memorize generalizations. Generalizations that are memorized but not understood are of no value in gaining meaning from new situations where the relationships expressed in the generalization apply.

Many adults can recall a picture displayed by a teacher or a textbook photograph that was used to illustrate a *desert* or a *bridge* or a *skyscraper* or an *island* or some other social studies concept that was unfamiliar to them at the time. Forever after, whenever that concept enters the individual's consciousness, he or she retrieves a mental picture of the exact illustration that was used when it was first presented! If we are to teach for a wide application of ideas, that is, for *generalized knowledge* that can be useful in new situations, children must be given as many broad and varied experiences with ideas as is possible. They need to view the ideas in a variety of contexts. Citing single examples should be avoided whenever possible because this presents too narrow an experience for the child. When pictures or illustrations are used, several should be presented. Tests of understandings should not be cast in the exact context as presented in the instruction but should be placed in new settings. The teacher needs to ask frequently such questions as these: "Where else do we see this happening?" "How is this like or different from the problem we discussed at news time?" "Can you give another example of that?"

It cannot be assumed that children will apply knowledge from one situation to another if left unaided by the teacher. A skillful teacher will pave the way for transfer to take place and, in so doing, will be teaching understandings with wide application. In the teaching of concepts and generalizations, the need is not to repeat, drill, and practice. Rather, it is to enable the learner to encounter the idea in many settings, each slightly different from the other.

THE ROLE OF FACTS

The practice of having children learn factual information in social studies has been subject to considerable criticism by educators. These critical comments often have been misunderstood to mean that factual information is unimportant. Actually, factual information is crucial to the understanding of concepts and generalizations because it provides the supporting detail and the elaboration that make them meaningful. For example, let us say that a child reads this generalization: "The livelihood of the people of this region depends on the seasonal cycle of rain to make their crops produce their maximum yield." This statement has meaning only if one has specific information needed to answer such questions as "Which crop?" "How much is a maximum yield?" "How much rain is needed?" "When does the rain come?" "What do the people do with their harvested crops?" These specifics will not be long remembered, but they are critical in understanding the larger ideas that children are expected to learn. Teaching for concepts and generalizations without being concerned about the supporting specific facts results in shallow learning.

Unfortunately, there is not a list of facts that all children should learn in social studies, nor is there even a satisfactory set of criteria that the teacher can use in making decisions about which facts should be learned. Thus, the teacher's judgment is critical in determining the specific facts children are expected to learn. In exercising that judgment, the teacher will want to consider such matters as (1) whether or not the factual information is needed to elaborate on or explain main ideas, (2) the extent to which it is frequently used in ordinary living, (3) whether or not the information is likely to remain important for a long period of time, and (4) whether or not the information is an important part of the *common culture* and is therefore something all people are expected to know.

TEACHING SOCIAL STUDIES SKILLS

The systematic and sequential development of skills is of utmost importance to children because skills are the tools with which they continue their learning. Consequently, inadequately developed skills tend to retard learning in many areas of the elementary school curriculum, particularly in the social studies. Inadequate achievement in the social studies can, in most cases, be traced to poorly developed reading skills, inability to handle the vocabulary of the social studies, inability to read maps and globes, poor work-study skills, inability to use reference materials, or retarded language skills. Therefore, a well-balanced program in the social studies needs to provide for systematic and planned instruction to ensure the development of these skills.

Skill implies proficiency, the capability of doing something well. To have a skill is ordinarily taken to mean that a person is able to respond more or less habitually in an efficient way. Skills are commonly classified as motor, intellectual, and social.

All skills have two characteristics in common: They are developmental and they require practice if they are to be mastered. To speak of skills as being developmental means that they are learned gradually over a period of years. They are never really learned to completion although there usually comes a time when the learner has mastered them sufficiently for

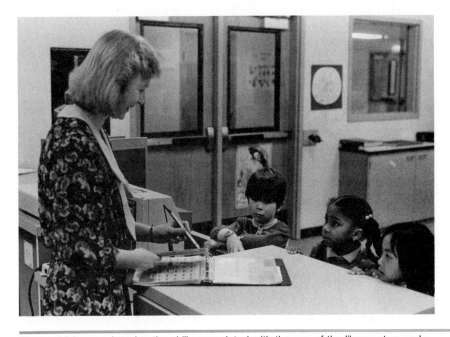

These children are learning the skills associated with the use of the library at an early age. The school librarian is an important member of a school's instructional team and can be enormously helpful to teachers and students in securing information resources for social studies. (Photo by Robb Mitchell, Tacoma School District.)

most purposes. However, one could continue refining these skills throughout one's lifetime. Thus, teachers should not assume that skills are taught and learned only once in some particular grade. All teachers need to assume some responsibility for the teaching and maintenance of social studies skills.

No amount of explanation or meaningful teaching will make children proficient in skills. They must practice and use the skills they have learned in order to build proficiency. This does not mean repetition or drill in the traditional sense, where a response was repeated over and over in exactly the same way. Instead, it is hoped that children will practice skills with the intention of improving. This also does not mean that skills would be practiced wholly out of their functional setting although there might be occasions when this would be necessary. In the ordinary study of a topic, there will be numerous opportunities to practice skills in the daily work-study activities of the class. In this way, the children improve their skills as they develop their understanding of concepts and subject matter. Skills are learned more effectively when they are closely related to actual situations in which they will be used.

Procedures in skills teaching are fairly clear-cut. The learners should first understand what is involved in the skill, how it is used, and what it

CHART 2. EXAMPLE OF STEPS IN TEACHING A SKILL APPLIED TO THE USE OF THE DIRECTORY OF A NEWSPAPER

Steps in Teaching a Skill:

Step 1   Make sure children understand what is involved in performing the skill. Show them how it is used. Provide them with a good model of the skill in operation. •———

Step 2   Break the skill into components and arrange them sequentially. Develop the teaching sequence step by step, having the children do each component as it is presented and explained. Supervise carefully to make sure their responses are correct. •———

Step 3   Have the children perform a simple variation of the skill under your close supervision. This is to ensure that they are performing the skill correctly. •———

Step 4   After it is established that the children are performing the skill correctly, provide for supervised practice, using simple variations that ensure success. •———

Step 5   Gradually increase the complexity of the variation of the skill, and begin having children apply the skill in situations in which it is useful. Continue this procedure until the desired level of proficiency is achieved. •———

Step 6   Continue to practice the skill at regular intervals, largely through functional application, in order to maintain and improve performance. •———

means. Providing a good model of its use is helpful at this point. Second, the learners need to work through a simple use of the skill under careful teacher guidance. This is essential to verify that they understand what is involved and are making a correct response. Third, they need additional practice in increasingly complex variations of the skill, applied in functional settings. Children need to use the newly learned skill in solving problems, thus demonstrating its value as a learning tool. Finally, they need continued practice in its use over an extended period of time to maintain and improve facility with the skill.

Teachers who help children develop skills do not depend entirely on incidental teaching of them. Rather, the skills are carefully identified,

CHART 2. Continued

Application of Each Step:

Step 1 Secure a newspaper, preferably a Sunday edition, and show how difficult and time-consuming it is to find some bit of information if one has to leaf through the entire paper to find it. Have children try their hand at finding items without using the newspaper directory. Show how easily one can find information with the aid of the directory.

Step 2 a. Make sure children know how to use the dictionary and the encyclopedia prior to teaching this skill.

b. Acquaint children with various sections of the newspaper: general news, classified ads, sports, editorials, weather, and so on.

c. Teach children the specialized vocabulary associated with the newspaper: vital statistics, obituaries, market quotations, masthead, dateline, syndicated, and so on.

d. Teach children what items are included in the various categories listed in the directory, and how they are arranged. For example, what is included in the Arts and Entertainment section, how are the classifieds organized, and how does one find out what arrangement is used?

e. Provide a newspaper for each member of the class, and have the children locate easy items using the directory. Such items might include the television schedule, sports, and the comics. Supervise to make sure everyone is performing the skill correctly.

Step 3 Follow Step 2 immediately with an exercise requiring children to locate items making use of the directory. Supervise and assist as needed. Check responses.

Step 4 Assign children to find information in the next day's newspaper. This should be done on their own without teacher supervision. Check responses.

Step 5 Bring to class copies of a different newspaper from the one used thus far in which a slightly different directory format appears. Assign children to find information in this paper without your assistance to see if they can transfer and modify their skill from one situation to another. Check responses.

Step 6 From time to time have children make use of the directory to locate needed information. Observe the accuracy and extensiveness of use of the directory.

systematically taught, thoroughly practiced, and widely used. This principle applies to such intellectual skills as critical and reflective thinking, coming to valid conclusions based on evidence, evaluating sources of information, and interpreting data as well as to work-study and group-process skills. These steps, along with an example of their application, are provided in Chart 2.

For purposes of focus and clarity of analysis, in the treatment of teaching methods, skills teaching is often discussed in a separate section. This separation should not suggest to the teacher that skills are taught or learned outside a content (i.e., subject matter) framework. The content connection is most obvious in the case of work-study skills such as finding information, arranging information in usable forms, using maps, globes, and graphics, and organizing information. Such skills have no purpose outside of a subject-matter setting. But the integration of content and skills applies to intellectual skills and group-work skills as well. Processes such as problem solving, critical thinking, inquiry, and decision making must have a content framework if they are to be taught with integrity. Teachers should not set out to teach these important processes without giving ample consideration to the subject-matter content in which they are to be used.

LEARNING AND TEACHING RESOURCES FOR CONTENT AND SKILLS

Children cannot learn content and content-related skills without valid sources of information. In recent years, a multimedia approach to social studies has been strongly encouraged, but the textbook remains the most widely used information source for children in social studies. The practice of using basic textbooks is often criticized because of their misuse. The challenge to the teacher is to learn how to make enlightened use of textbooks and to broaden the information sources available to children.

As we examine the potential of various media useful in teaching content and skills, we must be ever mindful that it is the *teacher* and not the media who produces exciting programs for children. The artistry of the teacher is enhanced when the necessary materials for creative teaching are easily available. But it is a mistake to assume that a generous supply of instructional materials will ensure inspired and creative teaching. It is the interaction of a talented teacher and a wide range of appropriate media that generates superior social studies programs.

Information sources for the social studies can be grouped into two categories: (1) reading materials and resources (textbooks, encyclopedias, references, computers, magazines, pamphlets, newspaper clippings, travel folders, classroom periodicals, and similar printed material) and (2) nonreading materials and resources (pictures, films, filmstrips, recordings, field trips, maps, globes, and community resources of all types). Together they provide the information base for social studies programs.

In the selection of any instructional resource, the objectives to be achieved should be uppermost in the mind of the teacher. The particular resource or material selected should be the one that will move children most effectively in the direction of those objectives. In short, instructional aids, materials, and resources are used to achieve specific purposes. The teacher is encouraged to use a wide range of instructional media for any or all of the following reasons:

1. Not all children learn in the same way; different media are able to appeal to the learning styles of different learners.
2. The reading ranges among children who are randomly selected to form classroom groups are great, averaging three to five years in the lower grades and five to ten years in the middle and upper grades.
3. Each of the media has peculiar strengths and limitations in the way it conveys messages.
4. The impact of a message is likely to be stronger if more than one sensory system is involved in receiving it.
5. Material to be learned varies greatly in its abstractness and complexity.
6. The use of a variety of media has motivating and interest-generating qualities.
7. Teaching modes that stress inquiry and problem solving require extensive information searches and sources.
8. Different sources may provide different insights on the same subject; there may be discrepancies or inaccuracies that go undetected if a single source is used.

Instructional materials need to be evaluated carefully before, during, and after they have been used. It is not a good policy to use any and all materials simply because they are available. The quality of the material or resource should be a primary consideration in deciding on its use. Maps that are out-of-date, films that are of poor quality, pictures that are inaccurate, or field trips that are poorly guided, for example, might better not be used at all.

The maximum value of any instructional resource requires skillful use on the part of the teacher. No instructional material is entirely self-teaching — all require a teacher to set the stage for learning to take place. A first-rate textbook in the hands of an unimaginative teacher can be devastating to the social studies program. The same book used by another teacher can become one of the most valuable resources available to the class. Materials of instruction can be no better than the teachers who use them.

Textbooks

The policy of school districts that calls for furnishing free of charge the same basic textbook for every child in a class is based on the legal principles of equal treatment and equality of opportunity. For this reason, textbooks are widely used and will doubtless continue to be widely used for years to come. It is apparent from their widespread acceptance that most teachers, especially those in grades three and above, perceive the textbook as a valuable teaching tool in social studies. It is important, therefore, for the beginning teacher to learn how to make the best use of these books.

Textbook development has tended to be consistent with changes in curriculum and teaching methods. Modern textbooks are attractive, inviting, a pleasure to look at and to read. There is better use of maps and visual materials; some social studies textbooks for elementary grades boast of at least one illustration on every page, many of the illustrations in color. Multiple authorship is common, with at least one author being a specialist in elementary education. This has served to retain high scholarly accuracy as well as to refine and improve the format and reading level of the books. Significant changes are apparent in the treatment of racial and ethnic groups and of women. In general, there has been substantial headway in presenting social reality more accurately in modern social studies textbooks.

Social studies textbooks almost always present problems of reading difficulty even though they are written at a level that is suitable for the average reader. The reason for this is that these books are designed to deal with substantive content, and this means that the terms and concepts relating to that subject matter must be used in explaining the ideas presented. For example, a book may be treating a topic such as *trade and commerce*. This subject cannot be meaningfully presented without including at least some of the following concepts and terms: *cargo, tariff, import, duty, international markets, ports, interdependence, hold, tonnage, trade, freight, shipping, stevedore, merchant, commercial, barge*. If these terms are eliminated from the selection in order to simplify the reading task, it is no longer an essay on trade and commerce. It is the complexity and frequency of concepts that often make reading social studies textbooks difficult, and there is no way this problem can be overcome entirely. An easy-to-read textbook is probably not a good social studies text because its purpose should be to provide information rather than be a simple storybook.

Textbook authors assume that the teacher will guide and direct children in their use of the book. Textbooks are highly condensed and factual presentations and are written with the thought that teachers will supplement and enrich the presentation through the use of other materials. Moreover, texts are not meant to be entirely self-instructing, and if children use them without guidance from the teacher, much of their value may be lost. This is especially true of accompanying visual material in the form of pictures, maps, charts, cartoons, graphs, and study helps.

Textbooks are written to be used as information sourcebooks and are not intended to become the social studies curriculum. They can be used in a variety of ways, and individual children may make different uses of the same book. For one child it may constitute a reading resource, for another child the illustrations may be more valuable, for a third child the map materials may be needed, and for a fourth child it may be a source of ideas for additional study. Similarly, different teachers may choose to make different uses of the same book, depending on their skill, experience, or method of teaching. Teachers are encouraged to make such differential use of textbooks rather than to "cover" the content uniformly and require all children to "master" the facts presented.

If the teacher keeps in mind that no single book can meet adequately the reading needs of all children in the class, the textbook can be a useful tool in teaching social studies. Four of the most common uses of the textbook are for (1) exploratory reading; (2) securing facts related to the study; (3) map, chart, graph, or picture study; and (4) summarization of learning.

What does a teacher look for in selecting a textbook? From the teacher's point of view, the most important criterion would seem to be *usability*. The book has to fit the teacher's style of teaching if it is to be used well. This means that the text has to be constructed in such a way that it lends itself to flexible use. A book that can be used in only one teaching mode or stresses only one approach to social studies is generally less useful than one that can be adapted to a variety of teaching modes. Readability always has to be an important consideration, and it is significant that one of the frequent criticisms of social studies texts is that they are hard to read. Good social studies texts include study aids; such study aids should facilitate learning the content and skills and, at the same time, encourage good study habits.

Many good social studies textbooks are available today. Some are better suited for certain purposes than others. Some more accurately reflect current curriculum developments than do others. Those who are charged with responsibility of making the selection should develop their own criteria for evaluating textbooks in social studies, but they will probably want to look critically at the following points:

1. *Authorship* — to ensure scholarly accuracy as well as suitability for use with elementary schoolchildren in terms of interest and appeal, reading gradation, and curricular consideration. How is the author identified with elementary school social studies?

2. *Treatment of Content* — to ensure adequate treatment of important concepts in sufficient depth as opposed to highly descriptive factual accounts or storybook approaches to significant content. Is subject matter selected from a broad range of sources, including history, the social sciences, the humanities, and science? Does the book provide readers with a global perspective? Is there a good balance in the treatment of objectives dealing with subject matter, skills, and values and attitudes? Does the book present realistic representations of societies both in prose and in illustrations? Does the book deal with ethnic minorities and women in a realistic way? Is there evidence of stereotyping or tokenism or both in the illustrations?

3. *Format and General Appearance*—to ensure an interesting and appealing book of proper size with good-quality binding and suitable type size. Are illustrations functional or simply decorative?
4. *Organization*—to ensure the book's harmony with the existing curricular pattern and see that it meets the needs of the instructional program within which it will be used. Is the book organized in a way to encourage good study habits?
5. *Visual Materials*—to ensure colorful, accurate illustrations of sufficient number and size. Are these related to the text or included only to enhance the attractiveness of the book?
6. *Instructional Aids*—to ensure their being an integral part of the text itself and of such nature as to be genuinely helpful to the teacher. Do study aids help explain and extend the meaning of important ideas?
7. *Literary Quality*—to ensure that the book is as well written as it can be consistent with the basic purposes of a textbook.

Other Learning Resources and Media

The numerous resources and media in addition to textbooks that contribute to a vital social studies program for children are discussed in context in other sections of this text. For example, the use of maps, globes, charts, cartoons, posters, and graphs is singled out for attention in Chapter 6. Other resources are discussed in connection with the teaching of history, geography, and other topics throughout the text.

Computers in Social Studies

The use of computers in education has been promoted so vigorously that it is estimated that, by the end of this decade, microcomputers will be a part of the instructional media of all schools. It is presumed, therefore, that the preservice preparation of teachers will familiarize them with the basic knowledge and skills needed to operate a computer, an ability currently referred to as *computer literacy*. In the social studies, as in other curricular areas, the challenge to the teacher is to integrate the use of this new technology into the ongoing instructional program of the classroom.

One of the major differences between the computer and other instructional media is that the computer has the capacity to *interact* with the student. The computer does not simply present the material to be learned as is the case with a film, filmstrip, or a recording. The computer requires the operator to *do something* in order for the process to proceed. This interactive characteristic of computers necessitates the active involvement of the learner. This has many implications for the pacing of instruction and for individualizing learning. For example, with conventional

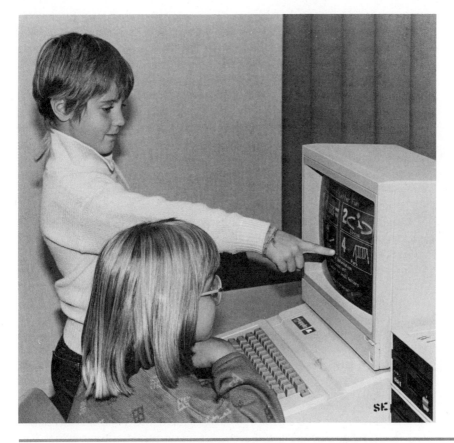

Although the computer is not likely to replace the book, as some of the more enthusiastic computer supporters claim, it is a device that will certainly be an important part of the environment of today's children for their entire lifetime. What are some of the ethical issues surrounding the use of computers? Should these issues be a part of the social studies program? (Photo by Edna Kellman, Seattle Public Schools.)

instructional materials, the program of what is to be learned is fixed. Only the time allowed to complete it can be varied from one student to the next. The computer, however, has the capacity to diagnose an individual learner's knowledge of the subject or skill, to call up a program appropriate for the learner, and to adjust the complexity of the presentation accordingly.

In the social studies, the contribution of computer-assisted instruction (CAI) falls into the following four categories:

1. Using the computer to obtain needed information (data) or to retrieve information stored in the computer. There is a growing number of collections of data, known as *data bases*, many of which are relevant to

social studies. These data bases will one day include most, if not all, of what is now found in libraries, government document centers, and other information collections. Being able to access information from data bases through the computer, as well as being able to use the Computer Catalog Service (COMCATS) in the library, are essential social studies skills in this "high tech" era.[4]

2. Using the computer to practice and apply social studies skills such as map reading, graph reading, chart interpretation, thinking, and problem solving. Computer programs of this kind are referred to as "drill and practice." The term *drill and practice* connotes the worst of the old-fashioned teaching methodologies of a bygone time and is an unfortunate choice of labels for computer use that actually involves the learner actively in improving performance.

3. Using the computer for tutorial assistance in providing a sequential program for the development and elaboration of concepts and knowledge that all students are expected to learn. These are essentially courses of study that have been programmed for the computer. So-called *courseware* is available for such social studies topics as the Constitution, basic economics, and United States history, but most courseware has been geared to the secondary school level.

4. Using the computer for specialized presentations such as simulations, decision-making situations, analysis of given data, interpreting information needed to solve a problem or a series of related problems.

Computer resources for social studies are now available from several sources.[5] Because this is a rapidly changing field, the teacher is advised to use a current list of sources in searching for computer software. Such lists are published, and materials are reviewed regularly in *Social Education* (National Council for the Social Studies, 3501 Newark Street N.W., Washington, D.C. 20016), *The Computing Teacher* (International Council for Computers in Education, University of Oregon, 1787 Agate Street, Eugene, Oregon 97403), *Classroom Computer Learning* (Peter Li, Inc., 2451 East River Road, Dayton, Ohio 45439), or *Teaching and Computers* (Scholastic, Inc., 730 Broadway, New York, New York 10003). The National Council for the Social Studies has published guidelines for evaluating social studies microcomputer software in the November–December 1984 issue of *Social Education.*

---

[4] One teacher relates how middle school students used the microcomputer to build their own data base for global studies. See Tama Traberman, "Using Microcomputers to Teach Global Studies," *Social Education,* 48 (February 1984), pp. 130–137.

[5] James O. Hodges, "Resources for Teaching with Computers," *Social Education,* 51 (January 1987), pp. 54–59.

DISCUSSION QUESTIONS AND SUGGESTED ACTIVITIES

1. Select three unit topics from the following list, and provide examples of five concepts that might be included in such units. Then, using two or more of the concepts you have identified, write a generalization that expresses a valid relationship between them that is relevant to each of the topics you have selected.

   People Change the Earth (K–8)
   School Living (K)
   Families and Their Needs (1)
   The Shopping Center (2)
   Life in the City (3)
   Our Home State (4)
   The Westward Movement (5)
   Crossroads of the World: The Middle East (6–7)
   Colonial America (8)

2. Interview individually four or five children from a grade in which you have a special interest to determine their understanding of selected social studies concepts. Use a straightforward procedure and everyday concepts. For example, you might ask, "What does the term *family* mean to you? What is a family anyway?" (or use *community, city, park,* and so on.) When the child responds, probe to get an elaboration of what the concept means to the youngster. You might vary the procedure by including abstract concepts such as *justice* and *freedom,* or quantitative concepts such as *several years later* or *long ago.* These experiences will provide you with firsthand knowledge of what it means to convert subject matter into thought forms appropriate for elementary schoolchildren. Report your findings to the class.

3. Select a grade of your choice. Suggest situations for that grade that would make use of the three strategies for concept development discussed in this chapter.

4. What are the essential differences between how one teaches concepts and how one teaches skills?

5. Use the left side of Chart 2 and apply each of the points to a skill of your choice for a grade in which you have a special interest. Share your example with others in class.

6. Provide examples of content and content-related skills that you believe are important for citizens to know, using the criteria listed on page 36. Why do you think there is such widespread disagreement over what is essential knowledge that all citizens should know?

7. Today the individual citizen has access to information sources that are almost unlimited in the scope of knowledge they can provide.

Does this increase or decrease the individual citizen's need to accumulate and store information in his or her own brain? Should the availability of information influence decisions about what is taught in school? Discuss and provide examples to support your points.

8. What are your reactions to the following?
   Ms. Dickens always insisted that students understand details. Some children even knew entire passages by heart. Those who were able to write such memorized answers to the questions on her tests were the ones who were given high marks.

9. Select a children's social studies textbook for a grade of your choice. Evaluate it in terms of items 1, 2, 7, 9, and 10 on Chart 1 in Chapter 1, pages 9–10.

10. Assume that a teacher were allowed to choose *not* to use a social studies textbook and made such a choice. What provisions would need to be made for children to get the basic information they need? Would this be easier to do at some grade levels than others? Explain.

SELECTED REFERENCES

ATWOOD, VIRGINIA A. "Data Sources: Tools of the Trade," and "Bubble-Good Data: Product Testing and Other Sources." *Social Education,* 49 (February 1985), pp. 140–141 and 146–149.

BEYERS, BARRY K. *Practical Strategies for the Teaching of Thinking.* Newton, Massachusetts: Allyn and Bacon, Longwood Division, 1987.

CHANCE, PAUL. *Thinking in the Classroom: A Survey of Programs.* New York: Teachers College Press, 1986.

CHARLESWORTH, ROSALIND, AND NANCY L. MILLER. "Social Studies and Basic Skills in the Early Childhood Classroom." *The Social Studies,* 76 (January–February 1985), pp. 34–37.

COSTA, ARTHUR L., ed. *Developing Minds: A Resource Book for Teaching Thinking.* Alexandria, Virginia: Association for Supervision and Curriculum Development, 1985.

Educational Leadership, 45 (April 1988). This entire issue deals with the teaching of thinking.

FELDMAN, PHILLIP, AND JOHN W. OSBURN. "Social Studies and Computer Technology: A Review of Recent Literature." *Education,* 108 (Fall 1987), pp. 9–26.

HART, LESLIE H. *Human Brain and Human Learning.* New York: Longman, 1983.

LIPMAN, MATTHEW. "Critical Thinking—What Can It Be?" *Educational Leadership,* 46 (September 1988), pp. 38–43.

MCKENZIE, GARY R. "The Importance of Teaching Facts in Elementary Social Studies." *Social Education,* 44 (October 1980), pp. 494–498.

MCKINNEY, C. WARREN, A. GUY LARKINS, MARY JANE FORD, AND JOHN C. DAVIS III. "The Effectiveness of Three Methods of Teaching Social Studies Concepts to Fourth-Grade Students: An Aptitude-Treatment Interaction Study." *American Educational Research Journal,* 20 (Winter 1983), pp. 663–670.

MCQUEEN, RICHARD. "Spurts and Plateaus in Brain Growth: A Critique of the Claims of Herman Epstein." *Educational Leadership*, 41 (February 1984), pp. 66–71.

NORRIS, STEPHEN P. "Synthesis of Research on Critical Thinking." *Educational Leadership*, 42 (May 1985), pp. 40–45.

PARKER, WALTER C. "Thinking to Learn Concepts." *The Social Studies*, 79 (March/April 1988), pp. 70–72.

PAUL, RICHARD W. "Critical Thinking: Fundamental to Education for a Free Society." *Educational Leadership*, 42 (September 1984), pp. 4–14. (This issue also contains fourteen other articles related to the development of thinking abilities.)

ROOZE, GENE E., AND TERRY NORTHUP. *Using Computers to Teach Social Studies.* Littleton, Colorado: Libraries Unlimited, 1986.

SCHUG, MARK C. "What Do Social Studies Teachers Say about Using Computers?" *The Social Studies*, 79 (May/June 1988), pp. 112–115.

SOLOMON, WARREN. "Improving Students' Thinking Skills through Elementary Social Studies Instruction." *The Elementary School Journal*, 87 (May 1987), pp. 557–569.

The Social Studies, 78 (January/February 1987). This entire issue is devoted to computers and the social studies.

3

Value, Moral, and Character Education

A class of elementary school children has been studying a unit on the early history of the United States. As a culminating activity, the children have prepared a series of dramatic skits that are being presented to their parents. We enter the classroom as the children, dressed in appropriate costumes, are dramatizing the origin of our country's flag. A committee headed by George Washington is meeting with Betsy Ross in her home. The time is June 1776, scarcely a month before the signing of the Declaration of Independence. The place is Philadelphia. George Washington speaks first.

> G. WASHINGTON: Mrs. Ross, now that we are soon to be an independent nation, we will need a flag for our country. George Ross is a member of our committee and an uncle of your late husband. He told us that you sew very well; that you would be able to make our new country's flag.

B. ROSS:　I would be honored to try, General Washington. It is true that I am a seamstress, but I have never made a flag before. What did you have in mind?

G. WASHINGTON:　We brought a design with us. The flag should have red and white stripes. Thirteen of them. One for each state. It should also have thirteen stars on a blue background.

B. ROSS:　I see your stars have six points, General Washington. I think stars with five points look better.

G. WASHINGTON:　Well, you do what you think is best, Mrs. Ross. The flag will have to be approved by the Continental Congress. The Congress does want the flag to have the colors red, white, and blue. We will check back with you in a few weeks. Goodbye, Mrs. Ross.

B. ROSS:　Goodbye, General Washington.

Each year skits such as the one just described are repeated in hundreds of classrooms throughout the country — Pilgrims celebrating the first Thanksgiving, Lewis and Clark exploring the western wilderness, a wagon train family along the Oregon Trail, rancho life in early California, plantation life in antebellum days. How does one evaluate these activities in terms of social studies education? Although the dramatizations may be based on actual historical incidents, the details of the representations are probably inaccurate. Is that important? Should teachers involve children in them? What purposes do such activities serve?

From a strictly pedagogical point of view, these activities have two important values. First, they are highly motivating for children. Children enjoy being involved in plays and pageants, and their natural interest in dramatic play can be used as a powerful vehicle when used in school learning. Second, the use of a dramatic activity to recreate a situation under study gives children tangible purposes for doing their information gathering. The children do their research in order to be able to recreate the situation as accurately as possible through dramatic representation.

But beyond their usefulness as teaching vehicles, activities of this type make a lasting impression on the affective development of children. When asked to recall their elementary school social studies program, adults most often mention experiences that were distinctly affective — a skit on George Washington's birthday in one of the primary grades, a play about the Pilgrims on the first Thanksgiving in the fourth grade, or those moving stories of courage and bravery that some teacher read to the class. These experiences are important because they provide ways for children to become acquainted with those common values, attitudes, and ideals that go into the making of our national character. They also provide important foundations for the moral and character development of children.

The attachment to and internalization of common core values by indi-

Here we see a group of children engaged in an exercise that symbolizes patriotism. What values do such exercises promote? What other activities or symbolic gestures are used in schools—and in society—to inspire feelings of patriotism? Is there a place for such activities in the citizenship education of the young? (Photo by James W. Johnson, *Northshore Citizen*.)

vidual members is an essential requirement for stable social life in a society. In a society with such a diversity of cultural legacies and origins as ours, the task of educating children in these common values and attitudes becomes both more challenging and more critical than it is in a more culturally homogeneous society. The process of socializing children for life in the common culture begins in the home but is continued and extended in the school, particularly in social studies education. Such education involves inculcation of values and related beliefs, the development of character, and the moral development of children. The dramatizations and skits described earlier call attention to those values and human traits that society likes to see in its citizens.

THE LANGUAGE OF AFFECTIVE EDUCATION

Affective education is a generic term that includes a variety of educational activities associated with the development of feelings and emotions. The well-known taxonomy of Krathwohl, Bloom, and Masia describes five levels of objectives in the affective domain: receiving, responding, valuing, organization, and characterization.[1] Affective education includes the study of the arts and humanities but is also related to the development of a system of values, attitudes, and beliefs, to the development of character, and to moral development.

Values can be defined as standards that individuals and social groups use to judge the worth of some behavior or some thing. Values are criteria that can be applied in making decisions. Values are associated with those things we perceive to be right and desirable. Values define for us what is worth striving for, what is preferred, what constitutes worthy life goals, what may be worth sacrificing one's life for. Values are abstract conceptions and, therefore, cannot be observed directly. We assume the influence of certain values by the way one behaves. Raths, Harmin, and Simon suggest seven criteria for defining a value, all of which must be present[2]:

1. *choosing freely* (This means that the individual is not coerced, pressured, or unduly influenced by others in making the choice. Choices made because they are suggested by the teacher or parents or as a result of peer pressure are not ones that are freely made.)
2. *choosing from among alternatives* (In order to make a choice, one must have available at least two options. If there is only one option, and the

---

[1] David R. Krathwohl, Benjamin S. Bloom, and Bertrum B. Masia, *Taxonomy of Educational Objectives — Handbook II: Affective Domain* (New York: David McKay, 1964), p. 95.

[2] Louis E. Raths, Merrill Harmin, and Sidney B. Simon, *Values and Teaching: Working with Values in the Classroom,* 2nd ed. (Columbus, Ohio: Charles E. Merrill, 1978), pp. 28–29. Explanations in parentheses are not quoted material.

Experiences such as the one shown here relate to the affective development of children. As living creatures, pets require care and humane treatment. A pet responds to love and affection and remains a faithful friend, qualities we admire not only in pets but in human beings as well! (Photo by Chip Van Gilder, Tacoma School District.)

individual is required to participate in the activity, there can be no choice.)

3. *choosing after thoughtful consideration of consequences* (This requirement rules out decisions made on impulse or on the "spur of the moment" because such choices cannot be said to represent one's values. Value-based decisions are arrived at thoughtfully with a full knowledge of the consequences insofar as they can be determined in advance.)

4. *prizing and cherishing* (This means that the person is pleased with the choice that was made.)

5. *affirming* (Because the individual is pleased with the choice, he or she says so. The affirmations are made freely and publicly.)

6. *acting on choices* (This is based on the ancient truth that actions speak louder than words. People act in accordance with what they value.)

7. *repeating* (When behavior is value based, it is consistent, and the individual will repeat it. Such behavior can be reliably predicted. For example, if an individual "loves to read," he or she will not read just one book but will continue reading many books throughout his or her lifetime.)

In terms of orderly social life, it is essential that most members of a society embrace those core values on which there is general consensus and lead their lives in accordance with them. It is important to note, however, that there is a big difference between knowing the *content* of social values and leading one's life in correspondence with them. The term *beliefs* often appears in the literature of affective education. Beliefs can be defined as *commitments* to certain values. There is a direct connection between one's belief system and one's commitment to specific values.

An *attitude* is an inclination or a predisposition to respond in a particular way. Attitudes are based on one's values and beliefs. To say that one has a "prejudiced attitude" is redundant, because an attitude is a prejudice, but it may have positive or negative value connotations. Thus, if educational programs are targeted to reduce racial prejudice in society, the programs have to be geared to deal with attitude changes in learners. This means that such programs will need to deal fundamentally with changing learners' values and beliefs related to various racial groups.

Moral development has to do with educating children in modes of conduct that are desired by society. Although the term *morality* is sometimes defined narrowly to mean only sexual behavior, it is a much broader concept. It includes not only knowing which values are accepted by the social group but also living accordingly. When we speak of people being faced with a "moral dilemma," we refer to situations in which the person is forced to choose between two alternatives, both of which may be right but in either case the unselected option results in unpleasant consequences. For example, a man might be presented with an opportunity for a well-paying job on an oil rig in the North Atlantic. As a father of four children, he has had erratic employment in West Texas for the past three years and he is deeply in debt. He badly needs the money that he could earn on the North Atlantic job. But if he takes it, he has to agree to a two-year assignment. He is deeply devoted to his family, and a two-year separation from them would be heartbreaking for him and for his wife and children. Should he take the job? Clearly, this conflict in his personal values must be resolved if he is to make a decision with which he will feel comfortable.

The test of one's moral maturity comes in the everyday choices in day-to-day living. Most people have no problem with those choices that are clearly wrong or clearly right. But it is in the gray areas that one is confronted with genuine moral dilemmas. Moreover, the strength of one's moral conduct is not known unless it is put to the test. The person who lives in a protected environment, sheltered from the necessity of making moral choices, may lead a virtuous life because he or she has not faced the need to consider alternatives and, therefore, is never confronted with a genuine moral challenge.

The term *character* is a summarizing concept that speaks to an individual's reputation as one who embraces those values and beliefs cherished by society and who has the moral strength to live in accordance with them. Character education has been a consistent goal of public school education in this century, much of it falling in the purview of social studies. These programs represented affirmative efforts to promote certain moral virtues and traits such as truthfulness, self-discipline, consideration for others, and trustworthiness. Earlier efforts used direct methods of instruction, focused on specific character traits, and used instructional resources that carried strong moral messages. More recent efforts stressed indirect teaching strategies with more subtle moral and ethical instruction. In general, programs in character education have not received enthusiastic support from the social science intellectual community mainly because historically these programs have relied on indoctrination, exhortation, and stories with strong moral messages to get ideas across to learners.

VALUES EDUCATION

Values education is concerned with both *general* values and *personal* values. Such values as liberty, justice, equality, honesty, consideration for others, individualism, human dignity, responsibility, and truthfulness are examples of general values on which there is consensus. This does not mean that everyone has the same values or interprets them in the same way. But there is general agreement that such values reflect the basic orientation of the society. These values are a part of our political and religious heritages. They are incorporated in our great historical documents and in our legal and judicial systems. They are apparent in our folklore and in our literature. Individuals who lead exemplary lives that reflect such general values are extolled as national heroes.

If children are to be socialized in accordance with these general values of society, they must be provided with examples of behavior that illustrate these values in action. That is, young people need to have encounters with idealized types — persons who illustrate by their way of life the values that society rewards and likes to see in its citizens. It is because these general values are internalized by the majority of citizens that orderly social life can take place. We expect our fellow citizens to behave in ways that are predictable and consistent with the basic premises inherent in those values on which there is general consensus. Law enforcement agencies are provided to protect society from the minority of persons who cannot or will not live in accordance with the general values embraced by the majority. But no police force could possibly monitor the behavior of all citizens if they were not willing to comply voluntarily with the accepted rules of the society. We are able to enjoy social order because a large majority of citizens have internalized general values on which there is accordance.

The lesson plan on page 59 dealing with symbolic values provides a good example of a lesson based on general values. General values are promoted through social studies in the following ways:

1. Daily life in the classroom that stresses consideration for others, freedom and equality, independence of thought, individual responsibility for one's actions, and the dignity of individual human beings.
2. The study of the history and development of this country stressing the ideals that inspired it and showing that a continuing effort is needed to move reality closer to those ideals.
3. The study of biographies of individuals whose lives reflect the general values of the nation.
4. The study of the law and the legal and justice systems.
5. The celebration of holidays that reinforce values and ideals associated with the holiday.
6. Thoughtful analysis of the meaning of such statements as the Pledge of Allegiance, the Preamble to the Constitution, and the Bill of Rights.
7. Building awareness to situations that are not in accord with values to which this society is committed.
8. Cross-cultural studies to illustrate differences in values from one society to another.

As we move from general values to *personal* values, the role of social studies becomes considerably different and, to some extent, less clear. Personal values are those values that affect the decision making of individuals in their own personal lives. To some extent they represent individual interpretations of general values, that is, the operationalizing of general values in the personal life of each individual.

Modern life involves an incredible amount of choice making: how to spend our time, what career to choose, what clothes to buy and to wear, where to live, what brand products to buy, what hobbies and leisure-time activities to pursue, and how to spend our money. The list could go on and on to include literally every facet of our lives. In each of these decisions, there are probably no absolutely right and wrong choices in the sense that basic general values are being compromised by either choice. Rather, these decisions are expressions of individual preferences. When selecting an automobile, one person buys a blue Ford sedan; another, a yellow Chevrolet stationwagon; and a third, a red Dodge Caravan. To ask which is *right* is inappropriate because right and wrong in the absolute sense are not issues in such choice making. This is really what personal values are all about — choice making concerning our personal lives.

It should be obvious that the social studies program cannot promote personal values in the same way that it can promote general values. What social studies *can* do is to help children think about the choices they make in terms of a values framework. This is often referred to in current literature as values clarification or the "process of valuing." Raths, Harmin, and Simon suggest that if adults seek to help children in the process of valuing, they should

1. Encourage children to make more choices and to make them freely.
2. Help them discover alternatives when faced with choices.
3. Help children weigh alternatives thoughtfully, reflecting on the consequences of each.
4. Encourage children to consider what it is that they prize and cherish.
5. Give them opportunities to affirm their choices.
6. Encourage them to act, behave, live in accordance with their choices.
7. Help them be aware of repeated behaviors or patterns in their life.[3]

Children need experiences in which they are confronted with a conflict of values, both of which are attractive, but a choice has to be made between them. These choices are between or among "goods" rather than between or among something that is desirable and something that is not. Similarly, the choice is *not* between options that are illegal, unethical, or contrary to social norms. Value clarification exercises that probe the sensitive, personal, psychological space of youngsters present serious psychological and ethical problems and are not recommended for use with elementary school children.

Almost any subject, topic, situation, or picture can be used to explore values. Questions of this type are suggested to elicit value responses for discussion:

1. If you return someone's lost billfold, do you think you deserve a reward?
2. Do you think you would like a job like that?
3. How would you like to live in such a place?
4. If you won a cash prize of $100, what would you do with it?
5. How did you feel when you read that paragraph?
6. If you could change *one* thing about this community in order to make it a better place to live, what would you change?
7. If the principal dismissed everyone at noon today and you could do anything you wanted this afternoon, what would you choose to do?
8. What do you think are the three most important qualities of a person who is president of the United States?
9. Can you name three decisions about which you think you ought to have something to say? Why do you think you should have something to say about these decisions?

[3] *Ibid.,* p. 38.

10. Can you think of some person you really admire? Why do you admire that person?

Expressing value preferences is a normal part of everyday life. Everyone makes choices based on values several times each day. Valuing exercises simply build an awareness of the value dimension of the choices we make. In the day-to-day work of the class, the teacher can use many situations to build such a consciousness of values and thereby get children to think more deeply about what is important to them.

LESSON PLAN 1

Topic:	Symbolic messages.
Grade:	Six
Time:	One class period
Objectives:	Children will deduce certain information about a country from symbols placed on its coins. Children will relate the symbols to basic values of that country.
Resources:	At least one coin for each child, preferably coins or facsimiles of coins, from several different nations.
Lesson Development:	TEACHER: Boys and girls, for the past few days we have been studying the use of signs and symbols. At the close of our discussion yesterday we came to an important conclusion. What was it?

CHILD: We said that we could tell what people considered to be important to them by the symbols and signs they use on their buildings.

TEACHER: Yes. Now today you will have a chance to test that idea in a slightly different way. Each of you will be given a coin to use. Study the coin carefully and see how many things you can tell about the country just from what you see on the coin.

Coins are distributed to the class. After they have had time to make their observations, ask the children what they have concluded. As these are presented, write them on the chalkboard. Have each child tell *why* the conclusion was made. Pass the coins about for other children to inspect. Items such as the following may surface in this discussion:

These people believe in God.
They want (or believe in) liberty.
They are able to read their language.
Men must be more important than women in this country.
They construct large buildings.
They speak more than one language.
It is an old country.
They have a queen (or king).
They are a peace-loving people.
They are proud of their wars and war heroes.
They want people to be courageous.

Follow-Up: Imagine that the United States is planning to issue a new coin and there is a contest to get the best design. You decide to enter the contest. The rules are these:

1. Write down two ideas that best describe what people in our country think are important to them.
2. Think of and draw symbols that could be used on a coin to show these two qualities.

Side 1   Side 2

MORAL AND CHARACTER EDUCATION

Educational goals having to do with moral and character education have been an important component of the educational enterprise even before the founding of the republic. Indeed, efforts to achieve such goals were more apparent in the practices of public schools in the nineteenth and early twentieth centuries than they are today. American schools were not unique in this regard. Edward A. Wynne refers to this practice as the "great tradition" and points out that, "The transmission of moral values has been the dominant educational concern of most cultures throughout history."[4]

The public schools of this nation operate as secular rather than religious institutions, and, consequently, the source of moral authority has had to be found in such imperatives of social organization as social order, justice, and the concept of the social contract. As a result, conventional approaches to moral and character education have focused on specific virtues and character traits to be developed. Historically, moral messages were conveyed to children through direct instruction, using stories or case studies to illustrate the harsh consequences that flowed from violations of the moral code. Although the presentations were made within a secular context, it is obvious that what was being transmitted was a code of Christian ethics and virtues.

This method of moral and character education was dealt a serious blow by research conducted between 1928 and 1930 by Hartshorne and

[4] Edward A. Wynne, "The Great Tradition in Education: Transmitting Moral Values," *Educational Leadership*, 43 (December 1985–January 1986), p. 4.

May and published as a book entitled *Studies in Deceit.*[5] These studies reported that character education as conducted in schools had little effect on the moral behavior of individuals as measured by objective tests of honesty, service, altruism, and self-control. The findings led the researchers to conclude that it was the situation that confronted the individual that made the difference in the kind of moral choice that was made. Following the publication of the results of these studies there was something of a thirty-year hiatus in moral and character education in public schools.

Alternatives to the traditional methods of moral and character education began to emerge following the Korean War. The search for effective ways to inculcate basic values that lead to desirable moral conduct and character, and, at the same time, doing so in ways that do not compromise democratic principles, continues to the present time. The strategies that have received the most attention in recent years have taken two directions: one that focuses on some variation of value analysis, and the other that builds on the "stage theory" of moral development. The value analysis thrust is best illustrated by the work of Louis E. Raths, Merrill Harmin, and Sidney Simon dealing with value clarification and the valuing process, discussed in the previous section of this chapter. The research of the late Lawrence Kohlberg and his associates is the most widely cited example of work dealing with stages of moral development.[6] These procedures have not been sufficiently well developed—nor accepted—to be given an unqualified recommendation as strategies for moral and character education.

Direct and Indirect Approaches to Moral Education

The transmission of knowledge and skills is most commonly facilitated through *direct* methods of instruction. The material to be taught is identified, appropriate objectives are specified, and the instruction proceeds step-by-step toward the attainment of the objectives. Because these procedures work so well in teaching knowledge and knowledge-related skills, we assume that they work equally well for character and moral education. This, however, is not the case. In character and moral education, we are not concerned only that the individual knows social values and can deal with them intellectually. We are concerned fundamentally that the individual's *conduct* reflects those social values. And as every teacher and preacher should know, there is a world of difference be-

---

[5] Hugh Hartshorne and Mark A. May, *Studies in Deceit* (New York: Macmillan Publishing Company, 1928).

[6] Lawrence Kohlberg, *The Philosophy of Moral Development: Moral Stages and the Idea of Justice* (New York: Harper & Row, 1981).

tween the two. Because one knows what to do and how to behave, it does not necessarily follow that the person will act accordingly. All of the world's great religions admonish their faithful not to kill, steal, lie, and cheat, but people continue to kill, steal, lie, and cheat as they have done for thousands of years. Surely the people about whom the late William V. Shannon wrote are well informed about social values, yet these are not reflected in their character nor in their moral behavior:

> . . . The hollow men are everywhere — on the television screens and in the pulpits, in the banking and brokerage houses, in board rooms and sports arenas. Their distinguishing marks are faces distorted by greed and actions disdainful of law and limits.
>
> Rival preachers struggle for control of lucrative television programs. On Wall Street, speculators bribe investment bankers to obtain inside information on pending deals. The governor of Texas admits he and fellow trustees bribed youth to play football in defiance of rules. A former Secretary of the Treasury admits he set up a bank in the Bahamas to handle hot money and evade his income taxes. If America goes under, some Edward Gibbon of the future will write our epitaph: 'In the midst of plenty, they died of avarice.' [7]

Because knowledge does not necessarily lead to more ethical and moral behavior, it does not follow that direct instruction on ethics, values, and morals is useless. It means simply that direct instruction is limited in its effectiveness in changing such behavior. Character education and moral development are complex processes that must include many opportunities to experience what is being taught. Eventually the individual must *want* to behave in the expected way; he or she must *willingly comply* whether anyone is watching or not; he or she must *feel uncomfortable* when not behaving in accordance with the value; he or she must have a conscience that guides behavior.

The kinds of learning experiences needed to internalize values that lead to improved ethical and moral behavior should take the form of *indirect* instruction. This has to do with engineering an environment that elicits the desired behavior. There is obvious wisdom in such simple sayings as "values are caught rather than taught" and "actions speak louder than words." Rather than relying only on verbal instruction and precept, indirect strategies instruct by example, by inference, by modeling, by emulating, by imitating, by identifying, by imagining, and by observing. That is why the selection of teachers is so important, especially in the elementary and middle school years. These adults are expected not only to instruct children in knowledge and skills but to provide *examples* and *models* of good character and moral conduct. The classroom and, indeed, the entire school environment should exemplify those values,

---

[7] William V. Shannon, *Boston Globe*, April 5, 1987.

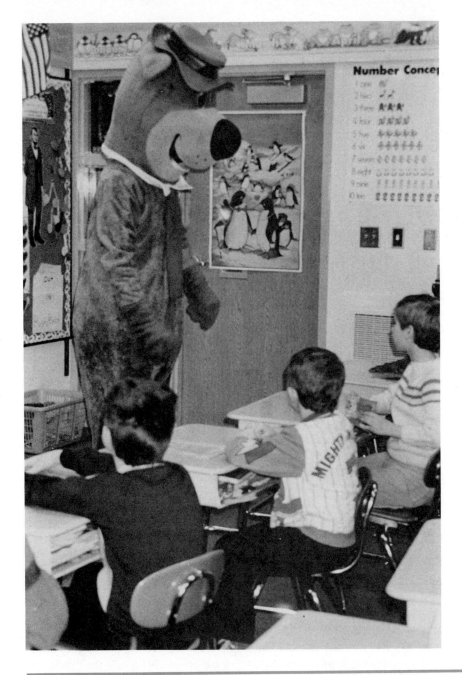

These children in a Tacoma elementary school are learning about earthquake safety from Yogi Bear. In this situation, we see the learning of substantive content enhanced because of the children's affective attachment to the presenter, who they recognize as a familiar and lovable cartoon character. They feel secure in the presence of their friend, Yogi, thereby making it possible for them to deal calmly and confidently with subject matter that could otherwise be quite frightening. (Photo by Pat Flynn, Tacoma School District.)

beliefs, and attitudes that the social studies program expects to see reflected in the conduct of the children who attend it.

The story is told of the person who was so struck by the play *1776* as a statement about freedom and democracy that she was moved to say that all Americans should be *forced* to see it! This is an example of the kinds of inconsistencies we often see in practices related to civic and citizenship education. Is it proper to use undemocratic methods to inculcate the basic social values of a democratic society? The answer to that question depends on the maturity of the learners that are being instructed.

In academic circles, there is a strong bias against anything that smacks of indoctrination. The term "to educate," we are told, is a derivative of a Latin word meaning "to lend out" or "to draw out." Thus, education is a process that *draws out* from the learner, not one that puts something in. Indoctrination and inculcation are, accordingly, not acceptable procedures if one is to "truly educate," especially to educate for life in a democratic society in which individual choice making is a cherished value. Although this perception of education seems attractive from a philosophical point of view, it does not easily convert into a plan of action for the conduct of character and moral education of young children.

The problem here is that a considerable amount of socialization, which is the foundation of character development and moral education, must take place *before* the child is capable of understanding the rationale for moral principles.[8] Teaching normative behavior and developing a sensitivity to what is perceived as right and wrong conduct simply cannot be postponed until the child has reached the "age of reason." The young child will not learn how to act and will not learn how to make judgments about the appropriateness of conduct unless there is adult intervention. The socialization process must begin early in the life of the child and a certain amount of inculcation or indoctrination of norms and values is inevitable. The teacher or the parent, however, must guard against being too heavy-handed in such teaching so as not to destroy the inclination to be critical and must not carry it on too long. As children mature, they need to develop some sense of ownership of the social values they are being asked to internalize. For example, they need to develop the attitude that it is *their* classroom, *their* school, and *their* community, that they are an important part of it, and that what happens there affects them directly. When they share in this investment in their surroundings, they are not apt to think of themselves as outsiders who are simply passing through someone else's "turf." It is at these more advanced levels that children need to think through reasons and rationales, and to have the opportunity to resolve moral dilemmas appropriate to their age level. Thus, in the end, we want children to be socialized into the moral values on which there is general consensus, while at the same time to cultivate their capacity for thoughtful criticism.

---

[8] Jean Piaget *et al., The Moral Judgment of the Child* (New York: The Free Press, 1965).

LESSON PLAN 2

Topic:	People of Prominence
Grade:	Five
Time:	Variable — three to five class periods

Objective: Children will develop an awareness of the qualities and traits that characterize persons of prominence.

Interest Building: Have children list as many names of "famous people"—living or dead—as they can think of in five minutes. Then have them discuss their lists in terms of what the individuals did to make them famous. Do a quick check on the number that were political figures, war heroes, sports figures, etc. Have children speculate on why these particular individuals became well known, whereas most of their contemporaries did not. Tell the class that over the next few days they will study the qualities and traits of famous people more carefully.

Lesson Development: Have wide selection of biographies of prominent people available for children. Ask each child to choose one biography to read. The books are to be read in the next week, and children are to answer the following three questions:

(1) What did you admire about the person?

(2) What qualities did the person have that made him/her come to the attention of others who knew him/her?

(3) What did the person do that made him/her famous?

At the completion of the assignment, have children discuss their ideas with classmates in groups of four. Have them try to find qualities or traits that were common to each of the persons about whom they read. Have each group report findings to entire class and discuss.

Summary: Generate a list of qualities that (1) applied to all; (2) applied to some; (3) applied to a few; (4) applied to none. Discuss reasons for differences. Solicit individual reactions in terms of how they might apply some of these qualities to their own lives.

Materials: Biographies of prominent persons at a reading level suitable for the class, to be secured from the school library.

Ideas for Additional Lessons:

1. Familiarize children with several well-known fables. In groups of four or five, have children dramatize the fable as it was originally written. Then have the children develop another skit illustrating an application of the message of the fable to some aspects of modern life. Discuss.

2. Have children develop a running list of proverbs. Place each proverb on an index card and post on the bulletin board. (*Example:* "The nail that sticks out gets hammered," "A rolling stone gathers no moss," "Where there's smoke, there's fire," "When pulling weeds, be sure to get rid of the roots.") Have children discuss those they find especially interesting and have them generate examples of applications in ordinary living. Relate the discussion to specific values or moral messages being conveyed in the proverbs.

THE LEARNING CONTEXT

When it comes to values, beliefs, attitudes, moral, and character education of children, one cannot escape the importance of a social context and the human teacher. Subject matter and skills can often be learned effectively through reading or by means of computer instruction or other sophisticated media. Working with classmates often facilitates the achievement of academic learning goals, but it is not critical to their attainment. Children who live in geographically remote regions may be home schooled and learn the basic subject matter and skills very well. But the kinds of learnings with which this chapter is concerned really need to be taught and learned in a social setting under the guidance of a human teacher. It is the teacher who is responsible for establishing the kind of classroom environment that embodies the values that children are expected to learn. It is the teacher who ensures that human relations in the classroom honor and respect the dignity and worth of all human beings. It is the teacher who provides the day-to-day adult model of democratic values in action. And it is the social setting of the classroom environment that provides the laboratory in which values and morals are nurtured and in which the child's character takes shape.

DISCUSSION QUESTIONS AND SUGGESTED ACTIVITIES

1. In recalling your own elementary and middle school social studies experiences, what values did your teachers stress? What activities do you remember that were particularly values oriented? Would such activities be worthwhile for today's children? Why or why not?

2. The use of plays and pageants is sometimes criticized, or even ridiculed, because such activities are not consistent with what the critic perceives as the true mission of schools. Do you think such criticism is soundly based? Discuss.

3. As you think about the world in which today's children live, can you think of situations they encounter or experiences they have that either reinforce or contradict character traits being promoted by the social studies program? What implications do you see in this for the teacher?

4. Examine report cards used by schools in your area. How do they report to parents on the learnings discussed in this chapter? If a checklist of traits is used, are the items stated in a negative or a positive way? Is the emphasis on building conformity or independence?

5. Select a nontext children's book that might be especially useful in illustrating a general value. Explain why you selected the one you did. Develop a set of values-oriented questions you would want children to respond to after they have read the book.

6. Why do you think parents often react negatively when the school deals with the development of personal values in children? Suggest guidelines that a teacher can use in order to handle personal values in ways that are educationally and ethically acceptable.

7. What values are being promoted when children engage in activities that symbolize patriotism, such as saying the Pledge of Allegiance? What are the advantages and limitations in using symbolic exercises to promote values?

8. What indicators might a teacher look for to determine whether his or her work with children in the area of moral and character education is being effective? Do this for a grade in which you have a special interest.

SELECTED REFERENCES

Association for Supervision and Curriculum Development. *Educational Leadership*, 43 (December 1985–January 1986). This issue contains twenty articles dealing with the school's role in developing character.

———. *Educational Leadership*, 45 (May 1988). This issue includes seventeen articles dealing with values, moral education, and related matters.

BYRNES, DEBORAH A. "Children and Prejudice." *Social Education*, 52 (April–May 1988), pp. 267–271.

CHAZAN, BARRY. *Contemporary Approaches to Moral Education.* New York: Teachers College Press, 1985.

DAVIS, E. DALE. "Should the Public Schools Teach Values?" *Phi Delta Kappan*, 65 (January 1984), pp. 358–360.

GRANT, CARL A. "The Persistent Significance of Race in Schooling." *The Elementary School Journal*, 88 (May 1988), pp. 561–569.

GRIFFITH, EMLYN I. "New Emphases on Basic Values." *American Education*, 20 (May 1984), pp. 14–16.

HOFFMAN, ALAN J., AND NANCY L. HOFFMAN. "Today's Tarnished Sports Heroes: Implications for Ethics-Based Instruction." *Social Studies and the Young Learner*, 1 (September/October 1988), pp. 14–18.

HOWE, HAROLD II. "Can Schools Teach Values?" *Teachers College Record*, 89 (Fall 1987), pp. 55–68.

JOHNSTON, MARILYN, AND CAROL LUBOMUDROV. "Teachers' Level of Moral Reasoning and Their Understanding of Classroom Rules and Roles." *The Elementary School Journal*, 88 (September 1987), pp. 64–77.

PARKER, WALTER C. "Why Ethics in Citizenship Education?" *Social Studies and the Young Learner*, 1 (September/October 1988), pp. 3–5.

PATE, GLENN S. "Research on Reducing Prejudice." *Social Education*, 52 (April–May 1988), pp. 287–289.

Phi Delta Kappan, 69 (February 1988). Authors Jacques S. Benninga, Thomas Lickona, Edward A. Wynne, Dennis F. Murphy, and Carolyn Pereira present five articles in a special section on emerging developments in character and moral education in the elementary school grades.

PIETIG, JEANNE. "Values and Morality in Early 20th Century Elementary Schools: A Perspective." *Social Education,* 47 (April 1983), pp. 262–265.

PYSZKOWSKI, IRENE S. "Moral Values and the Schools — Is There A Way Out of the Maze?" *Education,* 107 (Fall 1986), pp. 41–48.

RYAN, KEVIN. "The New Moral Education." *Phi Delta Kappan,* 68 (November 1986), pp. 228–233.

II

Social Studies Content and Content-Related Skills

4

History and Geography in the Social Studies

The sources of subject matter for the social studies curriculum have been broadened in recent years. Today many schools include concepts and subject matter from economics, political science, sociology, anthropology; from the humanities; and from current affairs and emerging social concerns such as environmental issues, uses of energy, and global relationships. Nonetheless, history and geography remain the backbone, or central core, around which most schools organize their social studies programs. History and geography are the integrating disciplines that serve as the basic framework for the social studies curriculum, especially in the third grade and beyond. In this and the succeeding four chapters, we will examine how the several sources of subject matter contribute to the elementary school social studies curriculum.

HISTORY AND THE SOCIAL STUDIES

In recent years there has been a revival of interest in history as a school subject because many lay persons as well as educators believe that history can and should contribute directly to attaining the broad goals of citizenship education. Most states have legislative requirements calling for the teaching of state and national history. A knowledge of history supported by actual experiences in the practice of responsible citizenship in the school and classroom unquestionably contributes to a strengthening of loyalties and helps children identify with their historical background. Persons develop love of country, loyalty, and fidelity through a knowledge, appreciation, and understanding of the struggles of the people who contributed to the building of this great and powerful nation. Hazel W. Hertzberg reminds us that "The improvement of history teaching in the schools is not just desirable: it is a national necessity."[1]

History teaching is valuable when it provides opportunities for the child to identify with the past. The historical experiences of the nation then become part of the heritage of individual children and, thus, a part of the common culture. This is amply demonstrated by the interest expressed by children when they dramatize events from our nation's history, events that may have occurred long before their own ancestors came to these shores. Because students can reflect on the known consequences of specific decisions that were made and can speculate on what outcomes may have occurred had other decisions been made, the subject matter of history provides many opportunities to teach critical thinking.

Knowledge of history does not lend itself to the practical solution of everyday problems *in the same way* as does a knowledge of spelling words or skills in reading or mathematics. Because little direct relationship between a knowledge of history and daily problems of living exists, it cannot and should not be thought of as an entirely practical subject. In this sense, history resembles literature, art, and music in that its contribution may lie along cultural lines rather than along strictly practical ones. Although children will not apply their knowledge of history directly to the solution of the many complex problems of the twentieth century, it will give them an insight, appreciation, and understanding of those problems.

Teaching Suggestions

The teaching of history in the elementary and middle schools occurs within the context of the social studies curriculum, and history contrib-

---

[1] Hazel W. Hertzberg, "Students, Methods and Materials of Instruction," *History in the Schools,* Matthew T. Downey, ed., National Council for the Social Studies Bulletin 74. (Washington, D.C.: National Council for the Social Studies, 1985), p. 40.

utes substantially to the program. The emphasis is on understanding the past, the people who lived during those times, their problems and ways of living, and their struggles to meet basic needs. History taught in this way helps the child develop a better understanding and appreciation of human growth through the years — not only along political lines but in all

The University of Texas Institute of Texan Cultures at San Antonio is an exceptionally fine instructional facility that features a special exhibit area for each of the 26 ethnic and cultural groups that have contributed to that state's development. Here we see a resource person from the Institute instructing children from a local school who are there on a field trip. Although the Institute for Texan Cultures is unique, all communities have some resources, however modest, that can be useful in studying the local community and home state. (Photo courtesy of the University of Texas Institute of Texan Cultures at San Antonio.)

ways—that contribute to a richer and more abundant life. This would include a study of the growth of the arts, sciences, literature, humanitarian movements, and other cultural aspects of human development.

An increasing number of teachers are discovering the exciting potentials offered by *social history*. Social history explores how ordinary people met the day-to-day challenges, pleasures, disappointments, and routines of everyday life in the period in which they lived. Children are fascinated in learning how people much like themselves made a living; engaged in leisure-time activities; raised their families; celebrated important holidays; punished criminals; educated their children; and observed such important milestones in life as birth, marriage, and the death of loved ones. In social history, the common persons—as opposed to those who have achieved prominence—become the central focus of study.

The following represent *samples* of major generalizations from the field of history that have been used as organizing ideas in developing programs in historical study:

1. The history of a country has a definite bearing on the culture, traditions, beliefs, attitudes, and ways of living of its people.
2. People are influenced by values, ideals, and inherited institutions as well as by their environment.
3. Several civilizations have risen and fallen in the history of human societies; many have contributed to existing civilizations.
4. Human societies have undergone and are undergoing continual, although perhaps gradual, changes in response to various forces, but not all change is progress.
5. Guidelines for understanding thought and action in contemporary affairs can be derived from the historical backgrounds of society.

A good social studies program will help the child build psychological bridges or links with the past through a series of planned experiences. The following are a few examples of activities that may be helpful for this purpose.

Opportunity to Examine Objects of Historical Significance. Children are usually interested in objects of historical significance, particularly if they can examine them closely and handle them. Items from the past that will be helpful in teaching are such things as Indian arrowheads, artifacts from past wars, a facsimile of a slave contract, a family Bible, deeds, photographs, church membership rolls, school records, a hymnal, and branding irons. Children may bring items of this type to school to share with their classmates. Such objects may have some monetary value and must be handled accordingly. If a particular item is highly valued, it is best for the adult owner to bring it to the school to show the children and tell them of its significance.

These children are observing candlemaking, a process of ancient origin, at Old Sturbridge Village, Sturbridge, Massachusetts, a recreated early nineteenth-century New England village. Experiences of this type help children develop a sense of appreciation for the ingenuity of human beings who lived in earlier times and had to depend on their own resourcefulness in meeting the challenges that faced them in a world without the conveniences that most families enjoy today. (Photo by Robert S. Arnold; courtesy of Old Sturbridge Village.)

In addition to historical *realia,* that is, real things or artifacts that can be brought to the classroom, or to those that may be in a school museum, the teacher should look into the permanent museum resources of the community. Most larger communities maintain exhibits of historical materials significant to the local community and state. School groups are usually encouraged to make visits to local museums and are frequently taken on guided tours through the exhibits. Some museums change their displays from time to time and will on request furnish schools with information about their current exhibits. These resources present valuable opportunities for teaching history and need to be used extensively.

The best use of the museum can be made by children after they have had an opportunity to develop a familiarity with the subject matter related to the material on display. This means that visits will be made after the children have been able to explore ideas and concepts in the classroom through reading, study, and discussion rather than at the beginning of a unit. They will then be ready to clarify ideas: They can ask intelligent questions and can enrich their understanding through the

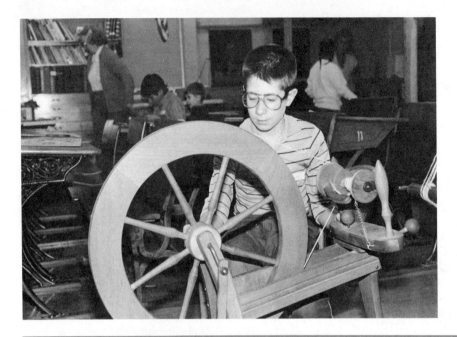

This student is learning firsthand about one important part of pioneer technology. Experiences of this type can help learners build an appreciation for the skills and resourcefulness of those who lived in bygone days. (Photo by Edna Kellman, Seattle Public Schools.)

museum visit. In taking children to a museum, teachers will want to ready the class beforehand by identifying a few relevant questions concerning the items to be observed.

Many museums in the country have assembled artifacts, pictures, and other items of interest into kits that are available to schools on a rental basis. Study kits ordinarily have a teacher's guide that provides background information as well as practical suggestions concerning the use of the material.

Opportunity to Talk with Older People of the Community. Children are fascinated when old-timers talk of their exciting experiences in the early community. They are surprised and electrified by the thought that the person now speaking to them served with General Eisenhower or shook President Kennedy's hand. These experiences make real people out of historical figures and remove them from the realm of myth and unreality. Interviewing persons who have had firsthand experience with an event under study is a technique often used by historians.

Almost every community has one or more persons who has devoted a substantial amount of time to the study of local history as a hobby. These individuals are excellent resources for the teacher, not only in their personally speaking to the class but also in directing the teacher's attention to other resources that might otherwise be overlooked. This provides an excellent opportunity to study the social history of the local community. To catch some of the enthusiasm and interest such persons ordinarily have for history is, in itself, a valuable experience for both the teacher and the children.

Oral History. The structured interviews or informal conversations with persons of historical significance in the local community can be preserved as oral history by using cassette tape recorders. This procedure has the added instructional value of involving children themselves on a firsthand basis in gathering historical data. The taped interviews should be structured to the extent that children have identified the questions to be asked and the sequence in which they are to be presented. Children should, however, be encouraged to include follow-up questions that emerge as the interview progresses. Often the interaction between the interviewer and the subject becomes stilted because the child asks only the questions that are prepared in advance. It helps if children simulate the interview or a portion of it in advance, with a classmate serving as the subject of the interview. The cassette recorder should be used for the simulation, too, just as it will be used in the real interview. A good-quality taped interview will result only if the interviewer has good interaction skills and if the substantive aspects of the subject matter and the technical elements of the recording are well planned and implemented.

If good classroom preparation precedes the interview, children may obtain taped interviews of a quality that can become a part of a central collection of local history materials. It is necessary to obtain a signed release from the person being interviewed if the material is to be used beyond the work of the class. Where it is possible to do so, children may also want to secure a photograph of the person being interviewed.

On the basis of several years of experience in helping teachers conduct oral history as an instructional activity, Professor John F. Ahern of the University of Toledo offers the following suggestions:

1. Conduct two interviews with the same person at least a day apart.
2. After the first interview, have children respond to the stem, "I wish I had said . . ." in preparing questions for the second interview.
3. Make use of the counter on the cassette to find the exact spot where something was asked or said.
4. Role play the interview in advance.
5. Brainstorm questions with students.
6. Be aware of noise in the environment that might affect the quality of the recording.

7. Test the batteries in the cassette before the interview.
8. Provide questions before the interview.
9. Get out a photo album, if there is one.
10. Interview one person at a time. (Important because one often wants to answer for or correct [modify] the response of the other!)
11. Ask ahead of time if it is o.k. to inquire about age.
12. Make sure names are spelled correctly.
13. Begin with easy questions, such as "Where were you born?" "Where did your family come from?" "Why did your family settle here?" Women like to talk about their last daughter's wedding; men like to talk about their first job.
14. Use techniques such as the following to elicit responses:
    "Tell me more about . . ."
    "Why do you think . . ."
    "Give me an example . . ."[2]

A STUDY OF LOCAL HISTORY

A combination fifth–sixth grade class used the publication of a magazine as the integrating activity for the study of their local community. Each student in the class selected a long-time resident in the community as one source of information. The students interviewed the resident and tape recorded the conversation using oral history procedures. Each student was then requested to prepare an article for the class magazine based on the information secured in the interview. In addition to the interviews, students used other local information sources, such as printed material and photographs from local libraries or personal collections. Also, numerous resource persons were asked to make presentations to the class on such topics as local history, interviewing procedures, journal writing, and procedures associated with the production of a publication.

Reading Materials. There is a plentiful supply of well-written, exciting books of a historical nature that have great value in helping children identify with the past. Children do this when they become "lost in a book." In the vivid accounts of the adventures of early explorers, the child relives the perils, dangers, and excitement of Lewis and Clark; the disappointments and trials of Abe Lincoln; the hazards of a trip across the western plains; or the rugged winters of Wisconsin. We are referring here specifically to "trade books"—books about Indians, airplanes, urban life, space travel, national parks, biographies of famous Americans, life in other lands, communities at work, and similar topics. Many contemporary children's books are not only informative but represent good children's literature. They have exceptional artwork and maintain high standards of literary quality.

[2] Professor John F. Ahern, in a presentation entitled "Making History More Meaningful," Hamilton County Shared Inservice, Cincinnati, Ohio, October 2, 1987.

Literary works useful for social studies instruction may be classified as (1) *informative accounts* — works that simply convey specific information in literary form on topics studied, such as books about trucks, trains, countries, printing, communication, homes around the world; (2) *informative fiction* — reconstruction of historical events that are built around a fictionalized plot or story; (3) *biographies;* (4) *nonfiction history;* (5) *poems;* (6) *locally produced materials* — consisting possibly of works falling in any of the preceding five categories.

Literature and literary materials should play an important part in social studies instruction because they convey so well the affective dimension of human experience. The realism that is achieved through vivid portrayals in works of literature stirs the imagination of the young reader and helps develop a feeling for and identification with the topic being studied. The relationship between literature and some of the subjects included in the social studies — particularly history — has been noted by numerous writers. Some great works of literature are also considered important historical documents, and the reverse is also true.

One reason that literary materials are so important is that they provide rich detail that is impossible to get in even a well-designed text or an encyclopedia. A textbook, for example, may simply mention women who spearheaded the movement to gain equal rights, such as Susan B. Anthony, Elizabeth Stanton Cady, Lucretia C. Mott, and Julia Ward Howe. However, the child can learn much about these courageous and determined Americans by reading children's biographies of their lives. Here the child can get a vivid word picture of the times in which these women lived. Such supporting details add richness and meaning to an understanding of the historical period studied.

The Joint Committee of the National Council for the Social Studies and the Children's Book Council has a Book Review Subcommittee that selects and evaluates trade books useful for teaching social studies in the elementary and middle schools. An annotated list of their selections is published each April or May in *Social Education* under the title "Notable Children's Trade Books in the Field of Social Studies." The books selected for these bibliographies "(1) are written for children in grades K – 8; (2) emphasize human relations; (3) present an original theme or a fresh slant on a traditional topic; (4) are highly readable; and, when appropriate, (5) include maps and illustrations." The annotations include a synopsis of content, publisher, price, and reading level. These lists are highly recommended to teachers and librarians.[3]

Films, Videotapes, and Filmstrips.   Films and videotapes have much to contribute to teaching history and geography. In a film or videotape,

---

[3] "Notable 1987 Children's Trade Books in the Field of Social Studies," *Social Education,* 52 (April/May 1988), pp. 312–319.

the children can traverse great distances and move through centuries of time, having before them a picture of places, persons, and processes that would be impossible to obtain in other ways. In many respects, the film has advantages over field trips because it singles out the most important aspects of a situation and eliminates the nonessentials. It is more selective in what it allows the viewer to see than is the human eye. It is a demanding medium and holds the attention of the viewer to a greater extent than do most other learning aids. A film can telescope great lengths of time into minutes, making it possible to observe a timeless process in a single class period. Its greatest asset, of course, is that it depicts motion, and the best use can be made of films showing situations involving motion. If motion is not a factor, a good photograph, a slide, or a filmstrip may be equally effective.

Filmstrips offer advantages over motion pictures in terms of cost, availability, and use. Because of the relatively low cost, schools ordinarily maintain their own filmstrip collection, and they are immediately available, therefore, when needed. A good instructional feature of the filmstrip is that it is possible to discuss its content as it is being shown. If it becomes necessary to refer to a picture previously shown, the filmstrip can be turned back to the frame in question. Filmstrips are easy to catalog and store and are simple to show. In this respect, they have many advantages over slides.

Filmstrips may be used to achieve a number of purposes in the social studies unit. A filmstrip on the New England States, for example, gives a clear picture of the physical features of this area and thereby assists in understanding map symbols and provides a good readiness for map reading. It may serve to introduce children to other countries of the world, showing how people in other lands live, work, and play. Filmstrips are useful in presenting material that follows a definite sequence — how a letter gets from sender to receiver; the steps in the production of milk; the history, growth and development of an area; the course of soil erosion; or the steps to be followed in the event of some emergency such as a fire, drowning, an accident, or a hurricane.

Interesting Study Projects.   In addition to the learning activities planned specifically to help the child build psychological bridges with the past, the teaching of history in the elementary school can be enlivened and made more meaningful through the use of a variety of other activities. The following are examples of only a few that have been used successfully by elementary and middle school teachers:

1. *Collect and exhibit* old photographs that show the history of the community.
2. *Collect and try* pioneer recipes; learn folk dances; investigate local cultural contributions of various nationality groups.

3. *Write items* of local history for the school paper or for the local newspaper.
4. *Write biographical sketches* of early settlers in the community.
5. *Investigate the history* of some important old buildings in the community.
6. *Trace the history* of some local industry such as mining, manufacturing, or lumbering.
7. *Make models* or sketches of oxcarts, prairie schooners, canoes, spinning wheels, or other pioneer equipment.
8. *Paint a mural* of some aspect of the history of the local community or state.
9. *Write and present* a pageant telling the story of some aspect of local, state, or national history.
10. *Collect songs* of various periods of history, and present a costumed recital of them.
11. *Make a model* of the town as it looked fifty, seventy-five, or one hundred years ago, or a diorama of life in the town at an earlier time.
12. *Make a topographical or relief map* of the local area, indicating points of historical significance.
13. *Use historical settings* for creative dramatics activities.
14. *Make pictorial time lines* tracing periods of national, state, or local history.
15. *Prepare bulletin boards* and other exhibits having a historical theme.
16. *Write, plan, and prepare* short plays or presentations in connection with holiday observances.
17. *Organize a junior historians club* in the classroom, and establish contact with the local and state historical societies.
18. *Have your class participate in the National History Day competition* (grades 6 – 12). Each state has a National History Day coordinator from whom information may be obtained. National History Day projects need to be started early in the school year. Local competition is usually held in March and April; state competition, in May; and national finals, in or near Washington, D.C., in June.
19. *Involve students in the Civic Achievement Award Program* (grades 5 – 8). See page 156 for information about the program.

Holiday Observances

Some of the most satisfying and long-remembered experiences children have in the elementary school are those associated with the observance of holidays. Many schools and states require observance of holidays such as Presidents' Day, Thanksgiving Day, Veterans' Day, Martin Luther King Day, and other days of import to the local community and to the state. Although school programs related to the observance of such historical holidays are often guided more by fancy than by historical fact, these occasions, nonetheless, present excellent opportunities to teach effectively history associated with the day.

The chief contribution that holiday observances can make to the education of young children is to acquaint them with their rich cultural heritage and help them grow in their appreciation of it. With this in mind, the teacher can plan a short unit related to the holiday, keeping the content simple but truthful. Commonly, such short units have as their culminating activity a dramatization that is shared with another class.

If the teacher does not plan to devote more than a class period or two to such an observance, reading an appropriate story or poem, followed by discussion, can be a profitable experience. After the reading, the children can participate in a suitable follow-up activity such as drawing, painting, singing a related song, writing an original poem or story, or listening to a recording; or they can use the story for creative dramatics. This is also an appropriate time to view a film dealing with some aspect of history related to the holiday or to listen to a recorded dramatization of a historical event. In this same connection, the teacher may discuss with the class the significance of a classroom picture or a symbol such as the flag, the Declaration of Independence, the Constitution, or the national anthem. The amount of time spent on activities of this type ought always to be weighed against their value as educational experiences.

LESSON PLAN 3

Topic:	Getting things in order: Making cornbread
Grade:	Two
Time:	Two class periods
Objectives:	Children will learn to identify a sequence of events and will learn the importance of following directions.
Interest Building:	Display pictures, out of sequence, that show the preparation and consumption of a Thanksgiving meal.
	Ask what is wrong with the way they are arranged. Have children rearrange pictures in a proper sequence.
	Discuss how order is important in lots of things we do. Ask for suggestions of things they do in a certain order (getting ready for school, playing a game, reading a book).
Lesson Development:	Read an account of the first Thanksgiving and discuss some of the foods the Pilgrims and Indians ate at the feast. Include discussion of products made of corn, stressing its importance in the diet then *and* now.
	Tell class that the next activity is one in which order is very important; they will be making cornbread.

Display large photos illustrating the process of making cornbread in the correct sequence. In random order, display sentence strips that describe each step in the process.

Ask children to look carefully at the photos and to read the sentence strips. Match them up, using clues in the pictures to help them understand the words in the sentences.

Discuss some possible consequences of not following the recipe in the correct order. What if we put in the wrong amount of milk or leave out salt? What if we decide to set the oven higher or lower? What would happen if we did not grease the pan?

Divide the class into two groups (or more, depending on size of class). With the teacher as leader, follow the recipe, step-by-step, giving each child a chance to participate actively. Prior to each step, ask for a volunteer to read the directions.

Summary/Follow-up: Eat the cornbread, and have each child rate it on a checklist. Make a graph showing ratings.

Give copy of the recipe to each child (who can make it for his or her own Thanksgiving meal at home).

Recommend that children try other recipes at home with adult supervision.

Materials: Story of the first Thanksgiving, photographs (Thanksgiving series, cornbread sequence), cornbread recipe, cooking utensils, ingredients, oven, checklist.

GEOGRAPHY AND THE SOCIAL STUDIES

Geography has traditionally occupied and continues to occupy a position of central importance in the social studies curriculum. Events in modern times have underscored the need to study geography from a global perspective at all levels. Social studies topics have a place in space, and geography is concerned with the character of those places. The qualities that distinguish an area and the way it relates to other areas are both of great significance in understanding human occupance and use of the earth.

The teaching of geography has suffered somewhat because of the persistence of traditional and often stereotyped ideas about the nature of geography. School geography has too frequently meant memorizing and naming various features of the physical environment: locating rivers; naming mountains; learning places, products, capes, and bays. Such teaching allows little, if any, opportunity to do critical thinking in the study of geography. Modern geography stresses the method of geographic inquiry as a major educational outcome. It is important to know place location, of course, but one must also have the intellectual tools to grasp the significance of such information and relate it to a broader

These middle school students are making an on-site exploration of the local environment, an important aspect of geographic education in the elementary and middle schools. In addition to learning geographic concepts and subject matter, these students have an opportunity to apply such skills as observing carefully, taking notes, and preparing a report. (Photo by Nancy Stutzman, Lake Washington School District.)

cultural and environmental context. Teaching children to think geographically must accompany the teaching of specific geographical information and facts.

Geography is a science that is concerned with the study and description of the earth. Traditionally, this has meant physical geography, with studies focusing on the unequal distribution of such phenomena as water, minerals, climate, productive land, vegetation, land forms, and so on. Undoubtedly, the intense interest that people have in the world in which they live and their desire to find out what lies beyond the immediate surroundings gave rise to the development of the science of geography. As early people began to move from one place to another on the earth, they noticed that one place differed from another and made observations of these differences. In time, these observations were systematically recorded and were gradually brought together into the discipline of geography. Geographic knowledge became extremely useful and, indeed, essential for travelers, explorers, military leaders, and those engaged in trade and commerce.

As people found their way into all parts of the world, knowledge of the physical geography of the earth greatly increased. All parts of the world were explored in a general way and were to some extent described and mapped. Then the emphasis in geography began to shift from simply describing phenomena to explaining the differences that were found from one place to another. In addition, the relationships between the physiographic and biotic elements within those areas were beginning to be explored. The study of the uniqueness of a particular area — the study of the factors that make an area different from any other area of the earth — is embodied in the concept of *areal differentiation*. Also, relationships between areas were explored, that is, the links and bonds, either natural or human-made, that develop between places. Such studies concern themselves with the concept of *spatial interaction*. These two concepts — areal differentiation and spatial interaction — are central to the understanding of the concerns and approaches of modern geography.

The National Council for Geographic Education and the Association of American Geographers have prepared a guidelines document that identifies five central themes on which the K–12 program in geography should focus. These are (1) *location,* the position on the earth's surface; (2) *place,* the physical, human, and observed characteristics that distinguish one setting from another; (3) *relationships within places,* the advantages and disadvantages that places have for human settlement, and how people have modified or adapted to natural settings; (4) *movement,* the relationships between and among places through the movement of people, ideas, and materials; and (5) *regions,* areas that display unity in terms of selected criteria such as a governmental unit, a language group, or a type of landform. The guidelines document also identifies learning outcomes for various grade levels.[4]

Teaching Suggestions

The primary-grade teacher will have no difficulty finding ways to include geography in social studies units. Much of the early geography teaching centers on the landscape of the local community. The primary-grade child may experience and observe firsthand in the local community various land and water forms—lakes, creeks, islands, gullies, slopes. The teacher should encourage children to explore the various forms of native plant and animal life and observe the characteristic changes of these with changing seasons of the year. With some help from the teacher, the children can build their understanding of ideas such as the following:

1. People adapt themselves to conditions in the environment.
2. Transportation plays an important part in the distribution of food.
3. Nature changes the character of the earth.
4. The same land can be used for many different purposes.
5. Every day we use things that have come from all over the world.

Local Geographical Exploration.   The opportunities for children to explore geographically in and around the school site should not be overlooked. A primary-grade class may visit a nearby basement excavation for a new home. The children observe the various layers of soil, and the teacher calls their attention to the many roots found in the fertile topsoil. The class is able to obtain samples of the various strata of soil to take back to their classroom for an experiment in seeing how well plants grow in the various layers—an early beginning in the appreciation and understanding of the value of soil conservation. The presence of earth-moving equipment suggests that human beings do things to modify the environment. Children learn that sometimes these modifications are helpful, but other times they are destructive and harmful. The imaginative teacher can plan similar experiences in purposeful exploration in connection with soil, water, water bodies, minerals, rocks, local vegetation, and surface features. Experiences of this kind provide an opportunity to learn and apply an important method of study used by geographers: careful observation of phenomena.

[4] *Guidelines for Geographic Education, Elementary and Secondary Schools,* published jointly by the Association of American Geographers, 1710 16th Street, N.W., Washington, D.C. 20009, and the National Council for Geographic Education, Western Illinois University, Macomb, Illinois 61455, 1984.

Weather and Climate. Weather and climate present another area of exploration. Children have viewed weather forecasts on television. The frequency of reference to weather in adult conversations indicates the degree to which weather and climatic conditions have an effect on the lives of people. In primary-grade classrooms, children will want to have their own charts on which they can record various weather data observed each day. The teacher reads the daily temperature, or the children report the official daily temperature that they have heard over an early morning radio broadcast. These temperatures can be shown graphically, thereby applying knowledge of numbers and graphs. Over a period of several weeks or months the graph will show the changes occurring in temperatures and seasons of the year. Children can also record data dealing with wind velocities, cloud formations, precipitation, and similar subjects. They can also make their own predictions based on the data they have collected. Sensitivity to weather changes will again call attention to the changes in native plant and animal life as well as to the adaptations people make to changing seasons. Here the teacher can apply another technique of the geographer: recording data and using simple charts.

Geography in Reading and Language Arts. A number of opportunities for teaching geography may grow out of the reading and language program of the class. In the basic reading series one will find many stories and selections with a geographical setting. The children read about the family that took a weekend trip to the lake or spent a summer in the mountains. They read about the antics of the monkeys in the zoo and wonder about their natural habitat. Brief explanations and discussions of accompanying geographic phenomena are helpful in gaining a better understanding of the meaning of the story. Primary-grade teachers often read to children, and many of these stories present opportunities for teaching geography. The selections children read in their classroom news periodical and the current affairs that they report also provide opportunities to develop geographic concepts and skills.

Teaching Geographical Relationships Through the Grades. Children in the middle and upper grades can delve more deeply into the relationships between the earth and the activities of human beings than they could in the primary grades. They learn that people the world over attempt to satisfy their basic needs in ways that are influenced by their environment, their past experiences, and present resources. Even though the methods various people use to meet these needs in specific regions of the world may seem strange to us, they are not unusual for those who inhabit that region. Although children should *not* be taught that geographic conditions *determine* how people live, they should learn that geography sets certain limits on the choices available to them. (For example, people in the Arctic are probably not going to find it cost effective to grow oranges and bananas there even though present technology would make that possible.) In this connection, children learn that historical and cultural components of a society as well as natural features are significant to the development of geographic relationships. A few examples of some of the key geographical ideas that should be stressed in the middle and upper grades are

1. Places on the earth have a distinctiveness about them that differentiates them from all other places.
2. Physical and human changes in one part of the world affect people's lives in other parts of the world.
3. The relationship between agricultural resources and human life is less direct in highly urbanized societies than it is in other regions.
4. Areas of the earth develop bonds, interconnections, and relations with other areas.
5. The wasteful exploitation and pollution of natural and human resources pose serious problems for the welfare of the earth's rapidly growing population of human beings.

In the study of various regions of the world, the middle-grade child will follow somewhat the same pattern of exploration and problem solving as in the primary grades. When studying a specific region, such factors as these will be included, although not necessarily in this sequence: (1) the surface features of the region, (2) the plant and animal life characteristic of the region, and (3) the relationship of this life to the climatic and weather conditions that affect the occupations and way of life of the people of the area. From this systematic study of communities in various natural regions of the world, the children can discover some relationships between various geographic conditions and the activities of human groups. For example, they might discover that in places where one finds similar physical geographic conditions, people may live quite differently. The reverse could also be true. How people use natural surroundings depends mainly on cultural factors.

The study of specific communities and regions (e.g. desert people, mountain people, polar regions, and so on) presents difficult instructional problems no matter what system is used in selecting them. Too often they are treated in a superficial or romantic way. It becomes easy to make unwarranted value judgments about the people studied, to arrive at hasty and inaccurate generalizations, and to develop stereotyped ideas of people. The tendency has been to stress traditional or legendary aspects of a people's culture rather than coming to grips with their way of life in modern times. The need for accurate information and a proper instructional emphasis is essential if valid understandings are to develop.

The geographic regions selected for study should be sufficiently different from one another to help the child learn the characteristic adjustments people make under varying conditions. These then may be compared with life in the local community, stressing the similarities in the basic requirements of life that people everywhere have to meet. Such a study should include historical and cultural elements as a natural part of geographic study.

Intensive studies of continents, with the exception of Australia, are usually not well suited for elementary school grades because the natural, cultural, and historical backgrounds of various sections are generally so diverse that it is difficult to select a unifying set of concepts for the study. Consequently, children often learn a number of facts about geographic features but fail to relate these to the people who inhabit the area. It is ordinarily better to select specific communities in representative regions of the world and study those intensively.

At the beginning of the study of a community or a region, it is helpful, however, to make an overview of the continent on which the region is located. This places the area properly in its larger geographical setting. At the beginning of such units, the teacher often will use a globe and a series of wall maps. Beginning with the globe, attention should be focused on the continent on which the place to be studied is located and relate its location to other known places on the earth. Then a wall map of the continent can be used to point out the particular area to be studied. This can be followed with a brief study of the geographical features of the entire continent in terms of their relationship to the particular area. Such a spot location of places will make it easier for the child to visualize the interrelationships and associations that are possible for a given place.

Some teachers cling to the concept of environmental determinism although geographers rejected it years ago as an explanation of differing ways of living. Geographic conditions should be taught as factors that relate to, or affect, ways of living but do not *cause* them. If geographic conditions caused people to live the way they do, everyone in a given area of the world would live the same way; and, of course, this is not the case. For example, some of the people of the world who inhabit the deserts live in tents, tend sheep, and live nomadic lives; others who live in desert areas have air-conditioned ranch-style homes, work in comfortable office buildings, and drive expensive automobiles.

The teaching of the earth's climatic zones also persists even though this concept, too, has been discarded by geographers. Traditionally, children were taught that the earth had climatic belts known as the Frigid, Temperate, and Torrid zones that encircled the earth at certain latitudes. The implication was that all places in these zones have the same climatic conditions. This conclusion is in error because there are places in the so-called Torrid Zone that have snow the year around; places in the so-called Temperate Zone that have winter temperatures as low as forty degrees below zero; and places in the Frigid Zone that record fairly mild temperatures even in the winter months. These zonal designations based on climate should *not* be taught. The terms *low latitudes, middle latitudes,* and *high latitudes* are acceptable in referring to these parts of the world because they do not imply that a specific climatic condition prevails throughout the area so designated. Climate should not be explained entirely in terms of latitude.

In the study of ways of living around the world, usually at the fourth-grade level, many programs focus on nonindustrialized societies because these people relate so directly to their surroundings in meeting their basic needs of food, clothing, and shelter. They make their homes and clothing from materials close at hand, and these necessities are usually entirely functional. All food is grown, gathered, or hunted. When there is trade or other contact with the outside world, children can see that the ways of living begin to change. Much of value can come from studies of this type, but the teacher needs to be careful not to develop the idea that just because these people meet their basic needs in simple ways, their social organization is easy to understand. Often the customs, mores, and taboos of these cultures are exceedingly complex. When studies of preliterate or preindustrial societies are undertaken, the units should be used to demonstrate specific points: People can live under a variety of geographical conditions; these people have less need for the great variety of resources required by industrial societies; certain human qualities are apparent in all people no matter how they live; people do not need great material wealth in order to be happy; these people spend a disproportionate amount of time meeting basic needs; ways of living change when people meet others from another culture; and so on.

In the fourth grade, one finds the study of home states to be fairly common. Many of the states are sufficiently diverse in geography to allow parallels to be drawn with similar places around the world. If the state has plains, for example, children might find out where else in the world one finds plains and how the people there make use of them. Or the state might have mountains or deserts or good harbors — any of these can be used to teach geographic concepts and relate such concepts to a broad, global context.

The same principles hold true in the fifth-grade social studies curriculum, which in many schools calls for the study of communities or sections of the United States, its history, and the movement of people from one section to another within it. In studying historical developments, life in early America, or contemporary life in various communities of the United States, the teacher should relate geographical factors to the topic. What did the geography of the region have to do with the way people lived and how they made their living? Why did large cities grow where they did? Why did the people moving west follow certain routes? How were people able to make use of the resources they found? All these questions relate to geography, and geographical understanding should be used to help explain them.

In the upper grades, many social studies units provide the opportunity to relate human activities to the environment. Children should learn how such social functions as making a living, producing goods, building homes, making clothing, transporting goods, and communicating ideas relate to the specific region in which people live. They should also develop skill in the use of the tools of geography — charts, graphs, sourcebooks, and, most particularly, maps and globes.

In the middle and upper grades, some attention should be given to the historical dimension of geography. For example, in studying the location of cities, teachers frequently have children explain why the particular place is a good location for a city. What is often overlooked in such an exercise is that the choice was made a hundred or two hundred or even more years ago. *At that time* in terms of the technology of the period, the site may have been a good one, but in terms of present-day technology it may be a bad site. If the choice of a place for a city were made today, perhaps it would be located somewhere else. Ghost towns are good examples of poor site selection for permanent settlement. The same applies to many other features of the environment that bear the imprint of human presence. Roads today were formerly cow paths and horse trails or old logging roads. Industrial centers grew up in places that were easily accessible to employees who walked to work or who rode trolleys. Downtown shopping centers were established before automobile parking became a problem. Instructive and interesting studies can be made of areas as they were in early days: Land division and use, the pattern of transportation, the location of processing and manufacturing facilities, the location and distribution of markets, and interactions with surrounding areas can be noted. The study then shifts to an examination and analysis of these factors in the same area as they are today; the children thereby gain an understanding and appreciation of the problems related to area growth and change.

In this connection, too, geographic thinking can be stimulated through the consideration of hypothetical propositions. For example, a fifth-grade class might consider the following proposition: Suppose instead of being located in northern Minnesota, the large iron deposits of the Mesabi had been discovered in southern Missouri. What effect might this have had on the location of northern cities? Would the major transportation systems and routes of the area be the same as they are today? Would major industrial and manufacturing centers be located where they are today? Teachers can easily devise problems of this type from time to time by selecting a situation and shifting a critical variable. Learners cannot arrive at final answers to such problems, but they can speculate on possible alternatives and can demonstrate their ability to apply their geographic knowledge. Hypothetical propositions, if well selected, provide good ways for a teacher to evaluate children's understanding of important concepts and their ability to transfer such knowledge to other situations.

One teacher used the place-names lesson (Lesson Plan 4) to alert children to the origins of place-names in the local area, which led the class to the development of the geographic concept of successive occupance.

LESSON PLAN 4

Topic:	Place Names: Where did they come from?
Grade:	Four
Time:	One class period and follow-up
Objective:	To explore the origin of names within a specific geographical area.
Interest Building:	Brainstorm a list of names of places with which you are familiar within a geographical area. After brainstorming, compile an additional list from maps that have been distributed (example: a map of the home state or local county). Perhaps a total of fifty or sixty names would be a good stopping point.
Lesson Development:	Categorize the names as to their origin: Indian names, names of explorers, famous people, early settlers, ethnic names, and so forth.
	Have the children decide on the fairest way of distributing the names so that each has two or three place-names to research.
	Each child will then research the names, using resource books, interviews, and letters to various city or community information sources to determine the origin of the name. This is done over an extended period of time.
Summary:	As each child obtains the information, display it on a bulletin board, attaching it with yarn to the particular geographical location on a map. Relate this information to the history and settlement pattern of the area.
Materials:	Maps of the area under study.

SPECIALIZED INFORMATION SOURCES FOR HISTORY AND GEOGRAPHY

Encyclopedias and Special References

In the middle and upper grades, all classrooms should have at least one and preferably two sets of encyclopedias suitable for children. Even in the primary grades, encyclopedias can be used to good advantage from time to time; and many schools are placing them in first, second, and third grades.

The value of an encyclopedia lies in the easy, quick way factual material can be obtained on a multitude of topics. It is an important source of information and one that will be referred to many times in the course of social studies units. When encyclopedias are available in the primary grades, the teacher will find the pictures and illustrations helpful in social studies instruction. Selected short portions of content may be read to the children from time to time, and some children at these early levels will be able to read portions of the encyclopedia independently. Perhaps the chief value of an encyclopedia in the primary grades is the contribution it can make to building positive attitudes toward the use of reference materials. Children learn fairly early that in the encyclopedia one can find answers to many questions on most topics. In this sense, early contact with this reference serves as a readiness for its more organized use at the upper levels. In the middle and upper grades, the encyclopedia is a constant source of factual information. Articles in an encyclopedia are highly condensed presentations, however, and this suggests the need for additional references—ones that may give interesting elaboration not ordinarily included in encyclopedia coverage.

The teacher should guard against the misuse of the encyclopedia. Children need to learn that the encyclopedia is only one source and, in some cases, may not even be the best source, of information. A children's biography, for instance, of Babe Didrikson Zaharias or Amelia Earhart might be more informative and more engaging for a 12-year-old than a factual, encyclopedia account of these women's lives. Children can become too dependent on the encyclopedia at the expense of not learning the value of other resources available to them. Thus, they may copy written reports verbatim from the encyclopedia or make oral reports based on encyclopedia accounts that are memorized but not understood. The difficulty, of course, lies not with the encyclopedia but with the way it is used. The teacher needs to make a conscious effort to discourage such misuse of this instructional resource.

For factual information there is also need for atlases, *The World Almanac,* and the state legislative manuals. Many local communities and cities also publish brochures, handbooks, and pamphlets. Local and state historical societies, museums, and art galleries may make available publications that are valuable for classroom work. These sources provide a storehouse of information, but children of elementary school age need a considerable amount of guidance and help from the teacher in their use.

Free and Inexpensive Materials

Free and inexpensive materials have become valuable resources in teaching history, geography, and social studies generally. There is a wealth of material in the form of posters, charts, bulletins, folders, booklets, films, filmstrips, and travel folders available free on request. In addition to the free material, an abundance of similar resources can be obtained at small cost. Much of the material available today is well prepared and useful for classroom work, but it does need to be examined carefully to ascertain whether or not it is suitable. Just because the material is available and free is no assurance that it is of value. Questions such as these should be considered in evaluating free and inexpensive material:

1. Is the material produced by a socially responsible organization?
2. Does the presence of advertising make the material unsuitable for use? A piece may or may not be rejected on this point, but it should, in any case, be considered.
3. Is the subject matter honestly and objectively presented? Is it consistent with democratic values and ideals? Is it free of racial and sex bias?
4. Is the material suitable in terms of readability, maturity of the children, technical qualities, and the topic under study?
5. Is the material up-to-date?
6. Are the sources of information given?
7. Does use of the materials carry any obligations with it?
8. In whose interest was the material prepared? Who benefits from its use in the classroom?

The teacher should not overlook the diplomatic offices of foreign countries based in the United States as a source of free material. In most cases, the best place to direct inquiries concerning the availability of such material is the embassy of the country in Washington, D.C. Some countries (for example, Japan) have excellent instructional packets available for school use.

Because the demand for free and inexpensive material is great and the quantity usually limited, the teacher is advised to use an up-to-date list of sources. Professional journals carry lists in almost every issue. In addition, there are compilations of sources of free and inexpensive material that can be purchased. The most comprehensive list of free and inexpensive instructional material is that published by Educator's Progress Service, Inc., 214 Center Street, Randolph, Wisconsin 53956.

Computer Applications

Computer programs in the form of tutorials, drill and practice, data base software, and simulations are available for teaching history and geography in the elementary and middle schools social studies programs. There are several comprehensive software directories and lists that provide titles, annotations, suppliers' names and addresses, and cost.[5] *Technology in the Curriculum Resource Material* produced by the California State Department of Education in connection with the state history/social

---

[5] See James O. Hodges, "Resources for Teaching with Computers," *Social Education*, 51 (January 1987), pp. 54–59; Gene E. Rooze and Terry Northup, *Using Computers to Teach Social Studies*, (Littleton, Colorado: Libraries Unlimited, 1986), Chapter 6.

science framework is especially useful because it recommends software programs that were evaluated by a team of fifty teachers.[6]

Community Resources

It is in the local community that the teacher should sow the seeds of a lifetime study of human society. Here the social processes that function a thousand times over in communities around the world may be observed firsthand. In the local community, the child is introduced to geographical concepts, to the problems of group living, to government in operation, to the production and distribution of goods and services, and to the rich historical heritage of the nation. In most American communities, the child can see evidence that it is possible for persons of varied backgrounds, nationalities, religious faiths, and races to live and work together harmoniously.

The teacher may make use of the local community in two basic ways. One is to bring some portion of the community to the classroom; the other is to take the class out of the school to some place or person of importance in the community. As a matter of principle, it is advisable to take elementary schoolchildren into the community only for the experiences that cannot be duplicated in the classroom. For example, it is usually better to arrange to have a person bring photographs of early life in the community to the school and to speak to the children there than it is to take the class of 30 children to a home. On the other hand, the process involved in canning tuna fish or cranberries cannot be observed in the classroom; the children must be taken to the cannery if this process is to be observed firsthand. Teachers make use of community resources when children bring materials from home for the bulletin boards, or for their construction projects; when parents are asked to assist in any way; when books are obtained from the public library; when the local newspaper is used; or when children bring items from home to share with others in "show and tell." The personal experiences children have in the community and share with the class are likewise a common use of community resources.

The teacher must always select with care the persons who are invited to spend time with the class for instructional purposes. Some people should not be asked to speak to children because they are not able to make themselves understood, they lack an understanding of children, they freely hold and express attitudes or beliefs that may be offensive to members of the group, or they fail to grasp the significance of their visit to the class. The teacher should plan to spend some time with the visitor sufficiently far enough in advance to brief the guest on the activities of the

---

[6] Available from California State Department of Education, Publication Sales, P.O. Box 271, Sacramento, California 95802, $95.00.

class, the purpose of the visit, and the points to be discussed and stressed. Likewise, the children must be prepared for the visitor, listing questions they should like to ask, and general courtesies extended to classroom guests. Handled in this way, persons from the community can make a significant contribution to the instructional program in the social studies. Those who might be used either for the purposes of interview or as classroom resource visitors might include

Persons with special skills: weavers, potters, jewelry makers
Armed forces personnel
Exchange students
Persons with interesting hobbies
Community helpers
Members of the local historical society
Newspaper reporters
Members of service organizations
County agent
County commissioner
Representatives of environmental and conservation groups
4-H Club leaders
Early inhabitants of the community
Professional persons: ministers, doctors, lawyers
Judges
Legislators
Members of the local business community: bankers, salespersons, shop
    owners
Local officials
Representatives of local industries
Travelers
Recent immigrants or other newcomers to the community
Authors
Commercial pilots

Whenever children are taken off the school site, the teacher must attend to a number of exceedingly important details. Adequate planning will help the teacher anticipate some of the problems that may arise in connection with the field trip and will help make the trip educationally worthwhile. Poorly planned field trips are worse than none at all, for they lack purpose, may jeopardize the safety of the children, may cause poor public relations between the school and community, and can break down learnings the teacher should have been trying to build in the classroom. Although the field trip should be pleasant for everyone including the teacher, it is first of all an educational experience, and its primary objective is not that everyone have a joyous outing. Good planning will ensure that the trip will be both a pleasant as well as an educational experience. The following suggestions will be helpful in achieving that goal:

FIELD TRIPS

Preparing for the Trip

1. Clearly establish the purposes of the trip, and make certain that the children understand the purposes, too. The excursion should provide opportunities for learning that are not possible in the classroom.
2. Obtain administrative permission for the field trip, and make arrangements for transportation. As a matter of policy, it is better to use a public conveyance or a school bus than it is to use private automobiles. In using private cars, the teacher is never sure if the driver is properly insured, is competent behind the wheel, or even if the driver has a valid operator's license.
3. Make all necessary preliminary arrangements at the place of the visit. This should include the time for the group to arrive, where the children are to go, who will guide them, and so forth. It is recommended that the teacher make the excursion prior to the time the children are taken. This will alert the teacher to circumstances and situations that should be discussed with the children before leaving the classroom. Make sure that the field trip guide is aware of the purposes of the field trip.
4. Study the literature on the subject. No teacher should approach a field trip unprepared. This knowledge will later be valuable in helping prepare children for the field trip and in initiating follow-up and study activities.
5. Obtain written permission from each parent for the child to go on the trip, and do not take children who cannot or do not return signed permission slips. Although this action does not in itself absolve the teacher of responsibility or liability in the event of an accident, it indicates to the teacher that the parent knows of the field trip and approves of the child's going. Most schools have forms for this purpose that are filled out by the teacher and sent home with each child for the parent's signature.
6. Prepare the class for the field trip. "What is it that we wish to find out? What things in particular do we want to look for? What questions do we want to ask the guide?" Through careful planning and preparation the teacher helps children to be more observant and makes a genuine research activity out of the field trip. The children probably will be taken to places to which many of them have been before. Most of them have seen trains, many have been to the airport, some have been to the harbor, and all have been to a filling station. Why, then, should the school take children to such places on field trips? The answer is that different purposes exist for the field trip than for incidental visits. The children are prepared to look for things they would not otherwise see. Discuss with the children how they will record the information obtained on their trip. If they are to take notes, teach the needed note-taking skills.

    The class should set up standards of conduct for the trip before leaving the school. Children are quick to accept the challenge that the responsibility for a good trip rests personally with each member of the group. Time spent on this part of the preparation for the excursion will pay dividends when the trip is underway. Nothing is more embarrassing for the teacher, more damaging to school–community relations, or more devastating to the educational purposes of the field trip than a group of rude and unruly children. This often happens when the children have been inadequately prepared for the trip.

7. If the trip is to be long, make arrangements for lunchroom and restroom facilities. Take along a first-aid kit.

8. Have an alternate plan in case the weather turns bad or something interferes with your plans.

Conducting the Trip

9. Take roll before leaving the school grounds, and "count noses" frequently during the trip to make sure that some of the children have not become lost or left in some restroom along the way. With young children it is a good idea to place them in pairs because a child will know and report immediately the absence of a partner. To assist with supervision of the children and to help ensure a safe trip, the teacher should arrange for other adults to accompany the group. Teachers can usually count on parents to assist in this way but should plan to meet with them prior to the trip and explain the purposes, standards of behavior, the route to be followed, and other important details. The adults accompanying the children must be prepared for the excursion also.

10. Arrive at the designated place on time, and have children ready for the guide. Be sure to introduce the guide to the class. Supervise children closely during the tour to prevent accidents or injury. Before leaving, check again to make sure all children are with the group.

11. Make sure that time is allowed for answering children's questions.

12. Make sure that each child can see and hear adequately. Be sure that a summarization is made before the trip is concluded.

Evaluating the Trip

13. Engage the class in appropriate follow-up activities. This should include writing a thank-you note to the firm and to the adults who accompanied the class. In the primary grades, the children should dictate such a letter to the teacher who writes it on the chalkboard or chart. Individual children then copy the letter, and one may be selected to be sent, or, in some cases, they may all be sent. The teacher and children will also want to evaluate carefully the extent to which the purposes of the trip have been achieved. "Did we accomplish what we set out to do? Did we get the answers to our questions? What did we learn that we didn't know before? What are some other things we will want to find out?" Finally, the teacher and children will want to evaluate the conduct of the class in terms of the standards set up before the trip was made. This evaluation should always include some favorable reactions as well as ways in which the group might improve on subsequent trips. A list might be made of these suggestions for improvement to be saved for review just before the next trip is undertaken.

14. Discuss enrichment projects in which children may engage for further study, such as construction activities, original stories, reports, dramatic plays, and diaries. Survey other resources available in the community for study.

15. Use opportunities to draw on information and experiences from the field trip in other subjects taught in the classroom.

Every community has places that can be visited by classes and thereby can contribute to the enrichment of history, geography, and all of social studies. These will differ from place to place, but any of the following could be used:

State historical society displays
Historical sites, monuments
Flood plain, eroded areas, dam sites
Razing of a building
Hospitals
Weather bureau
Warehouses
Airports
Railway station
Assembly plants
Post office
Broadcasting or telecasting station
Courthouse
Factories
Farms
Urban planning commission
Docks

Aquarium
Library
Refinery
Fish hatchery
Museum
Public health department
Local stores
Legislative bodies in session
Art galleries
Fire station
Newspaper printing facilities
Bakery
Observatory
Canal locks
The harbor
Police station
Zoo
Parks
Shopping centers

DISCUSSION QUESTIONS AND SUGGESTED ACTIVITIES

1. What are some ways that geography is important to the study of history? Is the reverse also true? Discuss these relationships in terms of the need for an integrated social studies program at the elementary and middle school levels.

2. Study your local community and suggest five community resources that could be used in teaching history and geography to a grade of your choice.

3. What specific out-of-school experiences of children enhance their ability to understand geography and history? Suggest television programs that would be useful in teaching history and geography.

4. Examine a social studies textbook and its accompanying teacher's manual. How are history and geography included in the book? Would the teacher and the child user clearly recognize the subject matter as history and geography? Is that important? Discuss.

5. What holidays are observed in the schools of your state? Develop a calendar of such days for the school year.

6. School librarians or media specialists or both frequently organize exhibits around selected themes during the year. For example, "Black History Month" in February provides an opportunity for librarians to draw attention to their black studies material. Visit an elementary school library. Ask the librarian or resource person about other special weeks or events during the year. How might these be tied to the social studies program?

7. What reasons can you give for the apparent revival of interest in the study of history in recent years? Are there potential negative as well as positive outcomes associated with this emphasis? Discuss.

8. Find out something about the methods of inquiry used by historians and geographers in studying their disciplines. Explain how — or if — any of these might be adapted for use with elementary and middle school students. Provide examples of such applications.

9. Secure a photograph of people at work in a culture outside the United States. By studying the photograph, answer these questions: (1) What features of the land appear to be most important to the people who live in this area? (2) What occupations seem to be most important? (3) What principal tools and machines do these people use? (4) What do the answers to these three questions tell you about the way of life of the people who live there? Can an activity of this type be used with elementary and middle grade students? Is this geography? Discuss.

10. History and geography are important in terms of their subject matter, but how can they be used to develop intellectual skills such as critical thinking and problem solving? Provide an example for a grade of your choice to illustrate your points.

SELECTED REFERENCES

AHERN, JOHN F., AND HUGHES MOIR. "Celebrating Traditional Holidays in Public Schools: Books for Basic Values." *The Social Studies,* 77 (November–December 1986), pp. 234–239.

THE BRADLEY COMMISSION ON HISTORY IN SCHOOLS. "Building a History Curriculum: Guidelines for Teaching History in Schools." Washington, D.C.: Educational Excellence Network, 1988, 32 pp.

BUGGEY, JOANNE, AND JAMES KRACHT. "Geographic Learning." *Elementary School Social Studies: Research as a Guide to Practice,* Virginia A. Atwood, ed. NCSS Bulletin No. 79. Washington, D.C.: National Council for the Social Studies, 1986. Chapter 4.

DOWNEY, MATTHEW T. *History in the Schools.* NCSS Bulletin No. 74. Washington, D.C.: National Council for the Social Studies, 1985.

DOWNEY, MATTHEW T., guest ed., AND SUZIE MCLEAN-BALDERSTON, PHYLLIS CLARKE, LILLIAN VALLE-CONDELL, KAREN GORDON, CAROLE CHIN, PETER S. O'CON-

NELL, PATRICIA A. LAVIN, KAREN JORGENSEN-ESMAILI, AND ROSALIND SARAH. "The Children of Yesteryear." *Social Education*, 50 (April–May 1986), pp. 260–293. A set of seven articles and an annotated bibliography telling about how children lived in earlier times.

FREEMAN, EVELYN B., AND LINDA LEVSTIK. "Recreating the Past: Historical Fiction in the Social Studies Curriculum." *The Elementary School Journal*, 88 (March 1988), pp. 329–337.

JEBSEN, HARRY, JR. "Integrating Sports History into American History Courses." *The Social Studies*, 75 (March–April 1984), pp. 62–67.

KINCHELOE, JOE L. "The Trouble with Geography." *The Social Studies*, 75 (July–August 1984), pp. 141–144.

LEON, WARREN. "Preparing a Primary Source Package on Your Community's History." *Social Education*, 44 (November–December 1980), pp. 612–618.

LOWDERBAUGH, THOMAS E. "Museums, Language, and the Hearing-Impaired Child." *Social Education*, 45 (January 1981), pp. 60–62.

MEHAFFY, GEORGE L. "Oral History in Elementary Classrooms." *Social Education*, 48 (September–October 1984), pp. 470–472.

METCALF, FAY D., AND MATTHEW T. DOWNEY. *Using Local History in the Classroom*. Nashville, Tennessee: American Association for State and Local History, 1982.

MUESSIG, RAYMOND H. "An Analysis of Developments in Geographic Education." *The Elementary School Journal*, 87 (May 1987), pp. 518–530.

NATOLI, SALVATORE J., ed. *Strengthening Geography in the Social Studies*. NCSS Bulletin No. 81. Washington, D.C.: National Council for the Social Studies, 1988.

PATRIARCA, LINDA A., AND JAN ALLEMAN. "Studying Time: A Cognitive Approach." *Social Education*, 51 (April–May 1987), pp. 273–277.

SEIDMAN, LAURENCE I., SHELDON BROWN, B. LEE COOPER, AND GEORGE CHILCOAT contribute articles to a special feature entitled "Studying U.S. History Through Songs." *Social Education*, 49 (October 1985), pp. 579–603.

SUNAL, CYNTHIA SZYMANSKI, AND BARBARA ANN HATCHER. "Studying History Through Art." *How To Do It Series* 5, No. 2. Washington, D.C.: National Council for the Social Studies, 1986.

WIEDER, ALAN. "Oral History in the Classroom: An Exploratory Essay." *The Social Studies*, 75 (March–April 1984), pp. 71–74.

5

Space and Time Dimensions of Social Studies: Maps, Globes, and Graphics

Suppose someone came into a roomful of people and announced, "There has been a disastrous earthquake!" What would be said by the others present? Most likely the next things to be said would be,

"Where did it happen?"
"When did it happen?"

Only after these questions were answered would there be an interest in whether anyone was injured and the extent of the damage. Events hold little meaning for us unless we know the *place* and the *time* of their occurrence. Consequently, in social studies we find ourselves constantly making references to *where* something happened and *when* it happened. Such references to time and place may be specific, such as Lexington, Massachusetts, April 18, 1775; or they may be general, such as "a long time ago, in the area where three continents meet." These definite and indefinite references to time and space also involve *quantitative* concepts:

SPACE	TIME
A great distance	Soon thereafter
Forty miles	A long journey
1,500 acres	Three decades
Largest continent	Four centuries earlier
55,000 square miles	A fortnight later
23½° north latitude	A four-hour interval

Definite and indefinite references to time and space can be bothersome for children. For example, if children read that Columbus' ship, the *Santa Maria,* was 98 feet long, such a reference to distance probably will mean something different to every child in the class. It might be conceptualized as a distance ranging from one not greater than the length of the classroom to one of several city blocks. When there is such confusion over a relatively simple and definite reference to distance, one can only speculate on the misunderstandings that must abound when we use such references as the following:

> A township was to be a square, 6 miles long on each side. Each township was to be divided into 36 sections. A section, therefore, was 1 mile square and had 640 acres in it.

The research that has been conducted on time, space, and quantitative concepts in social studies confirms that children often misunderstand them. The tendency is to overestimate the ability of children to handle such concepts. As a result, maps often are used that are more complex than they should be in view of the maturity of the children using them. Also children may make and use time lines that they really do not comprehend. Because children so easily verbalize quantitative concepts such as decade, century, thousands, hundreds, several miles, many years, and 10 percent, the assumption is that they are understood. Research on this subject indicates that such assumptions are often in error.

When the abstractness of these concepts is reduced, they are made meaningful to children. We try, therefore, to provide children with a concrete reference to space and time, preferably one that is a part of their experiences. This is why current news events provide such a good vehicle for teaching some concepts and skills. The children read about current happenings in the classroom periodical or hear and see them reported on radio and television news. Thus, finding places on a map is a natural extension of everyday experiences.

The social studies curriculum operates within a matrix that might be represented very simply as follows:

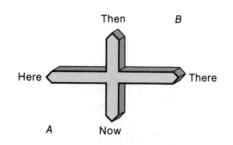

Experiences that could be charted at point *A* would be the least abstract and would usually be found in the early grades. Experiences at point *B* would be most difficult to make concrete for children because they are remote not only in space but also in time. Because many children today have firsthand experiences that acquaint them with places beyond their immediate environment, it is not as necessary to confine the social studies program to the local area as it once was. There can be more movement from the near at hand to the far away even at early grade levels. This is more difficult to do with the time dimension, however. The reality of events of the past needs to be tied to the present, again calling attention to the importance of using current news events.

There are many instructional aids that can help one teach and learn these complex concepts. For example, globes and maps are indispensable tools for working with space and spatial relationships. Time lines and charts can make time and chronology meaningful. Graphs and tables can make some types of quantitative relationships easier to comprehend. It is imperative, therefore, that the social studies program teach children how to use these tools.

MAP AND GLOBE SKILLS ESSENTIAL TO THE SOCIAL STUDIES CURRICULUM

Maps and globes are vehicles for representing space symbolically. The essential features of all maps and globes are a grid, color, scale, symbols, and a legend that explains the symbol system used. The ability to read and interpret maps and globes, like conventional reading, is a summarizing skill in that it represents a composite of several subskills. These subskills can be inferred by making an analysis of the behavior of someone reading a map who is skillful at it. Fortunately, this will not be necessary because it has been done by specialists several times and always with somewhat the same results. One list that has been widely used by school districts

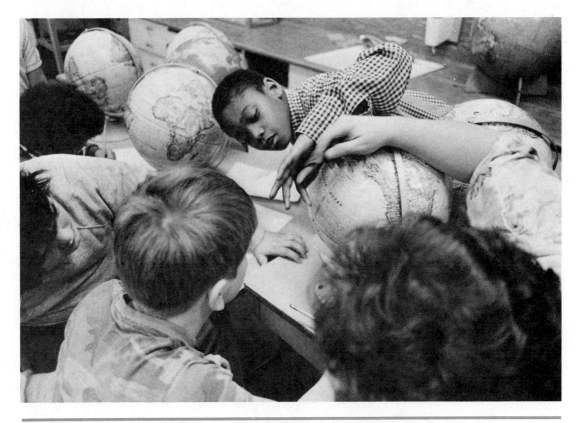

Schools are sometimes criticized for not teaching children place location. To develop such a skill, learners need to make frequent use of globes and maps. Moreover, they need to perceive the earth, as represented by the globe model, from many perspectives, including seeing it "upside down!" (Photo by Kay Engelsen, Tacoma School District.)

throughout the nation in developing their map and globe skill sequence appears in two yearbooks of the National Council for the Social Studies:

1. Ability to orient the map and to note directions.
2. Ability to recognize the scale of a map and to compute distances.
3. Ability to locate places on maps and globes by means of grid systems.
4. Ability to express relative locations.
5. Ability to read map symbols.
6. Ability to compare maps and to make inferences.[1]

[1] This list was developed by Professor Clyde F. Kohn for the 1953 NCSS yearbook. It is cited and elaborated on by Dean Lorrin Kennamer, "Developing a Sense of Place and Space," in *Skill Development in Social Studies*, 33d Yearbook. (Washington, D.C.: National Council for the Social Studies, 1963), pp. 157 ff. The chart in the appendix of that yearbook provides a list of related subskills along with a suggested curriculum sequence.

Directional Orientation

In order to deal with directional relationships on maps and globes, the child must first understand them in reality. The easiest directions to use are those that express relative location, such as close to, near, over here, and over there. These can be learned in the primary grades. The *cardinal directions* are also learned in the primary grades by having them pointed out and by referring to places that are known to children as being north of, east of, south of, and so on. Placing direction labels on the various walls of the classroom helps remind children of cardinal directions. They can associate east and west with the rising and setting of the sun. They can learn how a compass is used to find direction. While on field trips, children should be given practice in noting directions, observing especially the directions of streets and roads. Gradually, they learn the purpose of the poles, the meridians of longitude, and the parallels of latitude in orienting a map and noting directions. When maps with unfamiliar projections are introduced, children should be taught how to establish correct directional relationships on them.

Using Map Scales

In making a map, the cartographer tries to reproduce as accurately as possible that portion of the earth being represented. Because globes are models of the earth, they can represent the earth more correctly than can maps. No map can altogether faithfully represent the earth simply because the earth is round and maps are flat. The flattening process inevitably results in some distortion.

Scaling is the process of reducing everything in the same amount. When one works with children in the primary grades, scaling should be done in the relative sense. Some things are larger or smaller than other things, and the maps should show their *relative size* as accurately as possible. For example, a fifty-foot-high tree in the schoolyard should be about five times larger than the ten-foot-tall playground set. On conventional maps, three types of scales are used:

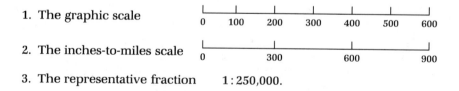

1. The graphic scale

2. The inches-to-miles scale

3. The representative fraction   1 : 250,000.

Of these, the graphic scale is the easiest to use and can be taught at about fourth grade. The inches-to-miles scale is more complex, but it can also be taught in the middle grades. The representative fraction is usually considered beyond the scope of the elementary school program.

As children become more global in their experiences, they will encounter map scales in metric measures. If metric measurement is used, the distance on a graphic scale would be recorded in kilometers. Likewise, rather than as inches-to-miles, the scale would show the relationship as centimeters-to-kilometers. The following graphic scale illustrates the same distance expressed in miles and in kilometers:

FIGURE 5.1. Middle-grade children can learn to use a grid in locating places by using road maps that have coordinates of the type shown on this map. Test your own memory of place locations by responding to these questions:
1. What major city is located in square C2?
2. What major city lies near the intersection of the squares D1, D2, E1, and E2?
3. Describe the location of Savannah by using the coordinates provided on this map. Check your answers by consulting a map of Georgia that shows cities.

Locating Places

The ability to locate places on maps and globes comes with a familiarity with these devices cultivated over a period of several years. Children first learn to locate places that are known to them on simple maps and layouts that they make in the classroom. In the early grades, too, children can learn the names and shapes of some of the major geographic features, such as continents, oceans, the equator, and the poles. The commercially prepared maps and globes designed for the lower grades are quite plain, having only a few features shown. Gradually, children increase their repertoire of known places they can find on the map and globe because of frequent references to the location of important cities, countries, rivers, mountains, and other physical features.

In the middle grades, children are taught to use coordinates to locate places. Local highway maps are well suited for use in teaching this skill because they deal with an area familiar to the children. One set of lines of the grid — perhaps the north–south lines — is identified with letters; the other set of lines is numbered as is done in Figure 5.1. The teacher can have the children (this is usually done in fourth grade) find several places located on or very near to a north–south line, say D. Then several places can be found on an east–west line, say 7. If the teacher is clever enough to pick two coordinates that intersect on a major point of interest, the children will discover that some city or other important feature is located at the point where D and 7 intersect. Figure 5.1 is an example of an exercise of this kind. This experience provides readiness for the use of meridians of longitude and parallels of latitude in locating places on wall maps and the globe. At this stage, children are mature enough to understand why reference points such as poles, the equator, and the prime meridian are essential in locating places on a sphere.

Reading Map Symbols

Maps use symbols to represent real things: Dots of varying sizes stand for cities of different populations; color is used to represent elevation; hash marks stand for escarpments; and lines are used to show boundaries, coastlines, and rivers. Naturally, the reader will not comprehend the messages of maps unless he or she knows what these symbols represent. Children begin to learn their meanings early in the elementary school social studies program. The development of this subskill closely parallels that of locating places on maps.

Map and globe symbols vary in their abstractness. Indeed, some simple maps for children in the primary grades use symbols that are pictorial or semipictorial. These symbols either look like the object being represented or provide a strong clue as to its identity, as shown in Figures 5.2

FIGURE 5.2. Children can be introduced to the concept of symbols through pictorial representations that they encounter in real life, such as the ones shown here.

and 5.3. It would not take much imagination, for example, to differentiate water areas from land areas on a globe simply on the basis of their color.

The instructional sequence to be followed in teaching the symbol system of maps is to move gradually from pictorial and semipictorial symbols on maps made by children to the abstract symbols used on conventional wall maps, globes, and maps that are included in the textbooks of the middle and upper grades. It is essential that children learn to consult the map legend or key in order to confirm which symbols are being used. In most cases, children in the middle and upper grades will be dealing with maps that use conventional map symbols; but special-purpose maps such as those showing vegetation, rainfall, population density, and so on, often use symbols that are unique to the particular map.

It is always a good idea to make generous use of photographs of the areas shown on a map in order to help the children associate the map symbol with what the place actually looks like. Similarly, when children go on field trips, they should be encouraged to observe carefully the appearance of landscapes and other features that are shown on maps. In time they will be able to visualize the reality that the abstract map symbols represent.

Understanding Relative Location

Understanding relative location is an interpretive skill that requires information beyond that provided by the map itself. It has to do with thinking about how places relate to each other in terms of political, cultural, religious, commercial, or historical perspectives. It has nothing to do with how close or how far away places may be in the absolute sense. For example, the non-Asian people — and even many Asians — of the British Crown Colony of Hong Kong feel closer to Great Britain (10,000 miles away) than they do to the People's Republic of China (less than twenty miles away) because of political, economic, and cultural ties.

Relative location may also be thought of in terms of the amount of time required to get to a place using the kind of transportation available. This is commonly expressed nowadays in ordinary conversation and small talk as people say, "It takes me thirty minutes to get to work," or "I'm about two hours from Washington." Distances that now take two hours to traverse would have taken two days a hundred years ago and two weeks or even more at the time of the founding of the Republic. Increasingly, we reckon distances in terms of time. Consequently, places may be thought of as being remote or near in terms of how difficult it is to get to them. Air crash survivors stranded in the High Sierras in the dead of winter, no more than fifty miles from Fresno, California, might be as far away from civilization in the relative sense as they would be if they were in Antarctica.

Comparing Maps and Making Inferences

Comparing maps and making inferences are also inferential skills because to some extent the reader has to project what he or she already knows on the map data. In this process the map reader discovers relationships among the sets of data presented by different maps. In the middle elementary grades, teachers often have children compare vegetation maps with rainfall maps. They also have them compare maps show-

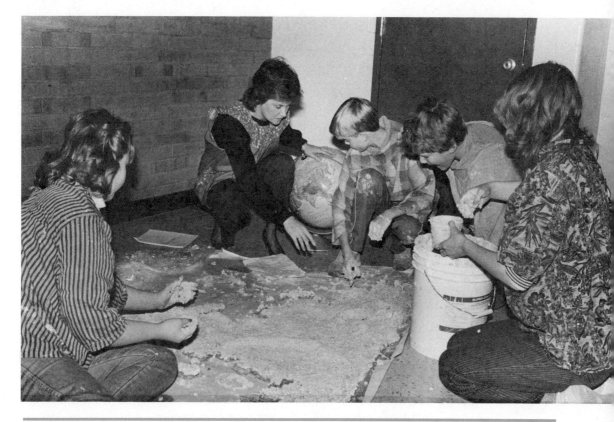

These sixth graders from the Westhill Elementary School, Northshore School District, Bothell, Washington, are expanding their global understanding through a map construction activity. The whole class, working in small groups, is creating a relief map of the world in segments. Their teacher, in cooperation with the art consultant, assists the children in moulding the mixture of sawdust, wheat paste, vermiculite, plaster of paris, and water into a raised relief map of one part of the world. When the project is completed, all segments will be placed together to form a world map. (Photo by Terri Malinowski, Northshore School District.)

ing the location of important resources, such as iron and coal, with maps showing the location of industrial centers, population densities, and so on. It is quite common to find special-purpose maps of the same region in the children's textbooks, making comparisons easy. These provide excellent settings for critical thinking as the children can study the data presented on two or more maps, make predictions or hypotheses about these data, and then go on to the next step of verifying or rejecting their speculations.

Children in the late middle and upper elementary grades should study maps based on different projections and compare the shapes and sizes of known areas with those same areas as shown on the globe. This will

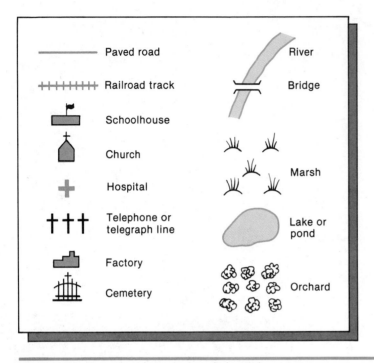

FIGURE 5.3. Examples of standard symbols used on maps.

familiarize them with the concept of distortion, which, in greater or lesser amounts, is present in all flat maps. Children should learn why distortion occurs and what cartographers have done to minimize its effect.

INSTRUCTIONAL EXPERIENCES WITH THE GLOBE

Every social studies classroom should have and use a globe. In grades one, two, and three a simplified twelve-inch globe is generally recommended because small children find this size easier to handle than the larger sixteen-inch one. For primary grades, the globe selected should have a minimum amount of information on it. It should not use more than three colors to represent land elevation or more than two colors to represent water depth. Only the largest cities, rivers, and water bodies should be shown. In the middle and upper grades, a sixteen-inch globe is recommended because of its easy scale of one inch to five hundred miles. Moreover, its larger size allows more detail to be shown without the globe's becoming a confused collection of facts. Globes for middle- and upper-grade children will ordinarily use seven colors to represent land elevations and three colors to represent water depths.

The chief value of the globe in grades one, two, and three is to familiarize the children with the basic roundness of the earth and to begin to develop a global perspective. The primary-grade child does not necessarily need formal lessons on the use of the globe. If the globe is in the classroom, it will provoke curiosity and a desire to know more about it and how to use it. Parents speak of places in the news, and the children wonder where those places are. They hear of earth satellites and wonder about their orbits. Perhaps a girl has just joined the class; her family has recently moved to this country from another part of the world, and she wants to show the class the location of her former home. The teacher will use situations such as these—and hundreds more like them—to acquaint the young child with the globe.

The teacher should help children discover other things about the globe—differences between water and land areas and that these are represented by different colors; the line that separates the water and the land is called the seacoast. Children may be shown pictures to help them visualize different kinds of coastlines. Similarly, the teacher extends their understanding of other concepts—oceans, cities, rivers, mountains. Children learn that most of the brown areas that represent land are on the half of the earth that has the North Pole and that it is here that the majority of the people of the world live.

In addition to the incidental references made to the globe, the teacher should make frequent use of the globe when teaching social studies and other subjects. For instance, in a reading lesson, children might find where their book friends "live." Thus, the globe can be used in a great variety of ways to lay a good foundation for more formal aspects of the teaching of these skills later on.

The following are examples of the *types* of learnings and experiences that can be planned with the globe for children in the lower grades:

1. Stress that the globe is a very small model of the earth. Good models look exactly like the real thing but are smaller. The globe is a good model of the earth.
2. Show the children how land areas and water bodies are represented on the globe. Have them find land areas and water bodies. Names of these need not be taught at this level, but children might already know the large water bodies such as the Pacific and Atlantic oceans. Similarly, they might be familiar with North and South America, Africa or the Antarctic, and these can be pointed out. Explain that all water bodies and land areas have names.
3. Have children discover that there is considerably more water than land shown on the globe. Ask children to find the half of the globe that has most of the land. Explain that this is the half on which we live

and is the part of the earth where most of the world's people make their homes.

4. Show children the location of the North Pole. Explain that most of the land of the world is on the same half of the world as the North Pole. We call this the northern half.

5. Show children the location of the South Pole. Explain that most of the water areas of the world are on the same half of the world as the South Pole. We call this the southern half.

6. Explain that our earth is a planet.

7. Show children how they can find their country, their continent, their state, and possibly their city on the globe.

8. Use the globe to find places that are familiar to the children — places they have visited on vacations, places in the news, homes of book friends and visitors from other countries, or places in the world from which some circus or zoo animals are brought.

9. Encourage children to handle the globe and to find places on it themselves.

10. Answer questions the children ask concerning the globe in simple, nontechnical language.

The following is an example of a plan used by one teacher to familiarize primary-grade children with geographic concepts and skills using the globe.

LESSON PLAN 5

Topic:	Using the globe to learn about the earth
Grade:	One or two
Time:	One class period
Objective:	To develop a familiarity with concepts relating to the globe.
Interest Building:	Give the children free time to manipulate a globe and explore it on their own.
Lesson Development:	The teacher directs the following questions to the children:

What shape is a globe?
Can you find the North Pole? Place your finger on it.
Where is north on a globe?
Where is south on a globe?
Is south the opposite direction of north?
What divides the north from the south?
Have any of you been to the equator?
Is the equator really a line?
How much of the globe is north?
How much of the globe is south?

What is half of a sphere?
Does anyone know what we call the northern half of the globe?
Does anyone know what we call the southern half of the globe?
How can we tell water from land on the globe?
Does anyone know what we call these large pieces of land?
Can you find a continent in the Northern Hemisphere?
Can you find a continent in the Southern Hemisphere?
Are there any continents that are in both hemispheres?

Summary: How is the globe divided?
Can you name the parts of the globe we talked about?
Can you point to the Northern Hemisphere?
Can you point to the Southern Hemisphere?
Can you point to a continent?

Materials: As many globes as are available in order that each child can easily explore and manipulate the globe.

As children move into the middle and upper grades, instruction in the use of the globe should take two forms. First, the teacher should take time from regularly scheduled unit activities to teach skills needed in reading and interpreting the globe. Second, in unit work and other classroom activities, there should be frequent reference to the globe and maps. Both of these aspects of instruction are important, and one should supplement the other. To hope that children will become skillful in the use of a globe or maps simply by making incidental references to them when the occasion presents itself is wishful thinking. At the same time, formal lessons in the use of these devices without application of the newly acquired skills in purposeful situations is equally ineffective. The best arrangement is to provide for systematic instruction in the use of map- and globe-reading skills as a part of unit activities, reinforcing this with direct teaching of these skills as the need arises.

Maps may be used to find distances between points only under certain conditions, but the globe represents distances accurately and true to scale at all points on the surface of the earth. It is easy to place a flexible ruler on the globe and measure directly the distance between two points in question, then refer to the scale and determine the actual distance between the two places. The air routes of the world use great circles because these are the shortest distances from place to place on the earth's surface. If nothing but flat maps are used, it is difficult to understand the concept of great circle routes, and, therefore, of airplane routes. The globe can help clarify this concept (see Figure 5.4). In this connection, the slated globe (sometimes called the project globe) is useful because it is possible to write on the surface of it with a piece of chalk.

Globes are helpful, too, in establishing concepts of direction. It is not

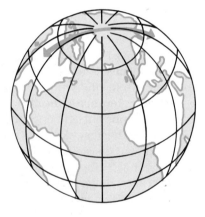

FIGURE 5.4. Notice how differently the map and globe portray global relationships. In the space age we need to think of the world more as it is shown by the globe than the map.

difficult to think of north as being in the direction of the North Pole when using a globe. On the other hand, this may be confusing if only a flat map is used. Furthermore, the relative direction of various parts of the earth can be better understood through the use of a globe. Many Americans are surprised, for example, when they learn that Great Britain lies in a more northerly latitude than do any of the forty-eight mid-continent states of our country; that Boston has nearly the same latitude as Rome; that our most westerly state is not Hawaii but Alaska; that our most southerly state is not Florida but Hawaii; that Moscow and Glasgow have approximately

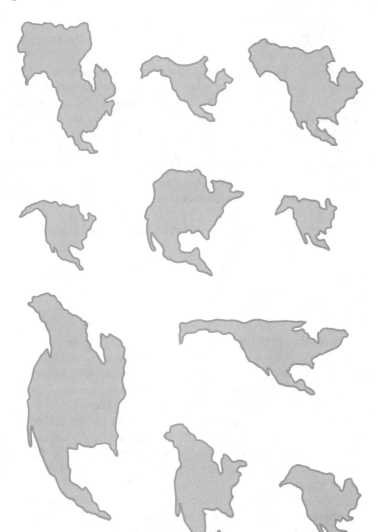

FIGURE 5.5. A land area such as North America may take a variety of shapes on maps, depending on the projection that is used. Professional cartographers continually search for more exact ways to show the earth's surface on flat maps. In 1988, its centennial year, the National Geographic Society selected a new map projection that more accurately represents the earth than did earlier projections. The new projection was developed by Arthur H. Robinson, Professor Emeritus of Cartography and Geography at the University of Wisconsin-Madison. The Robinson projection replaces the Van der Grinten projection that had been used by the Society for its world maps for more than five decades.

the same latitude, both being farther south than any city of Norway or Finland. These facts illustrate that one perceives the earth differently on a globe than on a flat map.

A definite advantage that globes have over maps is that they show the size and shapes of areas exactly as they appear on the earth's surface whereas maps cannot. The classical examples of distortions in the size and shapes of land areas are Greenland on the Mercator projection and Australia on the polar projection. On the Mercator projection, Greenland appears as a very large area—larger than South America. On a polar projection, Australia appears to have a greater east–west distance and a shorter north–south distance than is actually the case. Notice the different shapes North America takes on various maps as illustrated in Figure 5.5. A globe will show all these map shapes and sizes to be inaccurately represented. Therefore, a globe should be used with maps to prevent wrong conceptions.

INSTRUCTIONAL EXPERIENCES WITH MAPS

A number of complex skills are involved in map reading and interpretation; therefore, early experiences with maps should be kept simple. This can best be done through the use of diagrams and maps that the teacher and the children make of their immediate vicinity. These experiences may take the form of a layout on the classroom floor, using blocks and other objects for houses, streets, trees, and public buildings. The layout can be done on a sand table, or the map can be drawn on a large piece of wrapping paper on the classroom floor. When the floor surface will permit, masking tape can be placed on the floor itself to represent boundaries, streets, or roads.

Opportunities to teach and apply these skills often arise in the everyday life of the classroom. For instance, children in one class learned about map direction when a new student joined the group. Soon after the child arrived, the teacher used a map to show the class the location of the child's previous home. They determined the direction the child's family traveled to reach their new home. The teacher then used a map of the local area and had the children discover the direction they travel in going from their homes to school each day.

A fundamental skill in map reading is to learn that a symbol represents a real and actual thing. The symbol may be arbitrarily chosen and bear no resemblance to the object represented, or it may be one that would suggest to the reader what is intended. A school might be represented by a small circle or by a small square with a flag placed on top. It is easier to associate the flag and square with a school than to associate the circle with it. The flag and square are, therefore, less abstract. With young children, it is better to use pictorial or semipictorial symbols of this sort than to use completely abstract ones. In teaching mapreading skills, one must remember that both reading and interpretive skills are involved, and the interpretive skills depend heavily on maturity and background knowledge. Primary-grade children will do less with interpreting maps than they will with reading them.

DO-IT-YOURSELF MAP

This exercise can be used in the middle and upper grades for teaching, diagnosing, or evaluating map skills. The teacher can have everyone in class do the exercise as the directions are read, one step at a time. Directions can also be displayed with an overhead projector. When the maps are completed, the exercise should be discussed. Children can be invited to walk around the room to see maps drawn by their classmates. Maps can also be displayed on the bulletin boards.

Directions:

1. On a clean sheet of paper, draw an outline map of an imaginary continent. You may make it any shape you wish, but you must include at least one peninsula and one bay.
2. Show a scale of miles in your legend for the map.
3. Draw east–west and north–south lines on your map.
4. Draw a mountain range running east and west across your continent, but include at least one mountain pass. Place the symbol you use for your mountain range in your legend.
5. Show a city in the northern half of your continent and one in the southern half. Make each one a seaport.
6. Show a railway joining the two cities.
7. Show three rivers on your continent; show a lake and a swamp. Place all the symbols you use for cities, rivers, lakes, and swamps in the legend.
8. Place a third city somewhere on your map where you think a city should be. On the bottom of your map tell why you think a city should be where you have placed it.
9. Show boundary lines that divide your continent into three large countries and one small country.

The idea of objects representing other objects, people, or things is not new to the children; they have substituted symbols for the actual things many times in the imaginative play of childhood. The teacher can begin by explaining that they are going to draw a map of the schoolroom, schoolyard, or some segment of the immediate vicinity. It is best if this can be done on the classroom floor, so the layout can be oriented exactly as it appears in relationship to the classroom; this sidesteps the matter of orientation to directions at this early stage. Trees, doors, playground equipment, parking areas, and other objects appear in relation to other objects, and only the major ones should be included. The purpose of this experience is simply to show that it is possible to represent space symbolically and that symbols stand for real things. Their maps should have a title and a key to tell what the symbols stand for. This is the first experience in the development of skill in comprehending the significance of symbols, and it will be continued and extended as long as maps are used.

As the children become ready for more abstract symbols, such symbols will be introduced, taught, and used, as will more conventional map symbols. As a part of this instruction in the middle and upper grades, it is important to make generous use of pictures and other visual aids that will help children visualize the area represented. It is helpful, too, to take children to some high point in the community where they can look down on an area and see what it actually looks like from above. In most localities it is possible to purchase inexpensive aerial photographs of the local community, and these can be used in studying map symbols and in making maps of the local area. Some map companies have prepared wall charts designed to help children visualize things represented by map symbols; these are excellent devices for teaching this skill to middle- and upper-grade children. The teacher also should take advantage of the many fine photographs in social studies textbooks to acquaint children with the appearance of various areas, landscapes, surface features, land and water forms, and people-made things that are represented symbolically on maps.

For reasons of simplicity, orientation to direction may be avoided in the children's first attempts at making diagrams or maps. But the need to orient a map properly for direction will become apparent to them if their classroom map is rotated. Being able to note and read directions is a prerequisite to serious map study, and this skill should be introduced fairly early, perhaps in the second grade. Children can learn the cardinal directions by having the directions pointed out to them. They learn which wall of the room is north, south, east, and west because the teacher may have placed labels on the walls. They learn that if one knows the direction of north, the other directions can be determined; for if one faces north, the direction of south will be to one's back, east to the right, and west to the left. To extend their ability to orient themselves, children should be taken outdoors and the directions pointed out to them. If this is done at noon on a sunny day, the children's shadows will point in an approximate northerly direction. After the children have this basic orientation to direction, subsequent mapwork should include reference to direction and should become increasingly more complex as the children mature.

Finding directions on conventional wall maps can be facilitated with the aid of a globe and perhaps should not be taught much below the fourth grade. When this concept is introduced, it should be done through reference to north–south and east–west grid lines. Children are taught that north is in the direction of the North Pole and that south is in the direction of the South Pole. The poles can be easily found by following the meridians of longitude. The east–west directions can be found by following the parallels of latitude. Generalizations such as "north is at the top of the map" and "south is at the bottom of the map" should *not* be taught because they are not correct and because they may be confusing when one uses a variety of different map projections. Similarly, references to north as "up" and south as "down" should not be taught in connection with either maps or globes. When we speak of the earth, the term *down* means toward the center of the earth and *up* means away from the center of the earth, and both terms should be taught only in that way. The matter of associating *up* with north introduces many instructional problems as children learn more of the geography of the earth. For example, if north is up, how can so many of the world's rivers flow north? The children will invariably ask why we say "way down South" or "the Land Down Under"; these can be explained as being colorful expressions and figures of speech similar to "way out West" or "out at sea" that have crept into our language but have nothing at all to do with direction itself. (See Figure 5.6.)

There is merit in taking time to have children point out and discuss directions on the map. In the middle and upper grades, the teacher should duplicate maps on various grids and have the children place directional data on them. When this is done, the need to use east–west and north–south lines should be emphasized. This will give the children experiences noting directions on various map grids as well as keeping the teacher up-to-date on the progress that the children are making in learning this skill.

Children can be helped to understand the need for map scales by indicating to them that maps must be small enough to bring into the classroom or carry around. We cannot make maps as big as the area we wish to show because that would make the maps so large they could not be used. A map must, therefore, be made smaller, and everything on the map must be made smaller in the same amount. Just as a photograph of the family shows everyone smaller in the same amount, so must the map; otherwise, it would not give a true picture. Children should learn that maps are precise and accurate instruments. In primary grades, the scaling is not done in the mathematical sense, but the reductions are correctly made in the relative sense. That is, lakes would be larger than houses; streets, longer than driveways; cars, smaller than business buildings; and so on. In middle grades, when children have had sufficient background in mathematics, they can deal with graphic reductions more precisely. They learn that wall maps have the scale printed on them and are taught

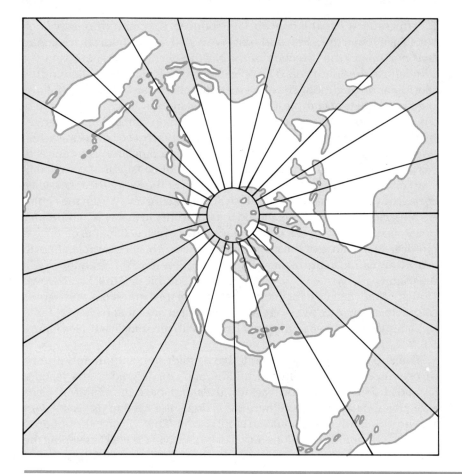

FIGURE 5.6. This map illustrates why generalizations such as ''north is at the top of the map'' are incorrect. East–west lines or parallels of latitude have been omitted in order to draw attention to north–south directions. What questions might you pose to students studying this map?

how to read the various ways by which scale can be indicated. The experiences children have using map scales provide a good context in which to call their attention to distances between various places. Children can be helped to visualize these distances through an appreciation of the amount of time needed to traverse the distances in question by air travel. These times may be obtained from commercial airlines.

When children have learned the meaning of map symbols, are skillful in orienting a map to direction, and can recognize and use map scales, they are well on their way toward an understanding of the language of maps. This does not mean, however, that they find maps especially useful or that they regard them as a valuable source of information. The development of skills that deal largely with map language must be accompanied by associated interpretive skills. Proficiency in interpreting maps will vary considerably among the children. One who is skillful in map use has developed the ability to visualize what an area actually looks like when it is seen on the map. Looking at the map color, one in a sense "sees" the rugged mountains of our West, the waving grainfields of western Montana, the rich farmlands of the Midwest, and the rolling countryside of Virginia. Because the child cannot visualize places not actually seen except in an imaginative way, the generous use of additional visual material along with maps is suggested. Good-quality pictures are especially important, and the class should see several pictures of an area in order to avoid fixing a single impression of the area in their minds. Filmstrips and slides can be used for the same purpose, and motion pictures and television are also excellent aids. As was previously noted, in the early stages of map reading, an excellent procedure is to have an aerial photograph of the local area as well as a conventional map. When these are placed side by side, the child can see how the area actually looks and how it is represented on a map. Stories and other narrative accounts also are helpful in assisting the child visualize areas represented on maps.

In the 1970s, the National Aeronautics and Space Administration (NASA) launched the satellite system called "Landsat," which uses remote sensing to obtain color images of the earth's surface. Landsat imagery is then used to construct maps of the earth's surface. Landsat maps are available for school use (NASA Code 130.3, Goddard Space Flight Center, Greenbelt, Maryland 20771, Attn. Elva Bailey). Because Landsat maps are based on actual images of the earth, they are useful in bridging the gap between the reality of the earth and the abstractness of conventional maps. One can *see* the actual shape and surface characteristics of the area shown on a Landsat map.

Activities such as the following can be used to relate the abstractions of maps to the reality they represent:

1. Observing local landscapes and geographical features, preferably from a high point.
2. Using pictorial and semipictorial symbols, especially at the lower grade levels.
3. Using three-dimensional models of the areas mapped; using blocks and models to represent buildings.
4. Making maps of the local area with which children are familiar.
5. Making generous use of pictures, films, and filmstrips of the areas shown on maps.
6. Relating aerial photographs (angle shots rather than perpendicular ones) to maps of the same area.
7. Comparing areas shown on the wall map with the same area shown in a picture.

8. Developing descriptive words (adjectives) that apply to a particular area shown on a map.
9. Making use of current events that relate to the area shown on a map.
10. Visiting places shown on the map, such as the airport, harbor, park, and downtown area.

Map- and globe-reading skills are learned through direct teaching and by application in situations in which the skill is normally used. In many instances, these processes can be combined. Let us say, for example, that children in a fifth-grade class read that "Permafrost is a condition found only in high latitudes." The teacher can use this encounter with *high latitudes* to teach map-reading in connection with that concept. That is, class time can be taken to teach the meaning of *high, low,* and *middle latitudes* on maps and globes, and the teaching would occur in what we refer to as a functional setting. Teachers are encouraged to teach as many map and globe skills as possible in this way rather than to isolate the skills from their relevant subject matter. After direct teaching there must be a generous application and use of the skills if proficiency is to be developed and maintained.

Because these skills are *developmental,* one cannot expect to teach them once and assume that they have been learned. Most skills are introduced early in the grades and then are retaught, reviewed, or expanded later on. We expect that children will show increased proficiency and maturity in their use of these skills each year that they are in school. Such development comes through continued teaching and use, not automatically through the natural process of maturation.

MAKING A TRIP MAP

The teacher showed children color photographs of several states and discussed the many interesting things that can be seen and done in the various states. Children shared some of their own travel experiences. The teacher provided the class with road maps of several different states and asked them to find places that might be of interest to someone visiting those states. These places of interest were discussed briefly. Children were then asked to think about and select a state they would enjoy visiting. Choices were to be made by the next day.

The following day the children made their selections of states they wanted to "visit." Using a road map of that state provided by the teacher and using references available in and outside the classroom, they were to plan a route of travel through the state of their choice, making at least five stops at places that would be interesting to a visitor. These places were to be marked with a large dot. A short narrative description was to be written to accompany the map telling about the travel route, state or national parks, natural areas of interest, historical landmarks, or other items of interest. If the children preferred, they could prepare a verbal rather than a written narrative by using the cassette recorder in the classroom.

The children responded to the teacher's encouragement to be creative in describing their imaginary trips, and several prepared travel brochures and recorded travelogs. They began a classroom exhibit of their trip maps and narratives, and in a week the room resembled a travel agency office. This generated a considerable amount of discussion and sharing of ideas and, of course, numerous opportunities to learn about maps. Also, through this activity the children acquired a great deal of information about their country, applied important skills (reading, research, writing, discussion, speaking), and developed an appreciation for the diversity and variety of their own country.

The use of color has caused confusion for children trying to visualize elevations. Children seem to believe that all areas represented by one color are precisely the same elevation, not recognizing that there are variations in elevations that occur within the limits of the interval used by the color representation. (See Figure 5.7.) Moreover, children develop the mistaken idea that elevations occur abruptly where colors change. Conventional color symbols give no impression of gradual elevations or depressions and create the illusion that changes are abrupt. The use of a relief map is helpful in showing that changes in elevation occur gradually. Comparing colors of a wall map with elevations on a relief map helps children gain a better understanding of map color as used to represent elevations. It is important to remember, however, that relief maps use two scales—one for vertical distances and another for horizontal distances. If the horizontal scale were used for vertical distances, the elevations would be imperceptible on a relief map of the size usually found in elementary school classrooms. Some maps combine shaded relief with altitude colors; this adds a third-dimensional effect to the mountains and valleys. Oblique shading and blending of color from one elevation to the other gives a graduated effect to land elevations that more accurately portray the surface of the earth. Children must also be taught that color may be used to designate political divisions such as states, nations, and territories and that the color chosen is an arbitrary one having nothing to do with the way the area actually looks. Pictures of state boundaries, for example, will illustrate that if it were not for the boundary marker, one would not be able to tell where one state ends and the other begins.

Landform maps are often used in middle- and upper-grade social studies textbooks. The usual land forms shown are *plains, plateaus, hills,* and *mountains;* each is represented by a different color. Difficulty in using these maps arises when the child mistakenly thinks of the colors as representing elevations in absolute amounts. For example, there are high mountains and low mountains, yet on a landform map they may appear in the same color. Some high plateaus are actually higher in absolute elevation than some low mountains. Some hills may be lower in elevation than plateaus and plains. Children need to learn that landform maps show only where the plains, plateaus, hills, and mountains are located, not how high they are above sea level.

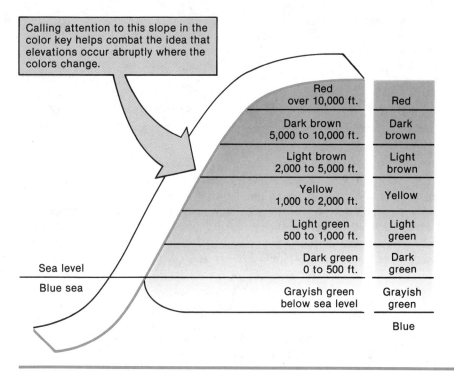

Calling attention to this slope in the color key helps combat the idea that elevations occur abruptly where the colors change.

Red over 10,000 ft.	Red
Dark brown 5,000 to 10,000 ft.	Dark brown
Light brown 2,000 to 5,000 ft.	Light brown
Yellow 1,000 to 2,000 ft.	Yellow
Light green 500 to 1,000 ft.	Light green
Dark green 0 to 500 ft.	Dark green
Grayish green below sea level	Grayish green
	Blue

Sea level

Blue sea

FIGURE 5.7. This diagram shows two methods of illustrating keys to colors used to express elevations on classroom maps. Some teachers find it helpful to construct a three-dimensional paper-mâché model of the key shown on the left.

Through years of experience with maps, children will develop skill in locating places and will become familiar with the shape and size of better-known areas. Places should be located precisely. In pointing to Chicago, for example, children should locate it exactly — not by sweeping a hand across the general location of Chicago, thereby including parts of Iowa, Illinois, Wisconsin, Michigan, and Indiana. But the location exercises must go beyond simply pointing to places and objects that appear on the map. It is these situations that provide ready-made opportunities to teach thinking skills in geography. For example, the teacher might pursue questions such as the following: What information can be obtained from the map that might account for the large settlement of people in the Chicago area? What features tend to encourage or discourage settlers? Such factors as natural transportation routes, waterways, waterfalls, mouths of rivers, coastlines, temperature, gaps in mountains, and outlets for products of the surrounding areas will become apparent as being important in population density and settlement. Why do certain areas of the Red River Valley in Minnesota and North Dakota experience frequent spring flood problems? The facts that the Red River is north-flowing and its headwaters thaw while the sections farther north are still frozen help explain this recurring problem. What is the relationship of the grazing lands of the West to the farmlands of Iowa to the meat-processing plants of Omaha, Chicago, and Kansas City? Map study, along with some knowledge of the geography of these areas, will help answer questions of this type. Children gain insights into geographical relationships by having a helpful teacher who can assist them in seeing possibilities for interpreting and making inferences from facts gained through map study.

The types of information that can be read directly or inferred from map study can be classified as follows:

Land and water forms — continents, oceans, bays, peninsulas, islands, straits.

Relief features — plains, mountains, rivers, deserts, plateaus, swamps, valleys.

Direction and distance — cardinal directions, distance in miles or kilometers and relative distance, scale.

Social data — population density, size of communities, location of major cities, relationship of social data to other factors.

Economic information — industrial and agricultural production, soil fertility, trade factors, location of industries.

Political information — political divisions, boundaries, capitals, territorial possessions, types of government, political parties.

Scientific information — location of discoveries, ocean currents, location of mineral and ore deposits, geological formations, air movements.

Human factors — cities, canals, railroads, highways, coaxial and fiber-optic cables, telephone lines, bridges, dams, nuclear power plants.

What follows is a list of map and globe activities that will provide the teacher with a few examples of the kinds of activities that can be used to stimulate interest and at the same time teach important concepts and thinking skills related to map and globe reading.

1. After an on-the-spot observation of the school grounds or the immediate vicinity, construct a three-dimensional floor map of the area.
2. Locate the place where stories about children in other lands take place or where news events are occurring.
3. Find pictures in magazines that illustrate various landforms: plains, plateaus, hills, and mountains.
4. Make maps of the same area, such as the local county, using different scales for each map.
5. Trace great circle air routes on maps and on globes, and compare the two.
6. Compare the shapes of known areas on different map projections.
7. Develop a classroom exhibit of maps found in current newspapers and periodicals, and compare them with conventional maps and globes.

8. Develop an illustrated glossary of concepts and terms associated with map reading.

9. Secure an outdated political map of the world (1950–1960 vintage), and have the class compare it with a current political map of the world.

10. Illustrate *mis*conceptions about maps such as "north is at the top of the map" or "the climate is temperate in the Temperate Zone."

11. Make use of computer programs designed to build or reinforce map and globe skills, such as *Maps and Globes* (Society for Visual Education) or *Exploring America* (Eye Gate Media).

Teaching map and globe skills does require some amount of special resources and equipment. Every classroom should have a globe along with wall maps appropriate to the curriculum content of the grade. In fourth grade and above, all classrooms should have a wall map of the world. Outline maps are needed in the middle and upper grades. It helps to have available a three-dimensional relief map of the United States and of the home state. Additional equipment might include charts showing conventional map symbols; slated maps and globe; and special-purpose maps showing vegetation, historical development, and natural resources. When children engage in map making, they will need to have available essential construction materials: boxes, blocks, butcher paper, black tape, tracing paper, colored pencils, pens or crayons, paints and brushes, papier-mâché, plaster, salt and flour, or other modeling material.

Regular social studies unit work and the current events program provide natural settings for teaching map and globe skills. Children can use maps to record their data or observations as they study unit topics. They can think through the significance of the relationships they detect in maps. They can use maps as a means of communicating ideas and findings to their classmates. It has been said that maps are the constant companions of geographers, and the same might be said about children as they engage in the social studies.

Children develop skill in map and globe reading in settings where teachers know which variations of the skills are to be taught at each level and where there is some method of accountability for such teaching. Regrettably, this does not occur as often as it should, and, as a result, the systematic teaching of these important skills becomes vulnerable to neglect. If we depend only on incidental references to maps and globes as a way of having children learn these skills, it will only be a fortunate accident if children become proficient in their use.

As a first step in developing a program of instruction in maps and globes, therefore, the teacher must determine which variations of the essential skills will be taught during the year. Naturally, it is helpful if the school district provides this information in a curriculum document. If such a document is not provided, the teacher should develop his or her own list of skills to be taught, looking for guidance to such sources as the textbook teacher's guide, the skills section of the NCSS Task Force Report on Scope and Sequence,[2] curriculum documents from other districts, or college methods books in social studies. The summary on pages 129–131 is an example of material that could be used for this purpose.

A SUMMARY OF MAP AND GLOBE SKILLS

Elementary and middle school children should develop map and globe skills associated with the following concepts and generalizations:

1. **Primary grades.**
   - A map is a drawing or other representation of all or part of the earth.
   - On maps and globes, symbols are used to stand for real things.
   - The earth is a huge sphere.
   - A globe is a small model of the earth and is the most accurate representation of the earth.
   - Half of the earth is called a hemisphere.
   - The earth can be divided into several hemispheres. The most common ones are the Eastern, Western, Northern, and Southern Hemispheres; land hemisphere and water hemisphere; and day hemisphere and night hemisphere.
   - Any part of the globe can be shown on a map.
   - Large bodies of land are called continents.
   - Large bodies of water are called oceans.
   - Terms such as *left, right, near, far, above, below, up,* and *down* can be useful in expressing relative location.
   - A legend or key on a map tells the meaning of colors and symbols used on the map.
   - Directions on a map are determined by the poles; to go north means to go in the direction of the North Pole, to go south means to go in the direction of the South Pole.
   - North may be shown any place on a map; north is *not* always at the top of a map.
   - The North Pole is the point farthest north on the earth; the South Pole is the point farthest south.
   - The scale on a map or globe makes it possible to determine distances between places.

[2] National Council for the Social Studies, "In Search of a Scope and Sequence for Social Studies," *Social Education,* 48 (April 1984), pp. 259–261.

- Maps are drawn to different scales; scale ensures that all objects are made smaller in the same amount.
- Maps and globes use legends, or keys, that tell the meaning of the symbols used on the map.
- The cardinal directions are north, south, east, and west; intermediate directions are northeast, northwest, southeast, and southwest.
- All places on the earth can be located on maps and globes. Different maps provide different information about the earth.

2. **Intermediate and upper grades.**
   - The larger the scale used, the larger each feature appears on the map.
   - The same symbol may mean different things from one map to another; the legend tells what the symbols stand for.
   - The elevation of land is measured from sea level; some maps provide information about elevation.
   - Physical maps can be used to determine land elevations, slopes of land, and directions of rivers.
   - Parallels of latitude can be used to establish east–west direction and are also used to measure distances in degrees north and south of the equator.
   - All places on the same east–west line (parallel of latitude) are directly east or west of one another and are the same distance north or south of the equator.
   - All places north of the equator are in north latitudes; all places south of the equator are in south latitudes.
   - The Tropic of Cancer and the Tropic of Capricorn are imaginary lines of latitude lying north and south of the equator. The part of the earth between them is known as the tropics.
   - The Arctic and Antarctic Circles are imaginary lines that define the polar regions.
   - The low latitudes lie on either side of the equator; the high latitudes surround the poles; and the middle latitudes lie between the low and high latitudes.
   - Parallels of latitude, parallel to the equator, get shorter as they progress from the equator to the poles.
   - Knowing the latitude of a place makes it possible to locate its north–south position on the earth.
   - Meridians of longitude can be used to determine north–south direction and are also used to measure distances in degrees east and west of the prime meridian.
   - The zero or *prime* meridian passes through Greenwich, a suburb of London.
   - Meridians of longitude are imaginary north–south lines that converge on both poles.

- Meridians of longitude are *great circles* because they divide the earth into two hemispheres.
- The shortest distance between any two places on the earth follows a great circle.
- West longitude is measured to the west of the prime meridian from zero to 180°; east longitude is measured to the east of the prime meridian from zero to 180°.
- All places on the same north–south line (meridian of longitude) are directly north or south of each other and are the same distance in degrees east or west of the prime meridian.
- The latitude and longitude of any place determine its exact location on a globe or map.
- Longitude is used in determining the time of day at places around the world. The earth rotates through 15° of longitude every hour; the earth is divided into twenty-four time zones.
- Globes give such information as distance, direction, relative and exact location, and sizes and shapes of areas more accurately than flat maps can.
- Maps and globes often use abbreviations to identify places and things.
- An imaginary line through the center of the earth, running from pole to pole, is called the earth's axis; the earth rotates on its axis from west to east.
- Night and day are the result of the rotation of the earth.
- Maps and globes provide data about the nature of areas by using color contour, visual relief, and contour lines.
- All flat maps contain some distortion because they represent a round object on a flat surface.
- Different map projections provide different perspectives on the sizes and shapes of areas shown.

DEVELOPING A SENSE OF TIME AND CHRONOLOGY

There is much in the modern, urban, industrialized world to remind one of the importance of time. Airlines, trains, and buses operate on time schedules, as do places of business, factories, churches, public institutions, sports events, and television programs, to name just a few. Benjamin Franklin said, "Remember that time is money," this being one of several such proverbs that equate time with economic gain. When we speak of persons making "wise use" of their time, we usually mean that they are busy at something perceived to be "productive." Because time is such an important commodity in the lives of most of us, we have little tolerance for time wasters and loafers.

In spite of the substantial amount of research that has been conducted on the ability of human beings to deal with time concepts and chronology, much about this phenomenon remains shrouded in mystery. There can be no question that one's perception of time grows out of cultural conditioning. There are few cultures in which people are as compulsive about punctuality as are Americans. To some extent, one's time orientation relates to one's social-class membership, but research suggests that human beings vary greatly in their ability to understand time concepts. Circumstances also condition one's perception of time so that in some cases we say that "time flies" whereas in other settings time seems to drag on endlessly.

Children, of course, learn much about time relationships through ordinary living outside of school. Undoubtedly most children would learn how to tell time, would learn the days of the week and months of the year, and would become familiar with terms ordinarily used in referring to units of time, such as noon, midnight, afternoon, and morning, even if these were not taught in school. The school program can ensure that these skills are correctly and are adequately learned, however, and can provide children the opportunity to practice using them. A few lessons with a simulated clock, supported by practical application in noting when things happen in the schedule of activities during the day, will be adequate to teach most children how to deal with clock time. It is rare to find a mentally competent grown person who cannot tell the time of day. In any case, the increased use of digital clocks should eliminate entirely any problems in reading clock time.

The main thrust of the school program should be, therefore, on those aspects of time and chronology that are not likely to be learned outside of school. This includes (1) the more technical language of time and chronology, such as century, decade, fortnight, fiscal year, calendar year, generation, score, millennium, A.M., P.M., B.C., and A.D.; (2) placing events in chronological order; (3) developing an understanding of the time spans that separate historical events. References to *indefinite* units of time — such as many years ago, soon thereafter, several years had passed, and in a few years — need special attention because they are apt to mean almost any amount of time to young children. Definite references to time can more easily be made meaningful by associating them with units of time that are known to the children: their own ages, the length of time they have been in school, when their parents or grandparents were children of their ages, and so on. The teaching of these relationships can and should take place within the context of social studies units, especially those that focus on history, and in connection with current news stories.

Time lines are often used to show how related events are arranged in chronological order and to show the relative amount of time that separates them. Though widely used, experts are not in agreement as to the value of time lines in clarifying time and chronology for young children. Research on this problem seems to indicate that below the sixth grade the use of time lines is questionable. Nonetheless, teachers report success in helping children arrange events in proper sequence by using time lines. Using only a limited number of events that are clearly and saliently a part of the subject matter studied seems to enhance understanding.

Children can develop the concept of representing time on a continuum by first charting events that they experience on a first-hand basis. This helps them arrange the events in the correct sequence. They can make time lines that show things that happened to them yesterday, today, or are being planned for tomorrow. The amount of time included on the line can gradually be expanded to cover several months and then years. Time lines are more interesting to children if events are shown pictorially rather than simply as dots and dates. With middle- and upper-grade children, frequent use can be made of time lines in connection with historical studies of their home state and their nation. Such time lines need not stop with the present date but may be projected into the future, thus illustrating that time is continuous and that the present stands between the past and the future.

The understanding of time in the historical sense represents a fairly mature level of dealing with time and, therefore, should not be expected of young children. The development of time concepts should begin with time situations that are within their realm of experience. Children should be given help in learning to read clock time and in understanding references to the parts of the day, days of the week, months, seasons, and the year. Even though primary-grade children make statements about things that happened "a hundred years ago," they have little comprehension of the real meaning of the expression and simply use it as a vague reference to something that happened in what seems to them a long time ago.

In the teaching of history, references to the past are often made through the use of indefinite expressions such as "a long time ago," "many years ago," and "several years later." These expressions are not well understood even by adults, and for young children they are often devoid of any specific meaning. To a child, "a long time ago" could very well be no more than a decade ago. Teachers need to build meaning into these abstract quantitative time concepts by discussing their meaning within the context of events of the period studied and by relating the time interval to things that are familiar to the children, such as the length of the school year, when their parents or grandparents were children, or the amount of time that has passed since they were born, and so on. (See pages 243–244 in Chapter 9.)

TEACHING CHILDREN THE USE OF GRAPHS AND CHARTS

Because of the widespread use of graphs and charts in social studies and in printed material outside of school, it is imperative that children develop the skills needed to read and interpret them. Just leafing through a daily newspaper or weekly news magazine reminds one of how commonly these graphics are used and how powerfully their messages are conveyed. Citizens today are "digest" oriented. They do not have the time or the inclination to wade through a mountain of narrative that explains social events or conditions. They want to see these ideas in summary form and in stark relief. Besides, the complexity of social data, much of which is in statistical form, lends itself well to a graphic format.

Graphs

Graphs are used to illustrate relationships among quantities. These relationships may be spread over a period of time, thus showing trends. The most commonly used graphs are some variation of the *bar graph*, the *pie* or *circle graph*, and the *line graph*. Any of these graphs may include pictorial representations, thereby making them more interesting to young children and making the content less abstract. For instance, with primary-grade children, stick figures can be used to represent children in a bar graph showing the number absent from class each day. It is easy to visualize the relationships of the parts to the whole in a circle graph, but to construct one accurately requires the ability to compute percentages, usually not possible in the elementary school grades. Modern elementary school textbooks make liberal use of graphs in presenting data, but children need to be instructed in how to read and interpret them. Because graphs can be designed to present distorted pictures of data, children in the middle and upper grades should be taught how bias is introduced in a graph. (See Figures 5.9, 5.10, and 5.11.)

Children can learn much about graphs and how to read them by constructing their own graphs. Such learner-made graphs can be used in making oral or written reports and for bulletin board displays. In the making of graphs, accuracy in the presentation should be emphasized rather than artistic perfection. (See Figure 5.8.)

Formal Charts

Like graphs, charts are widely used to present ideas in a vivid and forceful way. Formal charts are often designated as follows:

1. *Narrative chart:* Tells a story; shows events in sequence. (Example: how plywood is made, stages of the development of civilization, how to use a computer, or the construction of homes.)
2. *Tabulation chart:* Lists data in table form to facilitate making comparisons. (Example: data placed in tabular form to show infant mortality

Number of days the sun was shining at noon for the first five months

A class kept a record of the number of days the sun was shining at noon from the first of January through May. In January there were nineteen days when the sun was shining at noon; in February there were twenty-five; in March there were twelve; in April there were twenty; and in May there were twenty-eight days. These graphs show three different ways of showing these data. Graphs of this type can be constructed and used for study purposes by elementary schoolchildren. What inquiry questions might be based on these graphs?

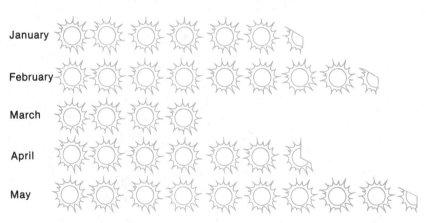

FIGURE 5.8. Examples of graphs and data suitable for use with elementary schoolchildren.

FIGURE 5.9. The drawing illustrates how the popular "pie" graph is sometimes used to create an incorrect impression. Because the sketch is shown in perspective, the sizes of the sections are distorted. Thus, sections that seem to be farthest from the viewer appear smaller than those in the foreground, although arithmetically they represent equal amounts.

rates, illiteracy rates, or per capita income among nations of the world.)

3. *Pedigree chart:* Shows events stemming from a common origin. (Example: a family tree, the development of a political party, or the history of language.)

4. *Classification chart:* Groups data into various categories. (Example: the various types of restaurants, types of personal services available, or different modes of transportation.)

5. *Organization chart:* Shows the structure of an organization. (Example: the three branches of government, the structure of a corporation, or the organization of a city government or a school district.)

FIGURE 5.10. It is important for children to learn that graphs can create false impressions. In these line graphs, the same data were used on three different grids, resulting in varying steepness in the slopes of the lines. Consequently, although the facts are the same, the rate of change appears markedly different.

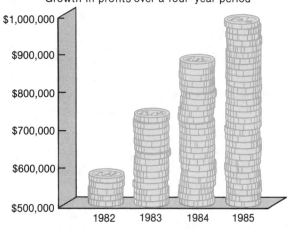

Growth in profits over a four–year period

FIGURE 5.11. How much larger were profits in 1985 than in 1983? The chances are that you have said "about twice as large." This graph illustrates how wrong impressions are conveyed when pictorial graphs are improperly constructed. Careful examination of this graph will show that the 1985 profits are not even twice those of 1982. The basic error in this graph is that it does not show the first $500,000 of profit. A more accurate perception of the growth in profits can be made if the correct position of the base line is established. Can you locate the place where the base line should be?

6. *Flow chart:* Shows a process involving change at certain points. (Example: how raw materials are transformed into finished products, the break of bulk in shipping as at a harbor facility, or how scrap iron is converted into a usable raw material.)

The frequent use of formal charts in children's books provides a good basis for inquiry learning. In the process children not only learn how to read and interpret the chart, but also broaden their substantive knowledge and build their understanding of associated concepts.

Informal Charts

Informal charts are charts that are developed and constructed by the teacher or by the children. They are commonly placed on wrapping paper, oak tagboard, newsprint, "butcher" paper, chart paper, or the chalkboard. They may contain diagrams, sketches, pictures, or other illustrative material or simply may be written accounts of experiences or activities related to the unit under study.

When charts are constructed for use with primary-grade children, it is essential that the mechanics and makeup of the charts conform exactly to the patterns that are taught in the basic language arts program. For example, the style of lettering used should be exactly the same as that used by the children in manuscript writing, capital letters and punctuation marks should be used only where they are used in ordinary writing, and the reading vocabulary should follow as closely as possible the vocabulary being developed in the basic reading program. Careful attention should be given to the format to facilitate ease of reading: uniform margins; well-spaced letters, words, and lines; natural phrases of appropriate length; and sharp, clear lettering. Phrases should not be broken at the end of a line such as:

Cross the street at
the crosswalk.

But rather:

Cross the street
at the crosswalk.

Middle- and upper-grade children can be encouraged to make and use charts in connection with their reports, committee work, and displays. As was true with graphs, the children need be less concerned with the artistic perfection of the chart than with the manner in which it conveys

CHART 3. DATA-RETRIEVAL CHART

Our Next-Door Neighbors		
Analytical Concepts	Canada	Mexico

Geographical features
  Size
  Climate
  Physical features
  Natural resources		

History
  Native people
  Foreign influences
  Relations with U.S.
  Type of government today		

Economic development
  Main occupations
  Average per capita income
  Exports		

Population
  Ethnic groups
  Density
  Major cities
  Levels of education
  Religious groups
  Languages		

ideas. Simplicity, vividness, concreteness, and accuracy of the idea presented are more important considerations than artistic finish.

Data-Retrieval Charts

The *data-retrieval chart* consists of a set of questions related to the topic under study and an indication of the groups or situations from which data are to be secured. It provides a convenient way for children to record information they gather in the process of study. It also has the advantage of displaying the data in a form that can be used or "retrieved" for study and analysis at a later time. The data-retrieval chart is useful in making comparisons and contrasts because comparable data can be secured from two or more samples. (See Chart 3.)

It is in the processing and presenting of data that the computer can be put to good use. Computers are excellent tools for making electronic spread sheets of graphs, data-retrieval charts, data displays, or other visuals. Commercial programs are available that help students transform raw data to visual forms on the microcomputer. Today a child with a microcomputer can produce graphics that just a few years ago would have required the talents of a skilled artist to create.

TEACHING CHILDREN THE USE OF CARTOONS

Cartoons are an accepted form of social commentary. Through a dramatic visual format, the reader projects meaning into the visual by virtue of his or her own experience. Cartoons are often humorous because they exaggerate, subjects are presented in caricature, and the cartoons are designed to show all the vices or virtues associated with a particular character in our culture. Cartoons are especially effective in calling attention to the ironies that surround our lives. They use an amusing way to make a serious point.

Editorial cartoons are not necessarily humorous. Indeed, they are often biting in their comment on social issues. The techniques of symbolism, the use of familiar situations, exaggerations, satire, and caricature are used to present forcefully a single point of view. The cartoon does not allow the reader or the person portrayed in it an opportunity for rebuttal. Recognition of the fact that only one point of view is represented in cartoons is important in their interpretation. Older children need to be taught the general makeup of cartoons that deal with social and political problems and need the experience of evaluating their message critically. It is well for the children to present an opposite point of view from the one depicted in the cartoon.

Field Newspaper Syndicate • 1703 Kaiser Ave. • Irvine, CA 92714 • (714) 549-8700

FIGURE 5.12. This cartoon is a good illustration of how much the reader must bring to such visuals if they are to have meaning. Ordinarily, we do not get new information from editorial cartoons. The artist relies on what we already know and provides a visual that places that information in a setting that conveys a powerful social, economic, and/or political message. (Reprinted with special permission of NAS, Inc.)

The symbolism used in cartoons causes much confusion in the minds of some children. When the characters are portrayed as animals, the children tend to associate those animals with various national groups. Cartoons use stereotypes of people that add little to the type of international understanding we are attempting to foster and encourage in the social studies program. Figurative terms such as *Iron Curtain* are represented as walls of iron, leading the child to believe that such a wall exists in a literal sense. Cartoons usually demand a high level of understanding of the issues involved if they are to tell their story accurately; thus, the child needs to be instructed and helped in developing the skill of interpreting cartoons. (See Figure 5.12.)

DISCUSSION QUESTIONS AND SUGGESTED ACTIVITIES

1. Select a topic for a grade of your choice, and plan specific map- and globe-reading activities that could be incorporated in a study of it.

2. Prepare a series of posters showing map symbols, and accompany each symbol with a photograph of the object being represented.

3. Make a list of words or phrases related to the understanding of maps and globes that are misleading (for example, *up, down*). For each entry, suggest an alternate word or phrase that would be more accurate.

4. What misunderstandings might develop when characters in charts and cartoons appear in caricature? What might be done to prevent such misunderstandings from occurring?

5. Develop an inquiry-oriented learning experience based on a map, chart, or cartoon. Arrange to teach it to your peers.

6. How might a data-retrieval chart constructed by the children be useful to them in unit study? Suggest a specific topic and variables that could be used in constructing such a chart.

7. Select a map-reading skill, and show by examples of learning activities how it is sequenced through the elementary grades on a simple to complex continuum.

8. Select a social studies textbook, and examine it in terms of its treatment of the skills discussed in this chapter.

9. If you are teaching or if you have access to a class, try these three activities:

   a. Have children find indefinite references to time and space in their social studies texts or in a newspaper (expressions such as "many years ago," "shortly after," "several ships," "few resources"). Discuss the meaning of these terms with the children. How accurate are their understanding of these terms? Report your findings to your classmates.

   b. Have the class discuss situations in which they think "time flies" and others in which they think time "moves at a snail's pace." Encourage them to identify reasons for this difference. Are the situations the same for all children?

   c. Have the class think of as many popular expressions or proverbs as they can that have to do with time. Conduct this activity for a period of days, and as expressions or proverbs are suggested, place them on the bulletin board. Have children make drawings to illustrate them. Discuss this in terms of the importance of time in our lives.

SELECTED REFERENCES

ATKINS, CAMMIE L. "Introducing Basic Map and Globe Skills to Young Children." *Journal of Geography*, 83 (March 1984), pp. 228–233.

BENNETT, CLIFFORD, DONNA BLISS, MARCIA S. DEFREN, WILLIAM RAY HEITZMANN,

BRENDA HOLUM, AND JOHN E. STEINBRINK. These authors contribute six articles to a Special Section on using political cartoons in the classroom. *The Social Studies,* 79 (September/October 1988), pp. 205–227.

CAREY, HELEN H. *How to Use Maps and Globes.* New York: Franklin Watts, 1983. (A children's book.)

CHEYNEY, ARNOLD B., AND DONALD L. CAPONE. *The Map Corner.* Glenview, Illinois: Scott, Foresman, 1983.

FRAZEE, BRUCE M. "Foundations for an Elementary Map Skills Program." *The Social Studies,* 75 (March–April 1984), pp. 79–82.

HATCHER, BARBARA. "Putting Young Cartographers 'On the Map.'" *Childhood Education,* 59 (May–June 1983), pp. 311–315.

MILLER, JACK W. "Teaching Map Skills: Theory, Research, Practice." *Social Education,* 49 (January 1985), pp. 30–33.

MONAHAN, DAVID P. "How to Stimulate Student Writing with Political Cartoons." *Social Education,* 47 (January 1983), pp. 62–64.

MUESSIG, RAYMOND H., ed. AND JACK W. MILLER, LINDA S. LEVSTIK, AND VAL ARNSDORF. "Building Map Skills to Advance Geographic Understanding." *Social Education,* 49 (January 1985), pp. 28–46.

MUIR, SHARON PRAY. "Understanding and Improving Students' Map Reading Skills." *The Elementary School Journal,* 86 (November 1985), pp. 207–216.

RUSHDOONY, HAIG A. *The Language of Maps.* Belmont, California: Pitman, 1983. (A book of map skill exercises for grades 4–8.)

TURNER, THOMAS N. "Using Maps That Move." *Social Education,* 48 (April 1984), pp. 275–277.

VAN CLEAF, DAVID W. "The Environment as a Data Source: Map Activities for Young Children." *Social Education,* 49 (February 1985), pp. 145–146.

WINSTON, BARBARA J. *Map and Globe Skills: K–8 Teaching Guide.* Western Illinois University, Macomb, Illinois: National Council for Geographic Education, 1984.

6

Contributions of the Social Sciences

The four social sciences — economics, political science, sociology, and anthropology — make essential contributions to the social studies curriculum of the elementary and middle schools. It would be a mistake, however, to place their importance on a par with history and geography as contributors of subject matter. For the most part, these disciplines do not have a secure anchor in the curriculum as do history and geography. Therefore, they must find their way into the program by infusion or by the integration of their important concepts and skills into the mainstream social studies units.

We deal with four of the social sciences in this chapter — economics, political science, sociology, and anthropology. Some programs add psychology, philosophy, and religion to this list. These latter three are not included here because psychology makes its contribution through the *process* of teaching and learning rather than by providing substantive content. Concepts and subject matter from philosophy and religion are such that they can be conveniently subsumed under history or anthropology for purposes of the elementary and middle schools' curriculum.

ECONOMICS AND THE SOCIAL STUDIES

Of the newer social sciences that are gaining a place in the social studies program, none has received more attention or been promoted with more enthusiasm than has economics. In one form or another, economic education has been a part of the American school curriculum for many years. The Joint Council on Economic Education, representing business, labor, education, agriculture, and other groups, was organized in 1948. Along with its affiliated local and state councils, it has actively promoted economic education in the schools. The Foundation for Teaching Economics, a San Francisco-based organization, has worked for the improved teaching of economics at the middle-school and junior high school levels.

Economics is the study of the production, distribution, exchange, and consumption of goods and services that people need or want. In a modern industrialized society such as ours, wants and needs are great because individuals have an expectation of a high standard of living. Moreover, the processes involved in the production, distribution, exchange, and consumption form an interrelated web of relationships. So directly are individuals enmeshed in it that almost everything they do is, in one way or another, related to our economic system. Economic education concerns itself with helping children achieve an understanding of some of the basic relationships between our economic system and our way of life, thereby enabling them to make informed decisions on economic matters. Another major purpose of economic education is to teach students a way of thinking about economics and economic issues based on orderliness and reasoning.

These samples represent major generalizations from economics that have been used as organizing ideas in developing programs in economic education:

1. The wants of people are unlimited whereas resources needed to fulfill wants are scarce; hence, societies and individuals have to make choices as to which needs are to be met and which are to be sacrificed.
2. The interdependence of peoples of the world makes exchange and trade a necessity in the modern world.
3. Economic systems are usually mixed with both public and private ownership and with decisions made both by the government and by individual members of society.
4. Increased specialization in production has led to interdependence among individuals, communities, states, and nations.

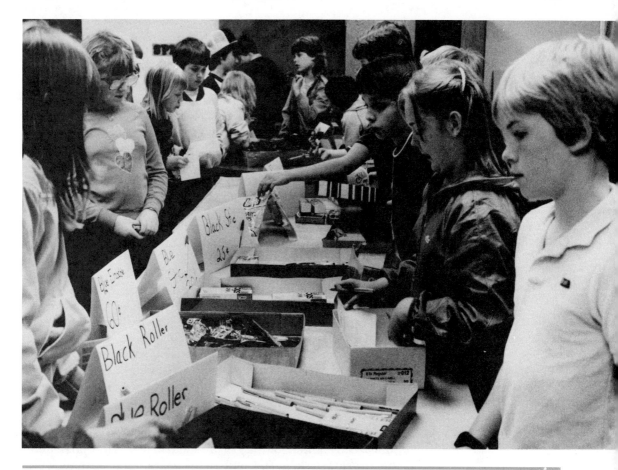

These fifth-graders at the Margaret Mead Elementary School, Lake Washington School District in Washington State organized their own "Fifthway Store." As a project in economic education, the children sold shares to get the store started. Stockholders received dividends on the profits that accrued from the sale of such items as pencils, pens, plants, and erasers to other students in the school. (Photo by Judy Mix, Lake Washington School District.)

5. In the complex, modern industrialized society of today, government plays an important role in the economic life of society.

Teaching Suggestions

The elementary and middle school program of instruction should be built around basic economic concepts (such as scarcity, production, distribution, exchange, and consumption) that are related to one or more generalizations of the type listed earlier. Each of these economic concepts can be developed in many of the topics included in the social studies curriculum. There may be times, however, when particular topics are selected because they have special usefulness in developing specific economic concepts. Units on The Market in the primary grades are of this type and ordinarily focus on the distribution of needed goods.

Learning resources and teaching materials for economic education in elementary and middle schools are available in increasing quantities. The best sources of such instructional materials are the Joint Council on Economic Education, 2 West 46 Street, New York City 10036, the Foundation for Teaching Economics, 550 Kearny Street, Suite 1000, San Francisco, California 94108, and the home state council for economic education. From these sources the teacher can secure sample units, scope and sequence charts, background information, and other teaching materials, as well as information concerning other sources of aids for teaching economic concepts.

Learning activities such as the following can be used in developing economic concepts:

1. *Examine ways that people depend on each other* in their families, neighborhoods, and communities. Relate this to the need for many different kinds of jobs.
2. *Compare work roles* of today with those in colonial times to discover differences between cottage-industry procedures with assembly-line production.
3. *Study different types of advertising* to learn how producers create consumer needs and wants.
4. *Compare wages* paid to workers in terms of such things as the *(a)* level of education required for the job; *(b)* extent to which the job requires highly developed skills; *(c)* length of the preparation or training program for the job; *(d)* amount of risk to the worker.
5. *Role-play negotiations* between buyers and sellers; employers and employees in a salary dispute; a consumer with a complaint about a product and a retailer; a customer who has been overcharged and the person who did the repair work.
6. *Use newspapers* to compare prices of items among various retailers. Relate this to factors that affect pricing policies.
7. *Study the concept of seasonal employment* as it relates to employment patterns in different parts of the country.
8. *Study government regulation* of business operations in terms of consumer protection, quality control, and ethical business practices.
9. *Familiarize children with local businesses* through the use of field trips and resource persons.
10. *Study personal and family budgeting procedures* to illustrate the relationship between income and expenditures, the difference between wants and needs, and the necessity of choice making.

11. *Participate in simulation games* designed to teach economic concepts (see pp. 383–385 for an example).
12. *Use computer programs,* such as *The Market Place* series (by MECC), *Economics* (by SVE), or *Stock Markets* (by Learning Arts), to build economic concepts and relationships.
13. *In grades seven and eight, involve your class in ECONOMICS TODAY,* an eight-lesson program that provides students with an introduction to the economy using news stories found in *USA Today.* Developed by the Foundation for Teaching Economics and *USA Today.* For information write to: Foundation for Teaching Economics, 550 Kearny Street, Suite 1000, San Francisco, California 94108.

The World of Work

The world of work is a subset of economic education, and elementary and middle schools have for many years included it in their social studies programs. Units on family life, neighborhood relationships, workers in the community, transportation and communication, food, clothing and shelter, and ways of living in societies past and present are familiar to elementary school social studies. Even though many changes have been made in the social studies program in recent years, these topics are still in the curriculum of most schools. These units and others like them stress work roles, jobs, the importance of work to the community and to the individual, interdependence, and simplified producer and consumer economics. In this context the social studies program is a natural vehicle to teach important ideas and attitudes relating to the world of work.

In the early 1970s, influential persons in this country argued persuasively that preparation for work, including the attitudes and skills needed to perform work, should be the primary emphasis of the school curriculum.[1] No less a figure than the U.S. commissioner of education challenged school leadership of America to attend to what he called "career education" of its children and youth.[2] By this he meant that the school experience should equip all children and youth with salable skills that would be useful to them in relating to the world of work. The term *career education* was and is used to describe the schools' effort to help children and youth relate to the world of work. Federal funds were made available to schools and colleges to encourage and promote career education. Presently, career education as an educational movement lacks the high priority it had a decade earlier, but concern for preparing individuals for the world of

[1] Larry J. Bailey and Ronald W. Stadt, *Career Education: New Approaches to Human Development* (Bloomington, Ill.: McKnight Publishing Company, 1973).
[2] Sidney P. Marland, Jr., "Educating for the Real World," *Business Education Forum,* 26 (November 1971), pp. 3–5.

work remains an important component of the economic education of students.

In teaching about the work world, as is the case with energy and environmental education, safety, law-related education, and other such topics, a systematic, integrated approach is probably more effective than special units spaced throughout the grades. This, of course, does not preclude the possibility of having special units with a world of work focus, but simply suggests that such an approach is not in itself adequate. Teaching is strengthened when concepts from the work world are built into many of the existing units of the social studies program. Most who have been involved in curriculum work in this field suggest that awareness building should be a major goal of a program relating to the world of work in the elementary school. The major components of such a program are these:

Information about the World of Work.   Persons are often uninformed about choices available to them when they decide on a vocation. They simply select from those few occupations they have learned about on a firsthand basis from a close relative or from a friend. This explains why some occupations seem to "run in families." Children should *not* be encouraged to make occupational choices when they are in the elementary school. But they can begin to build a background of knowledge about a broad spectrum of occupations that will one day help them make an intelligent career choice.

Opportunity to Explore Work Values.   Children need to see the connection between values that are stressed in school, such as responsibility, dependability, punctuality, cooperation, trustworthiness, and others, and the world of work. They need to develop a sense of appreciation for a job that is well done. They need to learn what it means to take pride in one's work.

Personal Choice Making.   Part of the awareness building of the world of work should include the opportunity to make decisions and to exercise choices. Decisions surrounding career choices will one day be an extension of decision-making skills the child has exercised throughout life.

Society and the World of Work.   Children need to learn about the relationship of the individual to society *through* the world of work. What one does for a living does not simply have to be a job that has no purpose other than as a way of earning enough money to pay bills and stay alive. Work contributes to the life and health of the larger society. Society's need to have jobs performed and performed well can be learned by the youngest children. All of us depend on others to help us meet our basic needs. Social studies units that deal with so-called community helpers provide opportunities for learning outcomes of this type. Work is so important to society that individuals are often identified by others in accordance with what they do for a living: "He is a data analysis specialist," "He is a United Airlines pilot," "She is a doctor in town," "She is the city manager at Augusta," and so on.

Many of the outcomes sought in career education are affective, dealing with attitudes, appreciations, and feelings. This means that children will need a broad exposure to the world of work and opportunities to respond to it in a variety of ways. Such experiences have feeling as well as knowledge dimensions. For example, children may want to express their own feelings about certain occupations, and the strength of those feelings should be explored. Children should be encouraged to find out the attitudes of their parents toward the jobs they hold. Why do they like them or dislike them?

Some attention should also be given to related economic concepts such as producer, consumer, goods, services, division of labor, and interdependence. Children must understand the importance of work both to the individual and to society. Instruction should stress society's need for a wide range of talents and abilities in order that the many jobs that need doing well get done. Society has a need for a constant flow of competent persons in order to operate the complex systems that go into making up our way of life. The study of basic economic concepts can help the child develop a sense of appreciation of our absolute dependence on others for the things we need in ordinary everyday living.

Education about the work world clearly must be sensitive to sex-role and ethnic-role stereotyping. Traditionally, women have been stereotyped along the lines of domestic roles, and a certain limited number of occupational roles—elementary school teaching, nursing, secretarial services, food services, and so on. School programs have often reinforced these stereotypes, with the result that women have a much more restricted set of occupational choices than do men. Boys and girls need to learn that the traditional ideas about what is "woman's work" and what is "man's work" no longer apply and that people now have greater opportunities to do the things *they* want to do to lead self-fulfilling, productive lives. Much the same can be said in connection with ethnic-role stereotyping. Although a great deal has been done in recent years to eliminate stereotyping in learning resources, the teacher still must be careful not to associate certain occupations with specific national, ethnic, or racial groups.

Activities for Studying the World of Work. *Conduct interviews* to find out how adults in the community earn money. Have the children compile a list of categories for their questionnaire such as these:

People Who Produce Things
People Who Fix Things

People Who Create
People Who Work with Ideas

Analyze these data in terms of different subpopulations in the questionnaire compilation, such as women, minorities, and so forth.

Brainstorm a list of reasons why people might have selected particular occupations. This list should include such things as "It provides me with a chance to be my own boss" or "I earn a good salary." Have this list refined and duplicated, and then use it in a survey with working adults in your community. Have the adults choose three reasons from the list, and ask them to rank them in order of most important to least important.

Administer an interest inventory on possible career opportunities. Then invite adults from the community to come to talk to your class in the areas in which the most interest was expressed.

Identify four or five careers that interest them (upper grades). Have them arrange to visit at least one of the work settings so they can see what the career is actually like. Create a checklist with such topics as Working Conditions and Job Requirements to use as a guideline for the children's investigations.

Brainstorm a list of occupations — say twenty-five to fifty. In groups have the children organize the data into four categories, using any system they wish to devise. Have each group explain its system. Discuss the standard career area classifications.

To sensitize children to sex-role stereotyping, *have them generate lists of occupations* that are associated with males, those associated with females, and those that are neutral. Discuss these in terms of equality of job opportunity and whether or not a person's sex has anything to do with performance of the jobs listed in the male and female categories.

Analyze television commercials and newspaper and magazine advertisements to detect evidence of sex-role and racial stereotyping in certain occupations.

Use "classified ad" sections of local newspapers to discover the types of jobs that are most available. Relate this to a study of changing needs of the work world over a period of time; for example, what jobs are available now that were not available ten, twenty, fifty, or one hundred years ago?

Study the relationship between the number of producers and consumers and the growing demand for increased social services. Relate this to taxing policies and the increasing need for persons employed by various levels of government; that is, local, state, and federal.

The following lesson illustrates how a primary-grade teacher developed the concept *division of labor* with a class.

Topic:	Division of labor
Grade:	Two or three
Time:	Two class periods
Objective:	Children will be able to give an example of division of labor.
Interest Building:	Have children discuss jobs they know about in their family or neighborhood by responding to these questions:

Do *you* have a job at home? What do you do?

What is the difference between your job and the jobs of grown-ups?

Explain that during the next few days they are going to learn about different kinds of jobs in the community.

Lesson Development: Have the children make a chart with the following headings:

Name of job   *Reasons for the job*

1. _____   _____
2. _____   _____
3. _____   _____

Instruct the children to take the chart home with them and complete it with the help of their parents, naming three different jobs in the community.

On the following day have the children compare and discuss their lists with each other.

Compile a list of as many different jobs as possible on the chalkboard. Children should pick one from their individual lists until everyone has had a turn to name one. Keep going as long as *different* jobs are named.

Have children discuss the need for a variety of jobs by responding to these questions:

Why is it that we have so many different jobs in our community?

Why couldn't each family do all these jobs itself?

Why do you suppose people in a community divide the work the way they do?

Do you mean that people who have these jobs have special skills? What do you mean?

Do you think people can do their jobs better when each person has a special job? Why do you think so?

Tell the children that when people divide work so that each one does something special, we call that *division of labor*. Write this term on the chalkboard. Discuss this term by having the class respond to these questions:

Does anyone know another word for *labor*? (Children suggest *work* as a synonym for labor. This is discussed and examples are provided.)

Can anyone tell us in his or her own words what division of labor means? (Children respond that "division of labor means dividing the work.") This is discussed and examples are provided.

Conclusion: Have children tell in their own words how they see the division of labor in these places

in their school	at the shopping center
in their families	in a hospital
in the supermarket	at the airport
at the post office	anywhere else they may have visited

Materials: No special materials are needed.

POLITICAL SCIENCE AND THE SOCIAL STUDIES[3]

For purposes of the elementary and middle school social studies curriculum, political science can be defined as a discipline concerned with the study of government, political processes, and political decision making. Some of this is handled through content in courses that are nominally history. In the upper grades, many schools have had courses called *civics*, comprised of instruction in the role, function, and organization of government with some attention to political processes, political institutions, and political decision making as these apply to citizenship behavior.

Three ideas are basic to the understanding of the organization of human societies. One is that all societies have developed ways of establishing and maintaining social order; the second is that the central order-maintaining instrument has great power over the lives of individuals subjected to it; the third is that all such systems demand and expect a loyalty to them when they are threatened by hostile opposing forces. It is apparent that if individuals are to function in a society, they must conduct themselves in politically appropriate ways. Not to do so might result in disastrous consequences. Therefore, societies provide ways of inducting the young into the political life of the society. Through this process, children internalize a set of values, beliefs, and attitudes that are consistent with the political system of the society. They learn how the system functions and eventually they contribute to its perpetuation. This process of learning has come to be called *political socialization.*

All this is relevant to the elementary and middle school teacher of social studies. Recent research suggests that the values and attitudes undergirding political socialization are formed fairly early in life. Children are able to add to their fund of information and knowledge, to be sure, but basic political orientation is well established during the early years. When children are in the elementary, middle, and junior high schools, they are still relatively flexible in their political outlook, making these years extremely important from the standpoint of their political socialization.

As is the case in all the other disciplines contributing to the social studies curriculum, certain organizing ideas from political science are used to provide a focus for studies. The following represent samples of major generalizations from political science that have been used as organizing ideas in planning units of study:

1. Every known society has some kind of authority structure that can be called its government; such a government is granted coercive power.

[3] Political science concepts and content are closely related to law-related education discussed in the next chapter, and it is reasonable to assume that the two would be combined in the social studies curriculum of the elementary and middle schools.

2. A stable government facilitates the social and economic development of a nation.
3. All societies have made policies or laws about how groups of people should live together.
4. The decisions, policies, and laws that have been made for a given society reflect and are based on the values, beliefs, and traditions of that society.
5. Throughout history human societies have experimented with many different systems of government.

Teaching Suggestions

The school program needs to begin early in helping children develop a political orientation. They need school experiences that familiarize them with the techniques of democratic procedures and that help develop a sense of appreciation for the liberties enjoyed by citizens of this nation. Such appreciations and skills must be built in part on a foundation of knowledge. Accompanying the development of these understandings, children should be given practice in using their knowledge and skills in the regular work of the class and the school.

Perhaps the best way to teach concepts drawn from political science at the early levels is to select those that can become a part of the immediate life of the child. For example, primary-grade children can learn that when people live together they must establish and observe rules. When people have rules, they know what they can and what they cannot do. Rules are made so that everyone is treated fairly. Children can understand this because they have rules in their classroom, in their school, and in their homes. They can learn that grown-ups have rules, too. These are written down and are called laws. When people break the rules, or laws, they are usually punished in some way. If some people keep on breaking the law or do things that are harmful to other people, they are not allowed to live with other people in the community. In this way, children learn not only that laws limit what one can do but also that laws have a protective function. As a result of instruction and firsthand experiences in group life, children's concepts of rules and laws, as needed for orderly living, develop. Naturally, such concepts are given increasingly greater depth as children progress through the grades. For example, later in the grades, they will learn that rules and laws are not exactly alike; laws are more binding than are rules.

The program for building civic competence begins with the introduction of the most elementary concepts relating to people living and working together under a system of order that preserves individual freedom. Great stress is placed on applying learnings as they are presented. Theoretical and complex explanations of the structure of government are inappropriate at this level. The main goals are to get children to handle themselves in responsible ways, to see the need for order in living, to govern their actions with consideration for the rights of others, and to realize that the whole realm of human activity is based on a system of rules and laws. Although children at this level are too immature to comprehend the meaning of freedom as an abstract concept, they can, nevertheless, understand it in terms of activities in which they can choose their own leaders or help to establish their classroom rules.

As children advance to the middle grades, more can be done in direct teaching of the ways our system of government functions. At this level, they also have greater opportunity to participate in school activities that promote civic learnings. For example, they can take a more active part in the school council if there is one, they can serve as members of the safety patrol or as playground monitors, and they can assume greater responsibilities for duties within their own classroom.

The exact concepts and learnings to be included in each of the three middle grades will depend on the content of the school curriculum. In the fourth grade, units on the home state are filled with good possibilities for civic learnings. Children can study the early beginnings of their state and learn how its government developed. The teacher will need to be careful not to make the concepts relating to state government too difficult for children of this age. Even the matter of differentiating between a city, a state, and a county, for example, may be quite difficult for some fourth-graders. Should the curriculum call for a study of communities around the world, a part of the study should stress that all of them have some type of government. Children should learn that governments are not all like ours, and the teacher will have to guard against having them make unwarranted value judgments about other governments. The essential points to be learned are that all people have some type of government; and although we would not choose their systems for ourselves, their governments may serve the people of those particular countries very well. There may be other cases, of course, where the teacher will want to call attention to actions of governments that clearly violate international human rights.

Grade five units dealing with the development of the United States emphasize ways of living during the periods of exploration, colonization, and the westward movement. However, this does not mean that early beginnings in representative government should be ignored. Youngsters at this level can achieve substantial understanding of some of the foundations of the government of this country. They are particularly interested in and ready to learn of the lives of some of the great champions of American freedom. Children can learn the differences in the way Spain, France, Portugal, and England ruled their colonies in the New World and relate these colonial attitudes to the kinds of governments that developed in the colonies ruled by these countries. They can learn how local representative government developed in the English colonies and can grasp simple concepts relating to the development of our own national government. It is easy to make such studies too technical and difficult for fifth-graders; ideas will have to be dealt with at a level of complexity suitable for ten-year-olds.

The sixth-grade program affords opportunities to learn something of the governments of other nations because, at this level, units often deal with countries in various parts of the world. Some schools include a study of early civilizations on the Mediterranean, and this affords an opportunity to show the origins of the democratic concept of government and law and how this idea found its way into our own system of government. If countries of Western Europe are studied, children can learn of the growth of freedom and that modern-day monarchies are based on democratic principles of government. They can also learn that in many nations of the world, individual citizens have little or nothing to say about the way they are governed. Units on Africa are popular in this grade, which makes it possible to show the problems of the governments of new nations.

A unit on the United Nations may be included in the sixth grade, in which case the need for lawful international relations can be developed. This will provide an opportunity to learn how and why national governments join together for the fulfillment of mutual self-interests. The concept of alliances and their purpose can be studied as it applies to the United States.

The program of the seventh grade depends on the sixth-seventh grade sequence followed in the school. If nations of the Western Hemisphere are studied in the sixth grade, the Eastern Hemisphere nations are usually studied in the seventh grade; or the order can be reversed. Some schools also include home-state studies in the seventh grade. Whatever pattern is followed, there will be many opportunities to include learnings related to government in connection either with other nations or with the home state.

In most schools, grade eight deals with the development of the United States, and there is ordinarily a heavy emphasis on the growth of the government of this nation. Attention is directed to the early Colonial governments, events that led to the American Revolution, and the formation of the new government. Children study the significance of such documents as the Declaration of Independence, the Articles of Confederation, and the Constitution. They learn about our political system and how it functions. They learn how the government of the United States grew in power and how it relates to the private lives of citizens. When students complete the eight grades, they should have a functional, citizen's knowledge of government and civic responsibility. They also should have had a great many experiences that will have given them the opportunity to learn, practice, and use democratic citizenship skills. This does not mean that they need not or cannot learn more; it means simply that they have completed the basic, introductory work in civic education that serves as the common foundation for all citizens of the United States.

In grades five through eight, the teacher may want to involve students in the Civic Achievement Award Program (CAAP) established under Public Law 100-158 in honor of the Office of the Speaker of the House of Representatives. It can be used as a supplementary segment to the regular social studies program in the classroom. The program consists of three parts: (1) The Learning Project; (2) The Research Project; and (3) The Civics Project. The program focuses on the development of a common body of civic knowledge and related skills. The research project and civic project components stress participation as an important aspect of civic competence. The CAAP is administered by the Close Up Foundation, and the Foundation will provide the materials needed to conduct the program. Information about participating in CAAP can be obtained by writing to Civic Achievement Award Program, Close Up Foundation, 1235 Jefferson Davis Highway, Arlington, Virginia 22202.

Lesson Plan 7 shows how a teacher could use an interesting local issue as a way to involve students in active citizenship.

LESSON PLAN 7

Topic:	Citizen participation in government
Grade:	Five or six
Time:	Seven class periods
Objectives:	Students will learn to formulate opinions based on facts.
	Students will learn how to participate in the resolution of a community problem.
Interest Building:	Explain that a group of citizens wants to ban limited hydroplane racing on our small urban lake. An opposing group of citizens wants limited hydroplane racing to continue on this lake.
Lesson Development:	Distribute to each student copies of the same recent newspaper articles on this issue.
	Have students read articles silently; discuss reactions.
	Have students reread articles sorting facts from opinions.
	Chart this information.

Hydroplane Racing on Our Lake: Facts and Opinions

Facts	Opinions
Hydroplane racing is a thirty-seven-year tradition on this lake.	Hydroplane racing on this lake does not cause health problems for human beings or for the animals at a nearby zoo.
(Extend the list)	(Extend the list)

Discuss information. Students correct or add to their charts as necessary.

Think of ways to verify the listed facts and find out if some of the opinions contain truths. Some ideas that students may think of include writing or phoning the city parks commissioners, the zoo director, and a newspaper reporter. Arrange for the students to act on these suggestions.

Invite to the classroom representatives of the groups involved: members of the community council, hydroplane racers, and zoo personnel. Brainstorm questions to ask each guest in advance of these visits.

Summary: Explain to children that now that they have the facts, they are prepared to express an informed opinion on this issue. Direct the students to formulate an opinion in a written statement. Ask them to share their statements with the class. Summarize each opinion on the chalkboard. Record the number of supporters of each opinion, including those who choose to remain noncommittal.

Group children according to opinion, and have them decide on a plan of action that might help to resolve the issue in their favor. Some possible actions include helping collect signatures on a petition, designing and distributing flyers, attending a public hearing and making a statement, and suggesting a compromise in a letter to an opposing faction. Discuss plans of action in class, and, if appropriate, arrange for children to carry out these plans.

SOCIOLOGY AND THE SOCIAL STUDIES

Sociology is a broad social science that deals with the study of the structure of society, its groups, institutions, and culture. Sociological studies often focus on the diverse societal and cultural phenomena that influence the behavior of individuals and groups. Sociology is especially concerned with social organization and the way people organize themselves into groups, subgroups, social classes, and institutions. It is difficult to draw a sharp line between the content of sociology and some of the other social sciences because their areas of concern overlap.

Social psychology and sociology concern themselves with somewhat the same social phenomena. Whereas sociology focuses on groups, social psychology studies the individual in a social situation. Social psychology is particularly concerned with the effects of group life on the behavior of individuals. Studies in social psychology deal with the problems of the individual's role in groups; the development of the self-concept; the effects of group pressure on individual behavior, attitudes, and how they are formed; leadership; followership; and the effects of social-class structure.

The following are representative samples of major generalizations from sociology that have been used as organizing ideas in developing social studies units with a sociological emphasis:

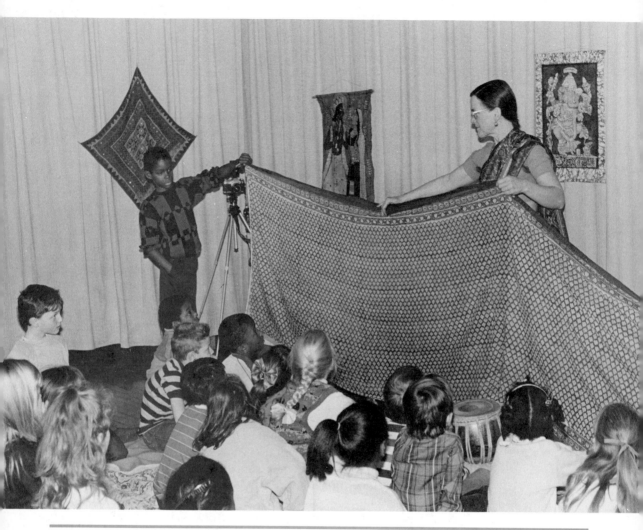

Students can learn about life in other cultures in many ways besides formal studies. Persons who have firsthand knowledge of and experience with the way of life of people of another culture are important and interesting sources of information for students making culture studies. (Photo by Edna Kellman, Seattle Public Schools.)

1. The family is the basic social unit in most cultures and is the source of some of the most fundamental and necessary learnings in a culture.
2. Social classes have always existed in every society although the bases of class distinction and the degree of rigidity of the class structure have varied.
3. Every society develops a system of roles, norms, values, and sanctions to guide the behavior of individuals and groups within the society.

4. All societies develop systems of social control; conflicts often arise between individual liberty and social control in societies where both values are sought.

5. The social environment in which a person is reared and lives has a profound effect on the personal growth and development of that individual.

Teaching Suggestions

A considerable amount of content of the elementary school social studies is drawn from sociology. This is particularly true in the primary grades. One of the units studied in first grade is "The Family." Children learn about the structure of this basic group in our society, some of its functions, and the roles of various members. This is usually followed in the primary grades by units dealing with the neighborhood, community workers, community living, and community institutions. As children study the diversification of work that is done in a modern community, they begin to see how various groups are formed and learn of the purposes of these groups. Later, in the higher grades, students will learn that the interests of such community groups are often in conflict and that this sometimes results in disorganization and community problems.

Studies of various cultures should focus on basic social processes rather than on the quaint ways used by the group to achieve them; that is, all groups have systems of communication, worship, education, and government. Much of value can be learned by showing what factors tend to disrupt conventional ways of living and cause people to change to other ways. Students in the middle and upper grades can also learn the consequences that befall cultures and do not make necessary changes in their way of living as external conditions change.

In units on the growth of the United States in grades five and eight, as well as in home-state units in the fourth grade, children should study the cultural, religious, and racial backgrounds of the people who live there. Such a study will show that the United States is pluralistic in its cultural legacy and has benefited from the contributions of a great many cultures of the world. Often it is possible for children to see concrete evidences of contributions of other cultures in the life about them in things such as the names of towns, cities, bodies of water, festivals, customs, language, and famous men and women in our history. A knowledge of, and appreciation for, the contributions of other cultures to our own can be a strong force in combating harmful aspects of ethnocentrism. Such studies provide a setting in which to deal realistically with pluralism and with the multiethnic quality of the United States.

Certainly, a problem that will be receiving increasing attention in the social studies is that of population distribution. In its simplest form, the study of population might call for the examination of the location of settlements and population centers. Which areas are densely populated? Which are more sparsely settled and why? In the upper grades, students can study more intensively some of the problems that develop in areas of high population density. They can trace the movements of peoples and discover why they move when and where they do. They can study population trends, birth and death rates in countries, and examine problems faced by countries with rapidly increasing numbers of people.

LESSON PLAN 8

Topic:	Family customs and traditions
Grade:	One
Objectives:	To develop the meaning of *customs* and *traditions*.
	To learn that families develop their own customs and traditions in celebrating holidays and other days associated with family life.
Interest Building:	Display the American flag, and ask if the children know any special days during the summer when people put the flag up in front of their homes.
	(If the children are not too responsive, show large photos depicting typical Fourth of July activities.)
	Lead the discussion toward the Fourth of July and the significance of the holiday as the nation's birthday.
Lesson Development:	**Part I**

Ask the children to remember what they did on the last Fourth of July.

Have them tell about it. (picnicking, swimming, watching parades, camping, watching fireworks, and so on)

Continue the discussion of holiday celebration by asking such questions as "Do you like this holiday?" "What do you like about it?" "Are there certain people you usually see on this holiday?" "Do you go someplace special on that day?" "Do you do something different on that day? Tell us about it. Are there special games you play or special foods you eat on the Fourth of July?"

Have the children draw a picture of something they did with their families and friends on the Fourth of July. If they cannot remember of if they did not celebrate the holiday, have them draw something they would *like* to do on the Fourth of July.

Have volunteers share their pictures with their classmates.

Display work on bulletin board.

Part II

Review the previous lesson, using displayed pictures.

Lead the children to a discussion of *other* holidays celebrated by their families (birthdays, Christmas, Easter, Rosh Hashanah, and so on.)

Encourage them to tell about what their family does together on those special days.

Write the concepts *customs* and *traditions* on the chalkboard. Have children pronounce the words and say them several times.

Explain the meaning of these concepts in terms of the things we do in somewhat the same way each time we celebrate an event.

Encourage children to talk about customs and traditions in their families.

Summary/Follow-Up: Summarize by making sure the children understand that each family develops its own customs and traditions. Have them ask their parents to tell them more about their own family's customs and traditions.

Materials: Photographs of Fourth of July activities.

Drawing materials for the children.

ANTHROPOLOGY AND THE SOCIAL STUDIES

Anthropology, with its several divisions, is often thought of as a unifying social science because it is by definition the study of human beings in their totality, their culture, and their growth toward civilization. Anthropology is concerned with the development of language, social institutions, religion, arts and crafts, physical and mental traits, and similarities and differences of cultures. Much of the research that has been done on the characteristics of various racial groups has been done by anthropologists. Anthropological concepts become a part of the social studies in the culture studies that are made of human societies.

Anthropological studies are often comparative. Such comparative, cross-cultural studies show the wide range of capabilities of human beings: modern medical practice and the tribal medicine man; affluence and poverty; humanitarian behavior and cruelty and war; urban living and rural life; life in extremely cold areas and life in hot, desert regions. People are, therefore, contradictory creatures, highly adaptive in their behavior, capable of remarkable achievements, rational yet often acting in irrational ways. They can, within limits, control and shape their environment and build a culture. They rely on their ability to think, imagine, and innovate to solve problems of living. This characteristic results in great diversity among the people of the world in how they live, what they believe, and how they conduct their affairs. Nonetheless, people are all part of the human family; all are a part of what is called humankind, and all have many common physical and social needs.

A considerable amount of interest has developed in the exciting possibilities for social studies programs with an anthropological orientation. This may be, in part, a result of the increased importance of the non-Western world in international affairs and the traditional interest of the anthropologists in non-Western cultures. The increased interest in anthropology may also stem from the concern of the discipline with concepts that are so closely related to the shaping of the human personality, human institutions, and the evolution of human societies.

The following are representative generalizations from anthropology that have been used as organizing ideas in developing social studies units:

1. Every society has formed its own system of beliefs, knowledge, values, traditions, and skills that can be called its culture.
2. Culture is socially learned and serves as a potential guide for human behavior in any given society.
3. Although people everywhere are confronted with the same psychological and physiological needs, the ways in which they meet these needs differ according to their culture.
4. The art, music, architecture, food, clothing, sports, and customs of a people help to produce a national identity.
5. Nearly all human beings, regardless of their racial or ethnic background, are capable of participating in and contributing to any culture.

Teaching Suggestions

Anthropological studies deal with the concept of culture from many different perspectives—cultural determinism, cultural relativity, cultural diffusion, cultural borrowing, and cultural change. Other concepts included in anthropological studies are environment, languages, tools, adaptation, technology, human variation, values, authority, institutions, socialization, and of course, many others. These concepts cut across several of the social science disciplines. Thus, social studies units often contain a substantial amount of information that could be defined as anthropological even though it may not be made explicit in the curriculum. The point is that there is already much in the social studies curriculum of most schools that is anthropological in content. Indeed, the unified concept of social studies has a closer kinship to anthropology, in terms of its attempt to deal with the totality of social phenomena, than it does to any of the other social sciences.

Activities such as the following have been used by elementary school-teachers in studies having an anthropological emphasis:

1. *Trace the development and use of certain tools;* associate ways of living with the use of tools.
2. *Follow the development of language and communication* systems from early signs and symbols to modern information dissemination devices.
3. *Identify ways that inventions have changed civilizations.*
4. *Have children serve as participant observers* in groups of which they are a part, such as their families.

5. *Prepare data-retrieval charts* to compare the use of resources, tools, technology, or other variables by different groups.
6. *Use role-playing, simulations, and creative dramatics* for cross-cultural comparisons of human behavior.
7. *Use music and art* to gain insight into the culture of a people.
8. In the upper grades *participate in a simulated archaeological dig.*
9. *Provide experiences in the exchange of goods and services,* as for example, a simulation game involving medium of exchange.
10. *Study artifacts from the local area* that provide traces of the early history of the community.

The following lesson illustrates how one teacher used a concept from anthropology in a social studies unit entitled "Changing Ways of Living."

LESSON PLAN 9

Topic:	Cultural borrowing
Grade:	Six
Time:	Two class periods
Objective:	To learn how contact with another culture changes ways of living.
Interest Building:	Begin the presentation by discussing with the class changes in ways of living with which they are familiar. This should lead to the idea that the ways of living of people all over the world are changing.
	Display a photograph of the tundra region showing a sled being drawn by a snowmobile with sled dogs and a tent in the background.
	Ask students whether they think the photograph is one that was taken a long time ago or in recent years and why they think as they do. This should lead to a discussion of the presence of the snowmobile, which means that the group has had contact with the industrial world.
Lesson Development:	Divide the class into groups of three, and using the resources available have students make an inquiry into the specific changes that have taken place in Eskimo life as a result of contact with the outside world and the impact of those changes on traditional Eskimo life. Their findings should be recorded on a chart as follows:

Change	Result
Motorboats	
Snowmobiles	
Guns and steel traps	
Canvas tents	
Sewing machines	
Schools	
Others (specify)	

Provide sufficient time for the groups to do their research, then reassemble as a whole group. Summarize the findings of all groups on a master chart on the chalkboard. Discuss the findings along these lines: How have these changes been helpful to Eskimo life? How have these changes been harmful to Eskimo life? Is it important to keep Eskimo traditions and skills alive? How might this be done?

Lead the discussion toward the more general problem of what happens when people of one culture have contact with another culture. This deals with the concept of cultural borrowing, although the term need not be introduced to the children at this time.

Summary/Follow-Up: Have the children, again in groups of three, find other examples of cultural borrowing in back issues of *National Geographic* magazines you have provided. Have them explain how their examples illustrate cultural borrowing.

Materials: Large photos of traditional Eskimo life.

Texts, supplementary books, and references on Eskimo culture.

Several back copies of *National Geographic* magazine.

DISCUSSION QUESTIONS AND SUGGESTED ACTIVITIES

1. Select one of the disciplines discussed in this chapter, and find out what particular methods of inquiry are used by scholars in that discipline. Explain how — or if — any of these might be adapted for use with elementary and middle school children.

2. Examine a social studies textbook and its accompanying teacher's manual. Which of the social sciences are included? Are any not included? Does the text or the manual explain how the content of the book relates to the social sciences?

3. Visit your curriculum library on campus, and examine two or three curriculum guides to see how the social sciences are incorporated in the program.

4. How can the study of the various disciplines discussed in this chapter help children learn social roles such as *family member, consumer, friend, worker, member of social groups, citizen,* and *self-identity?*

5. Much of the subject matter from the disciplines discussed in this chapter are brought into the program by *infusion* into existing units. What are the advantages and limitations of infusion procedures?

6. Why is it that the disciplines discussed in this chapter have not been institutionalized into the social studies curriculum as have history and geography?

7. Do you think it is a good practice for state legislatures to require that

aspects of economics and political science by included in the public school curriculum? Why or why not?

8. A year-long program entitled MAN: A COURSE OF STUDY (MACOS) was an anthropology-based program developed during the 1960s for the fifth grade. It was widely acclaimed by scholars as a fine effort to build social science concepts into the social studies curriculum. Yet, this program was thoroughly rejected by many parents and religious groups as being secular humanist in its philosophy, that it promoted relativism in teaching values, and that it taught children to question the authority of their parents and church leaders. Disregarding the specific issues of this particular program, discuss what you believe should be the appropriate role of parents in deciding the subject matter and procedures used in teaching social studies at the elementary and middle school levels. Do you have the same view regarding their role at the high school level? Why or why not?

SELECTED REFERENCES

ABRAHAM, KITTY G. "Political Thinking in the Elementary Years: An Empirical Study." *The Elementary School Journal,* 84 (November 1983), pp. 221–231.

ALLEN, WILLIAM F. "Mr. Goodberry's ECONOMICS." *Instructor,* 94 (January 1985), pp. 38–41.

BANAZAK, RONALD A., AND DENNIS C. BRENNAN. *Teaching Economics: Context and Strategies.* Menlo Park, California: Addison-Wesley Publishing Company, 1983.

DYNNESON, THOMAS L. "An Anthropological Approach to Learning and Teaching: Eleven Propositions." *Social Education,* 48 (September–October 1984), pp. 410–418.

HATCHER, BARBARA, AND R. TIM NICOSIA. "An Economic Education Program That Makes Cents." *The Social Studies,* 79 (January/February 1988), pp. 14–17.

Joint Council on Economic Education. *A Framework for Teaching the Basic Concepts,* 2nd ed. (A Master Curriculum Guide in Economics.) New York: Joint Council on Economic Education, 1984.

Joint Council on Economic Education. *Economics: What and When; Scope and Sequence Guidelines, k–12.* (A Master Curriculum Guide in Economics.) New York: Joint Council on Economic Education, 1988.

KOURILSKY, MARILYN L. "Children's Learning of Economics: The Imperatives and the Hurdles." *Theory Into Practice,* 36 (Summer 1987), pp. 198–205.

MILLER, STEVEN L. *Economic Education for Citizenship.* Published jointly by the Foundation for Teaching Economics, San Francisco; the Social Studies Development Center, Indiana University; and the ERIC Clearinghouse for Social Studies/Social Science Education, 1988. Available from Bloomington, Indiana: Social Studies Development Center, Indiana University.

MUESSIG, RAYMOND H., AND VINCENT R. ROGERS, eds. *Social Science Seminar Series,* 2nd ed. Six volumes. Columbus, Ohio: Charles E. Merrill, 1979.

NIELSEN, LYNN E., AND JUDITH M. FINKELSTEIN. "Citizenship Education: Looking at Government." *Social Studies and the Young Learner,* 1 (September–October 1988), pp. 10–13.

PALONSKY, STUART B. "Political Socialization in Elementary Schools." *The Elementary School Journal,* 87 (May 1987), pp. 493–505.

SCHUG, MARK C. "Children's Understanding of Economics." *The Elementary School Journal,* 87 (May 1987), pp. 507–518.

———. "Economic Reasoning and Values Education." *Social Studies and the Young Learner,* 1 (September–October 1988), pp. 6–9.

WRONSKI, STANLEY P., AND DONALD H. BRAGAW, eds. *Social Studies and Social Sciences: A Fifty-Year Perspective.* NCSS Bulletin No. 78. Washington, D.C.: National Council for the Social Studies, 1986.

7

Social Concerns as Priorities for Social Studies Education

Social issues and contemporary challenges that confront society do not always fit neatly within the subject matter boundaries of a social science discipline. Indeed, the effects of many of the problems of modern social life as so far-reaching that they must be studied from an interdisciplinary perspective that goes quite beyond any or all the social sciences. More-over, these problems and issues cannot be studied at one grade level and presumed to be learned adequately. If they are to be understood, the child must return to them time and time again at various grades, each time at an increased level of complexity. Often schools handle these topics as recurring themes that spiral at increased levels of complexity throughout the curriculums of the elementary and secondary schools. This chapter deals with several such vital topics that are thought by many to be priorities for society and, therefore, for social studies education.

GLOBAL PERSPECTIVES EDUCATION

Barring some global catastrophe, it is likely that international relationships will continue to grow among the people of this planet. This has many implications for social studies instruction. Today, international concerns are dominating the attention of our national political, economic, and cultural leaders. It could hardly be otherwise given the realities of the modern world. Consequently, social studies programs are being planned to equip the young citizen to deal thoughtfully and intelligently with problems of international import.[1]

We live in a world fraught with danger, which is likely to increase as modern instruments of destruction become available to more and more nations. Even a minor power, if armed with modern weapons, constitutes a threat to the entire world. To ignore the real danger that exists or to minimize it could result in disastrous consequences for the entire human race. But if nations can spare themselves from destruction during this delicate time of the present, perhaps more sensible approaches to human relations will eventually prevail. Perhaps through educational programs directed toward the understanding of others and toward a search for world peace, a more satisfactory method of resolving international disputes can be found than the oldest and least effective method, war. Many believe that a global perspective that engenders worldmindedness, therefore, is essential if humankind is to survive.

Although teachers should help children develop a sense of hope for the future, instruction for international understanding should not be allowed to become based on sentimentalism and naive optimism. The harsh realities of the world are ever present and must be faced. Teachers will want to help students develop feelings of goodwill, mutual trust, and understanding of others, but at the same time, it must be understood that these feelings cannot be one-sided in their application. No matter how strongly men and women of goodwill of *any* nation long for peace, it cannot be a realizable goal so long as huge sections of the world's people are taught to hate and distrust others. As has been said many times, we deal with the world the way it is, not as we wish it to be. Global perspectives education in American schools is crucial, therefore, when viewed in this context. American schoolchildren must be alerted to these realities, for it is they who will be representing the United States to the rest of the world in the years to come and who will be the decision-makers of the future.

When education for a global perspective is regarded as one of the

---

[1] See National Council for the Social Studies, "Position Statement on Global Education," *Social Education,* 46 (January 1982), pp. 36–38.

broad goals of education, it becomes apparent that the addition of a new subject to the curriculum is not necessary. Rather, it should represent an *extension and broader interpretation of what is already taught in most schools.* Teaching for a global perspective can occur through experiences the child has in music, art, science, literature, reading — in fact, in almost any of the various curricular areas.

In order to broaden instruction as described in the preceding paragraph, teachers will need to be imaginative in exploring and discovering new avenues to a worldview. For example, when children in the primary grades are studying homes and home life, that is the time to begin developing the understanding that people all over the world need homes and that they build them in a variety of ways. Or when the food market is studied, time might be spent on an examination of food markets around the world. Units on transportation and communication can, likewise, be expanded to familiarize the child with these functions on a broader basis than the local community. Almost any topic has within it such possibilities for teaching global relationships.

If a school accepts global perspectives education as one of its primary purposes, it will concern itself with ideas such as these:

1. The interdependence of peoples.
2. The need for peaceful relations among nations.
3. Basic similarities and differences in peoples because of geographical, cultural, and historical considerations, including an elementary understanding of the ways of living in the modern world.
4. The philosophy and practice of respect for the dignity of the individual irrespective of race or other factors over which he or she has no control.
5. The need to develop a sensitivity to and respect for the cultures of other people.

International Networks and Global Education

Social studies units that deal with international relationships ordinarily focus on specific nations. Children learn certain geographic, economic, and political information about a nation. They learn what the country produces and what it contributes to the world markets. They may even learn how our own country — or perhaps their specific community — interacts with specific nations through trade, through "sister city" arrangements, or through cultural exchanges. They learn how specific nations align themselves with other nations in forming power blocs and how our own nation fits into such international structures.

Children from Tashkent, Uzbekistan, in the USSR share traditional costumes and artifacts from their homeland with Seattle schoolchildren. The Soviet children visited this country as part of the sister-city program between Tashkent and Seattle. (Photo by Edna Kellman, Seattle Public Schools.)

What is described in the foregoing paragraph is a more or less conventional approach to building global awareness, and much of value can come from such learning experiences. The realities of the world today, however, are such that another dimension must be added to the study of the contemporary world and its people. In modern times international networks have been developed that are superimposed on the world of nation states, and these networks affect the lives of people almost everywhere in the world. Moreover, these effects are felt differentially even within a single country. For example, in our own nation, those who live and work in oil-producing and processing areas of the country may benefit when the price of oil goes up. Those who live in the northern tier of states and who heat their homes with oil are affected adversely by such a price hike. Furthermore, the price change may have been made by an international group of officials representing not only the Arab countries but oil-producing nations from several places in the world, including some in this hemisphere.

Because the things that people everywhere value and want are differentially distributed in the world and because increasing numbers of people want and value the same things, some systems for sharing those values and wants have to be devised. The result is a complicated set of systems and subsystems that are worldwide and extend into virtually every community and household in America.[2] Modern systems of production and distribution have little regard for national boundaries.

Some of these concepts can be illustrated with a familiar product, *blue jeans.* Here we have a fashion fad that began in this country during the 1960s and suddenly spread worldwide. Everyone wanted blue jeans, even the young people in the Soviet Union and other Communist bloc countries wanted good-quality blue jeans. Thus, there arose an unexpected international market for this product. Responding to this market, factories to produce blue jeans were established in several parts of the world — the United States, South Korea, Mexico, the Philippines, Hong Kong, Great Britain, and others. Clearly those responsible for marketing this product — bankers, shippers, distributors, and retailers — also represented the international community. Global perspectives education will need to focus on such international linkages that are a part of the everyday life of most of us.

The international networks are not limited to economic linkages. People of the world are linked through political systems and alliances, through international church affiliations, through their common ethnic heritages, and through the arts and humanities. When one hears a modern-day recording of Dvorak's "Slavonic Dances" or any other symphonic work, it may not be possible even for an expert to tell whether the performing group is the Cleveland Orchestra or the Bolshoi Ballet Orchestra in Moscow. Americans who return to the homeland of their forebears expecting to hear traditional folk music will find, instead, the same popular and rock music played on instruments with electronically enhanced sound that they heard back home!

---

[2] Robert B. Woyach, "Using the Local Community to Teach About the Global Community." Chapter 2. *Community Study: Applications and Opportunities.* Mark C. Schug and R. Beery, eds. NCSS Bulletin No. 73. Washington, D.C.: National Council for the Social Studies, 1984.

LESSON PLAN 10

Topic:	The Japanese meal
Grade:	Two
Time:	Five class periods
Objective:	Children will become acquainted with Japanese food, utensils, and method of eating and will compare these with their own culture.
Interest Building:	Have a sample of Japanese eating and cooking utensils and Japanese food items. Show them to the children, and have them try to determine what they are and how they are used.
Lesson Development:	View film or filmstrips of Japanese life.
	Take a field trip to a Japanese restaurant or an Asian food store or both.
	Invite a resource person to class.
	Practice using chopsticks for eating.
	Draw and label pictures of Japanese food and utensils.
Summary/Follow-Up:	In small groups have children assist an adult in preparing a Japanese dish to be shared with the class for lunch.
	Discuss: How did this compare with the meals you have at home? Do you think Japanese children would enjoy American food? Why are tastes different?

Materials:		
	teapot	rice
	teacups	tea
	chopsticks	assorted Japanese vegetables
	rice bowls	soy sauce
	wok	Japanese cookies and crackers
	slotted spoon	mandarin oranges
	pictures	cooking oil
	film or filmstrips	

Experiences to Help Build a Global Orientation

Use Experiences from the Everyday Lives of Children to Initiate Study Projects. The everyday experiences of children might include the return of a parent from an overseas assignment, the presence of a foreign visitor, a curio from another country, a story or television program about children in other lands, or a news item familiar to the children. Successful activities that grow out of ordinary life experiences usually begin in class discussions under the guidance of an alert teacher who can identify experiences of children that lend themselves to such a study. The local community and its ties with the rest of the world are logical springboards for building a global perspective.

Be Sure Information about Other People Is Accurate and Authentic. Misguided teaching resulting in erroneous concepts of other people, the development of stereotypes, or overemphasis on those aspects of the lives of others that are drastically different from our own leads to distorted ideas about other cultures and should be avoided. In order to get up-to-date information about the society being studied, the teacher might consult the local library or local travel bureaus, write to the appropriate embassy in Washington, D.C., or the nation's consulate, or request information about the country through the United Nations. Other sources of information are persons who were or are citizens of a foreign country — exchange students, recent immigrants to the United States, or foreign nationals visiting here.

Keep Instruction and Experiences for Primary-Grade Children Simple, Child-Oriented. Difficult concepts relating to international understanding, geography, and intercultural relations should be avoided in teaching young children. One of the major purposes of these studies at the primary-grade level is to develop the concept of friendliness and neighborliness among the people of the world. Learning activities should be simple ones, dealing with ideas and things that are consistent with the experience and maturity of the young child. Specifically, this means learning about the ways children in other lands live, play, dress, and eat. The primary-grade child can understand that everyone needs a home, a family, and friends; must go to school; and feels sad, happy, or angry at times.

Make Direct Contact with the Life of the Group Studied. One of the best learning experiences for young children in making a study of people in other lands is to have direct contact with a person from the country, especially a child their own age, who can answer questions about the clothes they wear, their schools, games, celebrations, homes, foods, stories, and similar ways of living. Other types of contacts include material things that have come from other countries. These are especially interesting to children if the items are similar to something they use in their own lives each day. A doll, an article of clothing, recorded music, a book, and a toy are examples of items that help children understand that there are differences in the ways of doing things but that children everywhere do many of the same things. With help from the teacher and their parents, even primary-grade children can carry on correspondence with children abroad, which invariably leads to the exchange of photographs and other objects. Teachers who wish to have their classes or individual members of their classes correspond with children in other lands may obtain information and addresses from the following sources:

International Friendship League
40 Mount Vernon Street
Boston, Massachusetts 02108

World Pen Pals
1690 Como Avenue
St. Paul, Minnesota 55108

Student Letter Exchange
RR 4, Box 109
Waseca, Minnesota 56093

League of Friendship, Inc.
P.O. Box 509
Mount Vernon, Ohio 43050-0509

Logo Exchange
ICCE
University of Oregon
1787 Agate Street
Eugene, Oregon 97403

Use Story and Literature Resources Related to Other Lands. The amount of fictional reading material dealing with children's lives in other lands has been increasing substantially in recent years. Typically, these little books are illustrated vividly, and primary-grade children get as much from the pictures as from the story as the teacher reads it to them. As children advance to the second and third grades, some of them can read the stories themselves.

In addition to the principles discussed in connection with the primary-grade program, the following suggestions apply to the middle and upper grades.

Explore More Deeply Some of the Reasons for the Differences in Ways of Living. People everywhere are products of their backgrounds — historical, geographical, sociological, psychological, and religious factors help explain how and why people live the way they do. Children in the middle and upper grades can begin to sense these relationships. They can learn, for example, how the presence of natural barriers such as mountains has tended to isolate people and that these barriers usually stabilize borders between nations; they can see the cultural impact of missionaries, explorers, and colonists; they learn that modes of dress or types of homes people select are related to climatic conditions of the region; they can understand why island people turn to the sea for their livelihood and why desert people move toward water and food. In studying other cultures, children need experiences that will help them perceive the world through the eyes of the people of that culture insofar as that is possible. They need to imagine how the world would look to them if they were a member of the culture studied. When children begin to see even partially how others view themselves and the world, they come to understand some of the reasons for differences in ways of living, and the differences tend not to seem unusual to them. Rather, they come to the conclusion that people the world over are resourceful, logical, and show considerable ingenuity in dealing with environmental factors and forces.

Teach about the United Nations and Its Specialized Agencies. Whether schools should teach about the United Nations has been a controversial issue in some communities in the United States. Because under our educational system such issues are resolved at the local level, teachers will need to decide how much emphasis should be placed on studies of the United Nations. As a nation, we support the United Nations and are members of it. Our national policy is to trust that it will be influential in averting wars and in settling international disputes equitably and peacefully.

Activities for Global Perspectives Education

Compile an international cookbook, a game book, a book of holidays, or a book of national sports.

Invite foreign-born local residents to the classroom to display traditional national costumes or skills.

Set aside one bulletin board for current events in other countries around the world. Associate such new stories with their map and globe location.

Write to embassies, consulates, airlines, or travel bureaus for material on the countries being studied.

Develop simulated situations and instructional games to teach about other countries. This can be combined with role playing for additional insights. Topics such as city life, education, agricultural problems, and government would be appropriate for this activity.

Teach folk songs, national anthems, poems, dances, and games of other countries.

Study the origin, growth, and change of languages. Examine the derivation of specific words.

Develop dramatic activities based on legends, myths, or stories of other peoples around the world.

Study contributions to American culture that have been made by immigrants.

Prepare a travel brochure on a country, continent, or region; role-play the part of a tourist representative from that country telling about a fifteen-day tour of the country.

Enter into correspondence with a class in another country.

Organize an International Club as a means of sponsoring all-school activities with an international emphasis.

Develop a tape exchange with children of another country.

Exchange artwork with a school in a foreign country or with children from a sister city if one exists.

Contact a local agency for foreign student placement, and arrange to have a foreign student spend a day with your class.

LESSON PLAN 11

Topic:	Conflicts around the World
Grade:	Five or six
Time:	Eight class periods
Objective:	Students will become aware of major conflicts in the world today.
Interest Building:	Ask students to watch the evening news on television for several consecutive days.
	Discuss locations where there are conflicts in the world.
	Using a symbol for conflict, have students mark these places on the world map.
	Tell class they will be making their own videotaped evening news.
Lesson Development:	Send teams of reporters "on location" to cover the identified conflicts.
	Have each team investigate, research, and prepare its report. Suggest they present it as an interview or live action report, but leave room for creativity.
	Allow two class periods for preparations.
	Videotape program.
Summary/Follow-Up:	Discuss reports as a class. List kinds of conflicts. List reasons they exist. Have children speculate about reasons for conflicts.
	Invite a reporter to the classroom. Include questions about experiences covering conflicts.
Materials:	Current news media, reference books, videotaping equipment, and wall map of the world.

ENERGY AND ENVIRONMENTAL EDUCATION

One of the essential characteristics that distinguishes a modern nation such as the United States from a less well-developed nation is its use of and dependence on various forms of energy. Modern nations have taken burdens off the backs of human beings and animals and have substituted inanimate sources of power and energy. The dependence on various forms of such energy — and in huge and escalating amounts — is absolute in modernized nations. Their economic systems cannot survive without it. They could not sustain their present standards of living if their energy sources were curtailed. The United States consumes more energy on a per capita basis simply to provide food for its people than developing nations such as the People's Republic of China use for the entire operation of the country. Perhaps no topic is related more directly to the day-to-day lives of citizens than is energy.

Energy is, of course, related to the environment. The relationship occurs at all stages of the energy production — delivery — consumption sequence. Extracting energy sources such as coal, gas, and oil from the earth either scars or pollutes the environment. Processing the raw materials of energy into usable forms and delivering the finished products also do violence to the environment. Similarly, the consumption of energy in most instances has some environmental impact. Thus, one of the major profound social issues of our time is that of providing for the vast energy needs of our modern industrial society while at the same time preserving an environment that can sustain human and other forms of life at an acceptable level of quality.

When European settlers first came to this country, the incredible vastness and abundance of resources they found produced no concern in their minds for the environment. There was fresh water aplenty. Forests and trees were in such abundance that they were perceived as obstacles to land use. There was no shortage of places to dispose of solid wastes. There were no internal-combustion engines or other devices creating large quantities of harmful hydrocarbons to pollute the air. The forests and streams were well stocked with wildlife and fish. What happened in the three hundred years that followed provides us with a shocking case study of unbelievable exploitation and waste and an almost total lack of concern for the consequences of this behavior. All this is now too familiar history.

Serious efforts to reverse this trend got underway about three decades ago. National and state leadership, combined with publicity in the popular press and, most importantly, concerned citizen groups, raised the consciousness of the general public to the violence being perpetrated on the ecosystem. More than that, these forces were successful in securing state, national, and local legislation that mandated a halt to environmental abuse. Scientific data relating to the use of certain energy-producing fuels raised the frightening possibility that the planet could experience something in the way of an "eco-catastrophe" in the foreseeable future. The most significant danger signals seemed to be those associated with (1) the use of pesticides, (2) the disposal of solid wastes, (3) air pollution, (4) water pollution, (5) radiation and radioactive substances, and (6) overpopulation.

The present concern for energy use and the related problems of environmental contamination are extensions of earlier efforts in the general area of conservation. The concept of conservation—meaning prudent use—has a reasonably long history in this country. Even during the colonial period some of the thoughtful men of the time (among them Washington and Jefferson) were concerned with conservation in the broad sense. During the middle of the nineteenth century, conservation efforts were institutionalized, largely as a result of rapidly diminishing forest resources. The U.S. Department of Agriculture established a Division of Forestry in 1880. Federal legislation during the latter half of the nineteenth century and extending into this century encouraged conservation and conservation education. The amount of federal, state, and local legislation dealing with environmental control has grown at a phenomenal rate in recent years.

It is clear that the turning point in the battle against pollution has now been reached and that people — in this country at least — will henceforth not be allowed to contaminate their surroundings with the same abandon as they have been able to do in the past. Almost everywhere in this nation local and state laws, following the lead of the federal authorities, are becoming much more strict in their control of human behavior that further contributes to environmental problems. More is being done to encourage citizens to be sensitive to the needless use and waste of energy. Similarly, educational programs are being implemented to help citizens use their surroundings more wisely. Recognition of the need for major remedial efforts to alleviate environmental pollution is growing.

Energy and environmental studies are, of course, not the sole province of the social studies. The subject is such a comprehensive one that it can be studied from many perspectives. It can be approached from the standpoint of science education, for, clearly, much of our polluted environment is a direct consequence of science and technology. Likewise, the subject is appropriate for health education because research has established relationships between air pollution and respiratory ailments such as asthma, emphysema, lung cancer, and bronchitis. Certainly, energy and environmental studies have geographical, esthetic, sociological, economic, and even political dimensions. Thus, the broad topic is highly appropriate for social studies programs because of its implications for human societies and human life. It is an ideal subject for interdisciplinary studies.

A program of energy and environmental studies should concern itself with three types of broad goals:

1. It should provide children with an opportunity to develop a basic understanding of the dimensions of problems surrounding energy and the environment, the causes and consequences of ecological disaster, the remedial measures now underway, the need for additional corrective legislation and action, *and* similar inputs of information that bear on these important topics.
2. It should help children develop an attitude of responsible concern for energy use and the quality of the environment. It should leave them with the feeling that they have a personal investment in their natural surroundings — that energy and environment truly are everybody's business.
3. It should provide children with the opportunity to do something themselves about improving the environment. That is, if goals 1 and 2

are concerned with knowledge, thinking, and valuing, this goal constitutes the action dimension of the program.

Studies of energy and the environment as broadly defined here should
be included in the social studies curriculum in at least two ways. First,
every unit studied should include attention to energy and related environmental problems throughout the entire curriculum when the topic
under study lends itself to such an emphasis. This will include most
topics, as can be seen by examining the typical unit titles on pages 14 – 16.
Second, every grade should include one unit of study each year devoted
entirely to the systematic treatment of energy and the environment. This
problem should be planned on a K – 12 basis in order to develop important learnings cumulatively as children progress through the grades.

Key Ideas in Energy and Environmental Education

The program of instruction in energy and environmental education
should focus on a limited number of key ideas. These ideas can be defined
along a continuum of complexity and be included in the curriculum at
several points. Such a basic idea as the need for food by all living creatures
can be dealt with in a simple way in the primary grades in the context of
the units on family living, the local community, changing seasons, or
meeting basic needs. In the middle school grades, this idea can be expanded and made more complex by getting into such dimensions of it as
food chains and webs of life. The planned curriculum should provide
ideas, identify emphases, suggest activities, and list learning resources,
but, at the same time, should allow for and encourage inspired teaching
and learning in this field.

What gives environmental studies vitality and freshness is a spontane-
ity and originality that are not often found when teaching conventional
unit topics. Children can easily relate to energy and environment because
these topics are so much a part of their day-to-day lives. Much of what
they hear discussed by the adults around them, what they see on television, and what they hear and read in the news has to do with subject
matter related to energy and the environment. Teachers can capitalize on
this readiness in planning interesting and engaging studies on these
topics.

The following key ideas are being suggested to provide a focus for
studies dealing with energy and the environment. They are not the only
ones that could be used; indeed, they are probably not even the best ones
for all parts of the country. They are, rather, a *sample* of ideas that can be,
and have been, used as central organizing ideas for energy and environmental studies:

Environment

1. People are now facing critical environmental problems of their own doing.
2. One of the crucial problems facing people of the world is food shortage.
3. The problem of food shortage is presently differentially distributed around the world but could ultimately affect all people.
4. Some rehabilitation of the environment and greater restraint of its use are needed in order to maintain an acceptable quality of life.
5. Most of what human beings do has a detrimental effect on natural balances because it interferes with natural communities.
6. The earth is a self-contained, self-sustaining life-support system, consisting of an infinite number of ecosystems.
7. All living organisms fit into a complex environmental interrelationship known as a *food chain.*
8. The food supply for all living organisms depends ultimately on sunlight, soil, air, and water; consequently, anything that destroys these essential resources disturbs the quality of life.
9. All living organisms in some way affect and are affected by their environment.
10. Living things must have minimum space requirements for optimum development.
11. The quality of human life depends ultimately on the natural environment.
12. Increase in human population, if continued at the present rate, will, in the long run, have disastrous consequences for human societies.
13. Waste disposal potentially is at least as severe a problem as is the fulfillment of basic food needs.
14. The effects of the presence of people on the environment has esthetic as well as survival dimensions.

Energy

1. All life depends on energy, the most basic being energy supplied by the sun.
2. Food provides energy for the bodies of human beings.
3. Energy is the ability to do work.
4. The amount of energy is constant; it cannot be created or destroyed; it simply changes form.
5. Energy can be changed from one form to another: mechanical to electrical, electrical to heat, chemical to electrical, and so on.
6. Through the years human beings have discovered new sources of energy.

7. Most of the serious environmental problems that we face are the result of economic growth that has a high dependence on energy consumption.

8. The standard of living of a society is related to productivity; productivity is related to energy use.

9. Energy resources and their use are related to the level of cultural and technological development; industrial societies place heavy demands on the earth's resources.

10. Economic development is highly dependent on industrialization, which in turn demands a high level of energy consumption.

11. The introduction and use of new energy sources often result in significant social changes.

12. Energy resources are unevenly distributed around the world; thus, as more nations become developed, interdependence among them is imperative if energy is to be shared.

These ideas are suggested as providing a focus for planning instruction. The specific subject matter should and probably will, in most cases, be selected from topics relating to the local region. Quite naturally, there will be a considerable overlap because many problems are common throughout the country. But case studies and examples should be drawn from the local area.

What follows is a series of specific types of energy-related environmental problems around which studies have been planned, along with a few examples of activities that teachers have used successfully with elementary school children. The activities are provided simply as examples of things that children can do. They are not meaningful unless they are placed within the context of a larger study. Just to do the activity would hardly be sound teaching and would probably not lead to good learning.

POPULATION

Activities to Build Awareness of Rapid Growth

1. Using *The World Almanac* or a copy of the U.S. Census, compare the population of the twenty leading American cities in 1940, 1950, 1960, 1970, and 1980. Are they still ranked in their original order? Which one has increased the most? Why?

2. Make a chart comparing the present-day population of a selected area with its population twenty years ago, one hundred years ago, two hundred years ago.

3. Make a chart comparing the present birth and death rates of a particular area with the birth and death rates of 1900.

4. Use the telephone directories of 1940, 1950, 1960, 1970, and 1980 to discover growth in such things as (a) schools, (b) hotels and motels, and (c) service stations.

Activities to Discover Population Distribution

1. Using a map and reference books, compare the populations of various parts of the United States. Why do people live where they do? What areas have the fewest people? Could people be moved to those areas? Why or why not?
2. Construct a map showing areas of heavy population in the city, state, nation, or world. Identify sparsely populated areas. Have children give reasons for both conditions.
3. Make a chart of the most rapidly growing areas of population in the state, nation, or world. Discuss the reasons for the rapid increase in these areas.

Activities to Understand the Meaning of Rapid Growth

1. Use a checkerboard or other similar squares and kernels of corn, and try doubling the number of kernels in each square, starting with one. How many kernels can be used before there is no longer room to double again? Discuss how this relates to population growth and its implications.
2. Encourage children to suggest problems that would be caused by an increase of twice as many persons in their environment.
3. Find pictures of the local area that were taken ten, fifteen, and twenty or more years ago. Have children compare those with the appearance of the same area today, noting especially reasons for changes and the effects of changes on the environment.

LAND AND WATER USE

Activities to Build Awareness of Need for Concern

1. Creative dramatics: A public meeting is held to protest closing of a lake to fishing. A biologist explains why it was closed. Have children discover what he or she should say. Conduct the drama, and include the discussion that followed the biologist's presentation.
2. Compare status reports of your state from the 1850s with those of the present day on some animal, fish, or bird. Identify the reasons for the change.
3. Collect pictures from newspapers and magazines showing misuse of land. Suggest remedial measures for improved use or what might have been done by foresighted planners to have prevented the misuse from occurring.
4. Obtain data on acres of land under cultivation in 1940, 1950, 1960, 1970, and 1980 in the local area. Find out why changes occurred.
5. List ways that productive farmland is used for other purposes, for example, for urban sprawl, for freeway construction, as land flooded or submerged behind dams. Consider other problems that might have resulted if urban growth had been stopped and no freeways had been built.

TRANSPORTATION

Activities to Understand Problems of Congestion

1. Construct a chart to compare the amount of space on a highway required to transport forty persons in forty cars as compared with that required to transport forty persons in a bus. Suggest differences in residential patterns and concentrations of workplaces that would result if everyone were required to ride a bus to work.
2. On a local map, identify points of congestion and hours of highest congestion. Study traffic flows, and suggest alternative routes.
3. Prepare a map of the local area showing existing transportation routes. Prepare another map showing an improved arrangement.
4. Show by illustration how air, water, and noise pollution are related to transportation.
5. Carry out a roadside improvement project. This could be a cleanup campaign or the planting of trees, shrubs, or flowers.

NOISE POLLUTION

Activities to Build Awareness of the Problem

1. Make a tape of various sources of noise pollution. Use this to build awareness of sounds in the environment.
2. Demonstrate instruments that measure the level of sound. Measure the level of sound in and around school at various times of the day.
3. Demonstrate familiar sounds of noise pollution such as that of jet planes, stereo rock music, motors, machines, horns, and construction.
4. Take a field trip into the local area to build an awareness of sound. Identify points of especially high noise pollution.
5. Make a map of the local area, and label the places with most noises.
6. Prepare guidelines to reduce noise at home and at school. Develop a program of action to reduce noise. Suggest costs of these measures. Where would money come from? What would have to be sacrificed?

AIR POLLUTION

Activities to Understand Dimensions of the Problem

1. Construct a map of the local region showing places of highest pollution. Explain why these areas have a high level of pollution.
2. Discover the major sources of air pollution. Present these on charts.
3. Have the class attend a meeting of the local Air Pollution Control Board. Discuss issues considered by the board.
4. Show by illustration why air pollution cannot be only a local problem.
5. Relate air pollutants to problems of health.

6. Discover effects of air pollution on vegetation.
7. Have class gather data associating smoking with lung cancer and other respiratory ailments.

WATER POLLUTION

Activities to Understand the Relationship of Polluted Waters to Recreation

1. Discover major sources of water pollution in the local area. Prepare a chart showing those sources. Discuss. Present the chart to local government officials.
2. Make a map of a specified area through which a large river flows. Find out if or to what extent the river becomes polluted as it flows.
3. On a map of the United States, identify water bodies that once were contaminated but that have been rehabilitated.
4. Select a water body in the local area that is not available for recreation because of contamination. Plan a strategy to have it rehabilitated. Present the plan to local officials. Begin a movement to mobilize public opinion in support of such an action.

ENERGY USE

Activities to Build Awareness of Energy Dependence

1. Through discussion, establish the relationship between increasing wants and needs and increased energy consumption. Find pictures from magazines to illustrate points.
2. Develop a class project to encourage energy conservation in the children's homes (turning off lights, turning down thermostats, shutting off TV and appliances not in use, and so on).
3. Prepare a bulletin board display of energy-related news stories. Through discussion, establish the importance of energy to the everyday lives of everyone.
4. Make a survey of their homes to identify energy uses that would not have been in homes fifty years ago, one hundred years ago. Discuss in terms of new demands on energy resources.
5. Secure data on sources of energy on which we depend, and construct maps, graphs, and other visuals based on the data.
6. Identify values that emphasize increased energy use and values that emphasize energy conservation.
7. Relate energy use to the production of goods and services and to standard of living.
8. Identify recreational activities that contribute to increased energy consumption and those that do not. Children can prepare displays to illustrate points.
9. Familiarize students with state and federal agencies that are concerned with energy matters.
10. Determine the relationship between energy cost and energy use. For example, what impact have higher gasoline prices had on gasoline consumption?

Not all schools in the country have instructional resource centers that provide the teacher with the tools needed for teaching. But in the case of energy and environmental education, every school does have an instructional resource center immediately at hand. All that is required is an imaginative teacher who will open the door of the classroom and step outside. What better instructional center is there for energy and environmental education than the local natural surroundings? Happily, it makes no difference if the school is located in the most congested section of our largest cities or in a remote rural area. Wherever one is, there is an environment that can profitably be studied, and we are all surrounded by energy resources.

Activities for Conservation Education

Some schools may choose to focus on conservation education rather than on the broader topics of energy and environment. Although it is not possible to suggest a great number of learning activities and resources for soil, water, wildlife, mineral, and forest conservation education because of space limitations, the teacher may find the following suggestions helpful. They are intended to serve as *samples* of activities that have been used with success with elementary and middle school-age children.

Use the many good films now available on the topic of conservation. They are thoughtfully prepared, use modern photographic techniques and color to present forcefully the problem of waste and the need for better conservation practices.

Take field trips to local conservation or ranger stations, fish hatcheries, farms, and local parks.

Invite speakers to class such as an environmentalist, the county agent, a ranger, an agriculture teacher from the local high school, or a member of an outdoor or recreation club.

Relate soil fertility in various ways to plant food elements and community prosperity.

Develop and exchange correspondence with children from different parts of the country, asking for firsthand information about their local conservation problems and what is being done to correct them.

Illustrate in various ways the time needed to recover resources and the impossibility of recovering some resources lost through waste.

Familiarize children with the interest and action of government (local, county, state, and national) in conservation.

Integrate conservation education of such groups as Boy Scouts and Girl Scouts, 4-H Club, Future Farmers of America, Camp Fire Girls, and other youth groups with the school program.

Place instructional emphasis on new developments in conservation through the application of scientific knowledge—new uses of resources, more productive farmland, new flood-control techniques, and new energy sources.

Conduct experiments dealing with conservation:
1. Collect runoff water and determine what it carries.
2. Discover how and why grass protects soil.
3. Demonstrate the effect of rapidly falling water on soil.
4. Test the productivity of various types of soil.

Contact various agencies that have an interest in, or dedication to, the cause of conservation for suggestions, teaching materials, or help. Such a list can be obtained from your local county agent, the Department of Natural Resources of your home state, or the U.S. Department of Agriculture Forest Service.

LAW-RELATED EDUCATION

The escalating rate of crime, the negative attitudes of young people and adults toward the legal system, the widespread and illegal drug traffic, and the evidence of widespread ignorance of the justice system among citizens are a few of the reasons why there is a growing interest in, and concern for, what has come to be called "law-related education." Law-related education seeks to help children develop an understanding of the legal and justice systems and to provide them with a functional knowledge of the operation of legal institutions. It stresses law as an essential component of social life, not as a set of abstract and theoretical concepts relating to the organization and structure of the legal system and government. Support for law-related education has come not only from educators and educational groups but from prominent jurists, the legal profession through the American Bar Association and local bar associations, political leaders, parents, and virtually every segment of responsible leadership in society.

This narrative may remind the reader of boring lessons on law and government endured in ninth-grade civics class. If so, the reader should have a sense of appreciation of the urgency for doing a more effective job on law-related education with the present generation of schoolchildren. Traditional approaches to teaching about the legal and justice systems were tied to courses in civics, history, and government. Often the learners would find little in these courses that would provide them with any practical sense of how the legal system actually operates. Learners might study the functions of the three branches of government, memorize the Preamble to the Constitution and the Bill of Rights, define a few legal terms, and know the difference between petty larceny and grand

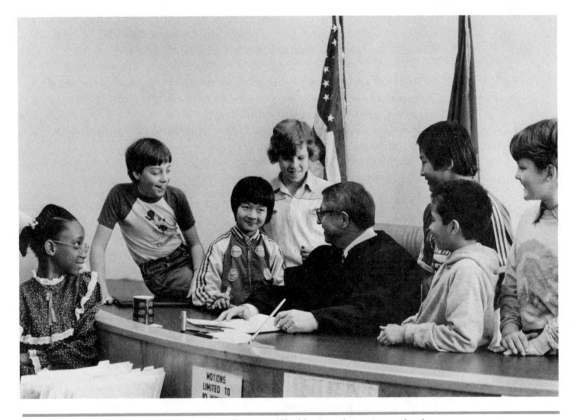

"Tell it to the judge!" These children from a Tacoma, Washington elementary school learn about the local courts on a firsthand basis from a judge in the local community while on a field trip to his court. Why is it important that each generation of schoolchildren have some firsthand contact with various governmental bodies at the local, state, and national levels? (Photo by Herb Williams, Tacoma School District.)

larceny, and yet be unable to relate such learning to their day-to-day living. School programs dealing with the law are often criticized because substantive content is either inappropriate or lacking altogether and because teaching methods are such that they engender no student interest in the subject. Recent thrusts in the law-related education field have attempted to correct both of these deficiencies.

The object of the school program of law-related education is not to make lawyers out of children. Nonetheless, a knowledge of the legal system and the skills associated with legal education and the practice of law are not beyond the grasp of ordinary citizens. These skills and this knowledge can no longer be reserved for those who have had legal training, namely, lawyers. When we live in a time in which aspects of the law touch our lives on a daily basis from our birth to our death, we cannot remain ignorant of its pervasive influence and uphold our responsibilities as free citizens. Accordingly, a program of law-related education should concern itself with broad goals such as the following:

1. Develop an understanding of concepts that are basic to the legal system, such as liberty, justice, fairness, toleration, power, honesty, property, equality, and responsibility.
2. Develop an understanding and appreciation of the constitutional basis of the American legal system.
3. Develop a functional knowledge of how the institutions of the legal and justice systems operate.
4. Develop an understanding of and respect for the need for a system of law and justice as prerequisite for orderly and harmonious living.

A vast number of national, regional, and local projects and centers have dealt with law-related education in recent years. Perhaps the best known are those projects conducted by the following groups:

National Street Law Institute
605 G Street, N.W.
Washington, D.C. 20001

Center for Civic Education
(formerly Law in a Free Society Project)
5115 Douglas Fir Drive, Suite 1
Calabasas, California 91302

Constitutional Rights Foundation
601 South Kingsley Drive
Los Angeles, California 90005

Special Committee on Youth for Citizenship
American Bar Association
1155 East 60th Street
Chicago, Illinois 60637

Key Concepts in Law-Related Education

There is no agreement on the exact list of concepts to be included in a law-related program, but the overlap of concepts identified by various projects is considerable. The Law in a Free Society Project developed its program around eight basic concepts: authority, justice, privacy, responsibility, participation, diversity, property, freedom. These are typical and are included in most programs. Such concepts as equality, power, honesty, fairness, and others could reasonably be subsumed in the eight listed by the Law in a Free Society Project. Instructional resources, stu-

dent materials, teacher training materials, study guides, and other related instructional materials that develop these concepts are available
through the projects and through commercial publishers.

Activities for Law-Related Education

Invite a local police officer to talk to the class about law enforcement
problems in the community.

Bring in news clippings describing acts of vandalism; discuss the effects
and costs of such behavior.

Discuss rights versus responsibilities along lines familiar to children such
as "Can we go to the movies and talk out loud even if we disturb
others?"

Research the latest legislation on drugs (upper grades). Find out if the legal
penalties for drug abuse are the same for adults as for juveniles.

Take a field trip to a court, the state legislature, or a city council meeting.

Find out how a jury is selected. Invite someone who has recently served
on a jury to speak to the class about the responsibilities and duties of
jurors.

Relate rules and laws to personal safety. For primary grades this could
include moving to and from school, bicycle safety, and safety in the
neighborhood. For older children this could be extended to laws relating to trespass, vehicle use, drug and alcohol use, assault, and other
activities that are at the edge of experience of preadolescents.

Find examples of advertisements from magazines, newspapers, radio,
and television that could be interpreted as being deceptive. Relate this
to consumer protection laws. Find out about agencies that deal with
consumer protection.

Make use of whatever services are provided the school by local law enforcement agencies and the local bar association.

With the help of a local attorney, *have students discuss the accuracy* of a
law-related television program (upper grades).

Develop classroom rules of conduct, and discuss the need for rules (laws)
in group life.

Conduct a mock trial in the upper grades.

Discuss citizens' rights and responsibilities in terms of specific cases that
appear in the news.

List legal needs of their community at the turn of the century. List legal
needs of their community today. Discuss differences, and have children explain why legal needs have changed.

Study the structure and functions of local community government, and
relate them to the daily lives of the people who live there.

Develop appropriate activities in connection with "Law Day USA," observed each year on May 1. Write to Law Day USA, American Bar

Association, 8th Floor, 750 North Lake Shore Drive, Chicago, Illinois 60611, or telephone (312) 988-6140 to receive information about Law Day USA.

MULTIETHNIC EDUCATION AND ETHNIC HERITAGE STUDIES

Multiethnic education and ethnic heritage studies should be directed toward the ultimate goal of improving the quality of human relations in this country. This purpose has become increasingly important since we have shifted our conception of American society from the traditional melting pot ideology to one of pluralism. Many implications may be found in this shift for all of education and most especially for the social studies. Race and racism remain serious problems for this society, and many believe that multiethnic education and ethnic heritage studies will help combat some of the evils that flow from racism and racist practices. Ethnic heritage studies are also intended to acquaint young people with the multiethnic composition of this society in order to help them become more fully aware of who they are as individuals and as a nation.

The society of the United States is multisocial class, multiracial, and multiethnic. Consequently, considerable confusion over terminology and meanings occurs when discussing issues relating to the pluralistic character of this society. Social class groups have to do with grouping individuals on the basis of income, occupation, life-styles, and, in the case of the upper classes, family background. These are status groups and represent a hierarchical arrangement from high to low on some basis of preference. Racial groups result from genetically transmitted physical characteristics that are innate and immutable. They are often visibly different from other groups on the basis of physical qualities. Ethnic groups, on the other hand, are formed on the basis of common cultural variables such as language, customs, religion, nationality, traditions, and history that give some groups a sense of "peoplehood." It should be clear that socioeconomic level or social class membership has nothing whatever to do with one's ethnic identity. All ethnic groups have individuals who are wealthy and those who are poor; all have individuals in upper social classes and those in lower social classes.

Race and ethnicity are often confused because in some cases they overlap. For example, the Japanese have physical characteristics that identify them as an Asian racial group. At the same time, the Japanese people have a language, tradition, common heritage, and history that give them an ethnic identity. A blond European baby boy who, at the moment of birth, was adopted and raised by a Japanese family would as an adult be ethnically Japanese in spite of his physical (racial) character-

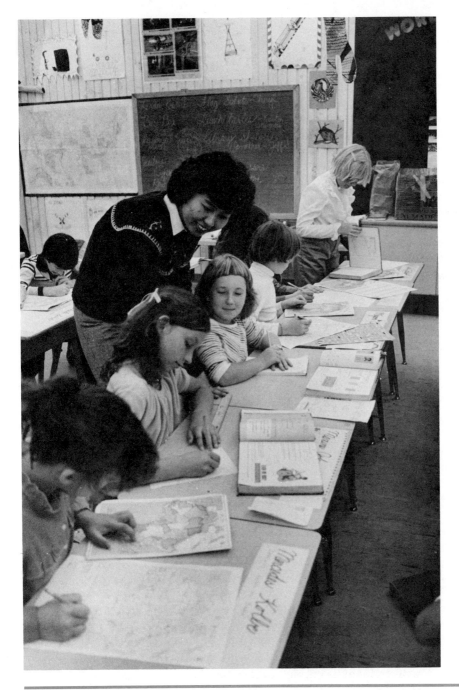

Today's children have contacts with persons from other cultures at an early age. Here we see a visiting teacher from Japan assisting children in the Northshore School District, Bothell, Washington with their social studies. What experiences outside of school do most children have that help them develop a global perspective on human affairs? (Photo by Terri Malinowski, Northshore School District.)

istics that he inherited from his European ancestors. Perhaps it would be difficult for such an individual to be fully assimilated by the Japanese society because of clearly differing physical characteristics. This is because negative social values are being associated with physical characteristics. This is an obvious illustration of *racism,* which is the practice of attaching nonphysical characteristics to physical qualities of human beings. It should also be obvious that this practice has been and continues to be quite common in the United States. *Race and racism are problems not because of the reality of physical differences between human beings but because there are social values attached to those differences.*

This country is exceptional among the nations of the world because it is composed of representatives or their descendants of almost all the world's many cultures. In terms of ethnic heritage, we are among the most diverse people on earth. But Americans vary greatly in the extent to which they retain their ethnic identity. Many have no knowledge or even interest in their forebears. Others lack a clear ethnic identity because of intermarriage, name changes, and migrations. Others may be nominally members of an identified ethnic group but do little more than attend a once-a-year picnic of such groups as Sons of Norway. Still others are more active in retaining their ethnicity by maintaining a fluency in the language of their ancestors, observing traditional holidays associated with their ethnic group, continuing traditional church affiliations, and so on. A small group remains totally immersed in its ethnic culture, as for example the Navajo people. Thus, the level of enthusiasm for ethnic heritage studies can vary greatly from one individual to another, and attempts to impose interest in such studies are not likely to be productive or even desirable.

The major purposes of multiethnic education and ethnic heritage studies ought to be along the lines of the following:

1. To present truthful accounts of the multiethnic composition of this society.
2. To develop a sense of pride in the multiethnic heritage of this nation.
3. To develop a respect for the contributions of all groups to the life and culture of this nation.
4. To develop harmonious social relations resulting from the use of acceptable methods of resolving social conflicts.
5. To develop a reasoned pride in one's own ethnic heritage.
6. To understand that much of the strength of this nation derives from the diversity of its ethnic heritages and cultural origins.

Multiethnic education and ethnic heritage studies should be firmly rooted in the local community but should not be limited to the study of ethnic groups of the local area. A broad spectrum of ethnic groups should be represented in the program in order to present social reality as accurately as possible. Much of the content of ethnic studies is affectively toned, and thus it can be expected that providing knowledge alone is not likely to be very powerful in achieving the goals of ethnic education. Activities need to be planned that will engender positive feelings toward others.

Ethnic studies can be interesting and enriching and can do much to build social cohesiveness by helping all children gain a better understanding of the diverse people we really are. There is much of which we, as a nation, can be proud that comes as a direct consequence of our multiethnic backgrounds. However, there is a potential danger that ethnic studies may contribute to social disunity and the development of ethnocentric attitudes. If ethnic studies are allowed to become rallying grounds for the advocacy of political and social goals of specific ethnic groups, if groups become polarized over issues that are ethnically based, or if these studies become politicized, they can do little to enhance human relations. It must be emphasized that there are common values that we embrace as a nation that are shared by all individuals and groups regardless of their cultural or ethnic identity. The concept of "one Nation under God, indivisible, with liberty and justice for all" must be made a reality if the nation is to escape internal conflict and strife of untold proportions.[3]

Instructional resources for teaching multiethnic education and ethnic heritage studies are available in generous amounts from many suppliers. The Council on Interracial Books for Children (1841 Broadway, New York City 10023) produces many materials useful to teachers, as does the National Council for the Social Studies (3501 Newark Street, N.W., Washington, D.C. 20016), and the Anti-Defamation League of B'nai B'rith (345 East 46 Street, New York City 10017).

Activities for Multiethnic Education and Ethnic Heritage Studies

Research contemporary groups that have been organized because of particular ethnic identities. Discover their purpose and identify their leaders, if possible.

Make a scrapbook of outstanding individuals in an ethnic group. Include their accomplishments and what they have contributed to the whole society, to their ethnic group, and to the individual.

Read a fiction book in which the main character is a member of an ethnic group. Have a discussion about the main character with another person who has read the book or with the teacher. How was the life of the main character affected by his or her ethnic background?

Create puppets and act out a folktale or legend from a particular ethnic culture.

[3] For a detailed statement of curriculum guidelines for ethnic heritage studies, see the National Council for the Social Studies position statement, *Curriculum Guidelines for Multiethnic Education* (Washington, D.C.: National Council for the Social Studies, 1976).

Write a newspaper article advocating the position of an ethnic group in a conflict situation, such as an Indian tribe in its land or fishing disputes.

Find out about class's own ethnic origins. Show on a world map where their ancestors came from. Discuss this in terms of the areas of the world represented in the class. Study settlement patterns in the United States of various immigrant groups. (Note: *Activities such as this one or studies of family genealogy ought always to be optional. Some parents and children do not wish to divulge personal family information, and their wishes must be respected.*)

Learn folk songs and folk dances of various ethnic groups.

Prepare a bulletin board or other displays that show the contributions of various ethnic groups to American life and culture. Have children bring newspaper clippings and photographs of various ethnic groups in the news.

Use the local telephone directory to find names that can be identified with a particular ethnic group, for example, French, Irish, German, Chinese, Slavic, Scandinavian. Try to detect a pattern in terms of the dominance of any group. Check also the yellow pages to find out which ethnic restaurants are found locally. If possible, compare data found in the local telephone directory with that found in a directory of a city in some other part of the country.

Invite representatives of various ethnic groups in the community to your class. Ask them about their cultural roots. Have them discuss their language and customs. Inquire about their connections, if any, with the homeland of their forebears.

Encourage children to view television programs or listen to radio broadcasts of ethnic groups in the local area.

Visit museums that display exhibits, artifacts, and collections of ethnic groups of the community and state.

Learn about holidays and festivals of ethnic groups in the community.

Conduct a survey of the school or the local area to find out the number of different languages spoken and identify each.

Survey the community to find places of business or service groups (food stores, funeral homes, specialty shops, churches) that cater to particular ethnic groups.

Study local community history to discover what ethnic groups first settled there, what groups came later, and what traces of their occupance are imprinted on the community.

STUDIES IN SEX EQUITY

In August 1920 the Nineteenth Amendment to the Constitution became the law of the land, and thereby women were given the right to vote, a right enjoyed by most white free men since the founding of the Republic.

The discrimination against women, however, did not end with the Nineteenth Amendment. The evidence is clear that women have not achieved full status with men in the business and professional worlds, in education, in political affairs, or in any field that has been traditionally dominated by men. For a variety of reasons, the traditional roles of men and women in society have undergone great changes in the second half of the twentieth century, resulting in the emancipation of women. The independence of women, which without question is one of the most significant social developments of our time, has many implications for social studies education in the elementary and middle schools.

Many believe that school programs of the past actually contributed to discrimination against women because they reinforced conventional sex roles that emphasized male superiority. Where this can be studied with a degree of objectivity, as, for example, in analyzing school textbooks, the evidence is overwhelming that males had a clear advantage. They have been consistently represented in positions of greater prestige and as being more courageous, more clever, more witty, and more skillful than women. Women tended to be represented in subservient positions and most generally in social-service roles or in roles that require serving men, as, for example, secretarial service and nursing. Thus, discrimination against women became institutionalized in that both boys *and* girls came to believe in the superiority of the male. Much of such blatant sexist portrayal does not now appear in recently published textbooks and other instructional material.

Discrimination on the basis of sex is explicitly forbidden by several pieces of federal legislation, the best known being Titles VI and VII of the Civil Rights Act of 1964, and Title IX of the Education Amendments of 1972. Title IX deals with discrimination in education, and the intent of the law is made clear by its opening statement:

> No person in the United States shall on the basis of sex be excluded from participation in, be denied the benefits of, or be subjected to discrimination under any education program or activity receiving Federal financial assistance . . .

Because nearly all schools receive federal financial assistance in some form, the law is for all practical purposes universal. In addition to these federal laws, many state laws and constitutions prohibit discrimination.

There is much greater awareness of sex-role stereotyping now than there was even a decade ago, and many of the practices that contribute to this attitude are being eliminated. The contributions of women to the life, culture, and development of this nation are becoming more visible in the curriculum and in learning resources. Women are seen in prestigious occupations as being coequal with men. Men and women are shown sharing responsibilities associated with maintaining a household, caring for children, and providing family income. Other forms of invidious distinctions between men and women are being eradicated from the printed and visual material used by children in school.

These changes obviously represent great gains for women in broadening the potential for their self-fulfillment. What is often overlooked is that it does the same for men. Both sexes will have greater opportunity for choice if neither male nor female role is stereotyped. This applies not only to career choices but to leisure-time activities, hobbies, reading interests, school activities, sports, and, indeed, all other aspects of life except those specifically limited by biological differences between the sexes.

Major Goals of Sex Equity Education

A major overall goal of the socialization of American children is that of engendering values and attitudes based on principles of equality among human beings. Many groups and institutions in the community contribute to the achievement of this goal, including the family, religious institutions, and the school. Regrettably, children may receive mixed signals regarding sex equity from these socializing agencies. Be that as it may, sexism and sex-role stereotyping are forms of discrimination because they are the result of arbitrary judgments based on the sex (or more correctly, the *gender*) of the individual. Social studies programs have a responsibility to combat the formation of such values and attitudes because they are contrary to the goals and purposes of the school curriculum and are contrary to the ideals and laws of the nation. Instruction in sex equity should be directed toward the attainment of goals along such lines as these:

1. To develop a sensitivity in children to the stereotyping of males and females along the lines of occupations, home life, life-styles, community life, recreation, and other life choices.
2. To learn about the contributions of both men and women to American life and culture, especially in areas that have traditionally been closed to one or the other of the sexes.
3. To have children become aware of the nature and impact of sex bias in all walks of life and have them become familiar with some of the more obvious examples of sex bias and inequities based on sex.
4. To stress the importance of providing both sexes with the right of *choice* in directing the affairs of their lives and in considering career options.
5. To gain an understanding of sex roles in terms of physiological and biological differences between males and females on the one hand and in terms of gender distinctions influenced by cultural beliefs on the other.

Activities for Sex Equity Education

Compare and contrast roles of men, women, boys, and girls in an earlier historical period, such as in Colonial times, with those same roles today. Similarly, compare and contrast those roles in other cultures with those in the United States. Discuss reasons for such differences. Have children provide reasons why roles change.

List as many different behaviors associated with males and females that are based on customs and traditions (e.g., ladies first, women wear dresses and men do not, and so on). Have children speculate on how these customs may have originated. Discuss items on the list in terms of changes that may be taking place in them.

Generate a list of different tasks members of the family do at home. Have children identify the person best able to do each task. Discuss whether or not the task could be performed by other members of the family.

Ask children to bring to school pictures from magazines or newspapers of men and women engaging in various occupations. Post these on the bulletin board in terms of those almost always performed by men and those almost always performed by women, and those performed by either. Discuss reasons why some occupations attract men, others attract women, and others are attractive to both men and women.

In a brainstorming session have children name as many important people in American history — living or dead — as they can think of in a ten-minute period. Write the names on the chalkboard. Then have the class group the individuals on some self-determined criteria (occupation, ethnic or racial minority, living or dead, men or women, and so on). Note discrepancy between the number of men and the number of women. Speculate on why this is so. Conduct an inquiry to test their hypotheses.

In the middle and upper grades, *have learners investigate* the daily lives of ordinary women one hundred to two hundred years ago; what they did; their roles in family life; and their contributions to their home, family, and communities.

Read children's biographies of prominent women who have championed the cause of sex equity.

Invite men and women who have made nontraditional career choices (e.g., male nurses, female airline pilots) to speak to the class about their experiences in pursuing their career goals.

CHILD ABUSE, AIDS, AND DRUG ABUSE

Child abuse, AIDS, and *drug abuse* are the great social tragedies of our time. Schools share in the responsibility with the rest of society for turning the tide against these scourges that are destroying the lives of so many

of our nation's people. Because these problems have severe social consequences, it can be expected that the social studies curriculum will give
some serious attention to them. These topics are so intensely sensitive
that the way they are handled in schools has to be guided by policies
generated and approved at the local and state levels.

It is a mistake to think of educating children about child abuse, AIDS,
and drug abuse as the sole responsibility of any single area of the curriculum, such as health, science, or social studies. The entire school program
needs to be infused with concepts and information regarding these social
problems as appropriate for each of the various curriculum areas. In
addition to such infusion, schools will need to provide some systematic
instruction specifically targeted on these topics each year the child is in
school, K–12. It can be presumed that some of these instructional units
would be incorporated in the social studies program. The teacher is
advised to seek assistance at the local level regarding policies and programs dealing with these problems.

DISCUSSION QUESTIONS AND SUGGESTED ACTIVITIES

1. What is *your* view of the role of global education in the schools, and
   how does it compare with that expressed in this chapter? If you were
   making a case for it to the school board, what would be the main
   points in your rationale?

2. Visit the curriculum library on your campus, and examine some of
   the newer materials related to the topics included in this chapter.

3. How are *racism* and *ethnocentrism* alike, and how are they different? What danger does each present in terms of desirable human
   relations?

4. How do you define *ethnicity?* Are all ethnic groups also minority
   groups?

5. What resource persons in the local community might be of help in
   teaching the topics included in this chapter?

6. Provide specific examples of how social studies topics in a grade in
   which you have a special interest can be studied from a global perspective.

7. Select one of the key ideas listed on pages 180–181, and show by a
   short example how it could be taught meaningfully to children in
   each grade of the elementary or middle school.

8. Locate a photograph relating to an environmental problem. Prepare
   six interpretation and analysis questions (see pp. 298–301, Chapter
   10) based on the photograph.

9. The inclusion of energy and environmental education, the world of
   work, law-related education, and multiethnic education in the social

studies curriculum is being challenged by a parent at a public meeting. If you were asked to respond to such a concern, what points would you make?

10. Explain how topics discussed in this chapter relate to the goals for social studies education listed on pages 6–8.

11. Some parents, for religious or other reasons, object to the teaching of sex equity. How do you define your boundaries of responsibility in dealing with this topic while at the same time respecting the right of parents to believe as they do?

12. In your view, what can social studies programs contribute to the education of children about AIDS that is different from that provided in science or health classes? At what age do you think such education should begin, and how explicit should the instruction be? Acquaint yourself with local and state policies in your community regarding these issues. Also, familiarize yourself with local and state regulations regarding the teacher's responsibility in cases of suspected child abuse and suspected drug use by schoolchildren.

SELECTED REFERENCES

BANKS, JAMES A. *Teaching Strategies for Ethnic Studies,* 3rd ed. Boston: Allyn and Bacon, 1984.

BRANSON, MARGARET STIMMANN, AND JUDITH TORNEY-PURTA. *International Human Rights, Society, and the Schools.* NCSS Bulletin No. 68. Washington, D.C.: National Council for the Social Studies, 1982.

CHAPMAN, JOHN (chairperson), JAMES M. BECKER, M. EUGENE GILLIOM, AND JAN TUCKER. "National Council for the Social Studies Position Statement on Global Education." *Social Education,* 46 (January 1982), pp. 36–38.

EVANS, CHARLES S. "Teaching a Global Perspective in Elementary Classrooms." *The Elementary School Journal,* 87 (May 1987), pp. 545–555.

GILLESPIE, JUDITH A., guest ed. "Teaching About the Energy Crisis." *Social Education,* 44 (April 1980), pp. 259–291. (Several authors contribute articles to this special section on energy and environment in this issue.)

HAHN, CAROLE L. "Promise and Paradox: Challenges to Global Citizenship." *Social Education,* 48 (April 1984), pp. 240–243+. (The NCSS presidential address.)

JOHNSON, JACQUELYN, AND JOHN BENEGAR. "Global Issues in the Intermediate School." *Social Education,* 47 (February 1983), pp. 131–137.

KNIEP, WILLARD M., guest ed. "Global Education: The Road Ahead." *Social Education,* 50 (October 1986), pp. 415–446. (Three authors contribute to this special section on global education.)

LANEY, JAMES D. "Learning about Aging: A Planned Inquiry for Intermediate Grades." *Social Education,* 51 (April–May 1987), pp. 269–272.

NICKELL, PAT, AND MIKE KENNEDY. "Global Perspectives Through Children's Games." *How To Do It Series* 5, No. 3. Washington, D.C.: National Council for the Social Studies, 1987.

ROSENZWEIG, LINDA W. "Law-Related Education and Legal Development." Chapter 7. *Developmental Perspectives on the Social Studies.* NCSS Bulletin No. 66, Linda W. Rosenzweig, ed. Washington, D.C.: National Council for the Social Studies, 1982.

SCOTT, KATHRYN P., guest ed. "Sex Equity in the Elementary School." *Social Education,* 46 (January 1982), Elementary Education Section, pp. 44–57.

SIMMS, RICHARD L., AND GLORIA CONTRERAS, eds. *Racism and Sexism: Responding to the Challenge.* NCSS Bulletin No. 61. Washington, D.C.: National Council for the Social Studies, 1980.

STYER, SANDRA. "Women's Biographies for the Social Studies." *Social Education,* 48 (November–December 1984), pp. 554–556.

TONKINS, HUMPHREY, AND JANE EDWARDS. "A World of Interconnections." *Phi Delta Kappan,* 62 (June 1981), pp. 695–698.

VOCKE, DAVID E. "Those Varying Perspectives on Global Education." *The Social Studies,* 79 (January/February 1988), pp. 18–20.

WHEELER, RONALD. "Law-Related Education." *Social Education,* 44 (May 1980), pp. 381–397. (This special Elementary Education Supplement on law-related education includes a list of children's literature with strong law-related content.)

WOOLEVER, ROBERTA M., AND KATHRYN P. SCOTT. *Active Learning in Social Studies — Promoting Cognitive and Social Growth.* Glenview, Illinois: Scott, Foresman, and Company/Little, Brown College Division, 1988. Chapter 16.

WOYACH, ROBERT B. "Using the Local Community to Teach about the Global Community." Chapter 2. *Community Study: Applications and Opportunities,* Mark C. Schug and R. Beery, eds. NCSS Bulletin No. 73. Washington, D.C.: National Council for the Social Studies, 1984, pp. 15–28.

ZARNOWSKI, MYRA. "Learning about Contemporary Women: Sharing Biographies with Children." *The Social Studies,* 79 (March/April 1988), pp. 61–63.

8

Current Affairs
in the Social Studies

"But they can't *do* that! It's against the Constitution!"

"What Constitution?"

"The *United States* Constitution!"

"What does the United States Constitution have to do with it?"

"I don't know; but it just doesn't seem right. If a person has some land with some trees on it, he shouldn't have to get permission from the Ecology Department to cut them. They're *his*."

This lively exchange took place between a boy and a girl in a fifth-grade class as a result of a story in the local newspaper under the following headline.

COURT STOPS FURTHER TREE REMOVAL
Orders Environmental Impact Statement

Opponents to the clearing of land on the Richards's property succeeded in getting a court order to stop the tree removal until a study is done to determine the environmental impact of such cutting.

The owner, Charles Richards has insisted that he has a legal right to harvest the timber on his property. The local . . .

The teacher brought this article to class because it dealt with an issue of local interest that had been in the news for several weeks and because it illustrated so well the conflict between individual rights and community values, something the class had been dealing with in social studies. The example also illustrates how the use of current affairs can add vitality and meaning to what might otherwise seem to be abstract and remote concepts. Although these children may not have the facts of the case straight, it is obvious that they have strong feelings about the issue. This discussion has motivated them to get additional information, and their teacher can help them and their classmates get the facts they need.

The point of view to be developed in this chapter is that the program of current affairs is a matter of importance in the school program and, as such, requires careful planning and teaching. Children cannot be subjected to several years of boring experiences with current affairs in school and leave convinced that they have any responsibility to keep themselves informed on the affairs of the world. It is not easy to persuade children of the importance of current affairs if during news sharing the teacher takes roll, collects lunch money, completes plans for another lesson, or does other things about the room that draw full attention from the news reports. The teacher could not successfully teach mathematics, reading, or spelling in this way, and there is no reason to believe that current affairs can be taught with success that way either.

If the nation expects its adults to have an abiding interest in news and current developments and have a desire to keep informed, the groundwork for these attitudes, interests, and skills must be laid in the elementary school. The first major purpose of current affairs teaching at the elementary school level is, therefore, *to promote interest in current affairs and news developments.*

Intelligent analysis of current affairs requires the use of a variety of skills and abilities: (1) to read news materials, (2) to discriminate between important and less-significant news items, (3) to take a position on issues based on a knowledge and a critical evaluation of the facts, and (4) to predict likely consequences in terms of present developments. *Promoting the growth of these skills and abilities represents the second major purpose of current affairs instruction at the elementary school level.* These skills evolve over several years through the study of current affairs under the direction and guidance of capable teachers. It is unrealistic to hope for an adult population that can exercise critical judgment regarding social problems and issues unless individuals have at their command the fundamental skills and abilities such action demands.

The third major purpose of current affairs teaching is *to help the child relate school learning to life outside school.* The constant reference to current affairs is good insurance against the separation of school activities from the nonacademic life of the child. Good teachers recognize that printed material begins to become obsolete shortly after it is written, and there is always a gap between the information contained in books and changing developments in the world. A generous use of current affairs materials helps to close this gap. Some encyclopedia publishers recognize the need for timely information and issue annual supplements that include changes that have occurred during the preceding year. Because textbooks and supplementary books usually are not revised each year, it is necessary to depend on such sources as newspapers and magazines for the latest information on some topics.

THE PROGRAM OF CURRENT AFFAIRS INSTRUCTION

The three most common methods of including current affairs in the elementary school program are (1) teaching current affairs in addition to social studies, (2) using current affairs to supplement or reinforce the regular social studies program, and (3) using current affairs as the basis for social studies units. A discussion of each of these methods follows.

Teaching Current Affairs in Addition to Social Studies

Ms. Hansen, who teaches fourth grade, plans to spend a few minutes each morning during the sharing period for the discussion of important news stories. She encourages children to bring news clippings from daily newspapers or from weekly magazines for the class bulletin board. Children are encouraged to bring news stories related to classroom work, and Ms. Hansen helps interpret these stories for the children by her comments and leading questions, such as

"How do you suppose the new highway will help our town?"
"What are the explorers looking for on these expeditions?"
"Why do you suppose the animals died when they were brought here?"
"Can you show the class on the map the exact location of the new airport?"

Ms. Hansen uses a classroom periodical and plans to spend a half hour on it with the children each week. This consists of reading the material or portions of it, with a discussion following. She varies the procedure from week to week and uses the suggestions provided in the teacher's edition that accompanies the classroom periodical.

This method has the advantage of providing a regularly scheduled time for news each day. Such periods can be useful in building interest in current affairs and in teaching skills of reading and interpreting news stories. It has the clear disadvantage of isolating current affairs from the remainder of the school program, most especially from the social studies. If current affairs teaching is handled as is done by Ms. Hansen in the example, time should be taken to relate news content to topics and units in social studies. This can be done by (1) interpreting news stories within the context of topics that have been studied or are under study; (2) extending the meaning of concepts developed in social studies; (3) applying social studies skills, such as map, graph, or chart reading to the news stories; or (4) comparing and contrasting events in the news with events encountered in social studies units.

Using Current Affairs to Supplement or Reinforce the Regular Social Studies Program

Mr. Ray schedules his social studies period immediately following morning opening activities for his fifth-grade class. As a part of the beginning activities, he provides time for reporting of news and encourages children to report news items related to social studies. He and his class maintain a news bulletin board as well as a small table on which are placed news articles, magazines, current maps, or similar materials of a timely nature related to the social studies unit. He uses current affairs materials in this way to augment other instructional resources and as a means of reminding his class of the need for up-to-date information.

Mr. Ray often suggests parallels between events that happened long ago and events that are occurring today, thereby illustrating recurrent problems in the conduct of human affairs. For example, in the study of the struggle for freedom and independence in America, he used examples from present-day affairs to show that some people of the world are still struggling for the right to govern themselves. When the class studied early explorers, Mr. Ray related this study to present-day exploration. In the unit on the Westward Movement, he called the attention of the class to current population movements and trends in the United States.

The difference between this method and the one used by Ms. Hansen is that Mr. Ray is more explicit in making the connection between current affairs and social studies. He is concerned mainly with those news stories that can be related to his social studies program. He builds an awareness of the relationship between what is currently happening in the world and what the class is studying in social studies. He is using the affairs of the world as reported in the news media as a current information source for social studies. This method has the advantage of keeping the information base for social studies up-to-date. It has the disadvantage of restricting the range of news stories that are appropriate. Therefore, if this approach is used, the teacher should provide some opportunity to examine news items that are significant and timely, yet may not be directly related to the social studies unit under study at the time.

Using Current Affairs as the Basis for Social Studies Units

Ms. Bell likes to develop social studies units with her sixth-grade class around topics that are currently in the news. She schedules these between the regular units she is required to teach. During her years as a teacher, she has found that units of this type must be carefully selected because it is not always possible to find a sufficient amount of instructional material suitable for children that deals with topics in the news.

Units that she has taught with success in this way in the past have dealt with alliances, such as NATO; meeting our needs for oil; migration of the world's people as a result of news of newcomers to the United States; twentieth-century explorers; progress in science, medicine, and industry; and elections. When Ms. Bell selects the unit topics carefully, she finds it possible to include much of the subject matter ordinarily included in her social studies curriculum under other unit titles. She believes that the use of current news happenings as a starting point for units does much to stimulate interest and discussion in her class.

This method has the advantage of being highly motivating because it deals with subject matter that is of immediate interest. It also bridges school learning with life outside of school. It has the disadvantage of being difficult to plan because news events may not relate directly to the social studies curriculum. Also, news stories may not provide a continuing or sustaining source of information on topics, and, therefore, other sources would need to be available. This method works best for short, minitype units as described in the example rather than as a structure for the entire social studies program.

TEACHING CURRENT AFFAIRS SUCCESSFULLY

Any of the three current affairs programs described here can be used successfully. In good programs there will be time during the school day devoted to the study and discussion of current affairs that may be entirely unrelated to topics under study in the social studies units or unrelated to any other curricular area for that matter. At the same time, in guiding unit work, the teacher will not ignore current affairs relating to the topic being studied but will, in fact, seek with enthusiasm the current affairs materials that will add strength to the unit. From time to time, too, the teacher and children can plan an entire social studies unit from current news developments. Units dealing with the topics of energy, environment, safety, intercultural relations, law and justice, housing, food, elections, discoveries in science, and items of local news may, and frequently do, grow out of current affairs. When the social studies program includes these three methods, the teacher and class will use any or all of the procedures described in the following sections.

Daily Discussion of News

Children enjoy discussing the news and should be given the opportunity to do so within the school program. It is a fairly common procedure for classes to have a morning meeting or sharing period at the beginning of

Children at the Browns Point School in Tacoma constructed this crystal radio as an enrichment activity in connection with a program entitled "Voyage of the Mimi," a curriculum that combines social studies, science, and technology. Much of the information needed comes from current news sources. (Photo by Robb Mitchell, Tacoma School District.)

each school day, during which time the children can report news items. Children in the primary grades frequently report only news that affects them directly: Daddy took a business trip, the family has a new baby, the pet cat had kittens, or other similar items of "news." As children mature, they move away from news items that are of concern only to them personally to news of more general interest.

In reporting, discussing, and analyzing daily news occurrences, elementary schoolchildren frequently report the sensational headline news that may or may not be particularly significant. Without guidance, children are likely to report murders or robberies or hold postmortems on the previous night's television programs. The teacher should help children evaluate the importance of news stories and teach them to discriminate between significant news and the sensational.

In general, the practice of reporting news should be encouraged by the teacher rather than required. Some teachers require children to bring a news clipping on specified days. This usually means a hurried breakfast for the child while Mother peruses the morning or evening paper hoping to find a suitable item that she can explain to the child before the child leaves for school. A better procedure is to build the children's interest in news to the extent that they voluntarily bring news clippings that they believe are important enough to bring to school. Similarly, in the reporting of news items, on some days there will be many items and much discussion; other days there may be none. The teacher must bear in mind that the purpose of this procedure is to *develop the children's interest* in current affairs and that this is usually not done by requiring children to spend specified amounts of time on news whether the content justifies the time or not.

As children approach the middle and upper grades, they will not only report news events but will also begin to include issues on which there are conflicting points of view. This should be encouraged, and eventually the emphasis can be placed almost entirely on problems and issues rather than on simple events. The movement from the consideration of simple events to simple issues to complex issues is a gradual one for the child.

When controversial issues are considered by the class, the teacher will find a number of special problems presenting themselves. Some teachers are so fearful of precipitating community ill will and pressure that they avoid consideration of any problems that are even mildly controversial. This is unfortunate and unfair to the child who needs to develop skill in handling controversy and conflict. The National Council for the Social Studies takes a strong position on this issue in its statement on academic freedom:

> It is the prime responsibility of the schools to help students assume the responsibilities of democratic citizenship. To do this, education must impart the skills needed for intelligent study and orderly resolution of the problems inherent in a democratic society. Students need to study issues upon which there is disagreement and to practice analyzing problems, gathering and organizing facts, discriminating between facts and opinions, discussing differing viewpoints, and drawing tentative conclusions. It is the clear obligation of schools to promote full and free contemplation of controversial issues and to foster appreciation of the role of controversy as an instrument of progress in a democracy.[1]

Good sense and mature judgment would suggest that the teacher avoid issues that may cause severe and intense feeling among parents and that can cause the wrath of the community to descend on the school.

---

[1] "Academic Freedom and the Social Studies Teacher" (a policy statement of the National Council for the Social Studies), published in C. Benjamin Cox, *The Censorship Game and How to Play It*, Bulletin No. 50 (Washington, D.C.: National Council for the Social Studies, 1977), p. 42.

Problems of this type are usually not well suited for study by the elementary schoolchild anyway. The best problems for discussion are those that are mildly controversial but that deal with subject matter that is significant and within the realm of experience of the child. This does not mean that issues must be limited to local problems. Teachers often comment on the extent of knowledge that elementary schoolchildren have on problems of national or international import and the intelligent way that they are able to discuss them.

In teaching controversial issues, the teacher has a special responsibility to help children develop habits of critical judgment and open-mindedness, to evaluate sources of information, and to appraise the soundness of facts. Young children are impressionable, and the habit of insisting on getting multiple sides of a question before taking a stand can be taught to youngsters by the teacher's example. There has been some discussion of the necessity of keeping the teacher's stand on issues unknown to the children. This is not possible or entirely desirable. To be sure, the teacher does not begin the discussion of an issue by stating his or her own bias to the class. It is the teacher's responsibility to see that all sides of the issue being discussed are presented fairly and impartially and that the reasons underlying points of view are thoroughly aired. If the class requests the teacher's own views on an issue, it is clearly the teacher's right to express them and to state the reasons for the position taken. The professional obligation remains, however, not to attempt to impose a personal point of view on the children on issues that are unsettled and on which there may be honest differences of opinion among well-informed persons. In such cases, the teacher should encourage children to discuss the matter with other adults whom they respect whose views may be different. The child thus learns that there may be honest differences of opinion among intelligent, well-educated persons who consider problems in good faith. The children will respect the teacher who is willing to take a stand on issues, who gives reasons for the position taken, and who accepts and honors the differences in points of view of others.

Teaching Suggestions for Controversial Issues

The news story on page 210 is a good example of the types of controversial issues that can be found in nearly all communities, large or small. Here are a few other examples:

Whether or not to

- Allow an area to be rezoned for a shopping center.
- Permit freeway construction through a residential or farming area.
- Close an elementary school.
- Build an athletic stadium.

HOMEOWNERS PROTEST AIRCRAFT NOISE

More than two hundred irate homeowners jammed the chambers of the Metropolitan Airport Commission last evening to protest noise from jets at the International Airport. Property owners are demanding that the commission secure funds to purchase homes immediately adjacent to the airport. They insist that the noise has reached a level that is intolerable and that it is endangering the health of residents.

"When a plane flies over our home, all conversation must stop," claimed one resident. Similar complaints were made by other homeowners. "It is impossible for us to conduct instruction when planes fly overhead," said Brian Sorokin, a teacher at Stevens School, located near the airport.

Marvin Sherwin, attorney for the homeowners, said his group would resort to legal action if appropriate measures are not taken immediately by the Airport Commission. He could foresee no satisfactory solution to the problem short of clearing the area of homes. "These families bought their homes without knowing that an international airport was to be placed next door to them," he said. "They cannot sell their homes and they cannot live with the present noise level. The commission must deal with this problem," he added.

Members of the Airport Commission refused comment except to say that the problem is a serious one and that funds were not presently available for the mass evacuation being proposed by the residents. Robert Randall, chairman of the commission, said he did not know whether federal monies are available for such removals, but that "all possibilities would be explored."

- Allow a golf course to be built.
- Pass a dog leash ordinance.
- Allow animals to be used for medical research.
- Allow certain forms of gambling.
- Restrict trash burning.
- Construct a new hospital.

These issues present good opportunities for teaching how to deal with controversy. A teacher might proceed as follows:

1. Have the children identify the facts of the case. In an examination of the airport news story, some of the facts are these:
   a. Jet aircraft produce objectionable noise.
   b. A sizable number of homeowners are disturbed over the noise level.
   c. The homeowners are insisting that the Airport Commission do something about the problem.

    d. The homeowners have engaged an attorney to represent them.

    e. The noise problem reduces the possibility of sale of the homes in the affected area.

    f. Money for the purchase of the homes by the Airport Commission is not now available.

    g. Modern urban areas must have conveniently located jet plane air service.

In identifying facts, it is important not to confuse them with opinions or with issues. For example, one would need further documentation that the noise "is endangering the health of residents" as is claimed in the story. Also, it is *not* a fact that the only solution to the problem is the purchase of the homes by the commission.

2. Have students identify the *issues* in the case. In looking for issues, one is seeking to find out why there is a problem. Usually, this involves conflicts of values. In the airport case, for example, the following are some of the issues:

    a. Is it possible to locate metropolitan airports completely away from residential areas?

    b. Have the dollar values of these homes been reduced because of the airport location?

    c. Should the homes of those residents who moved into the area *after* the airport was in operation be purchased?

    d. How can the residents insist on the commission's purchasing their homes when there is no money available?

    e. Who should bear the cost of the purchase of the homes? The local taxpayers? Travelers who use the airport? The airline companies whose planes make the noise? The federal government?

    f. Does a public facility that results in a nuisance to nearby residents require that the homeowners be paid for damages?

    g. How severe must the nuisance be before a claim can be justified?

3. Have students identify alternative solutions to the problem and list the consequences of each alternative. In this type of analysis it is not necessary to come to consensus as to the best solution. In the airport case, these alternatives might be proposed:

PROPOSALS	CONSEQUENCES
a. Reduce jet noise by reducing landing and takeoff speeds.	a. May not be safe; would not solve the problem completely.
b. Develop less noisy jet engines.	b. Would take too long to develop quieter engines. May not be possible to develop such engines.
c. Relocate the airport.	c. Would be very costly. Would simply move the problem somewhere else.

d. Purchase homes and relocate only those residents who owned their property before the airport location was established.

d. Does not solve the problem for the remaining residents. It is unfair and probably not legal.

e. Purchase all homes in the affected area.

e. Would require huge sums of money not now available. Would establish a precedent for other cases of a public facility creating a nuisance.

f. Do nothing.

f. Commission would be subject to legal action and would eventually have to do what the court directs rather than making the decision themselves. Would generate additional public ill will.

Cases such as this lend themselves well to role playing and simulation. For example, some children could play the parts of the commission members, the homeowners, the attorney, the teacher, and others. The information could be secured by the students from the point of view of the role they are playing. If a local issue is the focus of the study, children can get information from the community by interviewing individuals, researching background information on the problem, and through local news stories. If the airport case were used, the teacher would need to provide data for the various roles. For example, each player or group of players would receive information prepared by the teacher such as:

Homeowner. You have owned your home ten years. The airport planning began three years after you made the purchase. You and your wife have three children, ages eight, six, and two. You are worried that your children's hearing will be damaged by the noise. You have had your home for sale for a year. Three buyers looked at it, but decided not to buy when they found out about the jet noise problem.

Similar instructions would need to be prepared for all other players in the simulation. Directions for developing simulation games along with an example are provided on pages 383–385.

Situations such as this also can be used to have students speculate about the future. For example, how might we deal with the problem of jet aircraft noise (or any of several other issues) in a futuristic setting? Here the children do not need to be constrained by what is practicable and feasible—or even possible. They simply let their creative minds imagine what might possibly become alternatives at some future time.

Use of a News Bulletin Board

The teacher should prepare a display of interesting news pictures and stories to which the child can turn for information concerning current affairs. Because items on the news bulletin board should be changed frequently, it should be in a place in the room where children pass regularly. A point near the doorway is a good location.

It is good procedure to discuss the significance of the news articles in class before they are posted on the bulletin board. The display should contain items of national and international import as well as items of local interest, sports stories, developments in science, people in the news, perhaps even oddities and jokes for variety and spice. It is helpful to have various sections of the bulletin board specifically designated for such groupings as local news, science in the news, news of our country, and global happenings. This serves as a means of organizing the display in a meaningful way.

The following suggestions are offered as a way of making bulletin boards more effective as an instructional tool:

1. Use captivating captions of one type and color. Letters for captions might be made from dark construction paper, corrugated paper, cardboard, yarn, aluminum foil, or material that has a related design such as discarded book jackets, newspaper, or woodgrain.
2. Use sound principles of design, balance, order, and color. Too much material carelessly displayed gives a cluttered effect. Adapt the display to the physical makeup of the room. Take into consideration door and window heights, other displays, lighting, and the location of the display in terms of its basic purpose. Secure an organized effect by developing continuity in the display. Anchor material squarely and securely on all four corners.
3. Change the displays frequently, and use variety in the material posted. There should be a purpose for posting any material, and after it has served its purpose, it should be removed.
4. Take time to discuss the material on the bulletin boards; call attention to new material posted; teach directly from the bulletin board from time to time.
5. Encourage children to bring or prepare material suitable for bulletin board display. As soon as the children are sufficiently mature, involve them in the planning and preparation of some of the displays.

Use of a News Map

In the middle and upper grades, the news map can be used to teach current affairs. A world map is displayed in the center of a bulletin board allowing sufficient space around the map for the posting of current news clippings or pictures. Colored string can be used to connect the news story with the location of the spot where the event occurred. This has the value of combining the study of current affairs with map-reading skills. Children should have a major responsibility for keeping the news map up-to-date and for handling the mechanics of its preparation. It is also possible to subscribe to a commercially prepared news map published weekly during the school year.[2]

Use of a Classroom Newspaper

Many teachers consider the classroom newspaper or periodical an indispensable tool in the teaching of current affairs. These materials have a number of definite strengths as well as some limitations that are frequently overlooked. The limitations of classroom current affairs periodicals lie not so much in their makeup but in the way they are used. The papers themselves are generally well prepared. Companies producing these materials have editorial advisory staffs composed of nationally recognized educators in the field of elementary education, and their editorial staffs consist of carefully selected and highly qualified personnel. Two of the better-known sources of classroom periodicals are:

Scholastic Inc.
P.O. Box 3710
Jefferson City, Missouri 65102
Pilot Edition, grade 1
Ranger Edition, grade 2
Trails Edition, grade 3
Explorer Edition, grade 4
Citizen Edition, grade 5
Junior Scholastic, grades 6–8

WEEKLY READER
4343 Equity Drive
P.O. Box 16626
Columbus, Ohio 43216
Weekly Reader, kindergarten through grade 6
Current Events, grades 7 and 8

The chief strengths of the classroom newspaper are (1) its careful attention to reading difficulty, (2) its selection of current materials that are significant yet within the comprehension of children, (3) its unbiased presentation, and (4) the common background of information it presents to the class. These advantages cannot be obtained through the use of any

[2] WORLD NEWSMAP OF THE WEEK, General Learning Corporation, 60 Revere Drive, Northbrook, Illinois 60062-9821.

other single source. They are designed and published for use in a classroom, and, therefore, their writing style, readability, and illustrations are suitable to children.

Classroom periodicals also have some limitations of which the teacher should be aware. Even though the readability is carefully controlled, there is no published material that will meet the reading needs of every child in class. Some children will find the material too difficult; others will find it too simple. In a sense, the classroom periodical is the "textbook" for current affairs, and its use should be governed by the same pedagogical principles that apply to the use of textbooks generally.

There is a tendency for teachers to formalize the teaching of current affairs through the use of such a classroom periodical. One period a week is set aside for "current events" consisting of the reading of the paper followed by what is called "discussion" but amounts to the presentation of some questions by the teacher to be answered by the children. Overemphasis on the formal use of classroom periodicals crowds out the consideration of current affairs from the remainder of the curriculum.

A third limitation of classroom periodicals is that they select items of general interest either nationally or internationally and cannot deal adequately with local news. The teacher will find it necessary to turn to local sources for such news items. This is another reminder to the teacher not to depend entirely on the classroom periodical to carry the entire current affairs program.

Teaching Suggestions for Using Classroom Periodicals. The service bulletins that accompany classroom periodicals often suggest ways to make good use of the papers. A procedure similar to this should be followed:

The teacher prepares and preplans —
   Read the periodical and accompanying teachers' edition.
   Keep up-to-date on current affairs by regularly reading an adult newspaper and news magazine and by listening to radio and television newscasts.
   Build your own background on topics included in the classroom periodical.
   Plan how to use the periodical and vary the procedure from week to week.
The teacher prepares the classroom —
   Post related pictures, maps, and diagrams on the bulletin board.
   Have additional references available.
   Place new words and terms on the chalkboard.
The teacher prepares the children —
   Present the periodical to the class by calling attention to a picture, a map, or a particular story.

Discuss reasons why certain topics are in the news.

Develop meanings of new words and terms.

Use maps and the globe to orient children.

Develop purposes for reading.

Differentiate requirements to provide for individual differences.

Use the bulletin board, pictures, or other visual aids to motivate the class and to develop concepts.

Plan any special activities relating to the news stories, such as reports, dramatic presentations, and panels.

The children read the periodical —

Vary the reading assignments according to reading ability.

Have specific purposes for the reading.

Be available to assist with difficult vocabulary.

Direct the study of slower readers.

Have additional references on topics for more advanced learners.

The teacher and children conduct discussion and follow-up —

Discuss the periodical in terms of the purposes established.

Relate news stories to other classroom work.

Have children present any special activities that were planned.

Make generous use of maps and the globe.

Synthesize and summarize ideas and conclusions reached.

Plan further research or other creative follow-up activities.

Use of Daily Newspapers

Some teachers in the middle and upper grades find a daily newspaper helpful in promoting the goals of current affairs instruction. In units dealing with aspects of communication, the newspaper is an important learning resource. Students will profit from classroom instruction on the use of the newspaper that focuses on items such as these:

1. The organization of newspapers, purposes of various sections, where to look for certain kinds of information.
2. The nature of news stories, why some appear on the front page and others elsewhere.
3. The purpose and use of headlines.
4. Newspaper illustrations: wire photos, maps, charts, graphs, cartoons.
5. The editorial page and its function.
6. Detecting bias in news stories.
7. How to read a newspaper.

From time to time the teacher can devise practice exercises such as the following one to help students develop their skills in using a daily newspaper:

WHERE WOULD YOU FIND IT?

Features in Today's *Tribune*

Bridge	B-2	Horoscope	B-2
Business	B-3–6	Landers	D-6
Classified	C-7–15	Life-style	D-1–6
Comics	D-7	Marine	B-6
Crosswords	B-2	Obituaries	B-10
Dr. Colander	B-2	Sports	C-1–6
Editorial	A-14, 15	Television	B-9
Films/Arts	B-6–B-8	Travel	D-8, 9
Graham	B-2	Word Sleuth	B-2

In what section of the newspaper would you look if you wanted to know
the results of a major league baseball game?
what movies were showing at local theaters?
if your mother's "For Sale" ad was carried in the newspaper?
something about a person who had died?
the newspaper's position (or opinion) on some current issue?

OR

In what section of the newspaper might you find expressions such as these?
"the series of double plays along with the bases-loaded homer in the ninth . . ."
"nominated for five Oscars . . ."
"For Sale. Three-year-old duplex . . ."
"Dear Ann . . ."
"some influence from Gemini . . ."
"She died in a local hospital after a long illness."
"The market was sharply up today. . . ."

NEWS MEDIA LINGO

Persons who report the news often use expressions that are peculiar to their profession. Here are a few common ones. Can you tell what they mean?
"A usually reliable source . . ."
"The information was leaked to reporters . . ."
"The story was scooped by the *Post* . . ."
"The senator tried to extricate his foot from his mouth . . ."
"In a news release from the White House . . ."
"There is a touch of irony in the president's statement . . ."
"This is a live broadcast . . ."
"Both Moscow and Beijing said last night . . ."
"In its lead story this morning . . ."
"The story was first carried by syndicated columnist . . ."

Many teachers have found the Newspaper in Education (NIE) program sponsored by the American Newspaper Publishers Association (ANPA) Foundation to be a useful resource in teaching current affairs and, more specifically, in using the newspaper. For information about the NIE program and the several materials available through it, contact your local newspaper, or write to the ANPA Foundation, Box 17407, Dulles International Airport, Washington, D.C. 20041, or call (706) 620-9500. The NIE program provides many teaching and learning resources; two that are especially recommended are (1) *The Newspaper as an Effective Teaching Tool* 1975, 1977 and (2) *Bibliography: Newspaper in Education Publications*, 5th edition, 1984.

In grades seven and eight, the teacher may want to make use of the program called *ECONOMICS TODAY*. It combines the study of current affairs with economic education, using news stories found in *USA Today*. It was developed jointly by the Foundation for Teaching Economics and *USA Today*. For information write to: Foundation for Teaching Economics, 550 Kearny Street, San Francisco, California 94108.

LESSON PLAN 12

Topic:	Bias in news articles
Grade:	6–8
Time:	One class period
Objective:	To learn to detect bias in news accounts.
Interest Building:	Secure two accounts of the same news story, such as those included in the following example. Make copies and distribute one of each to members of the class.

Opposition to Gun Control Remains Strong

Legislation pending in Congress would ban possession of the kind of handgun used in the attempted assassination of President Reagan in Washington, D.C., in March, 1981. But opposition remains strong, especially in the House.

The present law banning imports of manufactured cheap handguns was passed in 1968 after the killings of Senator Robert F. Kennedy and Rev. Dr. Martin Luther King, civil rights leader. The law permits importing parts that can be assembled and sold in the United States.

Little Hope Seen for Gun Control Legislation

Long overdue legislation pending in the foot-dragging Congress would ban possession of the kind of vicious handgun used in the nearly successful assassination attempt on President Reagan in Washington, D.C., in March 1981. But the carefully coordinated opposition to tough gun control remains strong, especially in the politically sensitive House.

The present mild law banning imports of manufactured cheap handguns was reluctantly passed in 1968 after the ruthless murders of the popular and re-

A much tougher bill was approved by the Senate in 1972 after the shooting of Governor George C. Wallace, but the House never acted on it. Senate sources said that the members have shown a willingness to pass tough gun control laws but are waiting for some sign that the House is ready to do so, too.

Meanwhile, the lobbyists opposing gun control continue their efforts to stop such legislation. They remain consistent in their view that there is not necessarily a correlation between gun control and the actions of fanatics.

spected Senator Robert F. Kennedy and Rev. Dr. Martin Luther King, Nobel prize-winning civil rights leader. The so-called gun control law permits importing parts that can be easily assembled and freely sold to fanatics in the crime-ridden United States.

A much tougher bill was approved by the Senate in 1972 after the brutal shooting of Governor George C. Wallace, but, as usual, the conservative House never acted on it. Senate sources said that enlightened members have shown a willingness to pass much-needed tough gun-control laws but are waiting patiently for some hopeful sign that the House is ready to do so, too, however belatedly.

Meanwhile, the lobbyists opposing reasonable gun controls continue their clandestine efforts to sabotage such legislation. They remain consistent in their warped view that there is no correlation between gun control and the actions of fanatics.

Lesson Development: Have the children underline the *facts* in each story.

Using a chart, analyze the stories separately according to FACTS AND NONFACTS. Compare the facts in each account to determine if there are any discrepancies.

Analyze the two accounts sentence by sentence by having students identify all nouns and the words that describe them (adjectives). List these on the chalkboard or a chart as follows:

Account No. 1		Account No. 2	
Nouns	Adjectives	Nouns	Adjectives
opposition	strong	opposition	carefully coordinated strong
		gun control	tough
House		House	politically sensitive

Conclusion: Have children search newspapers and listen to news programs on television and radio on their own and bring to class examples of stories that contain elements of bias in the way they were reported.

Discuss with the class the conditions under which it is appropriate for news media to express opinions on issues.

Use of Television and Videotapes

Research on the television-viewing habits of children during out-of-school hours indicates that television viewing is a well-established pastime of nearly all American schoolchildren.[3] Studies consistently have shown that children view television from two to four or more hours each day during the week with some increase in this amount on weekends. The child in school, therefore, is well acquainted with this medium and is accustomed to viewing professionally produced programs even if the substance of such programs is not always of high quality.

There is an inclination to use instructional television in the same way a "live" teacher is used. This practice works to the disadvantage of television because the unique characteristics of the television medium are lost in the process. If television has instructional value, it is because it can do something more effectively than other media or because it can do some things that other media cannot do at all. Educational television can be of tremendous assistance to the elementary schoolteacher in enriching and vitalizing social studies providing it is used to achieve purposes the teacher cannot accomplish at least as well through the use of books and other conventional learning resources.

One valuable contribution television can make to social studies instruction is to motivate children. The television program has the total resources of the world outside the classroom to use in constructing programs that are highly interesting and motivating. Television can span both time and space in bringing relevant events into the classroom in capsule form. Television can visually transport children to the areas they are studying. It can also show them details they would probably miss if they were actually there. The most eminent authorities and world leaders can be their teachers through television. The dramatic capabilities of good television production can be used in making a subject alive and exciting for children.

A second contribution television can make is to provide information not available through other sources. Some of these possibilities were suggested in the previous paragraph. No other medium can make it possible for a child to witness the inauguration of the president taking place a thousand miles away. A young man from Africa cannot visit all fourth-grade classrooms in a large city and tell the children interesting things about his homeland. But he can share his ideas with them via television. A major strength of television is that it can assemble and distribute information widely and quickly.

[3] Based on data collected during 1983–84, the National Assessment of Educational Progress found that more than 40 percent of fourth graders, 25 percent of eighth graders, and 12 percent of eleventh graders watch five hours or more of television daily. Reported in *Education Week*, May 15, 1985, p. 6.

A third contribution of television to social studies is to clarify, elaborate, interpret, and enrich information that may be available through other sources. For example, a museum curator may be able to explain the religious significance of certain artifacts of early Indians who lived in the region. An authority or a traveler might be able to provide interesting details to help children understand why people of another culture do some particular thing the way they do. Television is an excellent medium for vitalizing knowledge because it can provide intimate, personal details that are not readily available through other sources.

Increasing numbers of schools have video cassette recorders available, and this has increased the flexibility of this medium. No longer is it necessary to view the program at the precise time it is telecast. In addition to television programs that have been recorded for classroom use, there is a growing amount of educational video available for social studies instruction.[4]

Use of a Variety of Activities

A number of learning activities can be used profitably to study current affairs:

Conducting round-table discussions — dividing the class into five or six discussion groups, each to discuss a question related to some item in the news. Each group would be responsible to present to the entire class a short four- or five-sentence summary of its major ideas.

Having panel discussions — selecting five children to prepare a twenty-minute presentation to the class on some topic currently in the news. These five children would be given a few days or a week to prepare the presentation and would be the class "experts" on the topic discussed. After the presentation, the remainder of the class could ask questions, clarify points, or add to what the panel has said.

Making charts, maps, graphs — showing increases in school population, steps in an event that led to a crisis, decline or increase in employment, the number of highway accidents over a holiday weekend, the route of a recent air flight of importance, and so on.

Constructing posters, murals — to emphasize safe living, progress in preventive medicine, changes in air travel, progress in space, and other topics.

Keeping scrapbooks of news stories or pictures — clipping and keeping the headlines from the evening paper for several weeks. This helps children to distinguish between news stories that are of continuing

---

[4] Amy Grotevant, "Social Education Resource List." An annotated list of selected distributors and developers of educational and instructional video. *Social Education,* 52 (September 1988), pp. 370–371.

interest and those that are transitory in nature. Collections of news clippings can be a valuable resource if the topic selected is one that is likely to be in the news for a period of several weeks or months. Careful selection of articles in the scrapbook will allow the class to follow the development of the news story on a continuing basis.

Drawing cartoons to illustrate news — can be used effectively with older children. Care must be taken to avoid having children draw cartoons that might be offensive to individuals or groups. Cartoons dealing with a community fund drive, a sports story, safety or health habits, conservation practices, good citizenship, and other topics can be used.

Giving reports — is a widely used technique for handling current affairs by having individuals report news items to the class.

Conducting television news programs — can be used from time to time to dramatize news stories. Children can take turns as reporters; variety can be obtained by using a tape recorder and playing the recorded "broadcast" for the class.

Dramatizing news events — when they lend themselves to dramatization. Not all do, but items dealing with festivals, meetings, conferences, and negotiations can be used.

Viewing telecasts of special events — reporting inaugurations, visits of foreign dignitaries, dedications, and other newsworthy programs can be used for in-school viewing in the elementary school. Children can also be encouraged to view news programs out of school and report on these to their classmates.

OTHER POSSIBILITIES FOR TEACHING SOCIAL STUDIES THROUGH NEWS STORIES

This chapter concludes with a created news story that is a typical example of the type of controversial issue that can be useful in teaching social studies concepts and skills. As you read this story, based on an actual incident in the Puget Sound area, think of (1) the issues it presents and (2) what possibilities it holds as a teaching vehicle in the middle and upper grades. What follows now are a few teaching suggestions based on the story.

How can a news story of this type be used for social studies instruction? Here are a few suggestions:

1. Use the procedure discussed on pages 210–212 in making an analysis of this situation — that is (a) have students identify the *facts* of the case; (b) have students identify the *issues* in the case; and (c) have students identify *alternative solutions* to the problem and list the consequences of each alternative.

WHALE CAPTURE CREATES WAIL

Six killer whales are being held inside the Aqua Life, Inc. nets at Cook Inlet while Bill Holberg decides which ones, if any, will be kept for aquarium exhibits. Hundreds of people watched the capture from boats and shore yesterday afternoon.

The huge mammals swam slowly round and round inside two purse seine nets today, surfacing to "blow" for only moments. They stayed under for five minutes at a time. A large bull whale and a small calf that escaped the capture were nowhere to be found.

Governor Reconsidering

Meanwhile, a political storm was gathering over the capture operation. The governor today interrupted his skiing vacation long enough to say that he was "reconsidering" the state's position on making the inlet a sanctuary for killer whales. The state's senior senator in Washington said that a declaration of support for the governor for a whale sanctuary would clear the way for protection of the sea animals. Earlier efforts to get support from state officials for the idea were unsuccessful. The senator also said, "Apparently this man [Holberg] had a valid permit. But there aren't going to be any more. This is the end!"

Depth Charges Used

An assistant to the State Game and Fisheries director, Jack Binns, watched the capture from about fifty feet away. Binns said Aqua Life, Inc. boats used "sonar, radar, and 'depth' charges" to drive the whales into smaller and smaller coves and finally into the nets. He said he watched three men in power boats racing across the water atop the whale school, "dropping 'depth charges' as fast as they could light them. I've never seen anything so disgusting in all my life," he said today. "This ought to be stopped right now."

A federal enforcement officer who supervised yesterday's operation said, "there is nothing in the permit that prohibits the use of such explosives."

Use of Charges Denied

Many citizens complained about the capture operation. An automobile dealer from South Harbor said he saw an airplane dropping "tomato can"-size cannisters that apparently exploded as the plane herded the whales. Bill Moss, veterinarian for Aqua Life, Inc. said no such charges were used. He said the whale chasers used "firecracker"-type explosives thrown from boats to herd the whales. Holberg himself was aboard the Aqua Life, Inc. boat, *KANDU*, and was unavailable for comment.

Court Action Threatened

Environmentalists and others bitterly opposed the capture of the whales. Fred Russell, president of the state's largest environmental protection group, PROTEX, demanded that the whales be released. He said his group was prepared to take the matter to court if necessary to prevent Aqua Life, Inc. from keeping the creatures. "This is an outrage," he said," and we are not going to sit by and let it happen."

Russell cited a Canadian biologist who found that only about sixty-five killer whales remain in the Straits of Georgia and Juan de Fuca and in Puget Sound. Earlier data had placed the number of whales at about three hundred.

Overlapping Jurisdiction

The power to create a whale sanctuary rests with the federal government, but federal law says the governor of a state that contains the sanctuary may veto its creation. This overlapping of jurisdiction sometimes creates confusion or results in no action being taken.

Until today, federal officials thought the governor opposed creation of a killer whale sanctuary in this area. The governor's staff said that no record could be found of the governor's ever having opposed such a proposal.

The senior senator renewed his call for a sanctuary, something he has advocated since 1974. There is no reason to believe that the governor will oppose the creation of the killer whale sanctuary.

2. Use this story as a springboard for an in-depth study of endangered species. More than *five-hundred* kinds of animals are listed as rare or in danger of extinction, including blue whales, Indian and Siberian tigers, Asiatic lions, snow leopards, eagles, condors, grizzly bears, alligators, and whooping cranes. Students should get into the values question of whether or not an animal has to be "useful" in order to be protected.

3. Have children study the roles of federal, state, local, and volunteer groups in decision making regarding issues of the type presented in this story. This should get them into local and state regulations concerning the conservation of natural resources and environmental contamination. It should also confront the matter of what individual citizens or groups of citizens can do when they see something happening that they believe to be unconscionable, even if legal.

4. This story provides an excellent setting for the study of the issue of capture of wild animals for use in circuses and zoos. Should zoos be allowed at all? Do animals benefit from zoos?

5. This story can provide the basis for the study of the web of life food chains — that is, how changes in the population of one animal change the number of another animal on which it feeds. This can be coupled with a study of wildlife management, hunting and fishing regulations, and the concept of *open season.*

6. Study the lives of individuals who have dedicated themselves to the preservation of wildlife and other natural resources: John Muir, Jack Miner, Gifford Pinchot, and local environmentalists.

7. Develop this news story into a role-playing activity in which the issues are highlighted and satisfactory resolutions played out.

8. Have children in committees develop "position statements" to represent the point of view of the various principals in this controversy: the whale hunter, the governor, the president of the environmentalist group, an irate citizen, the director of Aqua Life, Inc., who would receive the captured whales, and so on.

9. Use the story to build interest in developing a social-action project dealing with ecology or conservation. A second-grade teacher in Wisconsin reports the following activities that were developed in such a project:

   a. The children helped others become aware of the problems faced by endangered wildlife by sharing their research findings with their family, friends, schoolmates, clergymen, and neighbors.

   b. They wrote letters to state and federal officials to urge their support of legislation designed to protect wildlife.

   c. They presented programs that dealt with the potential threats to wildlife by land developers, trappers, poachers, snowmobilers, hunters, pesticide programs, campers, and so on.

   d. They compiled a list of guidelines and distributed them to each

child in the school, explaining ways individuals can help. These
are some of the guidelines:

(1) Refuse to shoot birds and other wild creatures "just for the fun
    of it."
(2) Refuse to participate in cruel and senseless "chases" of wild
    animals on snowmobiles, in cars, on bikes, on foot, or in boats
    or planes.
(3) Refuse to destroy animal homes.
(4) Refuse to disturb baby birds and animal babies in their nests.[5]

10. Find out about the purposes and activities of organizations con-
    cerned about protecting the environment such as the Sierra Club, the
    National Wildlife Federation, Nature Conservancy, and Greenpeace.

These suggestions provide interesting extensions of a news story. Of
course, no one class would engage in all of them; indeed, it is unlikely that
more than one would be used. Perhaps the teacher could create others
even more suitable than those provided here. The point of this list is
simply to illustrate the wide range of possibilities that inhere in well-
selected current news stories. They provide the excitement of controversy, they are relevant to the current stream of human events, they deal
with public policy issues, and they lend themselves exceedingly well to
social participation projects.

DISCUSSION QUESTIONS AND SUGGESTED ACTIVITIES

1. How can map and globe reading be related to the study of current
   affairs? What possibilities do you see for relating social science concepts to current affairs and vice versa?

2. What would be the strengths and weaknesses of a social studies program built entirely around current affairs?

3. Examine copies of a children's periodical such as those published by
   Scholastic Inc. What can a teacher do to ensure imaginative use of
   such material?

4. Develop appropriate exercises of the types on page 217 based on a
   newspaper story.

5. In what ways can current affairs topics be used for inquiry and valuing experiences for children?

6. Select a news story, and explain how it could be used as a springboard
   for a role-playing or simulation exercise.

7. Find a local news item that would be appropriate for teaching the
   skills needed to deal with controversial issues.

[5] Marsha Gravitz, "You and Me in the Classroom," *Instructor*, 82:8 (April 1973), p. 43.

8. In dealing with controversial topics, what issues relating to the teacher's academic freedom are involved?

9. How can the understanding of important social studies concepts and generalizations be expanded by the study of current affairs?

SELECTED REFERENCES

DONOHUE, JUDITH HIGGINS. "Beyond Journalism: The Newspaper as Universal Teaching Tool." *Media and Methods,* 16 (April 1980), pp. 57–58+.

FLEMING, DAN B., AND LARRY J. WEBER. "Getting the News in Virginia: A Provocative Study of How Students Find Out 'What's New?' " *Social Education,* 47 (March 1983), pp. 216–218.

FOLEY, ROBERT. "The Community's Role in Dealing with Censorship." *Educational Leadership,* 40 (January 1983), pp. 51–54.

FONTANA, LYNN A. "Television and the Social Studies." *Social Education,* 52 (September 1988), pp. 348–350. (One of seven articles in a special section on television and social studies.)

Junior Scholastic, Teacher's Edition. Scholastic Inc., P.O. Box 3710, Jefferson City, Missouri 65102. (Published biweekly during the school year.)

MOLNAR, ALEX, LOREN E. SANCHEZ, DAVID C. KING, HERBERT J. GROVEN, JOEL J. KUPPERMAN, AND MARK C. SCHUG. Each of these authors contributes an article to the theme Contemporary Issues in the Curriculum. *Educational Leadership,* 42 (December 1984–January 1985), pp. 60–78.

NELSON, JACK L., AND ANNA S. OCHOA. "Academic Freedom, Censorship, and the Social Studies." *Social Education,* 51 (October 1987), pp. 424–449. (Several authors contribute to this special section on academic freedom and censorship.)

OTTO, ROBERT (CHAIRPERSON), SARA ANDERSON, HELEN CAREY, NANCY ROBERTS, ROBERT SNAVELY, PHILLIP HEATH, AND BARBARA BARCHI. "Guidelines for Teaching Science-Related Social Issues." (NCSS position statement) *Social Education,* 47 (April 1983), pp. 258–261.

OTTO, ROBERT. "Teaching Science-Related Social Issues." *How To Do It Series* 5, No. 4. Washington, D.C.: National Council for the Social Studies, 1987.

WELLS, J., AND OTHERS. "Newspapers Facilitate Content Area Learning: Social Studies." *Journal of Reading,* 31 (December 1987), pp. 370–372.

9

Using Reading and Writing to Learn Social Studies

No doubt many beginning teachers, as well as those with several years of experience, share a sense of frustration in dealing with the "reading problem" in social studies. Reading remains the chief avenue to information needed in learning social studies, yet children are often unable to read well enough to secure that information. Inability to read well, therefore, is a major cause of poor achievement in social studies, and, unfortunately, the problem becomes worse each year the child is in school.

The usual recommendations for attending to the wide range of reading abilities among learners are these: (1) use multiple texts, (2) rewrite the material at a simpler level, (3) use a nonreading approach to social studies, and (4) secure simpler nontext materials for slower readers. But teachers on the job find these recommendations require resources, time, or skills that they do not have. The college methods courses in reading generally focus on the "basal" program and give minimum, if any, attention to reading in the content fields. In this chapter, we will examine in detail the relationship between reading and social studies and will provide suggestions for the use of reading and writing as effective learning tools in social studies.

Most elementary schools provide time during the school day when a major effort is made to teach basic reading skills. In this developmental reading program, children acquire a basic reading vocabulary and learn to use various word recognition techniques along with other skills and abilities that characterize the fluent, independent reader. But a strong basic reading program will not be able to meet all the reading needs of children because each area of the school curriculum requires reading tasks that are somewhat unique to that special area. *Helping children develop the specific reading skills and the abilities associated with each area of the curriculum must, therefore, go hand in hand with other instruction in the special-subject area.* This point of view is widely supported by authorities in the field of reading.

The special reading skills and abilities needed to handle social studies material may be identified by examining textbooks and supplementary references written for children. Chart 4 lists reading skills typical of those found in most programs.

CHART 4. READING ABILITIES AND SKILLS ESSENTIAL TO SOCIAL STUDIES

In social studies the capable reader

- Uses chapter and section headings as aids to reading.
- Uses context clues to gain meaning.
- Recognizes author bias.
- Adjusts speed of reading to purpose.
- Interprets what is read.
- Detects cause-and-effect relationships.
- Understands essential terms and vocabulary.
- Gains information from maps, pictures, and illustrations.
- Uses various parts of a book as aids to reading.
- Is able to skim to locate facts.
- Distinguishes between fact and opinion.
- Compares one account with another.
- Recognizes topic sentences.
- Interprets quantitative data accurately.
- Obtains the literal meaning of the material read.
- Relates what is read to reality.
- Uses reference aids and references to find information.
- Is able to locate a book in the library.

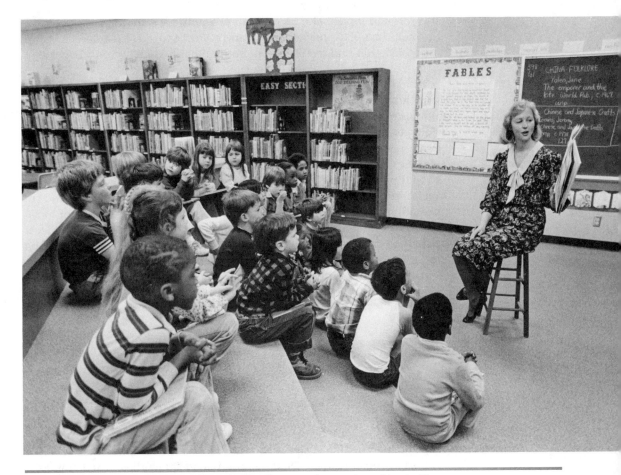

Children's books and stories housed in an inviting library environment combined with assistance from an interested and skilled librarian can take the teacher a long ways down the road toward building a rich social studies program for children. (Photo by Robb Mitchell, Tacoma School District.)

Reading in the social studies is an intellectual process and, therefore, requires the reader to think while engaging in it. Thus, problems in reading social studies in the middle and upper grades are often a reflection of a child's inability to conceptualize and to handle the ideas being presented through the symbolic system of print. Drill and practice on sounding out words are not likely to be of much help in dealing with this type of reading requirement.

This is not to say that the reading task cannot be simplified by careful attention to vocabulary and to reduced sentence length. The problem, however, is that explanations of specialized subjects and topics in print require the use of terms, words, and concepts that are peculiar to those subjects and topics. The reader will not comprehend the passage unless the meanings of the terms, words, and concepts used are understood. It is inevitable that children with limited conceptual ability will have difficulty reading social studies material.

The teacher's responsibility regarding reading in the social studies is, therefore, twofold. First, those special reading skills unique to social studies must be taught simultaneously with the subject matter and other skills relevant to the topic or unit under study. These are the skills listed in Chart 4. The teacher's second responsibility is to help children learn how to use reading as a tool in gaining needed information. Of course, reading should not be the only means through which children encounter new social studies information. Throughout this text, the idea is stressed repeatedly that a multimedia approach is vital to inspired teaching of social studies. But in that broad spectrum of media and activities that is at least potentially available to children today, reading remains undoubtedly the most important and, in the long run, the most critical to their success in learning social studies.

LEARNING ABOUT THE READING LEVELS OF CHILDREN

Elementary and middle school teachers in self-contained classrooms provide basic reading instruction to children and, therefore, should be well acquainted with their reading levels. Unfortunately, however, teachers who may be sensitive to differences in reading ability while conducting reading instruction may ignore those differences when it comes to social studies. Or they conduct social studies instruction as if those variations in reading ability did not exist. Most elementary schoolteachers have had adequate training in the teaching of reading, and although they are not expected to do intensive diagnostic analyses of the reading problems of learners, they should be able to make informal assessments of learner performance in reading. We are assuming here, therefore, that through daily contact with children in the basal reading program, through standardized test data, and through observation, the teacher already has some understanding of the ability of individual learners to apply word-attack skills and to comprehend what is read.

In social studies the teacher should regard diagnostic and instructional procedures as two essential components of the same process. Suppose, for example, the teacher wanted to teach a relatively simple skill such as learning to skim to locate facts. As an initial step, the teacher ought to prepare a diagnostic exercise that will indicate how well children are able to perform this skill. For example, an exercise such as the following might be devised:

SKIMMING TO LOCATE FACTS

Directions:

1. Open your book to the correct page.
2. Find the answer as quickly as you can.
3. Write your answer in the space.
4. You will have exactly twenty minutes to do the exercise.
   a. Page 117.   What does "VP" mean?_____
   b. Page 121.   The goods and services a worker can get in exchange for money wages are called_____
   c. Page 149.   The number of farm workers in 1870 was_____
   d. Page 152.   The percent of women doctors in the Soviet Union is_____
   e. Page 192.   The cause of the crisis was_____
   f. Page 209.   The number of miles of inland waterways in the United States is _____
   g. Page 209.   The cheapest transportation in the United States is by_____
   h. Page 230.   Places in cities that have no business buildings are called_____
   i. Page 241.   Towns and villages outside large cities are called_____
   j. Page 246.   The date San Francisco opened its Bay Area Rapid Transit System — BART — was_____

If a child cannot do such an exercise, it may be that the exercise itself is too difficult to read. In that case, the reading instruction must begin with attention to more basic skills and abilities having to do with decoding and simple comprehension. However, if the child can read the questions but does not know how to locate the answers quickly through skimming, this skill can be taught and practiced. This sequence — diagnosis, instruction, and follow-up practice — can be applied to any of the social studies skills listed in Chart 4.

A few other sample diagnostic exercises are these:

I. Using Context Clues to Gain Meaning

Select the words that belong in the blank spaces in this paragraph from the list of words that follows the paragraph.

The work of the TVA was started by building _____. A _____ is a wall or bank built across a river to stop its flow. The _____ hold back the water so the rivers do not overflow their banks and cause floods. Lakes, or _____, are formed behind the _____. Water from the _____ is allowed to flow into the streams when the rivers are low. This makes them _____ at all times. Power plants were built at the foot of some _____. These plants _____, or make, electricity. The electricity generated in the plants supplies _____ and _____ to factories, towns, and farms for a 200-mile area.

reservoirs	navigable	power
generate	dams	light
dam		

II. Recognizing Topic Sentences

Open your book to page 57. This page contains four paragraphs. Read each paragraph and find the sentence that best tells what the paragraph is all about. In the spaces here, write the beginning two words of the sentences you select.

Paragraph 1. _____ _____
Paragraph 2. _____ _____
Paragraph 3. _____ _____
Paragraph 4. _____ _____

III. Understanding Terms and Vocabulary

Acronyms (AK'-row-nimz) are words that are formed from the first letter of each word in the full name of something. For example, NOW is an acronym for *National Organization for Women*. Acronyms are abbreviated expressions.

Use your text to find the full title of the following acronyms:

1. MADD_____
2. OPEC_____
3. UNICEF_____
4. NASA_____
5. RADAR_____
6. AMTRAK_____
7. BART_____

USING STUDY AIDS AND STUDY SKILLS TO IMPROVE READING

In contrast to reading a library book simply for enjoyment, much of the reading in social studies involves a search for information. The design of social studies texts, almost without exception, provides many aids to make the job of reading easier. The teacher cannot assume, however, that children will make use of such aids unless they are taught to do so. The skills associated with the use of study aids must be taught, reviewed, and retaught each year throughout the elementary and middle school grades. Here are few teaching suggestions, each of which is discussed in turn:

1. Using various parts of a book.
2. Recognizing topic sentences.
3. Using the organization of the book.
4. Using pictures to aid comprehension.

Using Various Parts of a Book

The parts of a book should be taught as aids in getting information. For example, if a fifth-grade child, Sara, in her study of famous women in American history, wanted to know the name of the Indian woman who assisted Lewis and Clark, how would she find it? She might find a reference to the Lewis and Clark Expedition in the Table of Contents, but that would be less likely than finding the names of these two explorers in the Index. She looks in the Index and finds

legumes, 273–274
L'Enfant, Pierre, 114
levees, 346, 356–357
Lewis, Meriwether, 128, 304–305, 397, 415–416
Lewiston, Idaho, 397
Lexington, Battle of, 87–88[1]

She turns to page 128 and skims the first column quickly. At the bottom of the page, she reads, ". . . the explorers hired a French-Canadian fur trader named Charbonneau and his wife Sacajawea to act as their guides. A Shoshoni Indian, Sacajawea could understand the Indian languages."[2]

Thus, in a matter of moments, Sara is able to find precisely the information she seeks. Contrast this with the girl sitting next to her who needs the same information, but, lacking an efficient way of finding it, goes through the book page by page looking for a picture or a clue that will reveal the name of that famous Indian woman. She may never find what she is looking for.

Rather than teaching parts of a book in an expository mode, the

---

[1] Allen Y. King, Ida Dennis, and Florence Potter, *The United States and Other Americas* (New York: Macmillan, 1985), p. 595.

[2] *Ibid.*, p. 128.

teacher should use exercises that require children to apply these skills. Often such exercises are included in the book itself. The one following is an example.

LEARNING THE PARTS OF A BOOK

In the right-hand column are listed the parts of your book. In the left-hand column are listed some things you might want to find out. For each item in the left-hand column, tell what part of the book you would turn to *first* in order to get the information.

You want to know	Parts of your book
the number of chapters in the book	title page
the meaning of *treaty*	copyright page
how to say the word *bauxite*	preface
when the book was published	table of contents
the population of various states	list of maps
the date the Dutch bought Manhattan Island	list of illustrations
what a sod house looks like	glossary
the route of the first railroad to the west coast	pronunciation key
whether the book tells anything about Canada	appendix
	index

Other more complex variations of this exercise are possible. For example, the right-hand column can be omitted, and the child can be asked to find and supply the information. Or the child can be asked to indicate the specific page on which the information appears. Once learned, many of these skills can be transferred to many other situations. If the children can use an alphabetical arrangement, as in the case of an index, they should also be able to use the dictionary, the encyclopedia, and the card catalog. Also, if they develop the habit of knowing exactly what information they seek before beginning the search, information gathering will be more efficient.

Naturally, the complexity of activities of this type should be appropriate to the age and maturity of the learners. The examples provided were drawn from the middle grades. But even in the first grade, children learn that books have titles and that pages are numbered. They also learn that sections of their books and stories have titles. In the second and third grades, they can begin to make use of the Table of Contents to find a particular story. In the third and fourth grades they can learn simple variations of alphabetical arrangements that assist them in using an index.

Recognizing Topic Sentences

If children learn to recognize the main idea developed in a paragraph, they can organize the ideas developed by the author in some order of importance. They learn to separate the topic being discussed from the elaborative and supporting detail. Before they can deal with topic sentences, however, they have to understand that a paragraph is a group of sentences all of which deal with the same topic or idea. They learn that the *topic sentence* is the critical one in the paragraph because it tells the reader what the paragraph is about. A little practice will help them understand the singleness of purpose of paragraphs. Exercises such as the one on page 232 can be used.

An exercise of this type should be followed by practice in identifying topic sentences in paragraphs selected from the children's text. They should learn (1) that the topic sentence tells what the paragraph is about, (2) that other sentences in the paragraph elaborate on the topic, and (3) that the topic sentence is usually, but not always, the first sentence in a paragraph.

LEARNING HOW PARAGRAPHS AID COMPREHENSION

Read these selections, and decide which is easier to understand.[3]

A

As they drove on, he told them stories he'd heard about the old days on the Chathams, about the ships and the men who hunted the whales and seals, about the Morioris and how they had been almost killed out by the Maoris who came out here over a hundred years ago. "There's lots of people here with Maori blood," he said. "But there's not many with Moriori blood." The road curved round the lake, through hills, paddocks and beside smaller lakes. Ducks and swans were on all the lakes. They bumped across some paddocks and came to the airstrip. There were a lot of Landrovers and the yellow truck beside two sheds. They heard the plane before they could see it. It came low over the trees

B

As they drove on, he told them stories he'd heard about the old days on the Chathams, about the ships and men who hunted the whales and seals, about the Morioris and how they had been almost killed out by the Maoris who came out here over a hundred years ago. "There's lots of people here with Maori blood." he said. "But there's not many with Moriori blood."

The road curved round the lake, through hills, paddocks and beside smaller lakes. Ducks and swans were on all the lakes. They bumped across some paddocks and came to the airstrip. There were a lot of Landrovers and the yellow truck beside two sheds.

They heard the plane before they could

[3] From *The Chatham Islands* by Jack Lasenby. (A Bulletin for Schools) Wellington, New Zealand: Department of Education, undated, p. 32.

and bumped along on the grass of the air-strip. People got off, and others got on. Bags of mail and parcels of goods were carried off through the big doors, and others were put on. The fisherman was carried on.

see it. It came low over the trees and bumped along on the grass of the airstrip. People got off, and others got on. Bags of mail and parcels of goods were carried off through the big doors, and others were put on. The fisherman was carried on.

1. Why is one selection easier to read than the other?
2. Why did the author group the sentences the way he did in selection B?
3. Is there something about the grouping of sentences that makes them a paragraph?
4. Which sentence in each paragraph in selection B tells what the paragraph is about?

Using the Organization of a Book

Units, chapters, section heads, and subheads; ends of section, chapter, or unit study aids; maps, charts, or picture captions; introductory questions — all of these make sense to the mature reader who uses them as valuable aids in understanding the organization of a book. But left unguided, a child is not likely to make good use of them as aids to reading. Even teachers may not be familiar with the way a particular book is organized. Chart 5 on pages 238 – 239 illustrates organizational components that are commonly found in social studies textbooks. Research indicates that knowledge of text *structure* is a significant variable in children being able to recall information.[4]

Using Pictures to Aid Comprehension

The most widely used of all visual aids are pictures, photographs, and illustrations. These are used to obtain realism, to clarify ideas, to recall the real object, and, in short, to give meaning to learning. It is well known that words cannot convey meanings as accurately, vividly, or quickly as pictures. Pictures can also be helpful in promoting inquiry skills. For this reason, some textbooks now use questions for captions instead of a description of the content of the picture or illustration.

Publishers invest huge sums of money to provide instructive illustrations for social studies textbooks. Unfortunately, the full value of these aids to reading is not realized unless children are taught how to make good use of them. Illustrations are not simply cosmetic touches to make the book more appealing. They are, or should be, an integral part of the message system of the text.

[4] Barbara M. Taylor and S. Jay Samuels, "Children's Use of Text Structure in the Recall of Expository Material," *American Educational Research Journal,* 20 (Winter 1983), pp. 517 – 528.

Pictures and illustrations elaborate concepts presented in the narrative but usually do not repeat exactly what is said in the text. Neither do picture captions simply tell what would be obvious to the reader only by looking at the picture. Thus, captions should call attention to some element or relationship in the picture or illustration that might be missed by the casual viewer. Often this is done by using a question or series of questions. In this way pictures and illustrations can provide the reader with a wealth of information. In teaching children how to use pictures and illustrations, teachers will find questions such as these appropriate:

1. Exactly what is being shown in the picture?
2. What relationships are illustrated by the picture?
3. When was this picture taken? (recently, years ago, time of day, and so on)
4. How does the picture illustrate something we discussed in class?
5. What influences (causes or effects) can be detected in the picture?
6. What does the picture tell about the life-styles of the people?
7. How does the picture illustrate something valued by people?
8. How does the picture show conflicts between traditional and modern ways of doing things?
9. What does the picture show that illustrates the roles of men, women, and children in that society?
10. What characteristics of the culture are shown in the picture?
11. What can you say about the geography of the area shown by the picture?
12. What conversation might be going on between the persons in the picture?
13. What would you judge to be the educational level of the people who live there?
14. Would you describe this area as being technologically advanced? Why or why not?
15. Why do farmers make use of their land in this way?
16. Do you think the people use most of what they produce or sell their products outside their community? What makes you think so?

What makes a picture, photograph, or illustration suitable for instructional purposes in social studies? Certainly, the most important consideration is accuracy of the portrayal. The fundamental purpose of any learning aid is to convey accurate meaning; and if this is lacking, the picture, photograph, or illustration must be rejected unless, of course, it is being used to illustrate inaccuracy. Other factors that should be considered are that it be of sufficient size for the purpose it is to serve, appropriate to the age children with which it is to be used, of good artistic quality, impressive, of easy interpretation, and that it have a definite center of interest that is not subordinated by a great many details.

CHART 5. ORGANIZATIONAL STRUCTURE OF SOCIAL STUDIES TEXTBOOKS

Unit 3 — Life Ways Around The World

CHAPTER SEVEN–THE EARTH AS THE HOME OF MANY PEOPLE

How Do People Use The Earth?

Where Do People Live On the Earth?

How Are People Alike In What They Need?

How Are People Different In The Way They Live?

Soon the days become shorter. Often one can see birds flying south. Nearly every night the temperature drops below freezing. The *growing season* is over even though there may still be many warm days. The growing season is that time between the last killing frost in the spring and the first killing frost in the fall.

Finding the Main Ideas

Go back to the section called "How Do People Use The Earth?" on page 212. Which of the following is the main idea of that section?

a. All people must have certain things from the earth in order to live.

b. People who live in cities need the earth less than people who live on farms.

Understanding Key Words and Terms

Producer   Exchange   Culture

Use these words to complete the paragraph below

In every _____ people _____ goods and services.

How people _____ etc. . . .

Using What You Have Learned

On page 143 there are listed several fire hazards . . .

Getting the Facts

Skim the section "How Do People Use The Earth?" on page 212 and tell which of the following statements are true . . .

Thinking About What You Have Read . . .

Why do you suppose . . .

Unit divisions are usually longer than chapters. Sometimes teachers plan teaching units around units in the text they are using.

Chapters are numbered consecutively throughout the book. Notice this is Chapter 7, appearing in Unit 3.

These are section heads. In this case they are stated as questions. Such questions can be very helpful in setting purposes for doing the reading.

A short, representative paragraph of social studies prose. Notice that the term *growing season* is italicized, meaning that it is a new concept. Notice, too, that it is defined in the paragraph. Children should be alerted to the importance of italicized words, terms, or passages.

These are typical study exercises used in social studies texts. Notice that they deal with *literal comprehension* (Getting the Facts); *securing key ideas or main ideas* (Finding the Main Ideas); *vocabulary development* (Understanding Key Words and Terms); *application* (Using What You Have Learned); and *reflective thinking* (Thinking About What You Have Read). Other study helps might include inquiry exercises, cause and effect relationships, map reading skills, picture interpretation, hypothesizing, coming to conclusions, and others.

Select a children's social studies text and compare its organization with the one described here.

BUILDING SOCIAL STUDIES VOCABULARY

The vocabulary load of social studies reading material is one of the major causes of poor comprehension and faulty reading in social studies. Even with the more careful attention that contemporary authors give to word difficulties, the social studies vocabulary remains a stumbling block for many children. Although a degree of simplification is possible, it is true that there are limits beyond which the use of a specialized vocabulary cannot be avoided. If one is speaking or writing about social studies concepts, appropriate vocabulary must be used. This is not altogether undesirable if the teacher accepts vocabulary development as one of the goals of the total social studies program. The same situation exists in other areas of the curriculum; the child must learn the language associated with mathematics, science, art, music—all of which have their own peculiar words, terms, or phrases. The chart on this page shows some of the types of words and terms that are peculiar to social studies.

CHART 6. WORDS AND TERMS NEEDING SPECIAL ATTENTION IN SOCIAL STUDIES

Technical terms — Words, terms, and expressions peculiar to social studies and usually not encountered when reading selections from other fields of knowledge. *Examples:* veto, meridian, frontier, latitude, longitude, legislature, polls, franchise, temperate, plateau, hemisphere, mountainous, wasteland, balance of power, capitalism, democracy, nationalism, civilization, century, ancient, decade, pueblo, fjord, iceberg.

Figurative terms — Expressions that are metaphorical; having a different connotation from the literal meaning usually associated with the word. *Examples:* political platform, cold war, closed shop, Iron Curtain, logrolling, pork barrel, open door, hat in the ring, domino theory, Sunbelt.

Words with multiple meanings — Words that have identical spelling but whose meaning is derived from context. *Examples:* cabinet, belt, bill, chamber, mouth, bank, revolution, fork, court, assembly, range.

Terms peculiar to a locality — Expressions peculiar to a specific part of the country that are not commonly used elsewhere. *Examples:* truck, meeting, borough, gandy, draw, coulee, right, prairie, section, run, butte, arroyo, geoduck, goobers, grits, potlatch, bayou, haul cane road.

Words easily confused with other words — Words that are closely similar in general configuration. *Examples:* peasant for pheasant, alien for allies, principal for principle, longitude for latitude, executive for execution, conversation for conservation.

Acronyms — Words that are abbreviated expressions. *Examples:* NATO, NASA, OPEC, SALT, NOW, UNICEF.

Quantitative terms — Words and terms signifying amounts of time, space, or objects. *Examples:* shortly after, century, fortnight, several years later, score, one hundred fifty tons.

The teacher should anticipate likely word difficulties *before* children are asked to read a social studies selection. Two types of word problems must be expected. One is the inability to recognize the word in print; the other is not knowing the meaning of the word once it is recognized. Therefore, new words and terms should be presented and developed in the context of a phrase or a sentence rather than in isolation.

Vocabulary development should be conducted in relatively short, highly motivated settings. Having children look up a long list of terms in the dictionary prior to reading a selection is not productive. A better arrangement is to write the key terms in a phrase or sentence on the chalkboard and discuss their meanings. Better still, the sentence in the text in which the word or term appears can be selected for directed study.

Maintaining a sensitivity to, and interest in, new words and terms is essential. Children should be encouraged to use the specialized social studies vocabulary in their discussions. From time to time the teacher may want to involve them in word games. Devising riddles, providing synonyms or antonyms, making or completing crossword puzzles, or constructing variants of words are helpful in maintaining an awareness of new terms. Also, bulletin board displays and other classroom exhibits can feature new words encountered in social studies.

Teaching how known words can be used to construct new words can be of help in recognizing new words and understanding their meanings. Among the simplest variations are compound words or the addition of prefixes or suffixes. Some examples are these: construct, construct*ed,* construc*ting,* construc*tion;* consume, consum*er,* consum*ed,* consum*ing;* loyal, *dis*loyal, loyal*ist;* front, front*ier,* frontier*sman.*

One of the most useful skills in reading social studies materials is the use of context clues. A reader, for example, should have no problem gaining meaning from the following passage even though many of the words are missing.

At exactly 4:05 P.M. the _____ landed at the _____. Hundreds of _____ were waiting in the _____. It was the first time many of them had seen our nation's leader. When the _____ came down the _____, he _____. The crowd _____. He made a short _____. The crowd _____ again. In a few _____ he was on his way again, this time in a _____. As the _____ went straight up, the _____ could see the _____ through the window of the _____.

Gaining meaning through context is especially appropriate to social studies because it ensures that the reading is done thoughtfully. This contrasts with defining words and terms in isolation, in which case the wrong meaning might be selected. Many social studies terms and words have multiple meanings. For example:

- He established the first *bank* in the region.
- The river overflowed its left *bank.*
- "You can *bank* on that," he said.
- Directly ahead was a big *bank* of snow.
- As he looked west, he could see a large *bank* of clouds.
- Just before crashing, the plane seemed to *bank* to the left.
- The assembly line consisted of a long *bank* of machines.

When terms that have multiple meanings are encountered in a passage, only the meaning being used in the passage should be developed at that time, and it should be developed in context.

Glossaries do not provide the meanings of words and terms in context and, therefore, have some limitations in acquainting children with the precise meaning of new terms. For instance, a child may read the following sentence:

> Several well-known people from this city were killed in the crash of a charter flight.

Looking in the glossary of a text for the meaning of the word *charter,* the child finds

> **char′ter:** a paper giving a person or company special rights

It happens that the definition of *charter* given is only one of about five that correctly defines the word.

After anticipated word difficulties have been attended to and the purposes for doing the reading have been established, children will usually read selections silently the first time through (middle grades). The teacher should be available to assist those who encounter problems with words. Children should be encouraged to figure out the meaning of words for themselves, but if a child cannot do so in a couple or three tries, the teacher should explain the term, pronounce it, and have the child proceed with the reading. Reading of the entire selection should not be held up because of a problem with a few unfamiliar words or terms.

It is often helpful to keep a special social studies vocabulary list posted in the classroom. Lists can be developed by individual children, too, and made into a social studies picture dictionary. If a word is likely to be used frequently in writing, such a word might be added to an individualized spelling list. However, many social studies words are not often used by children in their writing and, therefore, do not make good selections for spelling lists. They are more likely to be a part of children's reading vocabulary than their writing vocabulary.

Most social studies texts provide extensive study aids to assist with vocabulary development, including any or all of the following:

1. Contextual definition of words and terms.

     Examples: Thousands of persons in this city earn their living by *processing* food. Processing means preparing food for marketing.

     In recent years people have become concerned about *pollution.* Pollution comes about when something harmful is placed into the water or air.

2. Use of boldface type and/or italics.

     Examples: The things from which products are made are called **raw materials.** Three *raw materials* — iron ore, coal, and limestone — are found in the Midwest.

3. End of unit, chapter, or section exercises.

     Examples: Matching exercises.

     Selecting terms for incomplete sentences.

     Finding definitions of key terms in the text.

4. Glossaries.

     Examples: **Pig iron:** melted iron that hardens into bars

     Pilgrim: a person who travels to holy places to worship

     Plantation: a large farm that specializes in one crop

     Polar regions: areas in the high latitudes

5. Pronunciation guide.

     Examples: **tropics** (trop′iks)

     volcano (vol-ka′no)

The teacher should give special attention to the meaning of quantitative concepts because they are used with high frequency in social studies prose and because research has repeatedly shown that they are not well understood by children. If a class reads in the text that "the Empire State Building reaches a height of 1,250 feet," individual children might think of 1,250 feet as meaning anything from a distance of perhaps 50 feet to 14 miles! Quantitative concepts deal with time, space, or objects (including people) and may be definite or indefinite. Chart 7 on page 244 provides examples of these categories.

The meanings of quantitative concepts need to be developed within the context in which they are studied and, whenever possible, related to the child's experience. For example, the area of a faraway place may be compared to that of their home state. Populations of places may be related to their own city or to a city in their state. An acre of space can be compared with their playfield or a football field. Indefinite references to quantity must be discussed in terms of the topic and period studied. For example, an hour's wait in the dentist's office would be considered "a long time," but a "long time" in terms of rehabilitating a polluted lake might be twenty-five years whereas a "long time" when referring to the

CHART 7. EXAMPLES OF VARIOUS QUANTITATIVE CONCEPTS

	Time	Space	Objects
Definite	10 years ago A century passed. two decades later	480 square miles the area of two football fields Each farm was 80 acres in size.	Columbus had a crew of 90 sailors. 2000 cars were manufactured each day. The explorers had only three canoes.
Indefinite	a short while later It took several weeks. Years passed before anything happened.	The Sahara covers a vast area. Much of the land is used for farming. The Miller family had a large spread.	The state produces a great amount of wheat. millions of barrels of oil Untold numbers of ships sailed into the harbor.

formation of the earth's surface would be millions of years. Through discussion, the teacher can help children gain greater meaning of these complex references to quantity.

IMPROVING READING COMPREHENSION

Reading with comprehension means that the reader is able to extract from the selection the essential facts and understandings, visualize details, and sense the relatedness of the facts. It is a process of obtaining an understanding of the meaning the author was attempting to convey. Comprehension depends on a number of factors, of which some reside within the reader and others relate to the selection to be read. Because of the complexity of the psychological processes involved in comprehension, as well as the limitations of printed symbols to convey meaning, it is doubtful that the reader is ever able to obtain the precise shade of meaning intended by the author. Teachers can help children read social studies materials with greater understanding, however, if proper attention is given to the factors known to affect reading comprehension.

It is obvious that the child who brings the most to a reading situation will receive the most in return. What the child brings that will enhance reading social studies materials are intellectual ability and experience background. Although there is not much a teacher can do about the intellectual capacities of children, there is a great deal that can be done to broaden their life experiences. Extensive use of field trips, films, pictures, stories, exhibits, displays, and real objects will materially assist the child in comprehending the ideas encountered in reading.

Comprehension is sometimes, but not always, related to the speed of reading. The poor reader may read at a snail's pace and also comprehend very little. The good reader, on the other hand, may read rapidly and have an adequate understanding of the ideas presented. Under ordinary conditions, the difficulty of the material *as it appears to the reader* should determine the rate of speed at which it should be read. Children should be taught to vary their rate of reading in accordance with the degree of comprehension required.

Some topics in social studies are more easily understood than others, and therefore, reading comprehension is more of a problem in dealing with some topics than it is with others. A narrative account of early plantation life in the South is straightforward and relatively easy to understand. Most children can read selections of this type rapidly and keep their comprehension high. On the other hand the child may encounter a passage that explains the topic "Why Seasons Change." This is an exceedingly complex idea and will require the most careful reading the child can muster if it is to be understood.

Reading comprehension in social studies consists of at least four components: (1) getting the literal meaning or a general understanding of what is being communicated, (2) understanding and remembering facts and details that support key ideas, (3) recognizing and remembering the sequence of ideas or events presented, and (4) following directions. Sometimes interpretation is regarded as a component of comprehension, but in this treatment, we deal with interpretation in a separate section. These procedures have been shown to be effective in improving reading comprehension; a discussion of each one follows:

1. Preview for the general idea.
2. Anticipate and attend to potential word difficulties.
3. Establish clear purposes for doing the reading.
4. Use study and organization aids provided in the book.
5. Teach children to vary their rate of reading.
6. Relate what is read to life experiences of children.
7. Check comprehension regularly and keep individual records.

Preview for the General Idea

Because comprehension involves getting meaning, it helps if the reader has a general idea as to what the material is all about before starting to read it. Such an overview will usually be directed by the teacher, but children should develop the habit of previewing material themselves. Let us say that a class is about to read *part* of a new unit entitled "The World of Carmelita and José." The teacher speaks to the class:

TEACHER: Boys and girls, for the next few days we will be reading from our social studies books. I would like to introduce you to two children we will visit in this unit whose names are Carmelita and José. Please open your books to page 86. (The children take time to find the page.) Notice that the large print says "The World of Carmelita and José." Just looking at this page, what do you think this unit is about?

FRIEDA: Mexico.

TEACHER: Why did you say Mexico, Frieda?

FRIEDA: Because Carmelita and José are Mexican names. Besides, it shows their pictures and they are dressed in Mexican clothes. . . . We learned that when we studied the community in Texas. . . .

DAVID: That doesn't mean they are from Mexico. They could be from several countries in South America and have names like that. They would dress like that, too.

TEACHER: Those are both good ideas. Perhaps if we page through this unit, we can discover the country it talks about. Turn to the map on page 88. . . .

It is established that the unit is, indeed, Mexico, and the teacher continues. . . .

TEACHER: As you look at these pages, what do you suppose you will be reading about in the world of Carmelita and José?

ERIC: Well, it looks like . . . uh . . . it tells like . . . you know . . . what they do every day . . . in school . . . at home, you know. . . .

LISA: It shows how they do many of the same things we do.

TEACHER: What do you mean?

LISA: Well, we have homes and families, we go to school, we go shopping, and things like that, and they do, too.

The discussion concludes after the teacher is satisfied that the children are oriented to the material to be read. Previews should do the following:

1. Help the reader get the general idea of what the selection is all about.
2. Help the reader understand how the material is organized and understand the nature of the narrative.
3. Help the reader see how the subject matter to be read relates to prior studies or experiences.
4. Help the reader understand how illustrations relate to the subject matter to be read.

Anticipate and Attend to Potential Word Difficulties

As has been indicated earlier, word difficulties and word meanings should be attended to before the reading is attempted. Often this can be done during the time the material is being previewed. In the example cited in the foregoing section, for instance, the teacher might have called the attention of the class to such words as *serape, fiesta, tortilla,* and *hacienda.* Specific suggestions for vocabulary development are provided on pages 240–244.

Establish Clear Purposes for Doing the Reading

Reading for a purpose is critical to comprehension. Children may pore over their social studies texts for endless hours without really knowing what they are looking for or why they are doing the reading. Clearly, it is the teacher's responsibility to make sure that the reading children do is purposeful. In directed study, these purposes may be given orally by the teacher:

> Find the sentence near the top of page 115 that begins, "Each time this happens. . . ." Put your finger on that sentence. (The teacher sees that all children have the correct place.) Now read the next three paragraphs to find out three different ways of controlling air pollution.

If the reading is to be done independently, that is, not directed by the teacher, as in the example given, the purposes of the reading can be written on the chalkboard:

> As you read the section "Dangers to Health" on pages 143–146, find the answers to these questions:
>
> 1. Why are scientists worried about air pollution?
> 2. Why has the government stopped the sale of some products?
> 3. What does the author mean on page 145 when he says, "Time is running out"?

The book itself may provide aids for setting purposes for reading. For example, the teacher says:

> For several days we have been learning about life in and around Big City. Today we will be doing some reading about how people get to work in Big City. On page 25 of your book there is a section that begins with the question "How Do People in Big City Get to Work?" Open your book to page 25. Can you find that question? Fine. As you read this part, find out as many ways as you can how people get to work in Big City. When you are finished reading,

we will talk about the ways you found. See if each of you can find all the ways the author tells about.

The teacher should vary the purposes from time to time to allow children to practice a variety of skills. Purposes can relate directly to the four basic components of comprehension; namely, getting the literal meaning, getting facts and details, sensing a sequence of events or ideas, and following directions.

Use Study and Organization Aids Provided in the Book

The use of study and organization aids was discussed earlier in this chapter (see pages 232–239). Attention is called to these aids again here because their use can be enormously helpful in comprehending what is read. It should be stressed that time must be taken to explain the organization of material and to instruct children in the use of the various aids presented. In learning about the organization of the material, children are also learning skills that are associated with organizing their own ideas to gain a better understanding.

Teach Children to Vary Their Rate of Reading

As a regular part of social studies instruction, the teacher should devise reading situations that require children to vary their rate of reading for a particular purpose. This may be in the form of questions, some calling for rapid reading or skimming, others for more detailed careful reading and rereading. Commonly, the answers to names of places, persons, situations, dates, and similar factual data can be obtained through skimming, whereas answers to reflective questions will require slower, more careful reading.

Relate What Is Read to Life Experiences of Children

Relating what is read to one's experiences not only helps comprehension but is motivating as well. It tends to give the material an added dimension of meaningfulness. Here are a few examples:

THE CHILDREN READ ABOUT:	THEY RELATE THIS TO:
1. Fire hazards.	1. Danger spots in their homes.
2. Discoverers, explorers, pioneers.	2. Present-day mountain climbers, adventurers, astronauts.

3. Ecology.	3. Local environmental contamination.
4. Occupations and careers.	4. Their own career interests and ambitions.
5. The law and justice systems.	5. Their own involvement with the law (in the civil, not criminal area).
6. The interdependence of nations.	6. The energy crisis, foreign-made products they use.

Check Comprehension Regularly and Keep Individual Records

When one wants to improve, it helps to record progress. In working toward improved reading comprehension, the teacher should follow a systematic cycle of instruction, practice, evaluation, and feedback to the learner. Social studies education is or should be more than reading. But beginning at about the third grade and continuing through the middle and upper grades, indeed, through high school, reading (especially reading *comprehension*) is critical to success in social studies. Comprehension suffers when the teacher assumes that the learner has the skills developed well enough to meet the reading requirements of the social studies.

Short teacher-made tests similar to several of the examples provided in this chapter can be used to assess student comprehension. Test questions should focus on those items of information that are believed to be important to learn and to remember.[5] It is recommended that time limits be set for such evaluations and that these be kept constant from one test to the next. Providing the children with information about the improvement they have made in reading over a period of time is likely to encourage greater effort on their part to improve their reading comprehension.

LEARNING TO INTERPRET IDEAS

Reading comprehension in the strictest sense involves getting the facts as they are presented by the author. Social studies materials often require that the reader interpret the ideas. This involves *making inferences, sensing relationships, noting cause-and-effect occurrences, detecting the emotional bias of the author, reading critically, evaluating the material, and being able to anticipate or predict likely outcomes.* It requires the reader to

[5] Karen K. Wixon, "Levels of Importance of Postquestions and Children's Learning from Text," *American Educational Research Journal*, 21 (September 1984), pp. 419–433.

go beyond the literal presentation of the facts and to sense the significance of them. This process is referred to as "reading between and beyond the lines." Consider the following example that might be a passage from a selection read by fifth-graders:

> All day long the wagon train moved slowly westward. The travelers were tired and weary from the long, dusty journey. The wagonmaster looked at his watch. It was four o'clock, but the sun was still high in the sky. Directly ahead was the river that had to be crossed. On the other side was high ground. Near the river bank was a fine grove of trees. The wagonmaster wondered if he should have the tired travelers cross the river yet today or camp on this side of the river and cross over the first thing in the morning. He decided to make the crossing that evening.

Now answer the questions: (1) In what season of the year were the people traveling? (2) Why do you suppose the wagonmaster decided in favor of crossing that evening? Notice that the material does not give the answers to either of the questions, yet the answers can be inferred from the information given. Many passages in social studies books lend themselves to questions of this type.

Making Inferences

Research in children's thinking supports the view that reasoning and problem-solving abilities begin at about age three and develop continually with increasing age and experience. Stimulating experiences in critical thinking and problem solving during the formative years of early childhood can do much to foster the growth of such skills. The example on pages 300–301 shows how two different kinds of questions can be based on the same piece of prose, each requiring different reading skills and different intellectual processes.

In a comparison of these two sets of questions, it is obvious that one set can be answered directly from the text and that the other cannot. In the latter case the readers must go beyond the information provided by the author; they have to bring prior knowledge to bear on the questions. They have to be able to speculate, to wonder, and to imagine. Moreover, there are probably no absolutely correct answers to these questions. In the case of the first set of questions, right answers can be established if one uses the authority of the narrative in determining correctness. Clearly, questions such as those in the right-hand column are best suited for discussion in class and should not be given as homework assignments.

Sensing Relationships

Social studies material often requires the reader to sense relationships among variables and to come to conclusions. Although factors may occur at the same time or follow in an established sequence, this does not mean that one *causes* the other. For example, areas of poor housing also show high incidence of law violation, but one would not conclude that crime occurs because people live in poor housing. There are, no doubt, other causal factors that relate to both housing and crime. Thus, the reader may not necessarily be searching for cause and effect but for things that seem to "go together." Or the reader may want to sort through the ideas presented in order to determine whether they are major ideas or supporting detail. In some instances, the reader is expected to use the information given and predict what consequences are likely to flow from the given situation. Here are examples to illustrate this type of interpretive reading:

UNDERSTANDING RELATIONSHIPS AMONG IDEAS

Suppose you start an outline of Chapter 3 of your text this way:

The Modern Western Dry Lands

1. How land use on the Great Plains brought trouble
   A. Climate of the Great Plains

The authors give a number of details about the climate to build the idea that climate is a problem in the region. As you read, you must put "small" details under "bigger" ideas. Here are two arrangements of the details given about climate.

Form A	Form B
1. Rainfall.	1. Rainfall
2. Average lower than on the land to east.	a. Average lower than on land to east
3. Varies from one period to another.	b. Varies from one period to another
4. Sometimes harmful.	c. Sometimes harmful
5. Thundershowers damage crops.	(1) Thundershowers damage crops
6. Summer storms sometimes accompanied by tornadoes.	(2) Summer storms sometimes accompanied by tornadoes
7. Occasional blizzards cause hardship.	2. Occasional blizzards cause hardship
8. Growing season.	3. Growing season
9. Varies from north to south.	a. Varies from north to south
10. Varies from year to year.	b. Varies from year to year
11. Winds.	4. Winds
12. Strong because not stopped by trees.	a. Strong because not stopped by trees
13. Sometimes blows away dry plowed soil.	b. Sometimes blows away dry plowed soil
14. Sometimes brings very cold weather.	c. Sometimes brings very cold weather

Which of these forms shows the relationship between "big" details and "smaller" details? How does it show this relationship?[6]

---

[6] Merle Prunty and Bertha Davis, *This Favored Land,* 2d ed. (New York: Macmillan, 1974). (Adapted)

SENSING CAUSE AND EFFECT

In each of the following situations, decide whether the price of the product is likely to (1) go *up*, (2) go *down*, or (3) stay the *same*. If unable to tell, give reasons for your answer.

A. Nearly one-third of the Florida nurseries are out of production because of citrus canker. There is no remedy for citrus canker. The only way to save the state's 761,000 acres of trees is to burn every contaminated tree, leaf, and twig. This disaster comes just as growers were beginning to recover from last year's killer freeze. How does this affect the price of oranges?

B. Scientists are not sure why the El Nino condition occurs. For unexplained reasons, the warm ocean currents of the tropics move in a northerly direction along the west coast of North America. The warmer water temperature, even though slight, is harmful to the food chain of certain marine animals. Thus, clams and crabs were nearly wiped out along parts of the west coast. Even the life cycle of the salmon was affected by El Nino. How does this affect the price of Alaskan king crab?

C. The United Automobile Workers union announced that is was ready to sign the contract offer made by General Motors. This ensures that a strike will not take place in the auto industry this year. Under the terms of the contract, management agreed to hold its profits to the same level as last year. How will this affect the price of cars?

D. The surgeon general's office announced today that there was a clear link between "the product" and cancer in laboratory animals. The surgeon general was advising against the use of "the product," particularly by young adults, until further tests could be made on human subjects. How will this affect the price of "the product"?

PREDICTING OUTCOMES

In a medium-sized city, a large company needed to hire 1,500 more workers. Would the population of the city increase by 1,500 or by more than that number? How can you tell? What problems would such a city face in taking care of this many people?

LOCATING AND USING REFERENCE MATERIALS

Children should make use of a wide variety of reference material in studying social studies topics. The value of such references depends not only on their availability but also on the ability of the children to make use of them. The teacher's responsibility in this respect is, therefore, twofold: teaching children (1) which references to use for various purposes and (2) how to use the reference efficiently once it is found. These are continuing responsibilities of the social studies program and cannot be completely taught in any one grade or any one year. A beginning will be made in the primary grades, but the child will continue to extend and refine the ability to use references throughout high school, college, and in later life. Instruction usually will begin as soon as the child develops a degree of independence in reading.

The reference materials used in the social studies may be grouped meaningfully as follows:

BOOKS

Textbooks
Supplementary reading books
Picture books
Biographies
Historical fiction

SPECIAL REFERENCES

Encyclopedias
Maps and globes
Atlases
Dictionaries
World Almanac
Charts and graphs
Yearbooks
Legislative Manuals
Who's Who in America
Junior Book of Authors
Statesman's Yearbook
Computers

REFERENCE AIDS

Card catalog
The Reader's Guide
Bibliographies
COMCATS

MISCELLANEOUS MATERIALS

Advertisements
Magazines and periodicals
Recipes
City and telephone directories
Labels
Guidebooks and tour books
Letters and diaries
Travel folders
Postcards
Newspapers and news clippings
Comic books
Pictures
Schedules and timetables
Pamphlets and booklets (such as those from the information services of foreign countries, superintendent of documents, conservation departments, historical societies, art galleries)
Weather reports
Manufacturers' guarantees and warranties
Money, checks, coupons for premiums, receipts
Reviews, government documents

Much of the instruction given on the use of references will have to be specific to the particular resource used. For example, one uses the *World Almanac* differently from the way one uses an atlas or a tour book. Moreover, the references may be used at varying levels of sophistication. The library may be used by primary-grade children under teacher guidance to check out books, to look at magazines, or to have stories read to them whereas upper-grade children should be able to use the library independently, making use of the card catalog and locating books themselves. The use of the various references should be taught as the need for them arises in the social studies.

The following suggestions will be helpful:

LEARNING TO USE REFERENCES

In the Primary Grades

1. Acquaint the children with the school library, and provide pleasurable experiences for them with this facility by having them look through books, check out books, look at magazines, and have stories read to them. Enlist the help of the librarian if there is one.

2. Provide learning centers that are well stocked with easy reading and picture books related to the topic under study.

3. Make frequent use of references in the regular work of the classroom. This may mean comparing a seashell that a child has brought with the picture of one in the book of shells; finding out whether we eat the roots, stems, or leaves of broccoli; finding out about the different kinds of boats and their uses; and hundreds of other questions that children wonder about during the course of the unit. It is helpful to have an encyclopedia handy for this purpose. Not all children will be able to use it, but its presence and use by the teacher provide an excellent means of developing positive attitudes toward reference materials.

4. Identify the children who are progressing rapidly in reading and teach and encourage them to use references such as encyclopedias, magazines, pamphlets, and other material from which they can profit but that may be too complex for the rest of the class.

5. Give children experiences in helping to locate materials — finding appropriate pictures, stories, or sections of books that relate to the social studies topic.

6. Develop prerequisite competencies for the efficient use of a dictionary: alphabetical ordering, use of guide words, antonyms, synonyms, multiple meanings of words. Primary-grade children could make a class picture dictionary of social studies words and terms they encounter.

In the Middle and Upper Grades

1. Make certain that children know how to use the various parts of a book. (See pp. 233–234.)

2. Take time out to teach children how to use the library, card catalog, the *Reader's Guide,* and other aids for the purpose of locating information, including COMCATS.

3. Teach the various skills needed to use each of the special references: encyclopedia, *World Almanac,* atlas. Provide for practice as well as application in purposeful settings.

4. Plan social studies activities that require the use of a wide variety of references.

5. Have children browse through the library and other sources to locate material that is appropriate for the unit under study.

6. Teach children how to identify key words in using reference material. Children may know how to use the references but not know what to look for with regard to the information they are seeking.

7. Teach children how to use titles of books as guides to their content, and select books that are appropriate for the purpose.

SIDE ONE

Find Out for Yourself

(If you cannot do any one of these, look for a clue on SIDE TWO of this card.)

1. Find the article on "Safety" in the *World Book*.

2. Into how many sections is the article divided? _____

3. Skim through the article to find these two facts:

   a. Where do most accidents happen? _____

   b. What do the letters *UL* on electrical wiring and appliances stand

   for? _____

4. Suppose you heard that someone had been killed in an accident in his or her home but you did not know what kind of an accident it was. You would be right most of the time if you guessed that the accident was a

   _____ or a _____ or _____

5. Suppose you questioned the accuracy of this article. What is there about the article that might renew your confidence in its authority?

   _____

SIDE TWO

CLUES

1. Select volume S–Sn. Look for the article according to the alphabet.

2. See the "Outline" at the end of the article.

3. a. Look under the section "Safety/Home."
   b. Look under "Safety with Electricity."

4. What does the article say about the major causes of accidental deaths in the home?

   _____

   _____

   _____

5. What group critically reviewed the article?

   _____

   _____

   _____

   _____

FIGURE 9.1. An example of teacher-prepared task cards.

Skills needed to use references can be practiced and learned on an individual basis or by children in pairs using *task cards,* as is illustrated in Figure 9.1 on page 255.

If teachers regard the teaching of reading as something that is done in three small groups during the reading period and ignore the reading needs of children during the remainder of the school day, they may expect children to have many disappointing experiences reading social studies material. The feeling that children learn to read in the basic reading program and read to learn in the social studies, for example, is not an entirely correct concept of the relationship between these two processes. Actually, the two occur simultaneously; children improve their reading ability *as they read to learn.* Children can extend and improve their reading skills and abilities quite apart from the basic reading program as they use reading for a variety of purposes.

The following lesson shows how one teacher organized a research project for a sixth-grade class.

LESSON PLAN 13

Topic:	China today
Grade:	Six or seven
Time:	Ten class periods
Objectives:	Students will learn basic information about the People's Republic of China.
	Students will refine research and small-group skills.
Interest Building:	For several days as the class is reading the text's overview of China, invite students to bring to school other recently published materials about China (books, magazines, travel brochures). Display these in a learning center.
Lesson Development:	Preview the resources.
	Using the text and resources for inspiration, brainstorm a list of topics that would be suitable for small-group information gathering projects.
	Have a member of the class list the topics on a chart in the learning center. See Sample Chart on top of page 257.
	Divide the class into study groups of five children each.
	Study group assignment: Elect a leader. Meet, discuss, and agree on and sign up for a topic.

Decide on subtopics to study.

Use outline format for taking notes.

Organize report into an introduction, main body, and conclusion.

Prepare visuals. Some ideas include charts, graphs, time lines, and illustrations from resources.

Practice giving the oral report.

Assign report dates.

Give students a copy of each evaluation form. Discuss expectations. See Sample Evaluation Forms at bottom of this page.

Summary: Groups give their oral reports with each member contributing to the presentation. They field questions and comments from their audience.

People's Republic of China

Topics	Names of Group Members	Report Date
Family life and education		
Geography and natural resources		
Economy: Agriculture and industry		
Political system: Leaders and history		
Holidays and festivals		
Cities		
Tourism and transportation		
Arts and athletics		
Science and technology		

China Today Report: Teacher Evaluation

	Yes	No	Comments
Was an introduction used?			
Were the main ideas presented?			
Were supporting details given?			
Was there a clear conclusion?			
Were visuals used?			
Was teamwork evident?			
Group Grade: _____			

China Today Report: Group Evaluation

Topic: _____

What did you do well?

How could you have improved your report?

List the resources that you used.

Evaluation: Complete the evaluation forms. Base the group's grade on a consideration of both evaluations.

Collect each student's notes. Evaluate these on an individual basis.

Resources: Text: *World Neighbors*, Macmillan Publishing Company

Recommended trade books:

China, Here We Come! Tang Yungmei

Two Chinese Families, Catherine Edwards Sadler

Red Star & Green Dragon: Looking at New China, Lila Perl

The People's Republic of China: Red Star of the East, Jane Werner Watson

USING WRITING SKILLS IN SOCIAL STUDIES

The learning activities associated with social studies present many opportunities to teach all of the communication skills, not only reading. Children read for information and often share that newly gained knowledge through oral reports and in class discussions. In such interactions, they use speech and speaking skills, and, correspondingly, others are listening to what is being communicated. Or children may prepare written notes or reports on what they have read or heard. We see, therefore, that there is a constant and close relationship between and among the several language arts — reading, speaking, listening, writing — as skills that are essential to learning social studies. The reverse is also true; social studies presents excellent functional settings in which to teach such skills.

The elementary school curriculum often becomes fragmented with bits and pieces of subjects and skills that are not tied into an integrated organized framework. Moreover, subjects and skills such as writing, reading, spelling, and listening often become make-believe exercises when they are taught in isolation, outside of a subject matter context. How much more meaningful these skills become for a learner when they are taught in purposeful settings. The child is then reading to find out something of importance to the subject under study. Or the child is writing something that will be shared with others as a contribution to knowledge about a topic. With greater attention to the inclusion of important communication skills in the units planned for social studies, the teaching of social studies *and* the language arts would be improved. We have discussed this subject as related to one component of the language arts, namely, reading; now let us direct our attention to writing skills.

Whereas reading has to do with the use of coded symbols to intake

The teacher here is checking the final draft of an essay dealing with the life of Dr. Martin Luther King, Jr. for the student. This eighth-grade project combined the study of history with art and creative writing. Students focused on the historical, social, and political events of Dr. King's life. They created montages based on their study and prepared compositions on some aspect of his life. The teacher, Beth Ashley, commented that "The integration of language arts and history has improved writing." (Photo by Sylvia Soholt, Lake Washington School District.)

ideas and feelings, writing reverses the process. Nonetheless, there is a reciprocal relationship between the two skills. One always reads what has already been written. One writes something with the expectation that either the writer or someone else will read what has been written. In addition to the skills associated with the mechanics of writing, such as capitalization, spelling, punctuation, and handwriting, Chart 8 lists writing skills that can and should be taught within the context of social studies.

CHART 8. WRITING ABILITIES AND SKILLS RELATED TO SOCIAL STUDIES

- Note-taking.
- Letter writing.
- Organizing and outlining.
- Preparing written reports.
- Record keeping.
- Summarizing ideas in writing.
- Preparing notices, announcements, advertisements.
- Expanding written vocabulary.
- Completing routine forms, for example, checks, deposit slips, applications, order blanks, library slips.
- Writing creative material, for example, poems, stories, plays.

Writing skill is developed when the individual engages in a considerable amount of writing and is provided instructive and supportive feedback on what is written. In short, writing requires practice with the intent to improve. Therefore, if the only writing children do in the social studies consists of filling in single words or short phrases in workbooks or work sheets, one cannot expect much progress in any of the important writing skills identified in the foregoing paragraph. Accordingly, the teacher must involve children in social studies-related writing assignments as a regular part of the work of the class. Such writing tasks need to be appropriate to the developmental level of the children.

Simply providing the *opportunity* for children to write is not in itself enough to develop writing habits and skills. They also need instruction, and they need to be motivated. Writing is often drudgery because the individual does not know how to go about doing it or has no inclination to want to do it or both. Consequently, school writing assignments frequently stifle writing abilities rather than encourage them. Teachers who have taught writing successfully create an environment or climate that places high value on writing and makes it seem an exciting adventure for young learners. A few techniques that have been used successfully by teachers follow.

Techniques That Make Writing Easier

1. List and post difficult, technical words that students might find useful in their writing.
2. Use imaginative springboards to encourage creative writing. For example (1) write a story about a pioneer girl, a pony, and a snowstorm; (2) keep a one-month diary of a newly arrived immigrant child; (3) describe how you ordered breakfast in a restaurant in a country where no one knew how to speak your language; (4) write what happened to you when you were lost in a large city. One teacher was able to get excellent creative written work from children by having them complete the following stem: "When Nancy wore her flour-sack dress as a child, never in her wildest dreams did she . . ."
3. Have students list main ideas about a topic. Have them order the ideas sequentially. Then have them write three more sentences about each main idea.
4. Remind children of forms and skills already learned (indenting paragraphs, using exclamation marks, using quotation marks for conversations, and so on).
5. Provide opportunities for children to share their written work with others and display it on the bulletin board.
6. Demonstrate writing skills through the use of group activity.
7. Use word games to develop more elaborate vocabulary—rhyming words, synonyms, antonyms, "happy" words, "sad" words, night sounds, city noises, and so on.
8. Develop and encourage children to use self-evaluating checklists.
9. Have children respond to questions that ask for an out-of-the ordinary answer. For example, after examining a portrait, ask, "What mineral do the eyes remind you of?" Or "Does the mouth tell you anything about this person?" In studying situations or photographs, such questions as these could be asked: "What colors do you think of when you see this (or smells, sounds, and so on)?" Or "Write a story about the Pilgrims from the point of view of the Indians." Or "Describe Columbus' place in history if there had been no North or South America."

Writing Activities for Social Studies

The best writing activities for social studies are those that children do within the context of what they are studying. Writing assignments take on a sense of importance and purpose when they are needed as a part of the process of achieving other objectives. A letter written to obtain information, for example, is likely to be more meaningful than is a make-believe letter written to a fictitious person. Thus, insofar as possible, writing activities in social studies should be functionally related to the classwork.

The activities on the following list have been used by elementary and middle school teachers who have successfully related the teaching of writing skills to social studies:

1. Write endings to reaction stories or situations in which the outcome is in doubt.
2. Prepare a classroom newsletter or newspaper.
3. Prepare an original script for dramatization.
4. Maintain a class or personal diary ("Today I learned how to jump rope." "Today I lost a tooth." "Today we had a visitor from China.")
5. Prepare outlines or notes for an oral report.
6. Prepare captions for pictures, illustrations, exhibits, cartoons.
7. Write explanations of events or exhibits or after a field trip.
8. Make holiday greeting cards, and write appropriate messages.
9. Write letters requesting information or material or both, letters inviting visitors to the classroom, thank-you letters, and get-well messages to classmates and teachers.
10. Create "news" stories about historical events; create descriptive headlines for historical events.
11. Keep minutes of meetings.
12. Write directions for doing something, such as making soap, reading a chart, or operating a machine.
13. Take notes from several different sources for use in a discussion.
14. Take notes while listening to a speaker.
15. Organize material, and prepare a written report for others to read.
16. Make lists of things studied, for example, rice, cocoa, oranges.
17. List questions during study period.
18. Label items on maps.
19. Write answers to questions.
20. Summarize ideas into topic sentences to be developed into paragraphs.
21. Prepare short annotations of trade books used in social studies.
22. Write a script for a tape-recorded program.
23. Write a short history of the school and the community.
24. List words that describe particularly well some event or period.
25. Write a poem to express feelings about a topic or period studied.
26. Write entries in a diary that might have been kept by an explorer or a pioneer.
27. Prepare maps of various types, and write accompanying explanations.
28. Write book reviews.
29. Write a short story based on subject matter studied in social studies.
30. Write a letter home as it might have been written by a member of the Lewis and Clark Expedition.

LESSON PLAN 14

Topic:	Members of our community
Grade:	Three or four
Time:	Two class periods
Objectives:	To reinforce the value of consideration for others.
	To learn how to write thank-you letters.
Interest Building:	The class was invited to and visited a senior center for the purpose of seeing a display of crafts prepared by the members. The experience was a positive one for the children, and the teacher has suggested that they prepare and send thank-you letters.
Lesson Development:	Ask children to brainstorm what they *liked* about their visit and what they *learned* from their experience. List these, in separate columns, on the chalkboard and save.
	Explain that thank-you letters are an appropriate way to express gratitude for visits, hospitality, and so on, and that is how each member of the class will thank the senior citizens.
	Review letter format.
	Distribute the assignment sheet in the form of a letter for the class to use as a reference. Review it with them. See Sample letter on page 264.
	Children write first draft of individual letters.
	Make corrections as needed.
	Children write final drafts of letters.
	Send letters.

DISCUSSION QUESTIONS AND SUGGESTED ACTIVITIES

1. If social studies textbooks are written for the average reader, why is it that all good social studies textbooks tend to be difficult for the average reader?

2. Select a children's social studies text, and examine it to find examples of the reading skills listed in Chart 4, page 228.

3. Select a children's textbook, and provide sample exercises based on the points made in the section entitled "Using Study Aids and Study Skills to Improve Reading."

4. Using the text you selected in your answer to question 3, find examples of the social studies words and terms listed on page 240.

5. Select a passage from a children's social studies textbook, and develop comprehension questions as is done on pages 299–301. Develop an equal number of interpretive-type questions.

6. What reference books do you believe are the most useful to children? Why do you think so?

7. Pick a social studies topic for a grade of your choice. Make a list of

January 8, 1989

Dear Member of Room 10,

    Your assignment is to write a thank-you letter to our friends at the Forest Park Center. Remember to include one thing you liked about the visit and one thing you learned. Your paragraph should be at least five sentences long. Please hand your rough draft in by Friday.

                      Sincerely,

                      Mrs. K.

P.S. Your letter may be longer if you wish.

poems, stories, biographies, and other reading sources that develop a strong mental set or mood appropriate to the topic. Read selected passages to your classmates.

8. Choose one of the references listed on page 253. What prerequisite skills must the child have in order to use that reference effectively and efficiently?

9. Prepare a lesson plan for social studies that incorporates the teaching of a related writing skill.

10. How might the teaching of writing be linked to a lesson designed to teach improved reading comprehension? Provide an example of such a lesson.

SELECTED REFERENCES

BECK, ISABEL L., MARGARET G. MCKEOWN, AND ELLEN S. MCCASLIN. "Vocabulary Development: All Contexts Are Not Created Equal." *The Elementary School Journal,* 83 (January 1983), pp. 171–181.

GARCIA, JESUS, AND JOHN W. LOGAN. "Teaching Social Studies Using Basal Readers." *Social Education,* 47 (November–December 1983), pp. 533–535.

HENNINGS, DOROTHY GRANT. *Teaching Communication and Reading Skills in the Content Areas.* Bloomington, Indiana: Phi Delta Kappa, 1982.

HERMAN, PATRICIA A., AND JANICE DOLE. "Theory and Practice in Vocabulary Learning and Instruction." *The Elementary School Journal,* 89 (September 1988), pp. 43–54.

LAMBERG, WALTER J., AND CHARLES E. LAMB. *Reading Instruction in the Content Areas.* Chicago: Rand McNally, 1980. Chapter 12.

NELMS, BEN F. "Response and Responsibility: Reading, Writing, and Social Studies." *The Elementary School Journal,* 87 (May 1987), pp. 571–589.

PARKER, WALTER, AND SAMUEL A. PEREZ. "Beyond the Rattle of Empty Wagons." *Social Education,* 51 (March 1987), pp. 164–166.

SCHNEIDER, DONALD O., AND MARY JO MCGEE BROWN. "Helping Students Study and Comprehend Their Social Studies Textbooks." *Social Education,* 44 (February 1980), pp. 105–112.

SQUIRE, JAMES R. "Language Concepts for Application to Social Studies." *Social Education,* 46 (October 1982), pp. 442–443.

III

Planning and Teaching the Social Studies

10

Preparing Teaching Plans for the Social Studies

Few teachers can plan and teach social studies completely on their own, unencumbered by forces beyond their own specific situation. In most cases, planning and teaching are influenced by a variety of factors, agencies, and organizations at the national, state, and local levels.

In the United States, education is legally under the jurisdiction of the various states. School programs, therefore, are not subject to the scrutiny and supervision of the federal government. Nonetheless, social studies education is influenced at the national level by federal social or fiscal legislation (or both), by projects funded by the Department of Education that may encourage certain procedures or emphases, by textbook and standardized test authors and their publishers who sell to a national market, and by national lay organizations whose special interests are aligned with social studies education. In the 1980s, the reports of several national commissions and study groups that surveyed the status of American education have been influential in shaping the policies and directions of education. National professional associations also speak to the nature of the social studies curriculum of the schools.

The largest and most significant professional association for social studies is the National Council for the Social Studies. This organization has given leadership and direction to social studies planning at the national level. Its committees study problems relating to the social studies on a continuing basis. Its journals, *Social Education* and *Social Studies and the Young Learner,* and its numerous other publications have been widely circulated and have proved to be valuable aids to teachers and curriculum planners. Membership in the National Council for the Social Studies is open to anyone who has an interest in any of the facets of the social studies at any teaching level.

State governments have the legal responsibility for directing educational programs of public schools. Typically, one finds certain curricular requirements relating to social studies in state education codes. These range from mandating the teaching of United States history and the Constitution to requiring the observance of state Admission Day. State education agencies often have a state framework for social studies that provides guidance to local districts in developing a philosophy and rationale, selecting subject matter for various grade levels (scope and sequence), recommending teaching procedures, and selecting instructional materials. In practice, state agencies have delegated much of their responsibility for education to local school districts.

Much choice making in curriculum is left to local districts. The feeling that the schools belong to the people of the local community and that schools should serve local needs has long been fundamental to educational planning in this country. Social studies programs must be tailored to the experience and background of children who live in a specific attendance area. State and national influences presumably ensure attention to common societal goals that are necessary for national unity; local influences should ensure that the children living in the area are well served by the social studies program.

As teachers design social studies programs, they should not be unmindful of the influences at the national, state, and local levels. It is helpful, for example, for the teacher to be familiar with the social studies guidelines and position statements published by the National Council for the Social Studies. Likewise, the teacher ought to know what is required by the state framework for social studies. The teacher should consult the local curriculum guide before the planning process begins.

TYPES OF TEACHING PLANS

In most instances, the school district will supply a curriculum guide, a list of suggested topics, a curriculum framework, a textbook, or some directive that provides the teacher with guidance as to which topics or units

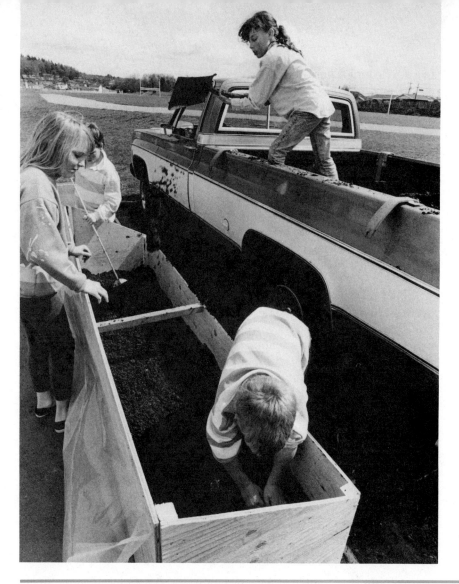

Teaching plans should provide for the integration of other subjects and skills with social studies. Here we see students preparing a solar greenhouse in connection with their social studies/science unit. (Photo by Robb Mitchell, Tacoma School District.)

are to be included in the curriculum. Often teachers can exercise limited choices within the established guidelines. It is not uncommon to find some topics required, some optional, and perhaps some to be chosen by the teacher. A teacher must be familiar with district policy in order to plan appropriately.

Thorough planning will not ensure successful teaching, but it will do much to give the teacher a margin of confidence that will enhance the possibility of more effective teaching. Many experienced teachers make use of three types of plans for the social studies: (1) unit plans; (2) short-range plans focused on a single topic, main idea, or skill; and (3) daily plans. The long-range plan, usually referred to as a *unit* or a *unit of work,* covers a period of six to ten weeks, during which time the class studies some broad topic on an ongoing basis. The unit plan is a way of organizing materials and activities for such an extended study. A unit might be thought of as a *depth study.* The following are examples of topics that would be suitable for parcels of work called *units:*

Living in Our Community
Families Around the World
The Exciting World of Lewis and Clark
The World of the Big City
Life in Early America
The Middle East — Crossroads of Cultures

Not all social studies instruction needs to be organized around comprehensive units of the type described. Many topics can be dealt with in a time span of no more than a week or two. These can often be sandwiched in between the larger units. Such topics, which call for short-range plans, might be organized around subject matter that is timely or is of especial relevance to a class. They might consist of unconventional subjects or topics on which there is not an abundance of learning resources for children to use. The following are examples of topics suitable for such shorter blocks of work:

Winners and Losers in the Election
Danger Spots in Our Home
Caring for Pets
Getting Information from Maps
Workers and Their Wages
Getting Your Money's Worth
Who Is the Me I See?

It is also possible to plan a large unit of work as a series of sequentially related miniunits of the type described here. When this is done, however, the teacher will want to provide some ongoing activities in order to give continuity to the larger study.

The third type of teaching plan is that which the teacher actually uses in doing the teaching. It is what is usually called a "daily lesson plan" and is really the teacher's "trip map" through the lesson. Such plans should extend and continue the instruction from one class session to the next. Naturally, these specific teaching plans are developed within the context of the more extended unit of study. Separate and discrete plans that do not tie into some larger framework are not recommended because of the resulting fragmentation of the topics studied. Plans should move the process of learning sequentially and continuously over a period of time.

Textbook-Based Plans

A textbook-based plan is one that is developed in advance by the teacher, who often relies on the textbook or other curriculum documents in determining the nature and content of the program. If children help in the planning, they do so minimally and usually in matters that do not alter the basic content and emphasis. That is, they might exercise some choice concerning individual activities to be performed but would not suggest alternative topics to be studied. Reliance on the textbook as the prime information source is complete. Variations in requirements to accommodate learner differences would include varying the lengths of assignments or varying the amount of time needed to complete them. All children deal with the same basic subject matter.

If we follow a teacher through the steps in planning and teaching social studies in this way, we would observe the following:

THE TEACHER

1. Surveys the text to find out which units are included and decides how to apportion the amount of time available to each one. The recommendations of the textbook authors may be used in making these decisions.
2. Studies the teacher's guide accompanying the text to find out how the program is organized and what major goals and objectives are stressed. These goals and objectives may be accepted as appropriate for the program.
3. Uses the teacher's guide for teaching plans and learner activities.
4. Uses additional resources and activities for enrichment, for extension of learning, and for individualizing learning. Some of these are suggested by the teacher's guide, including those provided by the publisher of the text series as supplementary materials such as workbooks or ''blackline'' ditto masters.
5. Evaluates learnings as suggested by the text and teacher's guide, focusing mainly on informational learnings, basic concepts, and related skills.
6. Uses formal teaching procedures consisting mainly of question and answer, some discussion, an occasional pupil report, and map making; there is infrequent use of drama, art, music, or construction activities.

Topic or Subject-Oriented Plans

A planning approach based on a topic or subject has some of the same characteristics as the one just discussed, but the reliance on the text is not as complete, more of the teacher's influence is apparent, and it is not so thoroughly preplanned and teacher-directed. Children are more involved in planning, and there is greater use of a wide range of instructional materials and activities. The formality that characterizes the textbook-based approach is missing. Learners feel freer to voice their own opinions and views on issues. Interactions are more along the lines of discussion as opposed to question-and-answer procedures. The teacher is sensitive to the individuality of children and provides for variations in ability and motivation. Children may be involved in expressive activities such as construction, art, music, role playing, and simulation games. This is not an altogether child-centered approach, yet it is not one that is wholly teacher-directed either.

If we follow a teacher through the steps in planning and teaching in this way, we would observe the following:

THE TEACHER

1. Examines the curriculum guide and the textbook to find out what topics and units are expected to be included in the program.
2. Establishes broad goals and objectives for the year; takes into consideration those suggested by the curriculum guide and textbook teacher's guide, but makes his or her own.
3. Tentatively selects topics to be studied; consults the teacher's guide and curriculum guide in this process, selects some that are suggested, omits others, and adds some. These topics may be modified as the program develops and as learner interests and capabilities are better known.
4. Decides on the sequence of units selected, time allotment for each, taking into account holidays, seasons of the year, and so forth.
5. Uses some teaching suggestions from the teacher's guide and curriculum guide but develops many of his or her own ideas for learning activities and teaching procedures.
6. Develops and uses learning packets, self-paced materials, learning centers, and learner contracts; also, individualizes learning through use of small groups.
7. Plans for and uses many instructional resources in addition to the textbook. This includes pictures, packets, library books, films, filmstrips, recordings, and artifacts.
8. Uses a variety of informal evaluative techniques and devices such as discussion, observation, student conferences, teacher-made tests, checklists, and experience summaries.
9. Maintains a relaxed instructional pace but stays close to teacher-learner planned treatment of the topic.

Child-Centered Plans

Some teachers prefer to plan the social studies program cooperatively with children, deriving the subject matter and skills from the interests and concerns of the children. Although it requires considerable preplanning by the teacher, the program itself is not structured in advance, as are the other two approaches that have been discussed. Study units and learner experiences are planned jointly by the teacher and the children in terms of their interests and backgrounds. Thus, the unit emerges under the guidance of the teacher, who relies on learner initiative and interest. Children help decide what they will study. They raise questions about the information they are interested in getting and search out relevant sources. They plan ways of working, activities in which they will engage, and ways of sharing ideas with one another. Children are encouraged to become involved in assuming responsibility for what they are to learn and how they will go about learning it. The boundaries between the various school subjects and skills are blurred; indeed, the social studies units may serve as the integrating center for the total elementary school curriculum.

If we follow a teacher through the steps in planning and teaching in this way, we will observe the following:

THE TEACHER

1. Formulates broad goals and objectives for the year in terms of anticipated social and intellectual development of the children.
2. Studies learner backgrounds; develops an awareness of the social milieu from which children come.
3. Prepares motivating or facilitating questions dealing with social issues and topics to arouse learner interest.
4. Provides books, artifacts, displays, visuals, construction materials, and other items to generate interest and curiosity.
5. Encourages children to suggest topics for study and to suggest possible questions and problems for exploration.
6. Guides children in exploratory information searches.
7. Assists children in developing an in-depth study of topics and problems selected; plans are refined and/or modified as the study progresses.
8. Individualizes the program in accordance with learner interest and ability using interest centers, individual study contracts, individual study materials, projects, and activities.
9. Closely relates social studies work to reading, language arts, mathematics, science, art, music, and drama.

PLANNING INSTRUCTIONAL UNITS

One must conclude from the foregoing discussion that the way units are planned and taught varies greatly from one teacher to another. For one, the unit may be no more than a chapter or a section of the textbook that deals with a single topic. For another teacher, the unit may be a comprehensive study that incorporates subjects, skills, and activities from all the rest of the school curriculum. One teacher may structure the unit in advance by thorough preplanning; another may plan the unit as the study evolves. Two teachers working on an identical topic at the same grade level may have their classes deal quite differently with it. The same teacher might handle the same topic differently with different groups of children. What follows is a description of the essential components of a comprehensive unit plan. The reader should understand, however, that a great deal of individual teacher judgment and decision making go into the planning and teaching of social studies units.

Making a Survey of Available Instructional Resources

If a school district includes particular topics in the social studies curriculum, it will ordinarily provide the necessary instructional resources. The amount of such resources that are available will vary, however, from no more than a basic textbook to a generous amount and variety of multimedia. As an initial step in planning, the teacher should inventory the availability and the adequacy of learning resources for the unit to be studied. What the teacher finds will have a direct bearing on how the unit will be planned. Whereas instructional materials should not entirely determine the social studies program, the availability of essential instructional resources necessarily affects the teacher's planning.

Much difficulty is avoided in securing and using instructional materials when teachers plan well in advance what they will need. Books, recordings, pictures, films, and filmstrips must be requested early enough to ensure their arrival at the time they are needed. Usually, instructional resources must be ordered, reserved, or even secured before the unit begins.

Establishing Objectives

Social studies instruction is almost always concerned with the attainment of multiple objectives. Facts, concepts, generalizations, principles, and general knowledge are derived from the encounter with the subject matter. Skills are learned during the process of study, including many of those discussed on pages 7–8 in Chapter 1. Affective outcomes deal with attitudes, values, and feelings that are important in studying most social studies topics. It is not likely that all the outcomes of a study will be formally defined by the teacher. Many outcomes are realized as side effects, meaning fortuitous learnings or unpredicted extensions of learnings associated with the unit.

We restrict our attention here to those few objectives that the teacher singles out for special attention. These are objectives that the teacher perceives to be the major purposes of the study. Our concern is not with those serendipitous outcomes that emerge as children read, interact with their teachers and with each other, prepare and give reports, and engage in various other activities. This is not to say that these latter outcomes are not important, only that it is not possible to know what they are to be in advance of the study.

Instructional objectives should be stated in ways that make clear what children are supposed to *learn.* This will enable the teacher and the learners to see more clearly how instructional activities relate to the purposes of the study. Insufficient clarity of objectives is likely to lead to the performance of activities that have neither purpose nor meaning. It makes little sense for teachers and children to try to solve a problem when no one seems to know what the problem is.

Objectives may be framed as broad, general statements that describe what it is the children are expected to learn. The following are examples, selected from several different units, of such descriptive objectives:

AS A RESULT OF A STUDY OF THIS UNIT CHILDREN WILL

- Learn the use of simple research skills associated with gathering information.
- Understand that certain basic needs must be satisfied if human life is to be sustained.
- Realize that decisions are based on one's value orientation.
- Learn to work in small groups, respecting the rights and feelings of others.
- Understand the interdependent relationship between geographical regions.
- Develop the skill of orienting a map to directions.
- Gain a knowledge of vocabulary associated with the legal system.
- Learn how advertising aids both the consumer and the producer.
- Learn to formulate and test causal hypotheses relating to community development.

These examples would provide purpose and direction for a study. Many teachers are comfortable with descriptive objectives of this type. Although they are general, they are, nonetheless, specific enough to communicate what the main concerns of the study are to be. Such objectives need further clarification, but most teachers prefer to make these statements more specific and explicit at the time the material is actually taught.

Another way to state objectives is in terms of specific observable learner behavior. Such statements are referred to as *behavioral objectives.* Prior to the time the instruction takes place, the teacher frames statements of expected student performances that are predicted to occur as a result of the proposed learning experience. These predicted performances are so precisely stated that their achievement could readily be assessed by an objective observer.

In order to achieve this degree of precision, teachers must use language that leaves no doubt as to what is wanted. Verbals such as "to comprehend," "to know," "to realize" are not well suited for this purpose because they do not specify what the learners are *doing* that would convince an impartial observer that the children do, indeed, "comprehend," "know," or "realize." Stems that are more suitable for behavioral objectives are these:

to name	to explain why
to choose	to identify
to illustrate	to cite
to provide examples	to define
to write	to locate
to place in order	to use

Examples of behavioral objectives are these:

AS A RESULT OF A STUDY OF THIS UNIT CHILDREN WILL BE ABLE TO

- Identify four different types of structures people use for homes.
- Provide five examples of consumer fraud.
- Locate a specific reference book in the library.
- List the main ideas in a passage of social studies prose.
- Show that they know how to use the index to find factual material in the textbook.
- Match causes and effects in an exercise relating to labor-management conflicts.
- Define the essential characteristics of the concept *region*.

The use of behavioral objectives has accompanied the growing concern for accountability in education. Advocates of behavioral objectives claim that such objectives encourage precision in teaching and learning by focusing on observable learner performance. They would argue that unless the child can actually do something to show what has been learned, that one can only speculate about whether or not learning has taken place. They argue, further, that unless the teacher can define what is to be learned in terms of the child's intellectual or physical behavior, it cannot be assumed that learning has actually occurred. The issue boils down to the question, "What can the child *do* that he or she could not do prior to the instruction?" In this framework, it is learner behavior that provides convincing evidence that intended learning has or has not taken place.

Those who do not favor the use of behavioral objectives say that many significant outcomes of social studies instruction, or any instruction, for that matter, do not lend themselves well to behavioral definition. For example, who can say precisely what happens to a child while reading an exciting account of life on the frontier? How does one define such learning behaviorally? Should it be the same for all learners? Besides, there is the question of whether or not such a degree of precision serves any useful purpose. Another argument against the use of behavioral objectives is that the practice encourages the narrowing of the instruction to those objectives that can easily be defined behaviorally, thereby neglecting other important learnings that cannot be so defined or that are difficult to manage in behavioral terms. Additionally, opponents claim that the use of behavioral objectives tends to fragment the social studies curriculum into bits and pieces of content and skills rather than to encourage the integration of learnings into larger wholes.

Perhaps there is a midposition that suggests a limited use of behavioral objectives for those components of social studies that lend themselves well to definition in terms of observable learner performance. For example, certain work-study skills would be of this type — reading maps, using references, gathering data, interpreting graphs and charts, reading for a specific purpose. Some content-related objectives can also be stated behaviorally, such as arranging events in a sequence, relating effects to causes, drawing a conclusion based on data, providing examples and nonexamples of concepts, and so on. In the case of social, intellectual, or affective learnings that cannot be easily defined behaviorally, the teacher may want to state instructional objectives in descriptive terms as illustrated by the examples on page 277. The types of objectives used will depend on local requirements and on teacher preference. Because there are philosophical differences among competent professionals as to the appropriateness of behavioral objectives, this is an issue that individual teachers will need to resolve for themselves.

Whatever form the teacher uses to state objectives, it is important to stress that the objectives should indicate clearly what it is the children are *expected to learn*, not what they will do. For example, the following are *not* appropriate instructional objectives because they simply describe procedures and activities that will be used by the children presumably to learn something that remains undefined:

The children will view a film.
The class will work in small committees.
The children will draw a map of the local area.
The class will discuss individual projects.
Children will make a model of a harbor.
Children will role-play workers in a shopping center.

Selecting and Organizing the Subject Matter

When teachers are asked what they are doing in social studies, they often respond by naming the title of the unit or topic under study, as for example, "We are studying Japan (or Canada, Mexico, the Community, and so forth)." The presumption is that this response will communicate the nature of the study. The fact is, however, that the title or topic of a unit tells us little about the focus of the study, the concepts being developed, the relationships being established, or the conclusions reached, if any. Any topic can be studied from several different perspectives. Part of the task of organizing subject matter, therefore, deals with establishing the focus of the study and determining which particular main ideas and concepts will receive priority.

Many social studies programs and most of the modern textbook series organize subject matter around basic ideas from history and the social science disciplines. These are usually called major generalizations, basic concepts, key ideas, or other similar designations, depending on the preference of the district. Examples of such ideas are listed in earlier chapters of this text where the disciplines are discussed.

There is some variation in school district policies, but typically elementary and middle school teachers have only a limited amount of freedom in selecting the subjects and topics to be included in the social studies curriculum. Topics and units are either designated by the school district curriculum guide or the district has adopted a textbook series that pretty much determines the subject matter and skills to be included. Teachers do, however, have a considerable amount of latitude in deciding how those topics will be developed and what ideas will be singled out for emphasis. It is those ideas that really determine the specific subject matter. An example will illustrate how this comes about.

Let us say that the fifth-grade curriculum guide calls for a unit on Canada. The guide also indicates what the emphasis is to be and the major generalizations that are to provide a focus for this unit:

CANADA: LAND GIANT OF THE WESTERN HEMISPHERE

This unit should provide children with a comprehensive view of Canada as it is today. This does not mean that historical information will be excluded, but simply that the stress is to be interdisciplinary with an emphasis on contemporary life. The unit should treat Canada as a whole rather than focus on a particular small sample of Canadian life and culture. Whereas the similarities between the United States and Canada should be studied, it is important to present Canada as a nation distinguished by its own nationality and culture. Some emphasis must be placed on how it is different from the United States. The long-standing tradition of cordial relations between the United States and Canada should also be stressed. The following generalizations should emerge as a result of the study of Canada:

1. The physical features of an area influence settlement patterns and transportation routes. (geography)
2. Maintaining an ethnic identity is important to most members of a cultural group. (anthropology)
3. The use of available resources depends on the nature of the economic system, the values of people, and their level of technology. (economics)
4. The early history of a country has a definite bearing on the present culture of its people. (history)

How does the teacher go about selecting subject matter about Canada that will be in accord with the focus suggested by the curriculum guide?

One option available to the teacher is simply to teach whatever is included in the children's textbook. If the textbook treatment is in harmony with the focus suggested and the teacher makes enlightened use of the books, this is not an altogether undesirable procedure. We would like to think, however, that the teacher will be able to develop a more imaginative approach and, in the process, make better use of the text and other learning resources that are available.

The basic question here is this: What is it that children are expected to learn about Canada that is consistent with the suggested emphasis? Or, what are the main ideas about Canada that will receive attention in this unit?

In order to respond to this question, the teacher should do some self-study with the thought of selecting six to eight major ideas to be included in the unit. The public library, *The World Almanac*, encyclopedias, and the instructional materials in the classroom can be used for this purpose. Let us assume that the teacher has done this research and decides that the following *main ideas* will be developed in the unit:

1. Canada is a country with a unique northern geographic location.
2. Canada is a large, regionally divided, and diverse country.
3. Canada is a highly industrialized and technologically advanced country.
4. Canada is an urbanized country, rapidly becoming a nation of city dwellers.
5. Canada is an exposed country, open to a multitude of external cultural, economic, and political influences.
6. Canada is a multiethnic country with two predominant linguistic groups.[1]

After the teacher has selected the main ideas, such as those listed here, it is possible to identify the essential related concepts and the specific subject matter, as shown by Chart 9, page 282.

[1] CONTACT, No. 60, Canada Studies Foundation, 252 Bloor Street West, Suite 3-390, Toronto, Ontario M5S IV5, Canada. December 1983.

CHART 9. ESSENTIAL COGNITIVE ELEMENTS OF A UNIT ON CANADA

Main Ideas	Essential Concepts	Subject Matter Synopsis
1. Canada is a country with a unique northern geographic location.	Arctic Latitude Coastline Heartland Natural boundary Political boundary	Location and size of Canada along with its dominant physical features, unique natural regions, and climatic characteristics; population distribution; location in terms of other nations of the Northern Hemisphere
2. Canada is a large, regionally divided, and diverse country.	Regionalism Prairie Maritime Offshore Province	Brief history of Canadian development; political and natural regions; occupations of its people; regionalism as a social, economic, and political factor in Canadian life
3. Canada is a highly industrialized and technologically advanced country.	Natural resources Minerals Raw materials Technological change	Development of Canadian resources for export and domestic use; rise of Canadian industry; transportation and communication systems in Canada
4. Canada is an urbanized country, rapidly becoming a nation of city dwellers.	Metropolitan area Trading center Manufacturing center Urban environment	Move toward urbanism with cities gaining in their influence over the lives of all Canadians; problems associated with urban sprawl and urban renewal: Toronto, a case study
5. Canada is an exposed country, open to a multitude of external cultural, economic, and political influences.	Foreign investment Nationalism Cultural influence	Influence of foreign investments in Canadian industry and agriculture; the American presence; cultural influences from the States; influence of immigration on Canadian development
6. Canada is a multiethnic country with two predominant linguistic groups.	Ethnic group Bilingual Bicultural Heritage Minority Cultural mosaic	Historical background of Canadian bilingualism; effect of bicultural life on social, political, and economic decision making; status of native people in Canada

Thus far we have discussed subject matter selection only in terms of informational outcomes — that is, cognitive objectives. But what about skills, attitudes, and values? How do they fit into the picture? Objectives that deal with skills, attitudes, and values are structured around the subject matter, too, and are developed concurrently with informational objectives. Unless the curriculum guide specifically indicates which skills, attitudes, and values are to receive attention — and usually it does not — the matter is left to the judgment of the teacher.

In the example of Canada, it is reasonable that map and globe skills would be a necessary part of Main Ideas numbers 1 and 2. All the main ideas will require information searches that will provide a way to teach and apply research and inquiry skills. The teacher will doubtless plan activities that require the children to use group-work skills. Attitudinal outcomes can hardly be ignored because the curriculum guide states explicitly, "The long-standing tradition of cordial relations between the United States and Canada should also be stressed." Values will come into the study as children begin to examine the trade-offs involved in Canada's becoming an urbanized country, exploiting its resources, assimilating its native people, and maintaining an official bicultural position.

The use of a planning format such as the one shown in Figure 10.1 on page 284 can be helpful for the coordination of information, skills, attitudes, and values objectives. The essential point is that it is around the basic subject matter that all these objectives are achieved. If a careful job is done in completing the four cells above the double line (Figure 10.1) for each of the main ideas included in the unit, the task of selecting resources and activities will be made easier.

Beginning the Study

Building and sustaining the interest of children in a topic are continuing responsibilities of the teacher, but are especially important when beginning a new unit of study. This involves more than simply getting started. It requires arousing the curiosity of the youngsters, exploring some of the possibilities for study presented by the topic, and, in general, setting the stage for learning to take place. In advance of the time the unit is actually undertaken, the teacher should post material in the room that will arouse interest in the anticipated study, and the relationship of the new topic to previous work should be indicated. There should be books and other appropriate materials in the room through which the children may browse. Materials can be brought to class that stimulate the thinking of the children. All these activities and others, which the imaginative teacher will use, serve to create interest and will help cause the children to want to learn more about the topic. Through procedures such as these,

SOCIAL STUDIES UNIT PLANNING

Unit Title _____ Date _____

Main Idea to Be Developed:	Related Skills:	Related Attitudes and Values:	Questions to Stimulate Reflective Thinking:
Key Concepts and Terms:			

Text References:	Oral and Written Language Activities:	Dramatic Activities:	Construction Activities:
Supplementary References:			
Audiovisual Resources:			
Community Resources:			

Related Curriculum Activities (Science, Math, Art, Music):

FIGURE 10.1. This form can be used in developing unit plans. Notice that it consists of four components: (1) the learnings to be achieved; (2) the references and resources to be used; (3) the activities to be performed; and (4) how to relate it to the rest of the curriculum.

the children have an opportunity to discover the new material gradually and will be ready to engage in productive teacher-guided planning.

Some teachers use dramatic representation successfully in the initial stages of the unit. Let us assume that a primary class is beginning a unit on transportation. The teacher suggests that the children show through creative dramatics what the workers at an airline terminal do. The children become excited about this and want to start immediately, which the teacher allows. Under the teacher's guidance, they begin to plan and to play the representation, but they soon discover that they do not really know enough about the situation to present it accurately. They do not know who the workers are at the terminal, let alone what each worker does. Now they have identified a problem they can understand and can go about their research and problem solving with genuine purpose. The children's purposes have to do with getting information to do the dramatic play whereas the teacher's purpose is to have them learn basic ideas about the airport and to learn important related skills. Although the example given applies to a primary grade, the procedure can be used at any level.

Other activities can be used in a similar way to motivate work, to develop purposes, and to give children reasons for doing the things they do. The projects are important in that they provide a child-oriented vehicle for learning. Construction activities are often used in this way. If an individual or a class is to build something, they have to learn what goes into it, how it functions, and how it is or was used. One has to be careful, of course, to make certain the time taken in such endeavors is justified by the learnings that result.

Properly understood, this phase of unit development consists of a *group* or *series* of experiences rather than a single experience. Sometimes teachers plan to initiate a unit through the viewing of a film. A film may be used in the introductory stages of a unit, but this experience should be supported by many others of the type previously described. In one sense, this unfolding process is continued throughout the unit in that each new learning is a readiness for the next.

Developing the Study: Problems, Experiences, or Activities

A distinguishing characteristic of a good elementary or middle school teacher is the ability to engage children in an interested way in activities that help them achieve important learnings. One unfortunate practice in teaching social studies is that of using activities without relating them to social studies purposes. This applies to traditional activities, such as reading textbook assignments and giving reports, as it does to the more informal activities such as committee work or some type of expressive experi-

"Dancing is not only for girls anymore!" We can be sure that it took a great deal of teacher encouragement and support to get these boys to participate in this ethnic dance. It is in the planning stages of the unit that the teacher needs to anticipate the types of activities that will be used during unit development. (Photo by Edna Kellman, Seattle Public Schools.)

ence. Activities are means to ends — they are used to help children learn something. It is thus imperative that the teacher define the objectives and know clearly what the children are supposed to learn *before* deciding what activities are to be used. If the planning format shown in Figure 10.1 is used as suggested, this will not be a problem because the upper portion dealing with objectives is completed before the activities are selected. As decisions are made concerning activities, the teacher must also select the information sources that will be used by the children. These can be listed in the space provided in the planning form illustrated by Figure 10.1.

Good unit development always makes provision for the involvement of children in planning instructional activities. Having them participate in planning can do much to overcome the feeling that they are only "doing assignments for the teacher." Such participation assists in clarifying objectives of learning for the children and allows them to identify psychologically with the unit activities. The many values of such planning have been well documented, and it is now generally recognized as sound teaching procedure by good teachers everywhere.

Teachers should plan with children many of the specific learning tasks undertaken in the unit: listing questions on which information is desired, making charts of what to do, finding and listing sources of information, appointing committees, reporting progress, pooling suggestions, and making plans for a construction activity. A fifth-grade teacher and her class summarized their plans for part of a unit on New England as follows:

JOBS IN A COLONIAL NEW ENGLAND TOWN

Each of us will select a different job from New England town life.

Each of us will find out what skills and responsibilities each person has.

Each of us will share our role with the others in the class by dressing up like the person, showing something one might have created or used, making a bulletin board or diorama, or preparing a dramatization.

Some of the jobs in a colonial New England town are:

candlemaker	homemaker – mother
blacksmith	merchant
weaver	shipbuilder
farmer	minister
schoolteacher	fisherman
miller	barrister
carpenter	tanner
slave	doctor
watchman	innkeeper
printer	cooper

WHAT WE WILL WANT TO FIND OUT ABOUT OUR JOBS

1. What skills did the person need?
2. What training was necessary to do the job?
3. How much money did the person make?
4. How was the person paid?
5. How many people will need the services?
6. How does the job relate to other jobs in the community?
7. What special equipment or resources did the people use in their job?
8. Would you like to have done this job or performed this service?

In general, the development of a unit consists of a sequence of procedures, each one emerging from the preceding one. In its simplest form, this pattern might be described as follows:

1. *Problem identification* and related information gathering; problem-solving activities such as reading, interviewing, listening, viewing, collecting, using references, doing map work.
2. *Application* through expressive activities such as discussing, illustrating, exhibiting, dramatizing, constructing, drawing, and writing.
3. *Summarizing, generalizing,* and *transferring* to new situations resulting in identification of new problems of a more complex nature; the cycle is then repeated.

This procedure includes both intake and expressive activities. Children not only take in knowledge but also must act on knowledge so obtained. Moreover, they must generalize and apply their knowledge to new problems and situations.

As the unit moves into the development phase, each class period should provide for three instructional operations: (1) readiness, (2) work-study, and (3) summary and evaluation. Teachers usually begin the social studies instructional period with the entire class in one group. At this time the previous day's progress is reviewed, plans for the day's work are outlined, and work objectives are clarified. The children then turn to their various tasks while the teacher moves from one child to the next or from one group to another, guiding, helping, clarifying, encouraging, and suggesting. The teacher will terminate the work period sufficiently early to assemble the entire group once again to discuss progress, to evaluate work, and to identify tasks left undone that must be continued the next day. As the children complete their various work projects and are ready to share them with the class, time will be arranged for them to do so. On some days the children may spend the entire period sharing, presenting reports, discussing, and planning. Other days may be spent entirely in reading and research or on work sheets the teacher has prepared because of a special need of the class. And on other days part of the group may be reading while others are preparing a mural and still others are planning a report.

The need to take time at the end of the work period to summarize what has been learned or to review work that has been accomplished should be underscored. Having a clear understanding of the objective or purpose of a learning activity and having knowledge of the progress go hand in hand. Unless the teacher spends some time crystallizing what has been accomplished or learned, the children may work for days without feeling that they have learned anything or that they are getting anywhere. Some teachers find it worthwhile to place these daily summaries on charts that serve as a log of the unit work as it progresses. Such logs are helpful in the culmination and may also be useful in evaluation activities associated with the unit.

The work-study or problem-solving phase of the unit is handled somewhat differently in the primary grades than it is in the middle and upper grades. Although children of all ages need many firsthand experiences to extend their understanding of social studies concepts, the older child has a greater familiarity with the world of things and people and can, therefore, profit from vicarious experiences to a much greater extent than the primary-grade child. Furthermore, the older child can make use of reading as a tool for learning in the social studies whereas the young child is less able to do so. The physiological and psychological makeup of the primary-grade child makes necessary the use of learning activities that involve the child actively on a firsthand experience basis. (See Chart 10.)

The following are a few examples of learning activities for all grade levels:

Sharing

Mr. Johnson's second-graders were studying their seashore community. Using a sandbox and things that each of them had gathered or collected with their families, they created a model of a seashore. The boys and girls talked about what they had brought and where their items had come from. They discussed whether or not the items were natural or artificially constructed.

Construction

Ms. Smather's class studied early people and constructed tools and utensils with sticks, rocks, and vines they gathered in nearby wooded areas. Each child demonstrated the use of the implement.

Experimenting

Ms. Womble secured samples of various grains — oats, corn, barley, wheat — while studying agriculture with her class. The children compared the appearance and taste of each type of grain and then planted some to compare germinating time and appearance of the first shoots.

Listening

In Mr. Potts' class, the focus of study was the American Indian. In motivating the children, Mr. Potts read an Indian legend and asked them to decide what the Indians valued in their lives, using the legend as a clue to their value system.

CHART 10. LEARNING ACTIVITIES FOR SOCIAL STUDIES

Type of Learning Activity	Examples	Purposes Served

Research	Reading
	Writing
	Interviewing
	Note-taking
	Collecting
	Map work
	Reporting
	Using references
		To
		  Gather information
		  Practice information-gathering skills
		  Answer questions

Presentation	Telling
	Demonstrating
	Illustrating
	Dramatizing
	Exhibiting
	Announcing
	Giving directions
	Pantomiming
	Relating events
		To
		  Share ideas with others
		  Practice communication skills
		  Clarify ideas
		  Encourage initiative
		  Apply information

Creative experiences	Writing
	Sketching
	Illustrating
	Sewing
	Soap carving
	Manipulating
	Comparing
	Drawing
	Modeling
	Painting
	Constructing
	Singing
	Dramatizing
	Imagining
		To
		  Express ideas creatively
		  Encourage creative abilities
		  Stimulate interest
		  Extend and/or enrich learning

Appreciation	Listening
	Viewing
	Describing
	Reading
		To
		  Develop attitudes and feelings
		  Provide valuing experiences
		  Extend and/or enrich learning

Observation or listening	Observing
	Visiting places of
	  interest
	Viewing pictures or films
	Listening to recordings
		To
		  Gather information
		  Build observation and perceptual
		    skills
		  Compare and contrast

CHART 10. LEARNING ACTIVITIES FOR SOCIAL STUDIES (continued)

Type of Learning Activity	Examples	Purposes Served

Group cooperation	Discussing
	Sharing
	Helping one another
	Doing committee work
	Conversing
	Asking questions
		To
		  Develop group-work skills
		  Use socialization skills
		  Engage in larger projects

Experimentation	Measuring
	Demonstrating
	Conducting experiments
	Collecting
		To
		  Clarify complex procedures
		  Develop inquiry skills
		  Gather information

Organization	Planning
	Outlining
	Holding meetings
	Discussing
	Summarizing
		To
		  Clarify relationships
		  Prepare a plan of action
		  Organize ideas

Evaluation	Summarizing
	Criticizing
	Asking questions
	Reviewing
		To
		  Clarify direction and purpose
		  Assess progress toward goals
		  Modify plans

Discussion

Ms. Perkle's sixth-grade class had a current events time, and a child brought an article from the evening paper telling about the sale of United States grain to China. A discussion that weighed the advantages and disadvantages of this action to the American people followed.

Written Language Experience

Ms. Thomas's class had written letters to their grandparents asking them to share their recollections of earlier schooldays. Those grandparents who lived nearby were asked to visit Ms. Thomas's classroom.

Dramatic Activities

During their study of Indonesia, each of the children in Ms. Monroe's class created a shadow puppet. In small groups they dramatized situations from Indonesian life.

Art Experience

In a first-grade class the children made a trip to a farm. On their return they painted a mural showing the animals, equipment, people, and buildings they had observed.

Field Trip

A day was spent at a fair during the study of the state. The children noticed what products were displayed and what their region of the state had contributed.

Processing

During a study of colonial history the class divided into groups to make soap, dip candles, bake bread, churn butter, make dyes, and weave.

Some of the unit activities will involve the entire group whereas others will be individual or small-group endeavors. In carrying out this part of the unit, the teacher should make certain that each child knows what is expected. Classrooms operating in this way are places where children are doing things; consequently, they will be moving about, asking questions, and communicating with one another; and a generally informal but task-oriented atmosphere will prevail.

Evaluating Learning

Throughout the study the teacher and the children should make frequent evaluations of how well the unit is progressing. This is *formative* evaluation conducted in order to diagnose student learning difficulties and to improve teaching and learning. Much of this day-to-day evaluation is, and ought to be, informal. The teacher sees children working well or poorly and adjusts the instruction accordingly. The teacher can also sense whether or not children are interested in what they are doing. Through observation and feedback, the teacher can gauge the extent to which progress is being made toward the achievement of objectives. An appropriate, short teacher-made test can be used to check how well specific areas of content and skills have been learned. Much of the informal evaluation that takes place on a day-to-day basis involves the children themselves. They should be encouraged through discussion to take stock of their work individually and as a group. Evaluation of learnings, therefore, should not be associated only with the conclusion of a unit, but should be an important part of the ongoing instruction. Of course, the end of a unit provides a time to examine the extent to which the overall objectives have been achieved. This is *summative* evaluation and both informal and formal evaluation procedures are appropriate for this purpose. (See Chapter 14.)

Concluding the Study

As a class nears the end of a unit, the teacher should plan a series of activities that encourage children to summarize what they have learned. This might involve opportunities to show what they have done or to share interesting things they have learned with other classes in the school or with their parents.[2] What is important about closing a unit of study is the opportunity to discuss conclusions, evaluate what has been learned, identify what children found to be of especial interest to them, and identify areas where additional study is needed. Concluding activities should include a suggestion of various interesting facets of the topic that were left unexplored and about which the children may wish to read and study independently. Concluding activities can and should serve as bridges to new intellectual pursuits.

INCORPORATING THINKING SKILLS

The usual assumption is that the development of thinking skills flows naturally as a result of the acquisition of knowledge. The belief is widespread that if one is well informed, the application of that knowledge to the solution of problems will pretty much take care of itself. Consequently, educational programs often emphasize the accumulation of information rather than a concern with its application. If there is a concern for application at all, the feeling is that it should come later, after there has been a period of knowledge accumulation, in high school or college or as an adult. Research indicates that this procedure is based on faulty assumptions and that knowledge accumulation and knowledge application go hand in hand and are part of the same process we call thinking.[3]

The process of thinking consists of a series of subskills, and, like any other skills, they must be practiced if they are to be applied with any degree of proficiency. These subskills can be identified as follows:

---

[2] The idea of a "sidewalk fair" in a local shopping mall could be a good outlet for sharing what has been learned with others. See Barbara Hatcher and Mary Olson, "Sidewalk Social Studies," *Social Education*, 48 (September–October 1984), pp. 473–474, 485.

[3] See Barry K. Beyer, "Teaching Critical Thinking: A Direct Approach," *Social Education*, 49 (April 1985), pp. 297–303.

1. Identifying problems and questions for study.
2. Making inferences and drawing conclusions from data.
3. Making comparisons.
4. Developing hypotheses.
5. Using evidence to test hypotheses.
6. Planning how to study a question or a problem.
7. Getting data from a variety of sources.
8. Predicting possible outcomes.
9. Deciding what evidence is needed in studying a problem.
10. Deciding what evidence is relevant to the study.

These skills must be incorporated in the ongoing work of the class if learners are to develop proficiency in their use. Occasional special lessons on inquiry are not in themselves adequate for building competence. Of course, not all these subskills will appear in social studies lessons every day. During a period of a few weeks, such as that of a study unit, one should see balanced and systematic attention being given to them.

Special instructional materials that are inquiry-based are helpful, but not essential, to engaging children in inquiry. Any of the standard materials can be used as sources of information, including textbooks. What is different when thinking is stressed, however, is the way these materials are used. The usual assumption regarding instructional material is that it includes essential information that must be learned. Nowhere is this more evident than in the use of textbooks. Textbook content often *becomes* the curriculum. In teaching for thinking, the textbook is a data or information *source*, and it should be used along with other information sources.

Not all social studies teaching need be, nor even should be, inquiry-oriented. The teaching mode selected must be consistent with the objectives to be achieved. If the purpose is to convey information to children or to teach a skill, exposition and demonstration are often more effective and efficient teaching modes than is inquiry. If the purpose is to teach thinking and problem-solving skills, however, an inquiry strategy should be used.

AN INQUIRY

Problem-Solving Behavior

Ms. Carroll's class is discussing problem solving in relation to their study of early societies. To increase their understanding of this concept further, she divides the class into groups of four and gives each group a carambola (any food that is uncommon — jicama, plantain, cherimoya, kiwi, and so on, would do).

Ms. Carroll: Pretend you are an early person and you have just found one of these fruits while food gathering. You do not know what it is because you have never seen one like it before. You are not sure whether or not you can safely eat it. In your group, discuss what decisions you can make concerning this "find" and the consequences of each decision.

The groups discuss this question, and then Ms. Carroll has each group present its decisions to the class. They conclude there are three options, and Ms. Carroll writes them on the chalkboard.

Decision	Consequence
1. Do nothing; pass it by.	1. Might lose a good and needed food source.
2. Test it by eating it.	2. Could become sick or could even die if it is poisonous; *or* could be a tasty nutritious food.
3. Develop some way of testing it before eating it.	3. Would take time but would be safe.

Ms. Carroll then continues: Suppose you made decision no. 3. In your group, develop a plan of action you could use to test whether or not you could safely eat the newfound fruit.

The children developed plans that involved testing the food on nonhuman subjects. These plans were discussed and compared with modern-day practices in testing food products, new drugs, and medical practices. This discussion raised many issues related to the use of human subjects for experimental purposes.

Ms. Carroll concluded the inquiry by asking the children to speculate on

1. The risks of trial-and-error behavior.
2. How such risks can be reduced.
3. Alternatives to trial-and-error, problem-solving procedures.

Almost any topic selected for unit study can be shaped to meet the requirements of an inquiry episode. However, topics that are to some extent controversial and problematic are best because they are consistent with the nature of inquiry. That is, there is clearly something to inquire about, and the outcome may still be in doubt. Subject matter and topics relating to current affairs, law and justice, the environment, energy, intergroup relations, economics, and geography are a few that lend themselves well to inquiry. As an example, the following case could be used as the basis for an inquiry into certain aspects of the legal and justice systems:

FARMER INDICTED IN ELK-KILLING CASE

Kenneth Reed was indicted in Sheridan District Court Tuesday on five counts of killing elk, a protected species in this state. Reed, a local farmer, did not deny killing the elk, but said they were damaging the grain crop he needed to feed his dairy herd.

Reed said that the animals began damaging his crop in midsummer and that he had repeatedly asked the Fish and Game Department to do something about it. Through his attorney, Reed said that he had contacted the department "at least a dozen times" by telephone. He also said that he sent three letters to the department warning that if something were not done, he would shoot the animals. Reed insists that he was justified in killing the elk to protect his property.

It is expected that the case will come to trial this fall. If found guilty, Reed could be sentenced to one year in jail and fined $1,000 on each of the five counts.[4]

This case raises some interesting legal questions relating to the right to protect one's property. Because television programs often show individuals using firearms to protect their property or themselves, children may have distorted ideas about the legal aspects of protecting oneself or one's property. Some of the issues raised by this case are these:

1. Why might the person be found not guilty in this case even though the specific action — that is, killing the elk — is clearly against the law in that state? Why should such a finding *in one case* not be interpreted by citizens as encouragement to break the law any time they think it is unfair or does not apply to them?
2. How does the fact that Reed had contacted the Fish and Game Department several times, without any apparent results, have any bearing on the outcome of the case?
3. Do individuals have the right to "take the law into their own hands" when appropriate officials refuse to or are unable to take corrective action?
4. Would the outcome of this case most likely be different if the trespassers were people instead of elk?

Intellectual skills such as critical thinking, reflective inquiry, problem analysis, and creative problem solving should not be taught outside a related subject-matter context. That is, to think critically or reflectively, learners must think about *something*. These are not processes that can either be taught or learned in isolation. Therefore, as the teacher is planning the social studies unit, some provision needs to be made to include instruction on and the application of critical thinking and other intellectual skills in order that they be perceived by the learners as a natural extension of what they are studying. This can be done by using the planning format suggested by Figure 10.1, page 284. Notice that space is provided in the upper right corner of the form to list questions to stimulate reflective thinking.

---

[4] This is a fictitious case, although in 1975, in a case much like this one, a Minnesota farmer was found not guilty by a district court jury.

PLANNING FOR EFFECTIVE QUESTIONING PROCEDURES

In using reading and writing activities, in conducting classroom discussions, and in challenging children to do critical and reflective thinking, the teacher will make frequent use of questions. Questioning strategies are among the oldest and most widely used methods of conducting instruction. The teacher uses questions to clarify procedures, to determine whether children understand what they are to do, to find out whether additional explanation is required, to get feedback on the effectiveness of a demonstration or explanation, and so on.

Questions may also be used to check the child's comprehension of concepts, generalizations, or subject matter. Often such questions require the learner to reproduce or recall factual information that has been read or discussed in class. Research of classroom-teacher behavior through the years shows that teachers use a high percentage of questions of this type. These questions are sometimes referred to as "lower-level" because they involve simple recall and memory rather than higher-order mental operations such as application, analysis, synthesis, interpretation, sensing cause and effect, or evaluation. So-called "lower-level" questions can be easily identified because they usually begin with who, what, when, and where. These questions are important, especially in checking reading comprehension or to ascertain that children are familiar with facts essential to the topic. The problem is that there is a tendency to overuse such questions, with a corresponding lessened use of other questions that do require higher-order thought processes. In terms of the development of intellectual skills, the most important questions to ask are those that require elaborative, reflective responses. These higher-level questions often begin, "Why . . ." "How . . ." "How do we know . . ." "Show that . . ." "If that is true, then . . ." The difference between the two is clearly illustrated by the example based on the narrative "Indian Old Fields" on pages 300–301.

These higher-level questions serve two general purposes relating to thinking skills. One is that they trigger mental operations that are in accord with a problem-solving discovery learning format. For example, what mental operations are involved if the teacher asks the question: What is the most important reason for a small population in the area? Before responding, the child has to (1) analyze the situation, (2) consider all of the reasons that might apply, (3) evaluate each in terms of its importance, and then (4) select the one considered to be most important. Mental operations of this type characterize higher-level, or reflective thought processes. Simply recalling a "correct" response is not adequate — the information has to be processed intellectually: analyzed, synthesized, applied, interpreted, evaluated, and so on. Thus, appropriate questions are essential in building reflective habits of thought.

Reflective or "thought" questions also serve the purpose of teaching the child improved habits of study. If the only kinds of questions encountered are based on recall of factual information, the child learns to study in accordance with such objectives. The child may not learn how to apply information or even to process it in terms of broader intellectual outcomes. For example, without such experience, a child may attach the same degree of importance to a trivial incident as to a major concept or a profound generalization. Also, problem solving requires the ability *to ask* appropriate questions, and children cannot develop this skill unless they encounter such questions in their study.

For what purposes are questions used in social studies? Examples of some of the more common ones are provided in Chart 11.

It is apparent that there is overlap among some of the categories of questions listed in Chart 11. For instance, a question for independent study might also be used to check comprehension, to analyze component elements, or to draw conclusions. The object of these examples is to show that questions can be used for many different purposes, not that the categories are mutually exclusive.

In order to improve questioning techniques, the following suggestions are provided:

1. Consciously reduce the number of factual recall questions asked. These are usually questions that begin with "Who?" "What?" "Where?" and "When?" Replace these with questions that require elaborative, reflective responses, for example, "Why?" "How?" "How do we know?"

2. Match the type of question with the purpose it is to serve. Questions that call for yes-no responses are not appropriate to stimulate a discussion. Reflective or discussion questions should not be used for homework or independent study.

3. State questions in ways that communicate precisely what is being asked. Sometimes children cannot respond to questions not because they do not know the material but because the question is ambiguous or otherwise poorly framed. The vocabulary level must be consistent with the age and maturity of the children. Although this may seem to be a trite reminder, it does constitute a problem for adults who have not been closely associated with children. Beginning teachers should write out in advance the main questions they plan to use.

4. Provide adequate time for the children to respond. Ask the question *before* calling on a specific respondent. This requires all children to form their own response intellectually.

5. Vary the way you acknowledge responses. In addition to "uh-huh," "all right," and "O.K.," which are commonly overused by teachers, try asking another question such as a probing or clarifying question. Avoid *always* acknowledging responses with evaluative comments

such as "right," "yes," or "that's good," although these should be used from time to time to encourage children to participate.

CHART 11. TYPES OF QUESTIONS USED IN SOCIAL STUDIES AND EXAMPLES OF EACH

1. **To establish procedures.** Examples:
   a. Does everyone have a copy of the map?
   b. Are you looking at the lower part of the picture?
2. **To analyze component elements.** Examples:
   a. How many steps are involved in the process?
   b. What land features are most important to the occupations of the people who live there?
3. **To check comprehension or general understanding.** Examples:
   a. Where was the first settlement made?
   b. What were the reasons for moving to a new location?
4. **To interpret data.** Examples:
   a. Why is there such a difference in climate between Rome and Boston even though they are on about the same parallel of latitude?
   b. Which income groups are hardest hit by a sales tax on food? Why?
5. **To predict outcomes.** Examples:
   a. What other products are likely to be affected by increased prices of steel?
   b. If everyone worked only four days a week, what businesses might be expected to grow?
6. **To probe for additional information.** Examples:
   a. Who can tell a little more about why the law was passed?
   b. Does this mean that one could not enter that country without a visa?
7. **To clarify meanings of learner responses.** Examples:
   a. Who can give an example of how daylight saving time benefits people?
   b. I am still not sure I understand your explanation of "duty-free." Is "duty-free" the same as tax-free?
8. **To explain something.** Examples:
   a. How might a winter frost in Florida affect the lives of people in northern cities such as Minneapolis, Milwaukee, Detroit, and Cleveland?
   b. If farmers make greater use of machinery and there is less need for farmhands, where do people in the rural areas find jobs?
9. **To describe something.** Examples:
   a. What was life like for an immigrant family from Eastern Europe living in Chicago at the turn of the century?
   b. Your book tells how the people felt when they arrived at their destination after traveling for several weeks in the wagon train. What were their feelings?
10. **To verify statements or conclusions.** Examples:
    a. Which paragraph tells exactly why environmental impact statements are required?
    b. That figure seems low to me. Would you mind locating the source of these figures and rechecking that second amount?

11. **To guide independent study.** Examples:
    a. What advantages does the author give for the use of checks instead of coins and currency?
    b. What reasons are given on pages 81–87 for our strong ties with Japan?
12. **To diagnose learning difficulties.** Examples:
    a. How would you find something about the cotton gin in this book?
    b. What is the main idea in the third paragraph on page 153?
13. **To summarize ideas or to draw conclusions.** Examples:
    a. Based on what we have learned thus far, what conclusions might we make about life in these early settlements?
    b. What is the relationship between the availability of a product and its price?

INDIAN "OLD FIELDS"

The Indians, we have seen, lived in villages. After eight or ten years in one place, an Indian village area became very dirty and had many rats, mice, and insects in it. The Indians knew, from long experience, that these conditions led to disease. Also they knew that, after a few years, their fields did not grow as large crops as did new fields. Therefore, every eight or ten years the people would find a new area, perhaps three or four miles away. There they would build a new village. They had to clear away the forest to build the new village and to start new fields around their new homes. The clearings and fields left behind became "old fields."

The records of all the colonies, from Canada to the Gulf of Mexico, mention large numbers of old fields. The early settlers called them "fair meadows," "broad grassy plains," "fine savannas," or "grassy glades." But there were few *natural* grassy places in this forest-covered land. All these names for open places referred to the same thing: Indian old fields.

By using Indian old fields, the settlers saved themselves the long, hard labor of cutting away the forest to start farming. Everywhere the old fields were a great help in getting settlements started.

The reason that there were so many old fields lies in an unhappy experience in Indian history. We believe that an epidemic swept through the Indian population in the 1500s. The disease was probably smallpox or some other disease to which the Indians had never before been exposed. They probably caught the disease from European fishermen who had gone ashore somewhere along the Atlantic Coast. Then it spread from one Indian group to another. The epidemic killed many — or even most — of the Indians from the Gulf of Mexico to Canada. As a result, there were many deserted clearings — old fields — where villages had once stood.[5]

Questions requiring comprehension of literal meaning

1. How often did the Indians move from place to place?

Questions requiring interpretation of ideas

1. If the Indians did not find the fields productive, how did it happen that the white settlers did?

[5] Merle Prunty and Bertha Davis, *This Favored Land*, 2d ed. (New York: Macmillan, 1974), pp. 26–27.

2. Why did the Indians move so often?

3. How far away did the Indians build the new village from the old one?

4. What did the early settlers call these Indian old fields?

5. Why did the settlers use the Indian old fields?

6. What disease caused the epidemic among the Indians in the 1500s?

7. How did the Indians get the disease?

8. What did the disease have to do with the Indian old fields?

2. How large would you say the Indian farms were?

3. What can you tell about the kinds of homes the Indians had?

4. Why would the Indians' old fields not be as productive as the new ones?

5. What time of the year would the Indians have cleared their fields?

6. What evidence would lead scientists to think that an epidemic swept through the Indian settlements?

7. Why couldn't these open areas have been caused by fires started by lightning?

8. Do you think that the smallpox disease might have been more deadly among the Indians than among the European whites? Why or why not?

PLANNING SHORT INSTRUCTIONAL SEQUENCES

Thus far our discussion has concerned itself only with planning a unit — a parcel of work that might take several weeks to complete. In order to implement such a plan, teachers must extract from the unit plan ideas that can be converted into shorter instructional sequences that may last anywhere from a single day to a week or more. Sometimes these are called daily lesson plans although there is some objection to that term because it suggests — and may lead to — fragmentation, rigidity, and old-fashioned teaching procedures. Social studies learning is, or ought to be, continuous from one day to the next. Children simply pick up where they left off in their study the day before. Lesson plans should be consistent with this continuous flow of learning. Short-range plans are a teaching trip map that the teacher has in hand and uses at the time the teaching is done. Because the teacher relies on these plans to implement the instruction, they must be complete in every detail, correctly sequenced, contingencies anticipated and accounted for, with as little as possible left to chance. As the teacher prepares such plans, it is helpful to rehearse mentally how the lesson is expected to proceed, step-by-step. This will help reduce the possibility of encountering surprises while the lesson is in progress.

There are four essential components of plans of this type. These are (1) the purpose or objective that identifies what children will *learn;* (2) lesson development to include (a) the readiness or interest-building procedures that indicate how the sequence is to *begin* and (b) work-study activities that indicate what children will *do* to help them learn; (3) summary and evaluation that indicate how the sequence will *close;* and (4) a list of the instructional materials and resources needed to teach the sequence. The following examples show how these plans can be constructed.

LESSON PLAN 15

Topic:	Group membership
Grade:	Two
Time:	Two class periods
Objectives:	Children will learn to identify human groups and will become aware of reasons why people are grouped together.
Interest Building:	Display five pictures of groups. Underneath each write what type of group is represented. (Ideas: soccer team, birthday party, family, class, scout troop)
Lesson Development:	Ask class to think of one word that describes all the pictures. Elicit the word *group.*
	Generate a simple definition of a human group.
	Have children think of the names of several more groups.
	Suggest that they include groups to which they belong. Write these on chalkboard.
	Focus the class discussion on the reason people are grouped together, and place ideas on a chart as follows:

Human Groups	
What are some groups that we know about?	*Why are these people grouped together?*
family	love, help each other
team	to play games
class	to learn
bithday party	for fun
scout troop	camping, making things, helping others

	Discuss ways that groups can be identified. Look at the five original pictures for clues. Some clues might be: clothing/uniforms, symbols/mascots, official names, special songs, distinguishing looks or languages.
Summary:	Bring the concept of group into the children's immediate experience by asking the following questions: Is this class a group? How do you know? Why are we grouped together? What are *your* reasons for being a member of this group?
	Have old magazines available, and ask children to cut out a picture of a group. Have each child tell something about what the group is doing. As they make their presentation, have them finish this sentence: "I think that these people make a group because . . ." Use the pictures to make a collage on the bulletin board.
Follow-Up:	Have children bring in personal photos of groups to which they belong and share them with the class.
	If possible, take a photo of the class group, and have a print made for each child.

Needed Materials: Five pictures of different groups for display purposes. White butcher paper and felt pen to make chart.

Old magazines or newspapers that have pictures of groups.
Option: Personal camera

LESSON PLAN 16

Topic: Futuring

Grade: Six

Time: Three class periods

Objective: Learners will be able to identify present trends and to project the consequence of a specific trend.

Interest Building: Suggest that the class has gathered together in the year 2025 for a reunion. Have them speculate on what their lives will be like then. Define *trends,* and have the students list current trends such as more mechanization in our daily lives or the increased use of computers.

Lesson Development: With the students working in groups of three, have them choose one of the current trends and brainstorm all of the consequences of that trend, such as more leisure time in the case of the mechanization trend, which leads to more recreation needs, which means an increase in the use of state parks and the like.

Ask the students to organize their ideas for sharing with their classmates.

Summary: In the next class period have each group identify consequences that seem to be negative.

Ask them to develop an ideal plan that could make this consequence beneficial to people in the future.

Materials: None necessary, but outside sources have commercial materials on this topic. Two possible references are these:

The Center for Curriculum Design
823 Foster Street
Evanston, Illinois 60204

Science Fiction Research Association
Box 3186
The College of Wooster
Wooster, Ohio 44691

JUDGING THE ADEQUACY OF A LESSON PLAN

A teacher is never as well prepared as he or she *might* have been, given more time and more resources. Lesson planning is an open-ended process that can go on endlessly. Many teachers can recall, as student teachers, staying up half the night preparing a half-hour lesson to be taught the next day. Although such effort is commendable, it cannot be sustained for any length of time. At some point, the teacher must decide that the lesson is well enough planned and then be able to turn to other matters with a clear conscience.

It is not always easy, especially for the beginning teacher, to know when one has reached the point of diminishing returns in lesson planning. The checklist that follows can be useful in deciding whether or not all important aspects of the lesson have been given appropriate attention in the planning process.

LESSON PLAN CHECKLIST

1. Do the lesson objectives state clearly what it is that the children are expected to *learn?*
2. Do the learner activities for the lesson relate in a direct way to the stated objectives? That is, will the children learn what they are supposed to learn by doing the things they are asked to do?
3. Do you know how the lesson is to begin? What is the very first thing you will do? Say? What next? What third?
4. Have you written down the questions you plan to ask? Do you have them in the order you plan to ask them?
5. Do you have all the needed instructional material? Equipment? If you are planning to use a machine, have you arranged to get it? Do you know where the electrical outlets are in the room? Will you need an extension cord? Screen?
6. Are there specific directions you are planning to give the children regarding what they are to do? If so, do you know what they are?
7. If you are going to group the children, do you have productive work planned for *all* the groups, *all* the time?
8. Do you know how much time will be needed for each component of your lesson?
9. Have you provided for differences in rate and level of learning among children? Do you have productive work-study activities planned for those who complete their assignments quickly? Have you provided additional help for the slower learners? Do you have appropriate learning activities planned for any children with handicapping conditions?
10. Have you considered whether or not the lesson will require changes in the room environment, movement of furniture, and so forth?
11. Do you know exactly how the lesson is to close—that is: What you will do? What you will say? What you expect the children to do?
12. Have you planned for any follow-up activity?
13. Have you taken into account how learning is to be evaluated?
14. Should the lesson be completed more quickly than you had

planned, do you have some "backup" activities ready that can be used?

DISCUSSION QUESTIONS AND SUGGESTED ACTIVITIES

1. Select a unit topic that would be appropriate for a grade of your choice, and identify six to eight main ideas that could be developed in such a unit. State these as declarative sentences (generalizations). Arrange them in the order in which they would be presented in the unit.

2. Select one of the main ideas you identified in your response to question 1. Develop it into a teaching plan, using the format suggested by Figure 10.1 on page 284.

3. Using the ideas you developed in your answer to question 2, prepare a teaching sequence (lesson plan) using the form suggested on pages 302–303.

4. Write behavioral objectives for a unit such as the one you identified in responding to question 1.

5. Suggest social studies learnings that lend themselves especially well to the use of behavioral objectives and some that do not. How would the teacher evaluate learner achievement of objectives that are not stated behaviorally?

6. Discuss teaching plans and how to prepare them with your supervising teacher or with some other in-service teacher you know. If possible, bring to class a sample of a social studies plan used by that teacher. Compare plans brought to class in terms of similarities in the items included.

7. Prepare a list of decisions that could be made in your classroom in which children could legitimately participate. Also, make a list of decisions in which they would not participate. What guidelines can you suggest regarding the involvement of children in classroom decision making?

8. Suppose as a teacher you were assigned to a school that had no social studies curriculum guide or any type of a planned social studies program. How would you go about planning the social studies program for your class?

9. Identify a few events, decisions, or actions that occurred at the national level that have had an impact on social studies education at the local level.

10. Prepare a lesson plan just as you would teach it to a grade of your choice. Apply the checklist on pages 304–305 to test for its completeness. Have the plan critiqued by a practicing teacher.

11. In the assignment of questions for independent study or homework, why is it important that the child be able to get the answers from the available books and resources?

12. Do you think the kinds of questions a teacher asks reflect the major objectives the teacher has in mind for the lesson? *Should* they? Explain your response.

SELECTED REFERENCES

BARRERA, ROSALINDA B., AND MAGDELENA ALEMAN. "Language-Centered Social Studies: A Natural Integration." *Social Education,* 47 (November–December 1983), pp. 528–532.

DILLON, J. T. *Teaching and the Art of Questioning.* Fastback No. 194. Bloomington, Indiana: Phi Delta Kappa, 1983.

FARRAR, MARY THOMAS. "Asking Better Questions." *The Reading Teacher,* 38 (October 1984), pp. 10–15.

GALL, MEREDITH. "Synthesis of Research on Teachers' Questioning." *Educational Leadership,* 42 (November 1984), pp. 40–47.

GRONLUND NORMAN E. *Stating Objectives for Classroom Instruction,* 3rd ed. New York: Macmillan Publishing Co., 1985.

HOLBROOK, H. T. "Writing to Learn in the Social Studies." *The Reading Teacher,* 41 (November 1987), pp. 216–219.

JAROLIMEK, JOHN, AND CLIFFORD D. FOSTER, SR. *Teaching and Learning in the Elementary School,* 4th ed. New York: Macmillan Publishing Co., 1989. Chapters 6, 7, 8, and 9.

MCKENZIE, GARY R. "Learning and Instruction." *Elementary School Social Studies: Research as a Guide to Practice,* Virginia A. Atwood, ed. NCSS Bulletin No. 79. Washington, D.C.: National Council for the Social Studies, 1986. Chapter 8.

ORLICH, DONALD C., *et al. Teaching Strategies: A Guide to Better Instruction,* 2nd ed. Lexington, Massachusetts: D. C. Heath, 1985. Chapter 5.

RYAN, FRANK L. *The Social Studies Sourcebook: Ideas for Teaching in the Elementary and Middle School.* Boston: Allyn and Bacon, 1980.

STEINBRINK, JOHN E. "The Social Studies Learner as Questioner." *The Social Studies,* 76 (January–February 1985), pp. 38–40.

VAN CLEAF, DAVID W. "Guiding Student Inquiry." *The Social Studies,* 75 (May–June 1984), pp. 109–111.

WOOLEVER, ROBERTA M. "A New Framework for Developing Classroom Questions." *Social Education,* 51 (October 1987), pp. 407–410.

YINGER, ROBERT J. "A Study of Teacher Planning." *The Elementary School Journal,* 80 (January 1980), pp. 107–127.

11

Adapting Group Instruction to Individual Learner Abilities in the Social Studies

The practice of moving children with handicapping conditions out of segregated educational settings and into regular classrooms has had the effect of sensitizing teachers to individual differences between and among *all* children. If the teacher is required to prepare an Individualized Education Program for a handicapped child, it is likely that the teacher will be more observant of the individual learning needs of the child's nonhandicapped peers as well. Much of the educational literature published in this century deals with variations in children and their effect on school achievement. Children differ one from another in their capacity to learn; in the rate at which they can learn; in their learning styles; in their methods of work; in their socioethnic, home, and family backgrounds; in their motivation to learn; in their physical fitness; and, indeed, on almost any variable we choose to examine. Some variations are more closely related to school achievement than are others, but the evidence is overwhelming that individual differences among children are so extensive and so pervasive that a group cannot be taught effectively unless some accommodation is made for such differences.

WHAT IT MEANS TO INDIVIDUALIZE INSTRUCTION

To individualize instruction means that each child is provided with personally meaningful learning experiences that are suitable to his or her capabilities, thereby enabling the learner to move in the direction of goals that are believed to be important. *Individualizing instruction does not mean that the teacher always works with individual children in a one-on-one tutorial setting.* Even if the teacher could work with children in a one-to-one relationship, this would not necessarily result in individualized instruction as we are defining it. Unless the teacher is sensitive to the unique learning requirements of each child, tutorial instruction can be just as impersonal and meaningless as whole-class instruction.

For a teacher to have an attitude of sensitivity to and caring about the idiosyncrasies and learning styles of individuals is critical. This means that a key element in the process is *flexibility*. Much of the instruction will, of necessity, take place in group settings. But membership in learning groups does not need to take the form of a permanent placement. Children can be moved from one group to another as is needed to help them learn in their own best way. There is no standard instructional format for individualizing instruction.

The teacher who individualizes instruction sees individual children rather than the class. Much attention is given to the identification of specific learning difficulties of individual children. The program requirements are open-ended. Children are neither restricted by so-called grade-level content, nor are they required to achieve grade-level standards. Achievement is assessed in terms of gains made by each individual. Interests and preferences are respected and, insofar as is feasible, are accommodated. Uniform assignments and uniform requirements for the entire class are, as a rule, not given. Learner initiative, independence, and self-direction should be generously rewarded.

Because of the flexibility that should characterize much of individualized instruction, it is easy for the teacher to become careless in setting requirements and standards. Levels of achievement expectations have to be set in terms of their appropriateness for individual children, and, once they are set, learners must be held to them. Records of learner progress must be kept if evaluations of achievement are to be made. Children need to be informed of their progress on a regular basis. A knowledge of one's status and progress is a powerful force in motivating improved performance. It is significant that there is hardly any game that human beings play that does not require keeping score. Games in which no score is kept

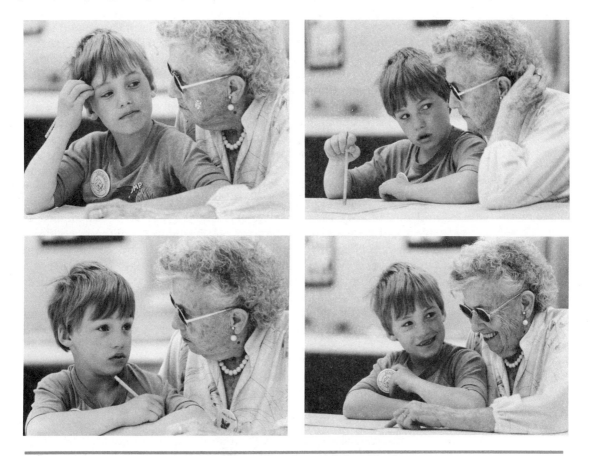

Adult volunteers can be enormously helpful to teachers in providing tutoring for individual children. But the use of volunteer tutors means that the child has to relate yet to another adult in the instructional setting. In this sequence of fascinating photographs, we see the development of a trust relationship emerging as the child relates to the volunteer. (Photos by Joel Schwarz, Tacoma School District.)

are frequently played carelessly and are less interesting to the players. And although school is not a game, the same principles apply. Teachers will usually get the level of performance they require and expect of children.

OBSTACLES TO INDIVIDUALIZING INSTRUCTION

If individualization is so important to good instruction, why don't more teachers do more of it? The answer to this question is not hard to find. Perhaps most important is the long tradition of whole-group instruction that is reinforced in many practices even today. The way children are grouped in schools often obscures important differences among them. Also, the belief is widely held that if children would just work harder, they could all achieve at the level required. Sometimes administrative and supervisory policies discourage individualization of instruction by mandating that teachers cover specific required material. "Covering" the textbooks and teaching for the content of the standardized tests also work against individualizing instruction.

At a more subtle level, the reality of individual differences runs contrary to our social philosophy of equality, that is, the conflict between a recognition of obvious differences among individuals on the one hand and the desire to provide for equality of opportunity on the other. These represent conflicting values, both of which are embraced by this society and, no doubt, by a large number of teachers. We sense a basic unfairness about setting different standards or requirements for different children. Yet we know that unless we do, some children cannot possibly succeed whereas others succeed too easily. Some believe that schools serve a sorting function and that individualization of instruction confounds this process. Others believe that schools *should* teach children how they compare in achievement with their classmates, and this can be accomplished by using the average achievement of the group as the standard for comparison.

There are other practical obstacles to individualization of instruction. There is no doubt it is demanding of teacher time. It necessitates a considerable amount of record keeping, requires a skillful teacher to manage it well, and also requires a considerable amount of instructional resources. Some teachers are not able to cope with the flexibility it demands.

These obstacles to individualization of instruction cannot be swept aside as being unimportant, and we are not unmindful of the problems they create for the teacher. Nonetheless, it is the teacher's responsibility to make the social studies program vital and relevant for *all* children. Because children come from a wide variety of home and community environments, and because they differ as much as they do in their intellectual abilities and motivations, they cannot possibly benefit equally from identical exposures to educational experiences. If everyone is treated the *same*, we simply institutionalize and perpetuate *inequality* because some individuals and some groups are better able to take advantage of opportunities than the others. Consequently, we would expect all teachers to do as much as they are able to do in reaching each child in the social studies.

APPROACHES TO INDIVIDUALIZATION

Because teachers have their own particular styles and preferences, each will develop ways of individualizing instruction that seem to work best for him or her. Most teachers, however, will find it necessary to use a combination of procedures in order to attend to the learning needs of individual children.

Management Approaches

Management and instruction are the two basic components of teaching. Consequently, the management aspects of a classroom have a great deal to do with the individualization of instruction. This becomes most apparent in such areas as the room environment, scheduling, the extent of "openness," and the amount and nature of teacher supervision.

Room Environment. If we visit a classroom in which learning is individualized, we are struck by the variety of interesting things children can do there that promote their opportunity to learn. The classroom is a storehouse of learning resources. We see areas of the room arranged for independent, quiet study. Other areas are planned for small-group interaction. We see interesting displays where children can handle and manipulate materials. There are learning centers where they can work at their own pace. There is easy access to books and other media that can be used as needed. There are work areas where children will find art materials, tools of various types, paper, boxes, and other raw materials needed to make things. The room is characterized by disciplined freedom where children can explore intellectually and move about physically. The environment is greatly varied in its appeal to children.

Learner Groups. In social studies, most groups should be temporary task-oriented clusters of children. Often these groups are formed on the basis of a common interest, as, for example, a group working together on a display, a report, or a small construction project. Other groups are formed on the basis of a common need. For instance, the teacher may work with a small group in reading their text, developing a map skill, or showing them how to use the learning center materials while other children work independently. With the class arranged in this way, it will be possible to group children in many different configurations in accordance with individual needs. What should be avoided are fixed groups that separate children into fast-, medium-, and slow-achieving clusters on a more or less permanent basis.

Scheduling. In traditional instruction, the time provided for learning is usually thought of as a constant fixed amount that is the same for everyone. Assignments are given on a specific day, and the completed work is due on a specific day. Because learners work at different rates, individualized approaches make time a variable rather than a constant. Within reasonable limits, children are allowed to work at their own pace. This requires careful supervision. Left entirely on their own, some would not make good use of their time, and this would work to the detriment of their learning. Nonetheless, the principle of providing for varying rates of learning is sound. This speaks against the use of rigid time schedules that apply to all, with penalties for "late" work.

Extent of Openness. We use the term *openness* to mean both intellectual and physical freedom to learn. It suggests an absence of unnecessary and artificially imposed restrictions on what children learn and how they go about learning it. Regimented management procedures, whole-class teaching, and the use of strict *grading* practices tend to reduce the extent of openness in social studies.

The term *grading* has two meanings. The first has to do with placing children in groups called *grades,* usually on the basis of common age; for example, most six-year-olds are in the first *grade.* The second meaning of grades has to do with the awarding of letters or numerical scores to represent a child's level of achievement, for example, an A, B, or C *grade.* The grade concept is often associated with certain curriculum requirements, hence the common expression "first-grade work," "second-grade work," and so on. There is not now, nor has there ever been, a consensus among teachers and educators as to precisely what constitutes "first-grade, second-grade, or third-grade" work. Nonetheless, it is usually interpreted to mean the average achievement of a child of average intelligence and motivation to do the work prescribed by the curriculum for that grade.

When grade standards are rigidly applied, as they often are, this practice has the effect of restricting learning opportunities. Children who are capable of doing so are discouraged from proceeding beyond what is specified because this would infringe on the curriculum content of the next grade. Meanwhile, the teacher intensifies efforts to get the slower-learning children up to the grade-level standard. Thus, by placing a lid on learning for some children and by requiring unattainable standards for others, the grade standard concept is clearly incompatible with individualized instruction.

These conventional ideas about grades and grade standards must be revised if we are to have the extent of openness needed to individualize instruction. The term *grade* should simply mean the group in which the child is placed and should be disassociated from an expected standard of achievement. That is, to say that a child is in the "third grade" should mean that he or she is in the third year of school. What each child knows or "should" know depends on the individual child. Some will know a great deal; others, very little. Once the issue of grade-level standards is set aside, the teacher can begin looking at the achievement levels of individual children and can set realistic levels of expectation for them.

Teacher Supervision and Guidance. Fairly early in the school year the teacher will be able to identify the children who are well on the way to self-direction in their study habits, those who need a moderate amount of supervision and guidance, and those who will need to be monitored almost continuously.

In building study habits, the teacher must, on the one hand, remain close enough to the situation to lend direction and support, yet, on the other hand, be far enough away to allow the child to experiment with independence. When five or six first-graders are operating the "store" in one corner of the classroom while the teacher is helping four or five others with a mural in another part of the room, it can be expected that help will be needed occasionally in the store to iron out minor problems. The same group as sixth-graders could be expected to work through the entire period without help if their tasks were well defined.

Children need supervision and guidance from the teacher in a great variety of ways. In every class some will need special help with reading. These children may be taken singly or in a small group while the remainder read independently. In this reading-study situation the teacher helps the children with word difficulties, helps them get meaning from visual material, calls their attention to picture captions and discusses the pictures, selects certain key passages and singles those out for special teaching, reads to the children short selections of special significance, and tries to build independence in reading. The teacher, through careful guidance, must help children make the best use of reading resources. This type of guidance is not limited to the primary grades but persists throughout the elementary school.

In most classes, too, there will be another group of children who can go much beyond the remainder of the class in their depth of understanding of the topics studied. With these children, the teacher points out possibilities for additional study, challenges them with provocative problems, suggests topics for additional research, helps them secure appropriate reading material, teaches them how to organize their ideas, and gives similar guidance. The teacher can be of most help to these children by suggesting, challenging, and holding them to high standards of achievement and yet expecting much of their study to be done independently.

The teacher's role in guiding and supervising social studies activities may be described, therefore, as a function of the needs of individual children. Children should not be supervised so closely as to discourage independent habits of work. But neither should the teacher fail to offer the kind of constructive help and guidance growing children need. The teacher should be actively involved during the social studies period — moving from group to group and child to child, assisting, encouraging, suggesting, and doing whatever else is needed to help children move in the direction of desired learning goals.

Multimedia Approaches

The intake of new information is an essential requirement of social studies education, and the conventional information sources have been the textbook and the teacher. For years teachers have been urged to expand these classroom information sources to include the many newer learning resources that are now available. The planned use of a generous and varied offering of learning resources greatly enhances the possibility of individualized learning. What is sought is the use of several different learning resources in combination, which is essentially what a multimedia approach does. Providing variation in the information sources available to children is one of the easiest first steps a teacher can take in individualizing the social studies program. Several specific suggestions are offered in this section.

Reading Materials. The differences in reading ability among individuals are apparent early in the grades and becomes greater as the children move through school. By the time they are in the fifth and sixth grades, the difference between the least capable and most capable readers is often as much as six to eight years. Accommodating these variations in reading ability is, therefore, critical to social studies instruction.

Usually, the teacher will have little problem in securing appropriate reading material for the more capable readers. Given a minimum of direction, they will be able to handle the textbook on their own. They can then be guided to other sources of information, most of which can be geared to their individual interests related to a topic under study or to individual or small group research projects. School and public libraries provide good selections of books that are relevant to many social studies topics. Additionally, the better readers can make use of special references, pamphlets, newspapers, and magazines. The teacher's role is not so much to assist these children with the reading task itself but to provide stimulating and challenging guidance that will motivate them to do the reading. The teacher should help those children develop advanced skills related to information gathering and processing.

With the less capable readers, the teacher will need to (1) provide direct assistance with the reading and (2) make available less difficult materials that deal with the topic under study. A third option is to provide ways for these learners to get needed information through listening, viewing, direct experience, or some other nonreading resource. In using nonreading resources, however, the teacher must recognize that this further reduces the opportunity for the child to practice using reading skills.

When working with less capable readers, either in small groups or individually, the teacher will want to select only those passages or graphic materials that are particularly vital to an understanding of the topic. The meanings of essential terms and concepts included in the passage should be developed prior to doing the reading. Carefully structured guide questions should be used in order to ensure that the reading is done with purpose. That is, children are reading to *find out* specific information. Have these children confirm their responses to literal questions by reading orally the sentence that provides the answer. These reading-study sessions should be kept short (15 to 20 minutes) and should be highly motivated. Additional suggestions relating to reading social studies content are provided in Chapter 9.

As one moves lower in the elementary grades, it becomes more difficult to secure simplified reading materials for social studies. There comes a point beyond which it is impossible to simplify the reading task and still have the narrative provide significant informational content. The teacher can rewrite some passages or create original selections for the slower readers. Because this is time-consuming and often difficult, the amount of such original material a teacher can produce is necessarily limited.

Often overlooked as valuable reading sources for social studies are trade books and literary works. Trade books are what children call "library books." Ordinarily such books can be secured from the school library or from the district instructional resources center. Children will use trade books as sources of information as well as reading them for enjoyment. In the middle and upper grades, simplified nontext books are available on many social studies topics. (See page 79.)

In addition to making these books available, the teacher must structure the learning environment in ways that will ensure that the children and books are brought together. This can be done by making the books an integral part of a learning center. Although some use can be made of book reports, this procedure can easily become routine, uninteresting, and self-defeating. Teachers can prevent this from happening by devising imaginative ways for children to share what they have read with each other. For example, teachers have made use of such follow-up activities as these: (1) evaluate the books children have read in terms of specific criteria (What did you like or dislike about the book? What is especially good about the book? What information does it provide? Would you recommend it to a friend? and so forth); (2) make an illustration that conveys some interesting feature of the book; (3) tape-record a short review of the book; (4) persuade a classmate to read a book found to be especially interesting or useful; (5) read orally to the class selected passages thought to be particularly relevant to the topic.

Learning Kits and Packages. A learning kit or package is a small collection of relevant materials that children can use on their own in studying a topic, concept, or skill. It will ordinarily contain instructions for use, information source materials (reprints, maps, pictures, pamphlets, or other appropriate resources), along with study guide questions,

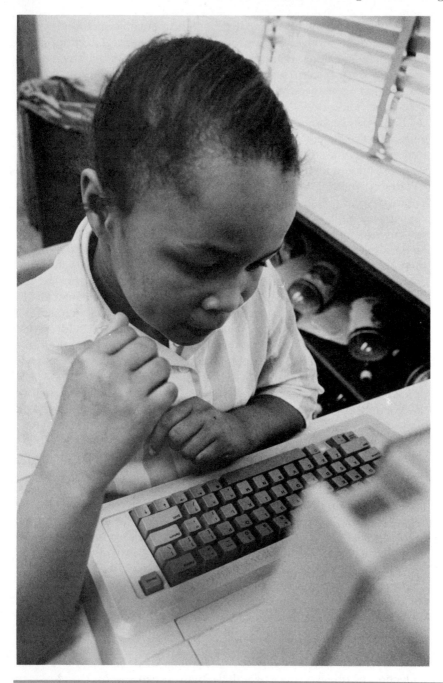

The computer can be a useful tool in helping to individualize instruction for students through the use of drill and practice programs, by developing and using data bases, by doing simulations and games, and by having students prepare spreadsheets and graphics. (Photo by Kay Engelsen, Tacoma School District.)

self-correcting work sheets, or other response formats or a combination of these. Directions must be clear enough to allow children to use the kit or package independently. Learning kits vary in the extent to which they can be used without teacher assistance, but insofar as possible, the kit or package is self-selected by the child; self-directed, self-paced, and self-

Components of a study kit prepared by a fourth-grade teacher on the subject of state parks.

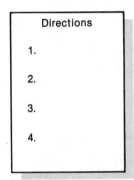

1. Directions to the student.

2. Road map of the state.

3. Tourist brochure entitled "Things to See and Things to Do."

4. Series of newspaper articles dealing with the state park system.

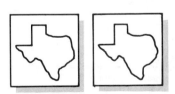

5. Outline maps of the state for student use.

6. A set of photographs; each bearing a one-paragraph caption on the back.

FIGURE 11.1. Components of a Learning Kit based on the subject of state parks.

corrected. Ordinarily such a kit could be contained in a file-size envelope or box. It can be constructed by the teacher or can be purchased from commercial sources. An example of a teacher-prepared, self-directed study packet is provided in Figure 11.1 on page 317.

Learning Centers. Learning kits, packages, and other self-directed materials can be assembled in a designated place in the classroom called a *learning center*. Usually, a learning center will contain multimedia materials focused on a specific topic, concept, or skill. Children are expected to work in the learning center itself rather than checking out materials that are to be used elsewhere. In a learning center one may find filmstrips and projectors, pictures, printed materials, cassette tape recordings, cartridge-type films, books, learning packets, maps, and other appropriate learning resources. They are designed to be used by children on their own as a means of (1) obtaining basic information, (2) practicing a skill, (3) following up on something taught to the entire class, and (4) enriching and extending basic instruction.

Learning center activities and materials must provide the children with specific and precise directions because they are expected to use the center with a minimum of teacher direction and supervision. If this is to happen, children will also have to be instructed on how to use the center. Children should be provided with some choice in what is to be done and should be allowed to work at their own pace. More than one child should be able to work in the center at the same time, and, in some cases, they may work cooperatively on the same activity.

It is important to emphasize that the learning center, as a collection of relevant learning resources, is an integral part of the total resources used by the class in studying a topic. *All* children can and should be expected to make some use of it. The learning center should not be perceived only as a "fun" place for those who complete their regular assignment quickly — as a reward for good work. Such restricted use limits the value of the learning center and denies its use to precisely those children who could benefit most from it.

EXAMPLE OF THE USE OF MULTIMEDIA IN AN INTERMEDIATE GRADE UNIT

Activities

In a unit entitled "The Challenge of Change," a fourth- and fifth-grade class used the following resources and activities that were in an activity packet:

1. Write a diary pretending you are in a Conestoga Wagon going from Independence, Missouri, to the Oregon Territory; have at least five entries. Then write a similar diary either for a trip in the present day or what you would imagine a trip would be like in the

year 2050. Again include five entries telling of things that you have seen and have done.

2. Research one of the following inventions, or choose a scientific discovery of your own. Be sure to include a discussion of how the invention changed the lives of the people at the time of the invention and how it affects our lives today.

   a. automobile
   b. cotton gin
   c. steam engine
   d. camera
   e. locomotive
   f. telegraph
   g. reaper
   h. phonograph

   i. telephone
   j. electric lights
   k. calculator
   l. computer
   m. airplane
   n. television
   o. satellite
   p. artificial body organs

3. Make a booklet of tools and utensils used by the pioneers; in a second part include tools and utensils that might be used in the daily lives of people today.

4. Interview someone who has immigrated to the United States. Try to find out what changes this made in the person's life. Decide on several (three to six) questions you wish to ask the person, and show them to your teacher prior to the interview.

5. Collect cartoons that deal with people making changes in some way. Perhaps the change might come as the result of some conflict or disagreement, or it might show the results of a changed attitude.

6. Make a collage showing change. Have a theme such as

   a. Changes in My Life
   b. Changes in Our Natural Environment
   c. Inventions That Change Lives
   d. Changes in the Status of Minorities and Women
   e. Changes in Recreation

7. Collect newspaper articles that deal with changes. Choose a theme around which to build your collection, such as political or physical changes in your state, city, or community. Arrange to display your collection.

8. Create a map that shows the places where several (three to six) of your classmates have lived during their lives. Be sure to have a key so you can clearly show which moves were made by which classmate. Your teacher has an outline map for you to use.

   Or take a poll to find out how many times each person in your class has moved. Compile your results and show them on a graph.

9. Make a photographic essay showing changes in your community. This could show natural changes or those made by people.

10. Contact a longtime neighborhood resident to find out how the area has changed over time. Use a cassette recorder to tape the oral history interview. Present a report to the class about changes that have taken place, making use of the taped interview.

11. Watch one of the films listed as resources in your packet. Create a poster or a five- or six-frame filmstrip showing the main ideas of the film.

12. Read a fiction book that deals with the changes in the lives of people your own age. Create a way to share your book with the rest of the class. Check the Reading Center for ideas. You might look for one of the following books:

Courage of Sarah Noble, A. Dalgliesh. A true story of a brave girl who in 1707 went with her father into the wilds of Connecticut.

Edge of Two Worlds, W. Jones. Sequoyah, an aging Cherokee leader, and fifteen-year-old Calvin, lone survivor of a Comanche raid, journey across the wilderness.

The Empty Schoolhouse, N. S. Carlson. A ten-year-old black girl in a small Louisiana town endures loneliness and abuse as the first to integrate her school.

Blue Willow, D. Gates. Janey is a child of migrant workers in the San Joaquin Valley in California whose greatest desire is a permanent home.

Bridge to Terabithia, K. Paterson. The story of a close friendship and coping with death.

But What About Me? S. Love. Lucy's mother decides to pursue a career. As a result, Lucy must adjust to changes in her own life.

A Month of Sundays, R. Blue. A boy comes home from summer camp and finds that his parents have separated. The story focuses on his feelings of guilt, confusion, and loneliness and on how he learns to cope with this new situation.

Changes, G. Rabin. This is a story of a young boy who, still mourning the death of his father, must adjust to a move, a change in life-style, new emotions of adolescence, and the loss of a grandparent.

Dear Mr. Henshaw, B. Cleary. Written in the form of letters and a journal, the book tells how a young boy struggles with some changes in his life in an attempt to find his place in the world.

Julie of the Wolves, J. George. This story sensitively describes the life of an Eskimo girl who resists both the old and the new ways of her homeland.

Dorrie's Book, M. Sachs. In her own words, the eleven-year-old narrator, a longtime only child, discusses openly many of the feelings she experienced with the arrival of other children in the family.

Toby, A. Wallace. A young boy has difficulties making friends after a move to a new home.

RESOURCES

Textbooks:

The United States and the Other Americas, Macmillan Publishing Company
Forming a New Nation, American Book Company
The United States of America, Prentice-Hall, Inc.

Resource books available in our library (only a few are listed):

The New Land, P. Viereck
Frontier Living, E. Tunis
New Burlington: The Life and Death of an American Village, J. Baskin.
The Changing Countryside (Vol. I); *The Changing City* (Vol. II), J. Müller.
Living Together in Tomorrow's World, J. W. Watson.
Pioneer Children of America, C. D. Emerson et al.
Sweet Land, Sweet Liberty, based on A. Landsburg television series "The American Idea."

Videotape:

"Think about . . . 60 Plan a City of the Future"

Films:

Age of the Buffalo
Inventions in American Growth: 1750–1850
Inventions in American Growth: 1850–1910
Factory: How a Product is Made
Maps for a Changing World
American Road
Our Changing Way of Life: Cattleman
Prairie
Good Morning Freedom
Ways to Settle Disputes
Understanding Stresses and Strains

Filmstrips:

"Loo Wit: A Changing Lady" (Mount St. Helens)
"America's First Factory"
"How Farming Has Changed"
"The Story of Alexander Graham Bell"
"From Kitty Hawk to Canaveral"
"How Automation Affects Your Life"
"Blazing the Oregon Trail"

Recordings:

"America's Men in Space: The Story of Project Mercury"
"Apollo II: Flight to the Moon"
". . . But the Women Rose . . ."
"We Shall Overcome"

Slides:

Early Hometown (Compiled by the local school district)

Study Prints:

Transportation—Includes photographs that tell the story of transportation from Indian canoes to airplanes.

Jamestown, Virginia — Color photographs of seventeenth-century people in authentic costumes.

Historic Williamsburg — Color photographs showing the social, political, economic, and family life of the Virginia colonists in the eighteenth century.

Mount St. Helens — Photographs of the mountain before, during, and after the volcanic eruption.

Field Trips:

Bell Telephone Center
Safeway Food Distribution Center
State Historical Society
Museum of History and Industry
American Bakeries Co./Langendorf Division

Current Newspapers and News Magazines.

Performance-Based Approaches

In using performance-based approaches to individualizing instruction, careful attention must be given to the specific objectives to be achieved by each child. For example, it is clear that ideas and skills can be handled at varying levels of complexity. Likewise, children vary in their ability to deal with complex ideas. In performance-based teaching, the teacher attempts to match the level of complexity of the objectives with the learner's ability to achieve them. This can be done by using behavioral objectives that are geared to various levels of difficulty, by using instructional material that is self-paced, or by using individual contracts.

Learner Contracts. A *learner contract* is defined as a cooperatively developed agreement between an individual and the teacher. The contract specifies precisely what the child will do and when the work is to be completed. Because contracts are individually negotiated, the nature and extent of the work to be completed can be well suited to the ability level and the interests of the child. Some teachers develop and use a contract form that gives the agreement an official appearance. Contracts are signed by both the child and the teacher. Examples of contract forms are provided in Figures 11.2 and 11.3.

The use of contracts has educational values beyond being an interesting assignment format. The children should learn what is involved in a contractual agreement and that there usually are adverse consequences when contracts are not completed as specified. Therefore, it is important

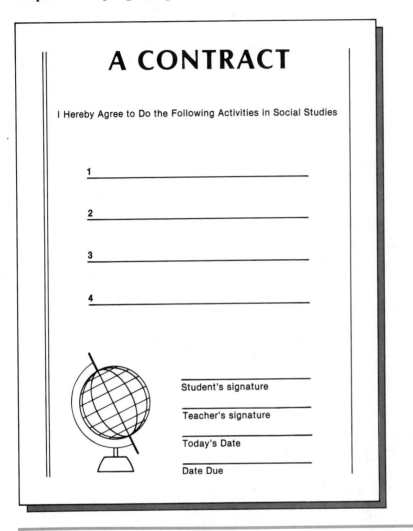

FIGURE 11.2. A sample learner contract format.

that children know what it is they are agreeing to do and what penalties may be attached to the failure to fulfill the conditions of the contract.

Special Assignments. A teacher may want to make special assignments to accommodate the particular interests or talents of certain children. For example, a child who is intellectually gifted may be assigned to do an independent research project related to a social studies topic. Children who have special talents and abilities in doing art, music, drama, or construction projects should be encouraged to apply these abilities in social studies. Social studies is the ideal area of the curriculum to make

AN AGREEMENT

As my contribution to the unit, OUR TOWN, I agree to do the project or projects checked:

_____ 1. Interview a person who has lived here a long time.

_____ 2. Conduct a survey of old buildings in our town.

_____ 3. Write a true story about our town.

_____ 4. Write a short play about our town.

_____ 5. Work on a mural with _____
                                              (Name other children)

_____ 6. Paint a picture of something in our town.

_____ 7. Prepare a TV program script about our town.

_____ 8. Do an original activity of my own: _____

_____

Today's Date: _____   _____
                                                          Student

Due Date: _____   _____
                                                          Teacher

---

INDIVIDUAL STUDY PLAN

I contract to do the following activities that are described on pages 157–158 of our text, to be completed by November 15:

(Check *two*)

_____ Using A Time Line   _____ Making History Real

_____ Building Ideas from Words   _____ Interesting Things To Do
                   and Pictures
                                            _____ Things to Think About
_____ Making an Outline   (Write out your answers)

_____ Making a Chart

Date: _____   _____
                                                       Student

                              _____
                                                       Teacher

FIGURE 11.3. Other variations of learner contracts.

adjustments to such special capabilities of learners. Children should not, however, always work on projects for which they have a special talent. Like all other children, they, too, need to have a balanced learning experience.

Individualized Education Program (IEP). Although the IEP is associated with and required for handicapped children, such plans can be used with any learner. The use of the IEP requires that the teacher assess the learning needs of individual children and draft a program plan consistent with that assessment. With class sizes being what they are, it is not feasible to think in terms of preparing IEPs for all children unless the teacher is provided considerable assistance. Nonetheless, this procedure may be just what is needed for particular children who have difficulty managing the regular instructional program.

Mastery Learning Based on Behavioral Objectives. Public concern over the quality of education has required schools to provide more documentary evidence of learner achievement than has been the case in the past. In responding to that concern for accountability, schools have turned to the use of minimum competency testing and to "precision teaching," meaning teaching targeted on the achievement of specifically defined objectives. Such "student learning objectives" are usually stated behaviorally and are interpreted as essentials that all children must learn. In other words, of all the potential things that *could* be learned, the teacher or the school authorities have said, "These items must be mastered at certain levels of proficiency by all learners."

Teachers can individualize the achievement of such objectives for children by varying the amount of time from one child to the next, by using different kinds of instructional materials, or by using different presentation modes for different children. What is important is that when the instruction is completed, all learners are able to demonstrate, through *performance*, that they have "mastered" the material.

Performance-based procedures require a close working relationship between individual children and the teacher. This means frequent conferences in order to monitor performance and progress toward specific objectives. An assessment of the child's status is essential if an individual study program is to be planned. Thus, a system for the diagnosis of learner needs is an essential component of performance-based programs. Much of this can be done informally as the teacher observes the work of individual children. In the middle and upper grades, the teacher can also make use of diagnostic tests.

It is important to stress that independent study, as characterized by performance-based teaching, is not the same as individualized learning. Individualized learning can and often does take place in group settings. Good social studies programs will not result if children constantly work by themselves without the opportunity to interact with others. Some provision must be made for small and large group activities during which time the results of individual study are shared, ideas are discussed, group activities are planned, and new areas of study are explored. This will ensure that the social dimensions of social studies education are not being overlooked.

Creative or Activity-Based Approaches

Much can be done to individualize social studies learning by encouraging children to imagine, to wonder, to act out feelings, to create, and to express their ideas and feelings through art forms and similar creative or activity modes. These approaches must be used in combination with some of the other approaches suggested in this chapter. The difference between this approach and the others is that it individualizes learning at the outgo or expressive level whereas all the others vary the ways children receive ideas or information. The use of creative and expressive activities is discussed in detail in Chapter 13.

Social studies activities should be sufficiently varied to appeal to the broad range of interests and capabilities of children. Some activities such as oral and written reports tend to be overused. Activities that are highly correlated with the usual academic skills and abilities are useful, of course, but other options should also be available. Not all children are able to perform these activities well, and consequently their involvement in the social studies program is limited. Most social studies teaching would be improved through the use of a wide range of activities, especially those that require the child to use creative imagination. The suggestions on pages 289–292 illustrate the types of learning activities that should at one time or another be included in social studies instruction.

This chapter has emphasized the need for taking a broad view of individualizing social studies instruction. Too frequently, individualizing instruction is understood to mean "doing something for the gifted" or "doing something for the slow learners." *The fact is that every child presents the teacher with the challenge of individual differences.* The teacher who accepts this broader concept of individual differences will take into account not only the child's IQ but also the other factors that influence the child's achievement of social studies objectives. This will ensure that some adjustments will be made in the program for the unique needs of every child irrespective of his or her mental ability. But because the problem of providing for exceptional children is a matter of special concern to many teachers, the next section addresses that subject.

INDIVIDUALIZING FOR EXCEPTIONALITY

The Congress of the United States enacted two pieces of legislation during the decade of the 1970s that had a profound effect on the education of persons with handicapping conditions. The first of these was Section 504 of the Vocational Rehabilitation Act of 1973. This law deals largely with the removal of discriminatory practices against the handicapped. Although it is basically a law that protects the civil rights of handicapped persons, it has a number of implications for education. It guarantees that an individual may not be denied access to education solely on the basis of a handicapping condition. As a result, Section 504 brought some greater extension of employment, training, and promotion opportunities to handicapped individuals.

Perhaps the most important contribution of Section 504 was its mandate to remove barriers in architecture and in transportation. The law requires that all *activities* (not all areas or spaces) must be accessible to physically handicapped participants and spectators. This meant that substantial structural modifications in existing school buildings had to be made in order to bring them into compliance. New structures must make provisions for these antidiscriminatory requirements in their design. Section 504 was instrumental in establishing "barrier-free" environments in schools.

In 1975 two Congressional Subcommittees held hearings in various parts of the country to determine what, if any, additional legislation was needed to accommodate the educational needs of the handicapped. Some of the findings of these hearings were astounding: Over 1.75 million children with handicaps were being excluded *entirely* from receiving a public education solely on the basis of their handicap. Over half of the estimated 8 million children were not receiving appropriate services. Many children with handicaps were being placed in inappropriate educational environments because their handicaps had not been detected. As a result of these findings and as a result of concurrent judicial intervention, the 142nd piece of legislation passed by the 94th Congress was the Education for All Handicapped Children Act, otherwise known as PL94-142. It passed both Houses of Congress by very wide margins — probably because the issue had already been settled by the courts. The bill was signed into law by President Gerald Ford on November 29, 1975, to go into effect in 1977, with no expiration date.

PL94-142 is one of the most lengthy and complex pieces of legislation ever enacted by Congress. Its main points, however, are easily summarized. The law requires

1. The availability of a free appropriate public education for all handicapped children between the ages of three and twenty-one, unless

inconsistent with state laws; school districts are obliged to search for and identify handicapped children.

2. The maintenance of an Individualized Education Program (IEP) for all handicapped children, prepared in cooperation with the parent or guardian, the teacher, and the school principal.
3. The guarantee of complete due process procedures.
4. The provision of special education and related services as needed in the "least restrictive" environment.
5. The nondiscriminatory testing, evaluation, and placement.
6. The placement in regular public school settings with nonhandicapped peers to the maximum extent appropriate and feasible.

PL94-142 is based on a philosophy of *inclusion* rather than *exclusion*. It embraces the "zero-reject" principle. It frowns on the segregation and labeling of human beings. It shatters long-held assumptions about who is educable.

Teaching Children with Handicapping Conditions

Traditionally, elementary school teachers dealt with the handicapped by referring them to special education classes. As we have seen, this type of arbitrary exclusion is no longer socially or legally acceptable. Today the teacher can expect one or more children with varying types of handicapping conditions to be present in most elementary school classrooms. This practice, known popularly as "mainstreaming," is the school's response to the mandate that children must be educated with their nonhandicapped peers to the maximum extent appropriate.

What the teacher can do and will do depends on the nature of the child's disability and the extent of support service provided. It is quite clear that a child who is orthopedically handicapped but is intellectually gifted will be handled differently from one who is physically fully functioning but is mildly — or severely — retarded intellectually. In this context, the Individualized Education Program makes good sense because the learning needs of children vary greatly from one to another. Likewise, what the teacher does or does not do will depend on how much technical assistance and support service is available. If the classroom has the services of an interpreter-tutor who can work with the handicapped child for part of the time in a one-on-one setting and who works with the teacher on a cooperative basis, it becomes easier for the regular teacher to integrate the handicapped child into the day-to-day life and activities of the classroom.

In the case of a child who is severely disabled, the chances are good that a teacher trained in special education will prepare the Individualized Education Program. The classroom teacher may be responsible for only a small part of the implementation of the IEP. On the other hand, if the teacher has a child in the class who is mildly retarded, that teacher may have full responsibility for the preparation and implementation of the IEP. Even in cases of mildly handicapped children, the regular classroom teacher may have available the assistance of a special education teacher in preparing the IEP. In those cases in which the handicapped child is attending both regular and special education classes, ordinarily the IEP goals and objectives will focus on compensating for the child's handicap, and it is the special education teacher who attends the IEP meeting. The regular classroom teacher, the special education teacher, and other support personnel must, of course, work in close cooperation with each other to ensure a coordinated program of instruction for the handicapped child.

The Individualized Education Program must take into account the child's present level of attainment or development. In other words, a learning needs assessment must be made, and the current status established. Based on that information, the IEP stipulates the long-range goals that are to be met by the end of the year and the short-term objectives to be achieved in order to attain the long-range goals. The short-term objectives should be listed in the sequence in which they are to be achieved. Although the regular teacher may exercise some initiative in preparing the IEP, the program planning and development *must* include, on a firsthand basis, the principal or other school representative and the child's parent or guardian. Teacher-prepared IEPs that are sent to the child's parent or guardian for signature are not acceptable in terms of the mandate of PL94-142.

The actual format of the IEP will vary from district to district although the substance of what is included will remain pretty much the same. The sample form provided on pages 330–332 illustrates a standard IEP that includes components required by federal regulations.

SUGGESTIONS FOR TEACHING SLOWER-LEARNING CHILDREN

1. Provide generously for firsthand, concrete experiences. These children learn best by handling, manipulating, sensing, feeling, and doing; and they learn least well by reading, analyzing, generalizing, and finding new solutions to problems.
2. Learning tasks must be specific and simple; learning objectives must be definite, clear-cut, and short-ranged. The children must know precisely what to do and how to do it. Use detailed study guides.
3. Learning experiences should be presented in one small step at a time with successful completion of each step before advancement to the next.
4. Recognize that lessons should be short in duration because of the brevity of the attention span of many slow learners.
5. Expect them to show less initiative and less ability to plan for themselves than

PIEDMONT PUBLIC SCHOOLS
INDIVIDUALIZED EDUCATION PROGRAM

Standard Form

Student _____ Birthdate _____
                                 C.A. _____

Address _____ (include zip) _____ Lives With _____ Relationship _____ Home Phone _____ Work Phone _____

Home School _____ Grade _____ IEP Conference Date _____ Projected Review Date _____

Teacher _____ Program _____ School _____ Date Enrolled _____ Terminated _____

I. SUMMARY OF PRESENT LEVELS OF PERFORMANCE
   (Include statements of progress in each area from last reporting period)

SCHOLASTIC:

PHYSICAL:

ADJUSTMENT:

II. ANALYSIS OF ASSESSMENT DATA
    (Report of significant changes since initial IEP)

ELIGIBILITY CRITERIA: _____

PLACEMENT OFFICE ONLY:

Date Enrolled
Teacher
Building
Program Assigned

_____
_____
_____

PROGRAM AND/OR REPLACEMENT CHANGE:

Team Leader: _____ Date: _____
Parent: _____ Date: _____

PROGRAM RECOMMENDATION:

Psychologist: _____ Date: _____
Parent: _____ Date: _____
_____ Date: _____

330

III. STUDENT GOALS & OBJECTIVES

Academic Year _____

Special Classroom Teacher _____

Support Services _____

(Specify Service)

Name of Student	B.D.	Grade	Program	Building	Teacher	Date Enrolled	
						Date Started	Date Completed
Initial Objectives:			Evaluation Criteria & Progress Notes (include pre-test, post-test data, and grades)				
Goals:							

_____
Signature of person or persons responsible for reporting progress on goals and objectives

_____
Parent Signature

_____
Date

Student: _____   Projected I.E.P. Review Date _____

IV. RELATED SERVICES

	Estimated Time/Week	Anticipated Start	End
Regular Education Program:			
Support Services: (C.D.S., P.E., Voc. etc.)			

Regular P.E. ☐   Adaptive P.E. ☐

My rights and responsibilities have been explained to me in a manner which I understand.

I have had the opportunity to participate in the development of this Individualized Education Program.

I understand all programs and services listed above and give my permission for my child/ward to participate in these programs/services.

I have been informed that the objectives listed on this form are initial objectives and that the person(s) responsible for implementing the objectives will revise and/or add objectives in keeping with the student's progress toward the stated goals.

Parent Signature: _____

Date: _____

V. I.E.P. Committee Members:

Name	Position

The School District shall provide the parent (or the adult student) a copy of the individualized education program.

average or gifted children. They are also less able to evaluate their own work, making close supervision and direction by the teacher imperative.

6. Reduce their load of abstract and verbal materials to a level they are able to handle. Work in references, if used at all, must be specific; reading and research must be held to a minimum.

7. Recognize that it will be difficult for them to sense relationships, to make generalizations, or to do inferential thinking. They are more skillful in dealing with *who, what,* and *where* questions than they are with *why* type questions.

8. When teaching crucial items such as those of health, safety, laws or conventions of society, or simple elements of social studies skills, plan to provide for much practice and repetition of the material to be learned.

9. Set realistic levels of expectation for them. Plan in terms of their most pressing needs with a view toward their future life as happy and productive members of society. Try to visualize what knowledge and skills will be most useful to the child in the future.

10. Above all, maintain a patient and encouraging attitude toward them. Help them establish security and status in the classroom. Provide opportunities for a degree of success for them.

SUGGESTIONS FOR TEACHING GIFTED CHILDREN

1. Provide a generous amount of challenging reading material that will allow them to read for informational purposes.

2. Plan learning activities that call for problem solving, making logical associations, making logical deductions, and making generalizations.

3. Give them many opportunities to plan their own work; allow for a considerable amount of individual initiative, commensurate with their degree of maturity.

4. Provide for individual study and research. This should include use of the library and references, as well as note keeping, outlining, summarizing, and reporting.

5. Expect and encourage much originality in self-expression — in discussions, dramatizations, projects, and activities.

6. Recognize that they have less need for extended firsthand and concrete experiences than do slow-learning or average-learning children because they are able to work with abstractions more easily, see associations and relationships more quickly, and have quick reaction time.

7. Encourage these children to develop self-evaluative skills; they are generally capable of effectively evaluating their own work.

8. Give them many opportunities for leadership responsibilities. Provide opportunities for gifted children to use their talents in helping slower-learning children on a tutorial basis. In some schools children of the intermediate grades with high intellectual abilities also work with primary-grade children.

9. Remember that gifted children have many of the common needs of all children. Although it is true that they are ordinarily accelerated in other aspects of their development as well, their physical growth, muscular coordination, social development, and emotional stability cannot be equated with their rate of growth in mental development.

10. The complete acceptance by the teacher of the high intellectual abilities of gifted children is essential to planning an effective program for them. The teacher who sees gifted children as a threat becomes defensive and is unable to work with them satisfactorily.

DISCUSSION QUESTIONS AND SUGGESTED ACTIVITIES

1. Do you believe that a teacher's expectations relate in any way to a child's achievement? Explain.

2. Develop a floor plan of a room environment that would lend itself well to the individualization of instruction.

3. How can the teacher ensure that the social values of social studies education are being attained in a program that individualizes instruction?

4. Prepare a small learning kit or package that could be used by children in a grade of your choice.

5. Design a sketch of a classroom learning center for social studies, and show what you would include in it.

6. Develop a learner contract suitable for use in a grade of your choice.

7. What procedures for individualizing instruction might be used in groups that (a) have a high percentage of poor readers; (b) have limited language ability; (c) have a high percentage of high-achieving, capable children; or (d) present difficult management problems?

8. If you visited an elementary school classroom, what would you look for that would suggest that individualizing of instruction is taking place in social studies?

9. What new knowledge and skills does a regular teacher need to have in order to work effectively with handicapped children who are assigned to his or her classroom?

10. What differences can you identify between the practice of "mainstreaming" and that of placing children with handicapping conditions in "least restrictive learning environments"?

SELECTED REFERENCES

BRANDT, RONALD S., ed. *Educational Leadership* 46(March 1989). Several authors contribute 16 articles on student differences to this issue.

BUTLER, KATHLEEN A. "Learning Styles." *Learning 88* (November/December 1988), pp. 30–34.

BYRNES, DEBORAH A. "Forgotten Children in Classrooms: Development and Characteristics." *The Elementary School Journal,* 84 (January 1984), pp. 271–281.

DOLGINS, JUDITH, MARCEE MYERS, PATRICIA A. FLYNN, AND JOSSIE MOORE. "How Do We Help the Learning Disabled?" *Instructor,* 93 (February 1984), pp. 30–36.

GUILD, PAT BURKE, AND STEPHEN GARGER. *Marching to Different Drummers.* Alexandria, Virginia: Association for Supervision and Curriculum Development, 1985.

HERLIHY, JOHN G., AND MYRA T. HERLIHY, eds. *Mainstreaming in the Social Studies.* NCSS Bulletin No. 62. Washington, D.C.: National Council for the Social Studies, 1980.

OCHOA, ANNA S., AND SUSAN K. SHUSTER. *Social Studies in the Mainstreamed Classroom*. Boulder, Colorado: ERIC Clearinghouse for Social Studies/Social Science Education, Social Science Education Consortium, Inc., 1980.

RIEDESEL, C. ALAN, AND DOUGLAS H. CLEMENTS. *Coping with Computers in the Elementary and Middle Schools*. Englewood Cliffs, New Jersey: Prentice-Hall, 1985. Chapter 10.

ROHRKEMPER, MARY, AND LYN CORNO. "Success and Failure on Classroom Tasks: Adaptive Learning and Classroom Teaching." *The Elementary School Journal,* 88 (January 1988), pp. 297–313.

SALEND, SPENCER J. "Factors Contributing to the Development of Successful Mainstreaming Programs." *Exceptional Children,* 50 (February 1984), pp. 409–416.

SHAW, TERRY, ed. *Teaching Handicapped Students Social Studies: A Resource Handbook for K–12 Teachers*. Washington, D.C.: National Education Association, 1981.

12

Skills for Group Interaction

"Nothing we learn is more important than the skills of collaboration," [1] and social studies education provides a natural setting in which to teach, promote, and practice social and group-work skills. The learning activities that characterize soundly based social studies programs require children to plan and work together; to strive toward common goals; and to share materials, tools, and resources. Although it is true that the total school curriculum assists in the growth of social behavior, the social studies program should contribute to its attainment in a special way.

The term *group* must be understood to mean something more than a collection of individuals. Groups develop a solidarity—a unity or cohesiveness—resulting from working and thinking together. A fourth-

[1] David W. Johnson, Roger T. Johnson, Edythe Johnson Holubec, and Patricia Roy, *Circles of Learning: Cooperation in the Classroom* (Alexandria, Va.: Association for Supervision and Curriculum Development, 1984), p. 52.

The "social" component of social studies is learned through experiences in interacting with others. Working together, sharing ideas and things with others, and engaging in study and play activities in a secure and caring environment are the conditions that foster growth in human relations skills. (Photo by Robb Michell, Tacoma School District.)

grade class at the beginning of a school year is an aggregate of individual children assigned to a particular room because of their similar chronological ages. This class of individuals may develop into a *group* as the year progresses and the children develop feelings of belonging to it, identifying with it, developing an esprit de corps, and growing in their concern for the welfare and success of the class. It will be a *group* to the extent that the actions of individuals are influenced by other members and the extent to which the behavior of individual members affects the group.

SETTING A DESIRABLE ATMOSPHERE FOR HUMAN RELATIONS

Why is it that some teachers are able to build a classroom atmosphere that is emotionally supportive, one in which children feel comfortable and secure, and other teachers have difficulty doing so? Doubtless, part of the reason can be attributed to personality variables. Some teachers have a greater tolerance for flexibility and ambiguity than do others. Quite apart from these variations in personalities of teachers, however, it is possible to identify teacher behaviors that contribute to or detract from setting a desirable atmosphere for human relations in the classroom.

We are not unmindful of the fact that groups of children also vary considerably and that the task of developing a wholesome classroom climate is more challenging with some groups than it is with others. Children who have developed hostile and aggressive life-styles outside of school bring those dispositions and behaviors to school with them. Groups that have been together for a few years may have formed in-groups, cliques, or bad feelings toward each other that persist from year to year. In some cases, children are so lacking in any sense of self-discipline and common courtesy that even the most skillful teacher would have a difficult time trying to develop some sense of group feeling based on unity and cooperation. Where such conditions prevail, effective teaching cannot take place unless and until basic problems of classroom management are resolved. We do not deal with such chronic problems of disruptive behavior because they are beyond the scope of this text.

An emotionally supportive atmosphere is one that is characterized by trust and by evidence that individuals care about each other. When a child volunteers, "Robin's group had more to do than the rest of us. They should have more time to finish," the observer senses that he or she is in a caring environment. Or when a minor classroom accident results in damage to material or broken equipment and the teacher treats the incident as an accident, one concludes that the teacher values human beings more than things. Teachers who develop comfortable classroom environments are concerned with a broad range of educational outcomes, including those that relate to the emotional and social development of children, in addition to attending to subject matter and skills goals. The classroom conditions that establish the *setting* in which children learn the basics of human relations is sometimes referred to as the *hidden curriculum.*

Perhaps the most significant characteristic of a desirable classroom climate is the lack of hostility between children and the teacher and among individuals within the group. The level of hostility and aggressive behavior in a classroom is related to what the teacher says and does. Teacher behavior can best be illustrated by such contrasts as the following:

DIMENSIONS OF THE HIDDEN CURRICULUM

PRACTICES AND PROCEDURES THAT TEND TO INCREASE HOSTILITY IN A CLASSROOM

1. *Negative statements by the teacher*—Here are a few examples of ridicule, sarcasm, criticism, neg-

PRACTICES AND PROCEDURES THAT TEND TO DECREASE HOSTILITY IN A CLASSROOM

1. *Positive statements by the teacher*—Friendly, constructive statements by the teacher tend to

ative, and tension-producing statements made by a teacher. Such statements to children invariably lead to hostility, emotional disturbance, selfishness, fear, and criticism of others:

"I wish you would start acting like fourth-graders instead of kindergartners."

"Someone is whispering again, and I guess you all know who it is."

"Most fifth-grade classes could understand this, but I am not sure about you."

"Sit up straight. Don't you have a backbone?"

"Why don't you listen when I give directions? None of you seems to know how to listen."

2. *Excessively competitive situations* — Fair competition in classrooms is highly desirable. It can stimulate good work, motivate children to do their best, and help children learn the graces associated with winning and losing. It becomes undesirable when it is of the "dog-eat-dog" variety where each child is pitted against every other child whether the competitive situation is fair or unfair.

3. *Disregard for individual differences* — Classrooms where some children are made to feel "this place is not for me" contribute much toward breeding hostility in children. Such rooms are characterized by one level of acceptable performance applied to all, uniform assignments, one system of reward, great emphasis on verbal, intellectual performance.

4. *Rigid schedule and pressure* — A rigid time schedule and constant

reduce tension and hostility in the classroom. Here are a few examples:

"We will all want to listen carefully in order not to miss anything Sue is going to tell us."

"All of us did our work so well yesterday during our work period. Do you suppose we can do as well today?"

"It is really fun for all of us when you bring such interesting things for sharing."

"It's nice to have Jason and Kendra back with us again. The boys and girls were hoping you would come back today."

2. *Successful cooperative enterprises* — The successful achievement of cooperative activities, involving all members of the class, tends to reduce hostility within the group because it demands the combined efforts of everyone in the successful attainment of a common goal. Children depend on one another in such situations and, therefore, feel a need for one another.

3. *Recognition of and adaptations made in accordance with individual differences* — In such classrooms, children are challenged at a level commensurate with their abilities. Boys and girls feel that they "count for something" in the classroom and that they belong to it.

4. *Relaxed, comfortable pace* — Good teachers working with

pressure associated with "hurry up," "finish your work," "you will be late," or stopping lessons exactly on time whether completed or not create insecurity in children that leads to hostility. A class that is always "one jump behind the teacher" is likely to be one in which children blame others for their failure to finish, invent excuses for themselves, and seek scapegoats.

5. *Highly directive teaching practices*—Teachers who must make every decision themselves, give all the assignments, allow for very little participation on the part of children in the life of the classroom are encouraging feelings of hostility. Such practices usually mean that teachers refer to the class as "my children," or in addressing them, say, "I want you to . . .," or more subtly, "Miss So-and-so wasn't very proud of her class this morning."

6. *Lack of closeness between teacher and children*—Some teachers feel they must "keep children in their place," meaning they must remain socially distant from them. This leads to a cold objective relationship between the children and teacher, causing the children to feel that the teacher lacks affection and warmth for them. This "holier-than-thou" attitude on the part of the teacher is likely to engender feelings of hostility in some children.

young children maintain a flexible schedule and will not place undue pressures on children. They will have a plan and a schedule, yet will not be compulsive in adhering to it. They will deviate from their plan and schedule now and then in the interest of the needs of the boys and girls they teach. Good teachers recognize that feelings of insecurity are related to hostility and will do everything they can to develop feelings of security in the classroom.

5. *Student involvement in planning and managing the class*—Giving children some opportunity to plan and manage the affairs of the classroom does much to develop feelings of "we-ness," of identification with the group. Children under such circumstances are less inclined to want to think of ways to disrupt Miss So-and-so's orderly room but will work hard to make "our" room a good place to work.

6. *Warm and friendly relationship between teacher and children*—One of the basic needs of children is that of love and affection. They need it in their homes, in their playgroups, and in their schools. The feeling that children will not respect the teacher who is friendly with them is in error. They are likely to respect the teacher more who they feel is a "human being" capable of cordial and warm personal relationships with others. This is a professional relationship, however, and teachers are advised *against* trying to develop a peer relationship with the children they teach.

7. *Lack of satisfying emotional experiences* — Some classrooms do not provide opportunities to express positive affect. Everything is deadly serious business — work, work, work. Even the music, art, story time, or dramatic activities are made to seem like work. Little time is spent on teaching children to enjoy one another, feel the inner joy that comes from a good poem or music selection, or express their feelings in some art medium.

7. *Many opportunities for pleasurable emotional experiences* — Teachers can reduce tensions that build up in children during the course of classroom life by providing opportunities for the release of these tensions through various emotional experiences. Children have the opportunity to express their feelings orally, in writing, or through art forms. They talk together and enjoy one another's company. They prepare skits, do creative dramatics, and role-play situations to help get the feelings of others. All these activities tend to reduce feelings of hostility.

ORGANIZING SUBGROUPS FOR SOCIAL STUDIES INSTRUCTION

Committee work or small-group enterprises are effective instructional procedures in the social studies and have many values for children. It is in the small group that the children get experience with and develop skill in group processes. These experiences should begin in a limited way even as early as the kindergarten. In block play, for example, the teacher can let some children choose the things they wish to build with blocks. Some will want to build an airport; some, a house; others, a post office; others, a supermarket; and so on. The teacher can let each of these children choose two other children to help build the project. The children proceed with the building and, when it is completed, tell the class or their teacher a story about their building. Early experiences in such block play will consist mainly of parallel play — three children may be building an airport but each is working independently of the other two. As the year progresses, there will be more evidence of cooperative endeavor. Children become more conscious of what others in their group are doing and will plan their own contribution in terms of the other children and the group goal.

A good way to familiarize primary-grade children with small-group work is to have committees responsible for various housekeeping duties in the classroom. Jenny's committee has the responsibility of keeping the library table neat, Paul's committee is in charge of the game shelf, Peter's committee is responsible for the care of the aquarium, and Kathy's committee keeps the coat corner orderly. Membership on these committees can be changed from time to time to include all the children in the class. Such experiences will help prepare children for the committee work that is done as a part of the instructional program. Small-group enterprises in the primary grades need careful supervision and direction. The goals or purposes of the group should be well defined, concrete, and easily understood. Materials needed for the group to do its work must be immediately at hand. Rules and responsibilities of working on committees should be discussed, explained, and posted conspicuously in the room. Group-work skills develop slowly and gradually and require practice as do any other skills. The skills of group work can be learned only by working in groups.

In the middle and upper grades, small-group work becomes an increasingly greater part of the social studies instructional program. At these grade levels, small-group work can take on more of the qualities of what some authors refer to as *cooperative learning*.[2] Cooperative learning occurs when small groups of students work together for the purpose of attaining a common goal. Each member has an assigned task in helping the group achieve its goal. Committees are used to prepare reports; discuss topics; plan activities; do construction, art, or dramatic activities; write plays; gather resources; interview resource persons; and so on. Through instruction and experience, children will learn responsibilities of committee chairpersons and committee members and will learn that the success of the group depends on the initiative and cooperation of individuals within the group.

When teaching is planned on a unit basis, there will be many occasions when the class will be divided into small work groups. These subgroups should be organized in accordance with the ages of the children and the nature of the task to be performed. Such subgroups are *task-oriented;* they are formed to do things that need doing. Task groups tend to be relatively flexible and short-lived. A committee may be assigned the task of finding out why pioneers moved westward. When the committee has obtained its information and has reported to the larger group, it can be dissolved, and its members can either join other groups or work on individual activities.

Teachers who have experimented with small-group instruction commonly feel that group work breaks down either because some children within the groups do most of the work or because the children waste time and accomplish very little. This is characteristic of immature groups and is an indication that the children have not yet developed the prerequisite skills for effective cooperative endeavors. Two kinds of skills are needed. First, it is important that members of the group have the appropriate skills necessary to carry through the assigned task to completion. It would be unwise, for example, to send a group of fifth-graders to the library to find

---

[2] *Ibid.*

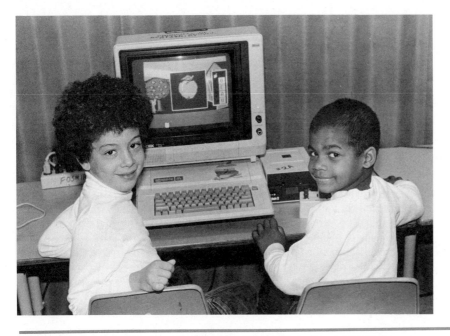

Computer use does not necessarily need to isolate children. By working at the computer in teams, children can develop social as well as intellectual skills. (Photo by Edna Kellman, Seattle Public Schools.)

information about population growth and food distribution if none of the children knew how to use the library for that purpose. Similarly, children who do not have well-developed reading skills should not be placed on group projects that demand a considerable amount of reading and research activity. The nature of the task assigned to a committee should be consistent with the ability of the individual members who comprise the group. Because the finished product presumably represents the combined cooperative efforts of all members, each must be able to contribute in some measure to its successful completion.

Second, the teacher needs to help children develop the social skills needed in order to function as a group: organizing, selecting a leader, designating responsibilities, deciding on controls, and various ways of working together. If, for example, the group sent to the library to find materials was unable to organize itself, plan how it would go about its work, assign specific responsibilities, decide who was the leader, and how it would report its findings, its efforts would not be that of a group but rather would be that of individuals working independently. It would be trying to move in several different directions at one time, making progress as a *group* impossible.

In organizing subgroups within a class, the teacher may find the following suggestions helpful:

GUIDELINES FOR ORGANIZING SMALL-GROUP WORK

1. Defer small-group work until the management of the class has been firmly established and until the work habits, capabilities, and special needs of individual children are known.
2. Begin cooperative group work slowly. Have children begin by working in pairs. Then select responsible key children for the first group and keep the group small — never more than five children.
3. Assign a task that is simple, well-defined, and one that the group is certain to accomplish successfully.
4. Have the remainder of the class engage in individual assignments while giving guidance and direction to the smaller group. Either designate a leader for the small group or have the children choose a leader. Explain the nature of their assigned task, and begin to discuss some of their special responsibilities when working in a small group.
5. Have resource materials available for the children. Later on, as they become accustomed to working in groups, they will be able to secure needed materials themselves.
6. Meet with the small group every day for a few minutes before they begin work and again at the end of their work period to make sure things are moving along as planned. If possible, have them make a progress report to the other, larger group during the summary and evaluation that should come at the close of each social studies period.
7. Give students specific help and suggestions in how to organize their work and how to report what they are doing.
8. Have their report to the class be short, concise, and interesting. Have members of the group explain to the class how they did their work as a group. Begin calling attention to some of the responsibilities of persons working collaboratively in small groups.
9. Follow the same procedure with another group of children as soon as possible. Gradually include other children, selecting some who have had previous experience in group work and some who have not. Observe carefully the children who need close supervision and those who are responsible and work well in groups.
10. After all the children have had an opportunity to work in a small group under close supervision, more than one group can work at one time. Eventually, the entire class should be able to work in small groups simultaneously. When this is attempted, it should be preceded by a review of the standards of group work, objectives should be clearly defined beforehand, and a careful evaluation should follow.

These principles are apparent in the following example of a teacher's getting a small group started on a task.

The children in Mr. Shigaki's class have been involved in a career awareness study and are going to have resource persons visit their classroom. The children have indicated careers they would like to have included. Mr. Shigaki has asked four children to meet him in the rear of the classroom and is now speaking to them.

"Because the four of you are particularly interested in learning about computer science careers, I am asking that you take responsibility for introducing Ms. Timms tomorrow. You will have to select some one person to actually do the introducing. The others can help by suggesting things that should be said about her in the introduction. Also, all of you should help develop some questions to ask her after her presentation. Remember one of our objectives is to find out what kind of training and skills computer scientists need and what opportunities there are in that field. Is there anything else you think you will need to prepare in order to be the host group tomorrow?'' (Pause)

One member of the group asked if they were to thank the visitor for coming.

"Yes. Good point! I'm glad you thought of that, Mark. You will need to select someone to thank Ms. Timms. Anything else?'' (Pause; no further suggestions are offered.)

"I guess you are ready to begin your work then,'' says Mr. Shigaki. "Lisa, would you act as the group leader and report to me when your group is finished planning?''

Mr. Shigaki then left the group to its task and supervised the remainder of the class who had been working on individual assignments.

It would be reasonable to assume that if children are given instruction and have many guided experiences in cooperative learning, that they are likely to develop group interaction and socialization skills. But do cooperative learning strategies have any positive effect on a child's overall achievement and cognitive growth? The evidence suggests that they do. Johnson, Maruyama, Johnson, Nelson, and Skon reviewed 122 studies that were conducted between 1924 and 1981 that addressed this question, subjecting those studies to three methods of meta-analysis.[3] These researchers concluded that the studies indicate that cooperative learning experiences tend to promote higher achievement than do competitive and individualistic learning experiences. The investigators claim that "These results hold for all age levels, for all subject areas, and for tasks involving concept attainment, verbal problem solving, categorization, spatial problem solving, retention and memory, motor performance, and guessing–judging–predicting. For rote-decoding and correcting tasks, cooperation seems to be equally as effective as competitive and individualistic learning procedures."[4]

MANAGING SMALL-GROUP INSTRUCTION

Careful attention to each of the following suggestions will facilitate the effectiveness of small-group endeavors.

[3] D. W. Johnson, G. Maruyama, R. Johnson, D. Nelson, and L. Skon, "Effects of Cooperative, Competitive, and Individualistic Goal Structures on Achievement: A Meta-Analysis, "*Psychological Bulletin* No. 73. Washington, D.C.: American Psychological Association, Inc., 1981, pp. 47 – 62.

[4] David W. Johnson, Roger T. Johnson, Edythe Johnson Holubec, and Patricia Roy, *Circles of Learning: Cooperation in the Classroom*, (Alexandria, Virginia: Association for Supervision and Curriculum Development, 1984), p. 15.

Help Children Learn Group-Process Skills

This text has repeatedly stressed the need to place children in group settings if they are to learn group-work skills. However, if they are only given the *opportunity* to work in groups without receiving instruction in how a group is supposed to go about its business, they may likewise not learn to function effectively in small groups. Simply dividing the class into groups, then assigning each a task, is not likely to help children grow in skills needed for cooperative learning.

Before attempting a small-group endeavor, the teacher should discuss with the class some of the responsibilities of the persons who are a part of a group. It is helpful if the children and the teacher can summarize these and place them on charts that are posted in the room. These standards can be used as evaluative criteria after the children have had an opportunity to work in small groups. Such standards would vary some depending on the age of the children, but, in general, they might include any or all of the following:

Group Members

1. Help the leader carry out plans.
2. Do your share of the work.
3. Work without disturbing other group members.
4. Ask other members for their ideas.
5. Select only the ideas that help the group do its best work.
6. Cheerfully take the jobs the group wants you to do.
7. Make other members of the group feel welcome.
8. Be courteous; respect the ideas of others.
9. Support the group's decisions.

Group Leaders

1. Help make everyone become a part of the group.
2. Let everyone have a turn at the "good" jobs.
3. Get ideas from all members of the group.
4. Let the group decide which ideas are best.
5. Keep the group moving to get its job finished in the best way it can.
6. Keep from being "bossy"; be a leader, not a dictator.
7. Help your group know what its job is.

Some teachers find role-playing to be a valuable technique in teaching the skills needed in small-group work. By selecting four to five children to serve as group members, the teacher can demonstrate to the class what it means to "help everyone become a part of the group" or any of the standards that have been discussed. When the role playing is completed, the remainder of the class can analyze the situation to determine why the group was functioning well or poorly. It is helpful to have children observe certain specific elements in the situation to be presented. For example, they might try to answer such questions as these:

1. What did individual members do to help the group do its job? What did members do that did not help the group?
2. What did the leader do to help the group get its job done?
3. How did the group find out exactly what it was to do?
4. Did the group use good resources in solving its problems?
5. Did the group seem to be working together as a team? Why or why not?
6. How could the group be helped to do its job better?

Following the role-playing, the class can discuss the situation in terms of the specific points being observed. It may then be helpful to replay all or a portion of the situation to help children appreciate the forces at work in group situations. With young children it may be desirable to have an older group demonstrate such things as a domineering leader, an unco-operative group member, a member who wants only the choice tasks, the noncontributor, the irresponsible leader, the member who must always have his or her own way, the member who talks too much, and so on. In teaching group-work skills, the teacher will want to do more than talk about what should or should not be done. Children really need an oppor-tunity to see and experience "how it works" as well as an opportunity to experiment and try their hand at doing productive group work. Role-playing can do much to sensitize them to the various subtleties and forces that come into play in small-group situations.

Increasing numbers of schools have video cassette recorders available for classroom use, and this equipment can be useful in teaching collabo-rative skills. The teacher can videotape a group role-playing certain skills needed for productive small-group work. The tape can then be used for study and analysis of the behavior required if small groups are to be effective in their work. The videotape provides a way to demonstrate over and over again the essential characteristics of group work. This teaching procedure is widely used in teaching athletes, and greater use could be made of it in regular classrooms today.

Keep the Size of the Group Small

The size of a subgroup within a classroom has considerable effect on its productivity. If groups are too large, there will be a duplication of respon-sibilities, less opportunity for individuals to carry their share of the group effort, and a tendency for some members to fade out of the group activity; and problems of management will become more severe. On the other hand, if groups are too small, the collective talent of the group is restricted, demands on individuals may be excessive, and the work product may represent little more than the effort of one or two individuals. In general, however, groups should be kept small, possibly not more than three to five children. In teaching group-work skills, teachers sometimes begin by placing children in pairs, and then combine compatible pairs into groups of four members. For maximum involvement of children, the optimum group-size number is three.

Keep in Mind the Status of Members within the Class

Within the classroom there develops a prestige or status system that reflects itself in the interactions among children. This status system involves every member of the group, including the teacher. Under favorable classroom conditions, the teacher is considered a high-status member, usually at the top of the status scale. The children distribute themselves on a continuum of status ranging from those who are generally well accepted and highly thought of by most members to those who are on the fringes of acceptance or may even be rejected by the majority of the class.

Some insight into the status of various members of the class may be obtained informally by observing the children in and out of the classroom. These observations can be made in any situation in which the children exercise a free choice of the partners they wish to play or work with. The teacher may observe, too, whether the preference is a mutual one or whether the child doing the selecting is simply attempting to identify with a high-status classmate. It is also possible to obtain information relative to the social structure of the class through the use of sociometric devices. More specifically, sociometric data may be used to

1. Identify leaders within the class.
2. Determine the social status or social position of any child with respect to other children.
3. Spot in-groups, cliques, or rival factions within the class.
4. Locate children who are rejected by others.
5. Obtain information that will be helpful in arranging the classroom seating pattern, forming committees, work groups, play groups.

The teacher will want to give careful consideration to status in setting up cooperative work groups. Children should be placed with others with whom they can work, but the selection should not be left entirely to the children. When this happens, high-status children are selected first, leaving the low-status children that no group wants. Even allowing children to choose the group with whom they wish to work is not entirely satisfactory. Possibly a combination of children's choices and teacher placement is the best course of action because the teacher knows the capabilities of each child and can make a sound judgment about how and with whom each is likely to work best and make the greatest progress. This also ensures that not all the most capable children are in the same group. Some teachers find the assignment of low-status children to group activities with high-status children has the effect of helping the low-status children obtain greater acceptance and prestige. A grouping of children that almost duplicates the "in-groups" and "out-groups" of a class rarely works well because it does not make for good human relations within the classroom.

Reward Group Work Appropriately

Part of the reason that group work is at times ineffective is because it is not rewarded as generously as are the academic aspects of the classroom work. This stems from the teacher's attitude toward the value of group activities. If the rewards (recognition, praise, value statements, reports to parents, grades) go only to those who do well in paper-and-pencil activities, children rightly conclude that group activities do not count much in the entire scheme of things. Group work will be enhanced if the teacher regards it as an important part of the instructional program and rewards appropriately the children who have done commendable work in group endeavors.

TEACHING AND USING DISCUSSION TECHNIQUES

One of the most widely used and most valuable techniques in social studies teaching is *discussion.* Its value lies chiefly in the fact that it represents a type of intellectual teamwork, resting on the principle that the pooled knowledge, ideas, and feelings of several persons have greater merit than those of a single individual.

Because the strength of discussion is obtained from the information and viewpoint of many members of the group, it is necessary that it be based on road participation. It is a thinking-together process that breaks down if one member or group dominates it. It is the responsibility of the teacher to encourage the more reluctant children to participate. Although there cannot be a single answer to the question of what to do with the child who dominates the discussion, skillful teachers usually take care of the matter with a statement such as "Jackie, you have given us so many good ideas today, and I know you have many more good suggestions, but we want to find out what some of the others think would be a good way to . . ."

In good class discussions, children should talk freely and voluntarily. There should be no set pattern of soliciting contributions, nor should letter grades be given on individual discussion contributions. It will take a while to develop effective discussions because the needed skills develop gradually.

The physical arrangement of the classroom may either contribute to or inhibit discussion. For example, it is difficult to interact with someone when one is not facing the person with whom one is speaking. When classroom seating is arranged so that all children face the teacher, the pattern of interaction will be *through* the teacher, that is, "child A–teacher–child B–teacher–child C–teacher." A preferred discussion pattern is to have children interacting directly with each other; this can be encouraged by having them face one another. This also can be achieved by arranging the seating in a semicircle for at least some of the discussion sessions. Through careful and patient teaching, a teacher can bring the class to a point where they interact courteously with one another—without always agreeing with each other—and do so without raising their hands to speak. Such maturity in discussion procedure, however, requires a considerable amount of good teaching, practice, and time.

If discussions are to have some purpose beyond ordinary conversation, the participants must have certain skills and attitudes, both of which can be learned. These skills should be taught through deliberate organized instruction. Skills and attitudes may be stated as standards or guides that characterize harmonious, productive discussion. For example, one participating in a discussion should

1. Listen attentively when others are speaking.
2. Remain objective and not become emotional.
3. Be open-minded, respect and accept the contributions of others, but think independently.
4. Assume responsibility for contributing ideas.
5. Prepare adequately for the discussion and be able to support ideas with factual evidence.
6. Speak loudly and clearly enough for all to hear.
7. Not be offended when one's ideas or suggestions are not accepted by the group.
8. Not dominate the discussion; contributions should be stated concisely and briefly.
9. Ask for clarification of ideas that are not understood; ask for evidence to substantiate statements.
10. Recognize the problem of semantics in arriving at group decisions or in discussing a controversial issue.

11. Assume responsibility for moving the group toward its goal; help keep the group from becoming sidetracked from the central issue.
12. Have confidence in the ability of the group to come to a satisfactory decision and support the decision of the group once it has been made.

Standards such as the ones listed here are not appropriately stated for use with children, but the ideas can be discussed and understood by them when stated more simply. It is generally more effective if children themselves contribute to the setting of standards. For example, children will state ideas, such as the preceding ones, in the following way:

1. Stick to the topic.
2. Be considerate of others' viewpoints and feelings.
3. Use facts to back up statements.
4. Ask questions when you don't understand.
5. Listen carefully while others are speaking.
6. Let everyone have a turn.

It is usually better to use positive rather than negative statements in developing standards. It is more helpful, for example, to say, "Speak clearly and loudly enough for all to hear," than to say, "Don't mumble." Positive statements help the child know what *to do* whereas negative statements tell what *not to do* but suggest no alternative.

Suggestions for Improving Classroom Discussions

Use a Variety of Springboards to Stimulate Learner Interest. Social studies content is loaded with issues that are emotionally toned and can serve as the basis for productive discussions. Additionally, the teacher can use issues raised in stories and books read by the children, news stories, sporting events, and child conflicts in school. Good topics for discussion are those with which children can identify. In relating themselves to the problem, they are able to gain some insight into their own behavior and at the same time maintain a measure of detachment.

Keep Discussion Groups Small for Greater Participation. If learner participation is wanted, discussion groups should be limited in size and preferably not larger than five or six children. Of course, there are other values in discussion besides saying something. Children also learn by listening to others discuss a topic. Therefore, a discussion that includes the entire class can be defended, but the teacher will have to expect some nonparticipation by children who are shy or who, for one reason or another, do not wish to talk in the large-group setting. Those same children might contribute their ideas in smaller groups.

Use Questions That Require an Elaborative Response. Discussion questions must be open-ended, suggestive of more than one point of view. They should require the respondent to provide an explanation. If questions can be answered by responding "yes" or "no" or with a single word or phrase, there is little to discuss. Questions that call for the reproduction of facts are not good for discussion, either, as for example:

1. By what three routes did people travel to the goldfields of California?
2. What are the Pacific states? Which is the largest? Which is the smallest?
3. Who was John Sutter?
4. Who were the forty-niners?
5. Who was the founder of the California missions?

As these questions are stated, there is nothing to discuss. However, the subject matter of these questions might be used for discussion if the questions were framed differently, as for example:

1. If you had been a gold seeker in 1849, what route would you have taken to the goldfields of California, and why would you have gone that way?
2. Washington, Oregon, and California face the Pacific Ocean. On the east coast of the United States, *fourteen* states occupy the same north-south distance as these three western states. What problems do you suppose are brought about by the size of a state?
3. How might the history of California and the United States have been different if John Sutter had found gold near Los Angeles instead of where he did?
4. How has the San Francisco Bay area changed since the days of the forty-niners?
5. What is there about California today that relates directly to the system of missions started by Father Junipero Serra and the Franciscan Fathers?

The two types of questions presented serve different purposes. For a quick check of literal reading comprehension, the first set might be appropriate but would not make good discussion questions.

Point Out Inconsistencies and Confusions in the Children's Thinking. Imagine a class discussing the merits of a law prohibiting smoking in public places such as meeting rooms, auditoriums, elevators, and restaurants. The discussion might proceed as follows:

CHILD: I think there ought to be such a law because a person has a right not to have to breathe someone else's smoke.

TEACHER: Is that a right?

CHILD: Well, if some people have the right to smoke, others should have the right not to smoke.

TEACHER: Isn't that the way it is now?

CHILD: Yes . . . but not really . . . when they have to be in the same room or in an elevator, the people who do not smoke do not have any choice, but the people who do smoke do have a choice.

TEACHER: Then you are talking about choices rather than rights?

CHILD: Yes, I think so. With smoking in the room, the people who do not smoke and *have* to be there have no choice.

This is an instructive example because it illustrates how the teacher moved the discussion toward a clarification of the main point the child was making.

Keep the Discussion Focused on the Topic.   It is difficult for discussants of any age to stay with the topic, but this is especially so with young children. Almost anything said reminds them of a personal experience that they want to share but is probably irrelevant to the topic being discussed. When the discussion strays away from the main theme, the teacher must refocus the group's thinking with a comment such as "But let's get back to our main question . . ." or "I wonder if we could look at this problem from another angle . . ."

Maintain a Low Profile in Leading Discussions.   If the object of discussion is to encourage participant talk, the teacher talk should be limited to whatever is needed to keep the discussion moving. Give children time to think about what they want to say. Allow extended periods of silence before calling for a response. Use nonverbal clues generously, such as a nod, an encouraging glance, or some other gesture along with verbal encouragement. Confine your own remarks to probing or clarifying comments or questions and to the acknowledging of contributions. Avoid having discussions become teacher lectures.

Discussion can be used to encourage children to speculate, to imagine, and to think of alternatives, as in the following example.

Ms. Fowler's second-graders have been making discoveries about changes in their community. To stimulate discussion, Ms. Fowler asked, "If you were a second-grader in the year 2050 and lived where you do now, what might you see on your way to school? Don't raise your hand for the next minute; I just want you to think."

After a minute, the children were bursting with ideas. Ms. Fowler was careful to accept all ideas and to try to hear a comment from every child. When a couple of the ideas were silly, she very adeptly brought the discussion back to the main focus by asking these children to clarify what they meant. Ms. Fowler was aware of the children who were too shy to volunteer and called on them, also. She encouraged all children to give evidence for their suggestions.

Many of the same principles and procedures used in group discussions involving the entire class also apply to other forms of discussion procedure. The advantage of smaller groups lies chiefly in allowing for greater participation by individual members. The teacher may find each of the following forms of discussion procedure helpful in social studies instruction.

Round-Table Discussions

A *round-table discussion* usually involves a small number of persons, perhaps no fewer than three and no more than eight. It requires someone to serve as a moderator to introduce the members of the discussion group, present the problem to be discussed, and keep the discussion moving. The leader's role is one of guiding the group rather than one of dominating it. A permissive atmosphere needs to prevail, and the presentations are conversational rather than oratorical.

Round-table discussions can be used in the middle and upper grades by having a group of children discuss a problem before the remainder of the class or by dividing the class into several small discussion groups that function without an audience. It is perhaps best to use this procedure with one group at a time, either with or without an audience, until the children have learned how to participate in discussions of this type. It will be necessary for the teacher to introduce the procedure to the class and to explain and demonstrate its purposes and the way it works. Such points as the following need to be emphasized:

1. **Responsibilities of the moderator** To be informed on the topic to be discussed, introduce the topic, keep the discussion moving, avoid having the group become sidetracked, ask members to explain more fully what they mean, avoid having members argue and quibble over irrelevancies, and summarize and state conclusions.
2. **Responsibilities of members of the discussion group** To be well informed on the topic to be discussed, especially some phase of it; speak informally while avoiding arguing and quibbling; stay with the topic under discussion; have sources of information available; back up statements with facts; and help the group summarize its conclusions.
3. **Responsibilities of the audience** To listen attentively, withhold questions until presentation is completed, ask for clarification of ideas, ask for evidence on questionable statements, confine remarks to the

topic under discussion, and extend customary audience courtesies to members of the round table.

Round-table discussions may be used for any of the following purposes:

1. To discuss plans for a major class activity.
2. To evaluate the results of a class activity, the merits of a film, school assembly on citizenship, or the decision of a student council.
3. To make specific plans, such as the best way to present the work of the class to the parents.
4. To get facts related to a topic.
5. To discuss current affairs.
6. To present differing views on a community issue or a school problem.
7. To make decisions and recommendations to the class (the student council wants to know how the class feels about a new play schedule. A committee of five children discusses this matter and presents its findings and recommendations to the class).

Panel Discussions

A *panel discussion* is similar to a round-table discussion in many respects, but there are also some important differences. The responsibilities of the moderator are approximately the same as they are for the moderator of the round table, as are those of the participants. The procedure is more formal than that of the round table. It usually begins with a short statement or presentation by each discussant before the panel is opened for free discussion by members. Panels are usually more audience-oriented than round tables, and frequently some provision is made for audience questions or participation at the end of the panel's presentation. A greater responsibility is placed on participants to prepare themselves well for their particular part on the panel, for each panelist is considered to be more or less an "expert."

One teacher made use of a panel discussion format in the following way.

The topic for the panel to discuss was a community problem involving the conversion of a military base into a community resource. Various special-interest groups were competing for the use of the newly acquired property. In class the teacher asked children to volunteer to represent one of the following special-interest groups:

1. city planner
2. golf enthusiast
3. representative of the local community club
4. condominium builder
5. representative of a local Indian tribe
6. moderator

The children were provided planning time in which to prepare a three- to five-minute statement explaining their point of view regarding the future of this property. Time was allowed for questions to clarify points made in the presentations or to raise other issues.

Buzz Groups for Brainstorming

The following is an example of a "buzz" group in operation.

The members of Ms. Kryzinski's class were asked to view a television special dealing with energy. The next morning they were anxious to discuss the program and even more anxious to do something about the energy problem.

"What can we do, Ms. K, to help other kids in our school know about some ways to save energy?" a child asked.

"Why don't you decide?" Ms. Kryzinski responded. "You are already arranged in small groups, so why don't you take the next ten minutes and come up with some ideas? Be prepared to give us two or three good ideas that would be possible for us to carry out in our school."

After about ten to fifteen minutes, the children's attention was refocused, and each group presented some ideas. There was no attempt to evaluate suggestions at that time.

All the suggestions were listed on the board and discussed. The class then voted on the list to determine which three they would implement.

We have here a brief description of a *buzz-group* or *brainstorming* technique. It is an informal consideration of ideas or problems where the chief purpose is to solicit the suggestions, feelings, ideas, or consensus of the members participating. In brainstorming for ideas and suggested solutions to problems, it is important *not* to evaluate each one at the time it is offered. If each is discussed, the list will not be very long. The objective of brainstorming is to get as many ideas to the surface as possible, no matter how outlandish they may seem. After the complete list has been generated, time can be taken to evaluate each one and select the best ones by consensus. It is usually best for the group to have a designated leader and recorder.

Talking things over in a buzz session can be helpful in clarifying ideas, getting a wide sampling of opinion and feeling, obtaining suggestions and ideas, and getting children to participate who might be reluctant or fearful in a more structured discussion situation. Likewise, it has some limitations. Buzz sessions can easily get out of hand and become noisy and boisterous where nothing is accomplished except the creation of confusion. There is need, therefore, for the teacher to have firm control of the class before such a procedure is attempted and to establish standards that are clearly understood beforehand.

MAKING USE OF REPORTS

Reports to the class by the children are commonly used in social studies to share information obtained through individual research and study. They serve the purpose of bringing to the group the knowledge and understanding obtained by individuals, as well as teaching children how to organize, plan, and present a report. This suggests a mutual value that accrues to the group as well as to the individual making the report. It also implies a responsibility that each must share if the procedure is to have value.

There is nothing quite so deadly or lacking in instructional value as the elementary schoolchild giving a "report" that has been copied from an encyclopedia. The speaker stumbles over every other word — meanings are not understood, and pronunciation is incorrect. The report lacks continuity and is hard to follow. The listeners become bored or disruptive. Under such a set of circumstances, no one likes to give reports or listen to them. They are a waste of time.

The primary responsibility for good reports rests squarely with the teacher. How to give reports and how to prepare them should be explained. Through discussion, the teacher and the class can establish standards that will be used in the preparation of reports and the evaluation of them after the reports are given. Examples of such standards are these:

RESPONSIBILITIES OF THE SPEAKER

1. Speak in a clear voice.
2. Be well prepared.
3. Speak in your own words.
4. Use charts and pictures to make the report more interesting.
5. Ask for questions at the end of the report.
6. Stick to the topic.

RESPONSIBILITIES OF THE AUDIENCE

1. Listen carefully.
2. Be courteous; do not interrupt the speaker.
3. Ask questions only at the end of the report.

Children can help each other improve the quality of their reports by holding brief evaluative discussions following the presentation. A good practice to follow is to ask for positive statements first — things that were especially well done in the report. Then, the children might offer suggestions concerning the way the report might have been improved. The teacher must set the stage for a positive attitude toward evaluation rather than only pointing out things that were wrong with the report. Care must be exercised so as not to make the evaluations destructively critical of a child's work.

It is the responsibility of the teacher to take an active part in assisting the child with the preparation of the report. This includes helping select a suitable topic, suggesting references, helping with its organization, and suggesting visual devices to use. The teacher should find a few minutes a day or two in advance of the presentation to sit down with the youngster and review what is to be included in the report. Once prepared, the child should be left alone while the report is being given unless help is specifically requested. It is unfair to the child and to the listening group to have the teacher continually interrupting and asking questions. The standards and responsibilities of good listeners apply to the teacher as well as to the children. Of course, when the report is completed the teacher can ask questions, call attention to points that need further clarification, or add pertinent information to the report. Positive comments and concrete suggestions as to how the child might improve future reports should also be offered.

Only a few reports should be scheduled on the same day. It is impossible for children to sustain any degree of interest if they must listen to a dozen or fifteen reports consecutively. A better procedure is to have two or three reports given at a time and to spread the reporting over a period of several days.

A common problem with reports given by children is the tendency for them to be "bookish." Some teachers encourage verbalism by being too rewarding, too complimentary of reports that are well presented but are not given in the child's own words. The dependence of the child on the language of the reference material is probably an indication that the topic is not understood. In order to combat the problem of verbalism in reports, the teacher should

1. Not fully accept bookish presentations that are meaningless to the child and are simply repetitions of what has been read. This usually can be handled by a comment such as "Jackie, I know you spent a lot of time and work preparing your report, but we would have found it much more valuable and interesting if you had told it to us in your own words."
2. Encourage children to make and use visual material in their reports — pictures, charts, diagrams, maps, graphs, the chalkboard, or an overhead projector.
3. Ask children to give concrete examples of what they are describing in words they use in everyday conversation.
4. Encourage children to use more than one source for their information.
5. Be more lavish in praising those who avoid bookish presentations.

Oral and written reports are among the most common ways children share ideas in social studies. In many classrooms these activities are overused and, in some cases, misused. It is important for children to share ideas with each other, however, and if some variation is made in the traditional reporting format, these experiences can be both interesting and informative. Here is an example.

To culminate a unit in which the class studied North American Indians, the children were asked to create an illustrated documentary on a tribe of their choosing.

Ms. Pang brought in art materials for the children to use in creating their visuals and several cassette tape recorders. The children planned a narration and tape-recorded it. Then they made illustrations to accompany their narrations and presented their completed "documentaries" to their classmates.

The following are suggested as still other alternatives to the traditional oral and written reports.

SUGGESTIONS FOR IMPROVING CLASS REPORTS

1. Dramatize an incident, sequence, or situation relating to the topic and incorporate essential data to be communicated in the dramatization.
2. Use children's own drawn illustrations, charts, and graphs as the basis for a presentation or use illustrations found in newspapers, magazines, or other sources.
3. Pretend to be a tour guide taking the class through the area studied.
4. Use the overhead projector for visual aids in a presentation.
5. Role-play the part of a newscaster making an on-the-spot report.
6. Interview a classmate who is role-playing the part of someone who is an expert on the topic under study.
7. Collect pictures, arrange them in sequence, and use them as the basis for a report.
8. Write a diary or letter that might have been written by someone in an earlier period.
9. Use artifacts or realia as the basis for a report.
10. Prepare and explain a bulletin board display or diorama.
11. Prepare a narration for a filmstrip.
12. Do an original narration for a motion-picture film with sound turned off.
13. Write news stories that might have been appropriate to a particular period or prepare and publish a single issue of a newspaper that might have appeared in some historical period.
14. Tape-record a presentation for playback to the class.

DISCUSSION QUESTIONS AND SUGGESTED ACTIVITIES

1. Under what circumstances might a teacher *not* want to clarify in great detail the objectives of a small group?

2. How might a teacher build readiness for small-group activities with a class that has always worked on a whole-class basis?

3. Develop a role-playing exercise designed to teach group-work skills.

4. Select a topic that is appropriate for a grade of your choice, and develop questions that could be used to stimulate a discussion.

5. The chapter suggests the "use of a variety of springboards to stimulate learner interest in discussion." Provide examples of such "springboards" in addition to those included in the chapter.

6. Prepare an informal chart that might be used with children to illustrate points to keep in mind when preparing and making oral reports. Illustrate your chart in a way that you think would appeal to children.

7. In visiting a classroom, what specific things would you look for that would provide an indication of the quality of interaction taking place there?

8. Examine the chart on pages 338–341, and add examples from your own experience that tend to increase or decrease the level of hostility in a classroom.

9. Suggest topics or questions that could best be discussed in a *dyad* configuration (a group of two), a *triad* (a group of three), and by a group of five children. What reasons do you have for selecting certain topics or questions for a particular group size?

10. Discuss similarities and differences between traditional small-group instruction as used in the teaching of reading, and cooperative learning groups as used in social studies.

SELECTED REFERENCES

HAMILTON, STEPHEN F. "The Social Side of Schooling: Ecological Studies of Classrooms and Schools." *The Elementary School Journal,* 83 (March 1983), pp. 313–334.

HAZEN, NANCY, BETTY BLACK, AND FAYE FLEMING-JOHNSON. "Social Acceptance: Strategies Children Use and How Teachers Can Help Children Learn Them." *Young Children,* 39 (September 1984), pp. 26–36.

JOHNSON, DAVID W., AND ROGER T. JOHNSON. *Joining Together: Group Theory and Group Skills.* Englewood Cliffs, New Jersey: Prentice-Hall, 1982.

JOHNSON, DAVID W., ROGER T. JOHNSON, EDYTHE JOHNSON HOLUBEC, AND PATRICIA ROY. *Circles of Learning: Cooperation in the Classroom.* Alexandria, Virginia: Association for Supervision and Curriculum Development, 1984.

KREIDLER, WILLIAM J. *Creative Conflict Resolution.* Chicago: Scott Foresman, 1984.

——— . "How Well Do You Resolve Conflict?" *Instructor, 93 (January 1984), pp. 30–33.*

OLINER, PEARL. "Putting Compassion and Caring into Social Studies Classrooms." *Social Education,* 47 (April 1983), pp. 273–276.

PASSE, JEFF. "Citizenship Education: Its Role in Improving Classroom Behavior." *Social Studies and the Young Learner,* 1 (September–October 1988), pp. 19–21.

SLAVIN, ROBERT E. "Cooperative Learning: Where Behavioral and Humanistic Approaches to Classroom Motivation Meet." *The Elementary School Journal,* 88 (September 1987), pp. 29–37.

——— . "Cooperative Learning and the Cooperative School." *Educational Leadership,* 45 (November 1987), pp. 7–13.

TURNER, THOMAS N. "Following the Clues: A Group Discussion, Hypothesis-Making Technique." *The Social Studies,* 75 (May–June 1984), pp. 124–128.

VAN SICKLE, RONALD L. "Practicing What We Teach: Promoting Democratic Education in Schools and Classrooms." Chapter 4, in *Democratic Education in Schools and Classrooms,* Mary A. Hepburn, ed. NCSS Bulletin No. 70. Washington, D.C.: National Council for the Social Studies, 1983.

13

Learner Involvement Through Activities, Expressive Experiences, and Social Participation

It is a common assumption that when learners are involved in creative activities, less in the way of "real" learning takes place. Traditional attitudes toward learning suggest that it must be accompanied by a hard-nosed discipline that is joyless. The feeling is widespread that if children enjoy what they are doing in school, the program is not intellectually rigorous. The following narrative describes a parent's attitude on just this point:

> At first we were quite concerned when we found out that Lori was to be placed in Mr. Allison's room the next year. His room had such a relaxed atmosphere about it, and he was very popular with the kids. We just assumed, I guess, that a teacher who was so well liked by all the children could not be very effective in maintaining a disciplined environment for learning. I must say this assumption was wholly unfounded.
>
> Mr. Allison was clearly the most creative, imaginative, and overall the

Visits to places that encourage students to become actively involved in their use of pioneer technology make a unique contribution to social studies education. Experiences of this type are important not only for the information gained but in giving today's children some sense of what it felt like to have lived in those earlier times. (Photo by Edna Kellman, Seattle Public Schools.)

most effective teacher Lori had during the seven years she attended that school. He always had the most unusual things going on in that room that would so hook the kids that they spent hours of unsupervised study on what they were doing. Schoolwork seemed to be a sheer delight, strange as that may seem. They analyzed advertising techniques in a unit on consumerism; they simulated law and justice procedures; they studied the effects of immigrant groups on American life and culture; there were art, poetry, music, and dramatic activities galore. Once they constructed a whole set of authentic models of Indian villages representing various tribes that inhabited this part of North America in pre-Columbian times. This involved the children in an incredible amount of research and information gathering in order to do the contructions. There were always games, puzzles, inquiries — tremendous interest grabbers. It was the only time I can recall that children had literally to be told to go home after school. If not, they would stay until dinnertime.

Mr. Allison convinced my husband and me that disciplined learning did not have to give the appearance of rigidity and drudgery. He seemed to embrace the philosophy that a teacher should obtain "maximum learning with minimum effort." But the "minimum effort" only seemed that way because of the tremendous motivating power of the creative activities he used. Actually, I have not seen children work any harder nor be more productive in their efforts than their year with Mr. Allison.[1]

How does a teacher develop this type of stimulating program for students in social studies? In part, this comes from an imaginative teacher who is able to capitalize on the natural interests and curiosities of children. The teacher encourages them to raise questions and to suggest ways of working. These, then, are converted into interesting study activities. In this chapter we will discuss ways that creative and expressive activities can be used in social studies for any or all of the following purposes:

1. To stimulate children's interest.
2. To develop various aspects of thinking.
3. To give direction and purpose to learning.
4. To encourage initiative, exploration, and research.
5. To aid in applying factual information obtained through research to concrete situations.
6. To provide a setting in which to use socialization and human relations skills.
7. To clarify complex procedures.
8. To aid in developing an understanding of concepts and generalizations.
9. To relate various components of the school program to one another.
10. To provide opportunities for thinking, planning, sharing, doing, and evaluating.
11. To provide an outlet for creative abilities.
12. To provide an opportunity for recognition for the nonverbal, nonacademic child.

The shortage of funds has forced cutbacks in the services of special teachers for art, music, drama, and even physical education in many schools. This means that the regular classroom teacher has to assume more responsibility for these subjects if anything at all is to be done with them. This set of circumstances provides the regular teacher with the opportunity to do a considerable amount of meaningful teaching of these subjects and skills within the framework of the social studies curriculum. In those districts where special teachers *are* available in these fields, it is

---

[1] An actual case from Minneapolis, Minnesota, reported to this writer.

to the regular classroom teacher's advantage to work closely with them in integrating these subjects and skills in the classroom curriculum in social studies.

CONSTRUCTION AND PROCESSING ACTIVITIES

Most children love to make things. They build villages and castles in the sand at the beach; they build boats to float in a nearby pond; they construct birdhouses, model airplanes and cars, and wigwams. These natural sensory-motor play and creative-building activities are valuable for children in and of themselves. They give countless opportunities for thinking and planning as well as for creative expression, use of tools, physical activity, and the development of coordination. Children need many experiences of this type. In social studies, however, these values are only incidental to the chief purpose, which is *to extend and enrich meaning of some aspect of the topic being studied.* The excellence of the final product is, likewise, not a major concern. What is important is the learning that has occurred as a result of the construction activity. This being true, authenticity, genuineness, and truthfulness in the representations are important considerations in conducting construction activities. If constructions are inaccurate, contrary to truth and reality, they may be detrimental to learning because they reinforce incorrect concepts.

It is possible to use construction activities to motivate children's work and to establish more clearly children's purposes for doing things. For example, the teacher of a primary grade conducting a study of the dairy farm might suggest that the class construct a model farm in the classroom. Naturally, the children will want to make their model as authentic as possible; therefore, a considerable amount of research will be necessary as they proceed with the building of the farm. In fact, they cannot even begin unless they know what it is they want to do. This gives them a genuine need for information. The children's purpose in this case may be to learn about the dairy farm to be able to build a classroom model of it. The teacher's purpose, however, is to have children form accurate concepts and understandings of a dairy farm; the construction activity is being used as a vehicle to achieve that goal. Under this arrangement, both learner objectives and teacher objectives will have been achieved.

In selecting a construction activity for social studies, the teacher should make certain that

1. It is useful in achieving a definite objective related to social studies.
2. It clarifies, enriches, or extends the meaning of some important concept.
3. It requires children to do careful thinking and planning.

4. It is an accurate and truthful representation.
5. It is within the capabilities of the children.
6. The time and effort expended can be justified by the learnings that occur.
7. It is reasonable in terms of space and expense.
8. The needed materials are available.

There is no limit to the items that children can make in projects related to the social studies. The following have been used successfully by many teachers:

Model furniture
Books
Musical instruments
Simple trucks, airplanes, boats
Puppets and marionettes
Paper bag dolls
"Television" set with paper-roll programs
Looms for weaving
Animal cages
Animals of art materials
Maps (pictorial, product, relief, floor)
Candles
Soap
Baskets, trays, bowls
Preparation of foods (making cookies, jelly, butter, ice cream)
Ships, harbor, cargo
Retail food market and equipment
Scenery and properties for stage, dioramas, panoramas
Holiday decorations
Jewelry
Pottery, vases, dishes, cups
Covered wagons, churns, butter paddles, wooden spoons, and other pioneer gear
Post office
Bakery
Fire station
Dairy farm and buildings
Oxcarts
Circus accessories
Playhouses
Model Indian villages
Purses, hot pads, table mats, small rugs
Birdhouses and feeding stations
Seedboxes, planters

Tie-dyeing
Production of visual material needed in the unit, such as pictorial graphs,
    charts, posters, displays, bulletin boards
Block printing

The following suggestions are offered to help the teacher use construction activities in teaching social studies:

Discuss the Purposes of the Activity with the Children. The practice of having children make stores, build boats and covered wagons, or do Indian crafts without knowing why they are performing these activities is open to serious question. Children may not have any idea of the real purpose or significance of the construction. It is suggested, therefore, that at the beginning of such an activity, the reasons for planning it should be discussed and understood by all. The purposes for the construction should be reviewed from time to time during the activity.

Plan the Method of Procedure with the Children. The initial planning will take a considerable amount of time if every detail is to be taken into account. Such extensive planning is not necessary or entirely desirable, for it tends to make children impatient. Decisions must be made, however, as to the basic materials needed, the major responsibilities and who will assume them, the committees needed and who will be on them, where the construction will take place, where needed information may be obtained, and a general overall plan. After the construction project is underway there will be time each day to do additional specific planning. It is best to plan in a general way and get started and leave the details to be worked out at a later time.

Plan Methods of Work with the Children. Construction activities involve working in groups, using tools, perhaps hammering and sawing or other noisy activities, and somewhat more disorder than is usually found in regular classroom work. This means that unless rules and standards concerning the methods of work are established and understood, there is likely to be much noise, commotion, and general confusion. Therefore, it is recommended that the teacher and the children discuss and decide what the rules of work are to be. These might include

1. How to get and return tools and construction materials.
2. Use of tools and equipment, including safe handling.
3. Things to remember during the work period: talking in a conversational voice, good use of materials to avoid waste, sharing tools and materials with others, consideration for others, doing one's share of work, asking for help when needed, and giving everyone a chance to present ideas.

4. Procedures for cleanup time. It is well to establish a "listen" signal to get the attention of the class. It can be playing a chord on the piano, turning off the lights or ringing a small bell. When the listen signal is given, children should learn to stop whatever they are doing, cease talking, and listen to whatever announcement is to be made. In this way, the teacher can stop the work of the class at any time to call their attention to some detail or get them started at cleanup. Cleanup is one procedure that can be done in a routine way. When the signal is given, all work stops, and the children listen for directions, restore the room to its prior condition, and assemble at the circle or go to their desks.

Provide Plenty of Time Each Day for Planning, Working, Cleaning Up, and Evaluating.   Before work on the construction activity is begun each day, time should be spent in making specific plans. This is to ensure that everyone will have an important job to do and that the children will know their responsibilities. It also is a time when the teacher can go over some of the points the class talked about during its previous day's evaluation. "You remember yesterday we had some problem about which group was to use the tools. Which group has the tools today?" Or "Yesterday our voices became a little loud at times. Perhaps we can be more careful about that today."

During the work period the teacher will want to move from group to group observing, assisting, suggesting new approaches, helping groups in difficulty, clarifying ideas, helping children find materials, and supervising and guiding the work of the class. Children will be identified who need help in getting started, those who are not working well together, those who seem not to be doing anything, or others who may be having difficulty. The teacher will keep an eye on the time and stop the work of the class in time to ensure a thorough cleanup.

An important part of each period is the evaluation that occurs after the work and cleanup. During these times, the teacher will want the class to evaluate the progress it is making on the construction as well as the way children are working with each other.

> "Were we able to make progress in building our store today?"
> "How do you think we might change the color to make it look more real?"
> "Does anyone have any ideas how Steven's group could show more action in their mural?"
> "Did anyone see signs of unsafe handling of tools today?"
> "I wonder if the mountains aren't too high on Julie's group's map? Did you check that against the picture in your book?"

The precise points discussed in such an evaluation will depend on the class and its work. In any case, some attention should be given to (1) progress on the construction, (2) methods of working together, and (3) problems that need attention the next day.

Make Use of the Construction in Some Way, Relating It to the Unit under Study. When constructed objects are completed, they should be put to good use. In the primary grades such a project may serve well for dramatic play activities. A market in the classroom, for example, gives the children an opportunity to play customer, grocer, checkout person, or other personnel associated with a market. They read labels and prices, rearrange the material on the shelves, keep the store clean, and so on. In the middle and upper grades, objects made can be examined, discussed, and displayed. A mural can be used for study purposes. A child can explain the way some object is constructed, its main features, how it was used, its history, why it is no longer used, and similar information. In some instances, children can share the information learned and the object they have constructed with other classes in the school. Constructions are of value only insofar as they relate to the work of the class; when they have served this purpose, they should be removed.

EXAMPLES OF CONSTRUCTION ACTIVITIES

Primary Grades

After a study of both the urban and rural communities, the class was divided in half. One group was assigned the project of constructing a rural community; the other, an urban community.

Ms. Stillwater planned with each group separately, starting with the development of a list of services and facilities needed in each community. Each child was responsible for constructing at least one part of the community.

For several days before construction was to begin, the children brought in cartons, shoe boxes, and other "building materials" that were to become their communities.

Using paint, construction paper, shellac, and team effort, the children transformed the cartons into urban and rural communities and placed them on butcher paper streets on the floor around the classroom.

Intermediate Grades

Mr. Russo's class had been studying the state's history, and he believed that there was a need for the children to understand better the role that geographical differences had played in the state's development. He thought that the construction of relief maps might be a good method for the children to achieve this understanding.

Because such a construction was too large a project for individual children, he asked them to organize themselves in groups of two or three with whomever they could work best.

Mr. Russo provided the children with a papier-mâché recipe and the necessary construction materials. He encouraged them to be innovative in adding things to their maps that would highlight the significance of relief features.

After he was satisfied that the children understood what they were to do, he had the groups begin planning their maps. He provided a regularly scheduled work period each day and supervised and assisted the groups as needed. The completed relief maps were displayed and discussed in terms of the role of geographic features in the development of the state.

Closely related to construction activities are those that help the child understand the various steps or stages in the production of some material item. They deal with the *process* of changing raw materials into finished, usable items and, hence, involve *processing of materials.* These activities help children understand and appreciate the complexities of producing some of the basic material items that most persons use in everyday living. They are commonly used to illustrate the hardships, labor, skill, and ingenuity required of pioneers and early people in a time when it was necessary for them to produce basic materials for themselves. The most common processes used for this purpose are making butter, candles, paper, sugar, salt, bricks, natural dyes, jelly, ink, books, ice cream, soap, and weaving and dyeing cloth.

There are some instructional problems, however, in processing materials in the classroom. For example, is it appropriate to demonstrate the hardships experienced by pioneers in making candles by dipping, by using such modern-day conveniences as an electric hot plate as a source of heat and an aluminum container for the wax? In most classrooms it is, in fact, impossible to duplicate conditions under which candles were made in the seventeenth century. Almost any raw material the class uses in its processing will in all likelihood *already* be semiprocessed. The child may, therefore, leave such an experience with a lack of appreciation of the complexities involved in the process — a misfire of the precise learning the teacher had hoped to put across.

Some processes require extremely careful supervision by the teacher because of physical danger to the children. Candlemaking means heating tallow, wax, or paraffin that can ignite if allowed to become too hot and cause severe burns if dropped accidentally on one's person. Soapmaking calls for the use of lye, always potentially dangerous. These points are mentioned not to discourage the use of construction and processing but to alert the beginner to the real need for careful supervision while such activity is taking place.

MUSIC ACTIVITIES

Music activities make an important contribution to social studies instruction. Through the universal language of music, the child may extend communication to other peoples, races, and cultures, both past and present. Various songs and music forms are associated with periods in our national history, and many songs relate directly to heroes or great historical events. Musical expression is an emotional experience, piercing through everyday inhibitions and extending into the inner reaches of one's personality. Music inspires patriotism, love of country, loyalty, and fidelty. It is for this reason that marching bands are used in holiday parades and between halves at football games. Nation-states have used music effectively in building a feeling of national solidarity. Music has a profound effect on individuals as well as on groups.

Music educators have worked diligently to break the shackles of the "music period" concept of music education and have consistently recommended a greater integration of music in the total life of the classroom. Music activities, therefore, not only contribute to social studies instruction but support the music program itself. The material that follows suggests some possibilities for the use of singing, rhythmic expression, listening, and creative music activities in social studies units.

Singing. For almost any social studies unit, the teacher will find appropriate and related songs for children to sing. One of the chief values of singing is its affective quality; it gives the child a *feeling* for the material not likely to be obtained in any other way. Through singing, the child senses the loneliness of the voyageur, the gaiety of a frontier housewarming, or the sadness of a displaced people longing for their homeland. Folk songs can be springboards to the study of a period in history, to the contributions of ethnic groups, to the life-styles of a group, and to many social studies topics. Singing is an experience that can broaden children's appreciation of people everywhere. In the study of communities around the world, the teacher will want to use the songs of various national groups. This provides opportunities to learn more about a culture through the language of music.

Some educators have recognized the rich learning resource folk music provides, and they have promoted the use of folk songs in social studies classrooms.[2] Contemporary folk songs such as "Little Boxes," "We Shall Overcome," "Detroit City," and "Sittin' on the Dock of the Bay" convey powerful social messages. Cowboy songs such as "I Ride an Old Paint," "Colorado Trail," "The Night Herding Song," and "Git Along Little Dogie" have both lyrics and melodies that are hauntingly reminiscent of the lonely life of this American folk group. "The Yellow Rose of Texas," "When Johnny Comes Marching Home Again," and "Over There" are associated with significant conflicts of this nation (Texas Independence, Civil War, and World War I, respectively). Teachers interested in learning more about the use of folk songs in the classroom should write to Dr.

[2] Laurence I. Seidman, C. W. Post College, and John Anthony Scott, Rutgers University, have made several presentations at NCSS annual meetings since 1977.

Laurence I. Seidman, 140 Hill Park Avenue, Great Neck, New York 11021, for information about the newsletter entitled *Folksong in the Classroom.*

Rhythmic Expression.   Rhythmic and bodily expression tend to release one from the crust of convention and formality of everyday life and provide a means of self-expression. Through rhythms, bodily expression, and folk dances, the child develops grace and poise and learns the amenities that are characteristic of such social activities. Folk dancing and folk games in themselves are pleasurable and legitimate social activities for children. They provide for teamwork and allow the child to participate in the activity with several other boys and girls. Folk dancing and folk games usually involve eight or more children with a continual shifting of partners. For this reason, folk dancing is well suited for children in the elementary and middle schools.

In social studies, the teacher will want to use the various folk dances and rythmic activities that are characteristic of many countries, as well as those associated with various periods of our national history. Because ethnic heritage studies have become popular in schools, activities of this type can be particularly meaningful. Far from being solely a recreational activity, rhythmic expression provides a wide range of possibilities for social learnings in general and especially for the social studies.

The following lesson plan describes a method of incorporating and teaching folk dancing as part of a social studies unit.

LESSON PLAN 17

Topic:	Folk dancing (Select a dance from the culture being studied.)
Grade:	Kindergarten through six
Time:	One class period
Objectives:	Children will grow in appreciation of another culture.
	Children will extend social skills.
Notes:	Some children may not wish to dance for religious reasons. Provide an alternate activity —perhaps operating the sound equipment.
	Circle, line, and trio dance formations often are better accepted by children than dances requiring couples.
Preparation:	Learn the dance well before attempting to teach it.
	If some of the motions seem too difficult, eliminate them, and plan to repeat the easier motions.
Interest Building:	Wear the appropriate folk costume; display pictures of dancers in costume; involve children in rearranging classroom in preparation for dancing.
Lesson Development:	Discuss previous (especially positive) folk dance experiences.
	Use map or globe to show place of the dance's origin.
	Share information about the dance or that culture's dance customs.

Link dance name or motions to characteristics of the culture. For example, the dance "Mayim" means water in Hebrew. This is a particularly meaningful concept in arid Israel.

Explain customary singing or shouting.

Display a poster that gives the name of the dance and an outline of its movement pattern. If possible, display a poster or posters showing dance positions.

Play music and demonstrate dance. (Optional: Teach a small group the dance in advance so that they can help demonstrate.)

Teach the dance in sections.

Stand with your back to the class. Children can mimic motions of your feet more easily this way than if you are facing them.

Repeat each section several times before moving on.

Encourage children who have caught on to help those who have not.

Tell children to relax; it is not imperative to get every motion exactly right.

Walk through entire dance without music. Repeat at tempo.

Dance with music. Help children by counting and summarizing the motions out loud. Signal important position changes.

End dance with a bow, curtsy, or clapping — as appropriate.

Summary: Ask children what impressions of this culture they have formed as a result of this activity and what inferences they can make about this culture.

Follow-Up: Teach other folk dances. Occasionally, repeat dances previously learned.

Materials and Resources: Records: "Folk Dancing," HLP 4027, Hoctor Records
　　　　　　 "American Indian Dances," Folkway 6510

Books: *International Folk Dancing U.S.A.*, Betty Casey
　　　　Folk Dance, Lois Ellfeldt
　　　　Dance a While, Jane A. Harris, Anne Pittman, and Marlys S. Waller
　　　　The Dance of Africa, L. Warren

Record or tape player

Volunteer adult to fill out a dance formation requiring an odd or even number

A room with ample space

Mainstreaming and Bilingual Considerations: Folk dancing is a medium for learning that does not require reading or writing. Bilingual children or children with language handicaps should not be frustrated by this lesson. Though oral instructions are used, children can also learn the dance by imitating the teacher's motions.

Creating. Social studies topics provide many opportunities for the child to create musically. This can be done on an individual basis or as a class project and can be used with almost any topic by any age group. Perhaps it is not used more frequently by teachers because they feel that a considerable amount of technical knowledge of music is necessary. The need for the technical skills of music is greatly overestimated, but if the teacher feels insecure, there will ordinarily be someone available who does have such skills and can be of assistance. This person might be a music supervisor or teacher, the high school music director, another classroom teacher, or a parent volunteer.

In its simplest form, creative music is a melody or sounds children learn to associate with the topic being studied. For example, the children may make sounds that remind them of a factory, a circus, or a train. Later these sounds can be used in the development of an actual melody. Children commonly produce creative verse to which they may add an appropriate melody. In the middle and upper grades such creative music activities may include the development of words and music for pageants, plays, puppet shows, or simple musicals. These original numbers are frequently of good quality musically and are favorites of the children for years afterward — an indication of the satisfying and long-lasting quality of creative music.

Children can also be encouraged to create their own lyrics for melodies with which they are familiar. Such an activity is especially appropriate when the class is preparing an original play or pageant associated with a topic in social studies. Or, children may find the writing of lyrics to be worthwhile simply as a creative experience. Children can be encouraged to develop lyrics that convey a funny message, or that tell a story about the topic (a ballad), or that speak to the qualities of some person or character, or that use language associated with a particular place or historical period, or for other interesting purposes.

Listening.   Although singing, creating, and rhythmic expression involve *performing* or *doing* aspects of music, listening places the child in the role of a consumer of music. This role deserves more attention than is usually given it because it is the type of musical experience that continues throughout life. Long after most persons stop performing musically, they enjoy listening to music. Relating music listening to the affairs of life and living is, therefore, essential.

Listening to music should be an imaginative experience for children. The teacher can help them learn of mood in music and contrast what is bright, happy, and lively with music that is quiet and restful. Through listening the child learns to identify the use of music by different groups throughout the world — it provides for another direct cultural contact with people of many lands. The teacher will have no difficulty obtaining recordings for the purposes described.

EXAMPLES OF MUSIC ACTIVITIES

Primary Grades

During a unit on the children of Mexico, Ms. Juarez shared some of her own ethnic background with her class. She was able to teach them a few simple folk dances and folk songs she had learned as a child in Mexico.

After learning the words to the songs in Spanish, the children asked her to teach them other words and expressions in Spanish. By the end of the year, many children had developed a fair speaking vocabulary of greetings and commonly used expressions in Spanish.

Intermediate Grades

Mr. Cole's fifth-graders were studying the development of the United States. He thought it was important for them to learn how music reflects the mood of the nation at a particular time. He was also able to get examples of popular music from the middle of the nineteenth century to the present time. The lyrics of these songs were analyzed in terms of national events and concerns of the time. Mr. Cole was also able to get recordings of some of these songs and, without telling the class the period from which the song came, asked them to try to determine when the selection was popular.

CREATIVE ART ACTIVITIES

Creative art is widely used in social studies instruction because many topics and activities inspire creative expression. A trip to a farm, airport, zoo, post office, or fire station all give impetus to the desire to create. Observing bulldozers, cranes, demolition crews, as well as going on a hike to a nearby park or stream, are the types of experiences from which come the creative artwork of children. Through an art medium the child may be able to symbolize experiences, express thoughts, or communicate feelings that cannot be done through the use of conventional language. For a young child in the primary grades, a picture or painting is likely to tell a whole story, and all the action is happening in the picture as it is being shared with others. For example, a first-grader's painting may show children playing with a dog while a jet is flying overhead and a police patrol is chasing a speeding motorist. But the action is not stopped at the time the painting was made; it goes on all the time. That is, the children really are playing with the dog, and the airplane is actually flying. Children's artwork tells a story; it can be useful in recording social studies experiences.

Many parallels could be drawn between art experiences and music experiences in social studies. Like music, art provides a cultural link with the many peoples of the world, past and present. It also places the child in the roles of creator and consumer as does music. It deals directly with feelings, emotions, appreciations, and creative abilities of children. In addition to the many desirable outcomes associated with any creative endeavor, creative art experiences have much to offer in stimulating and strengthening learning in the social studies.

The teacher can take advantage of the natural interest that children have in the arts by using art activities to enrich the social studies program. We see here only two examples of the many types of such art activities that can be used in connection with social studies. (Photos by Robb Mitchell and John Ringler, Tacoma School District.)

In the course of the social studies unit, the teacher might use any of the following art activities:

Preparing murals
Free painting
Making illustrations
Weaving
Block printing
Clay modeling
Potato or stick printing
Chalk, charcoal, and
    crayon drawing
Pencil sketching
Making properties for
    plays, pageants
Making puppets and
    marionettes

Poster making
Making models
Making cartoons
Making booklets and books
Crafts related to some
    locality or country
Constructing dioramas to
    illustrate scenes
Planning and preparing
    exhibits
Sewing
Making designs and
    costumes
Wood carving

Soap carving	Toy making
Basket making	Finger painting
Indian beadwork	Indian sand painting

Creative art expression as used in social studies may take two forms. The first of these might be described as *personal* and is performed by the children because it expresses an idea or gives personal satisfaction. Having the experience is its own reward, and the child need not share such a piece of art with anyone although children often want to. Artwork of this type is not evaluated in terms of the product produced but in terms of the satisfactions the experience itself gives the learner. Any of the art mediums can be used for personal expression.

A second type of creative art expression can be thought of as *functional* in that the product is used in connection with some other activity. It might be a mural to be used as the background for a dramatic activity. It might be a model of something that will be used to illustrate an explanation. It could be a visual aid the child plans to use in making a report to the class. In artwork of this type, the representation has to be reasonably accurate and authentic; consequently, the teacher will need to guard against having the children copy exactly the illustrations they find in reference materials.

The poorest of all art experiences are those that are patterned rather than creative. The teacher might, for example, ditto a diagram of a turkey and have children color certain feathers red, others brown, and others black. Children who follow the directions precisely and who can color within the lines are highly rewarded with teacher praise. Then the twenty-five turkeys, all alike, are posted on the bulletin board under the caption "We Do Creative Work." Such conspicuous misuse of art may also take the form of black profiles of Lincoln, hatchets and cherries, covered wagons, or Christmas trees. Teaching of this type tends to depress any creative art ability or interest in art expression that an imaginative child may have, and should be avoided.

EXAMPLES OF CREATIVE ART ACTIVITIES

Primary Grades

Third-graders peeled and dried apples to make apple-head dolls. They added yarn hair and formed bodies of wire. Each doll was dressed to resemble some well-known historical figure.

Intermediate Grades

In a study of India, fourth-graders constructed movable rod puppets. They used the puppets to dramatize folktales from India.

LESSON PLAN 18

Topic:	Sandpaper deserts
Grade:	Four
Time:	Seven class periods
Objectives:	Children will increase their knowledge about deserts.
	Children will enjoy this nonverbal approach to the subject.
Building Interest:	Tell class that they will soon begin illustrating some deserts of the world, using sandpaper as one of their art materials.
	Discuss how sandpaper suggests a desert environment. Elicit ideas such as "Sandpaper reminds me of materials found in deserts — rocks, gravel, and sand. Its colors are common in deserts. It is rough like desert life."
	Ask children to bring in assorted grades of sandpaper.
	Send a group of children to the school library to find and check out resources pertaining to deserts.
	Have another group prepare a display of the resources, adding other desert-related items such as small cacti and toy reptiles or rodents whose natural habitat is the desert.
	Have another group make bulletin board labels for five or six deserts under which the compositions will hang.
Lesson Development:	Preview the reference materials. Ask questions that remind children how to find specific information using book titles, tables of content, indexes, and so on.
	Instructions:
	Choose a desert to illustrate from among those that are given bulletin board labels. Find specific facts about that desert.
	Select a cardboard rectangle for the backing for your composition.
	Cut a piece of newsprint to fit your backing exactly.
	Sketch a desert scene on the newsprint. It must contain accurate information about the chosen desert.
	Make pattern pieces out of the large shapes in the newsprint drawing, for example, sky, mountains, and dunes.
	Paper-clip pattern pieces to sandpaper or colored paper, and cut out shapes. (Cut a bit outside the pattern's edge to allow for errors in cutting.)
	Glue sandpaper or colored paper shapes to the cardboard backing, completely covering the backing.
	Draw the details of the desert when the glue has dried — as you sketched them on the newsprint — using crayons. (Crayons on sandpaper give an unusual color intensity and texture.)
	Hang each composition under the desert name it represents.
Materials:	Resources that include pictures of deserts, sandpaper, cardboard or tagboard rectangles, colored paper, tacky-style craft glue, scissors, plain newsprint, crayons, pencils, world map and globe.
	The Earth and Its People, Macmillan Publishing Company.
Summary:	Have children show location of each desert represented on a world map and a globe. Have them describe the terrain of that desert.
	Use each labeled collection of desert compositions as an art essay about that particular

desert. Ask for volunteers among the artists to "read" each art essay.

Mainstreaming Considerations: The nonverbal mode of art would enable children with limited hearing or other communication skills to participate in this activity. Using sandpaper would allow vision-impaired children to feel the composing process.

DRAMATIC ACTIVITIES

Dramatic representation in any one of its many forms is a popular activity with children — one in which they have all engaged during their early years. What child has not "been" a fire fighter, a cowhand, a jet pilot, or a doctor during the fanciful and imaginative play of early childhood? Dramatic activities have great value in promoting social studies learnings by helping sharpen the child's power of observation; giving purpose to research activities; giving insight into another's feelings; providing experiences in democratic living; helping create and maintain interest, thereby motivating learning; and affording an excellent opportunity for the teacher to observe the behavior of children.

The most structured dramatic activity is the *dramatization,* which requires a script, staging, rehearsal, and an audience. It may be used to show some historical event, to represent the growth of a movement or idea, to represent life in another period, or to demonstrate some problem of living. Children are usually involved in a considerable amount of creative work in productions of this type. They may plan and prepare costumes, do the artwork necessary for staging and properties, plan a program, send invitations, and make all arrangements attendant to the project. This requires that the children do a great deal of planning, working together, evaluating, and participating.

The least structured dramatic activity is the spontaneous acting out or reliving of situations from the child's world. It is called *dramatic play.* As this activity is used in social studies, the term *dramatic play* is an unfortunate one because it suggests entertainment. Perhaps the terms *creative dramatic representation* or *representative living* would describe more accurately what is involved in the activity. When kindergartners and first-graders are playing various roles of mother, father, sister, brother, doctor, and nurse in a corner of the classroom, they are engaging in dramatic play. Free dramatic play is a natural activity for young children, and they participate in it with little or no stimulation from adults. During the periods of free dramatic play, the teacher can learn much about the personalities of individual children — with whom they identify, their attitudes toward others, their willingness to share, and their emotional maturity.

Plays and pageants representing life in other times are perennial favorite activities of children. Preparing the dramatization can provide purposes that children can understand for doing a great deal of information-gathering about the historical period and place being studied. (Photo by Edna Kellman, Seattle Public Schools.)

As children move into the second and third grades, there is less evidence of spontaneous dramatic play. At this stage of growth, dramatic play usually requires more suggestion and stimulation from the teacher and may be used profitably to help the child understand or appreciate some phase of human relationships. These slightly more structured dramatic activities are referred to as *role-playing, sociodrama,* or *creative dramatics.*

Role-playing, sociodrama, or creative dramatics is used to present a specific situation for study and discussion. There is no prepared script, it is unrehearsed, speaking parts are not memorized, and properties, if used at all, are held to a minimum. Some small amount of properties may be used simply to help children remain in role. These activities are used to teach or clarify social values, to focus attention on a central idea, to help children organize ideas, to extend vocabulary, and to gain a greater insight into the problems of others by casting themselves in another's role. Because they portray problems in human relationships, they provide an excellent basis for discussion and evaluation. They should be followed by a discussion of questions of this type: "Which character did you like best? Why?" "Which one did you like least? Why?" "How do you suppose the person *felt?*" "If you had been in the wagon master's place, what would you have done?" "Have you ever known anyone like that?"

This final discussion and analysis requires that the situation be cut before the problem has been solved and before the outcome is a certainty. Otherwise, there would be little room left for thoughtful consideration of the problem.

Closely related to creative dramatics is the use of *reaction stories.* Reaction stories are brief, narrative accounts dealing with human relations that are used to uncover various attitudes and emotions. They may be written by the teacher or may be passages selected from published works. They deal with a variety of topics such as sharing, teasing, responsibility, peer pressures, respect for property, and intercultural relations. The story is read to the children, and they are asked to tell their feelings about characters, situations, what they would do under similar circumstances, what alternatives were available to the characters, and other comparable reactions. This critique is similar to the one held at the conclusion of a creative dramatics activity.

EXAMPLES OF DRAMATIC ACTIVITIES

Primary Grades

Ms. Beatty wanted the children to be able to cope with situations that might arise while they were shopping. She listed situations that could present a problem, such as returning faulty merchandise, knocking over displays, becoming separated from their parent, or inquiring about the location of the restroom. The children added other situations to the list.

Ms. Beatty asked the children to role-play the situations. These were discussed in terms of possible and responsible actions in such situations.

Intermediate Grades

Ms. Hall's class had been doing research on the signers of the Declaration of Independence. Each child had been responsible for finding out about at least one of these historical figures.

Ms. Hall then asked various groups of children to reenact the signing of the document. She encouraged them to react as the person they represented might have done.

The following music and drama activity was planned for the purpose of enhancing children's understanding of the lives of American workers after the Civil War.

LESSON PLAN 19

Topic:	The American worker
Grade:	Five
Time:	Two class periods
Objectives:	To become aware of the lot of America's working people, including types of work, working conditions, and life-styles.
	To develop imagination and creativity.
Preparation:	Select about five American work songs that are available in recorded form and that depict an assortment of types of work.
	Make copies of the lyrics.
Interest Building:	Distribute copies of the lyrics.
	Play each song while the class listens, reads the lyrics, hums along, or joins in on the chorus.
Lesson Development:	Discuss the content of the songs.
	Discover what these songs have in common.
	Determine the kind of work associated with each song.
	Is this type of work still done today? If so, how has it changed? If not, what types of work replace it?
	Identify words or ideas that are out-of-date. Figure out what they mean.
	Discuss subtleties, symbolism, and double entendre. (For example, in the prison work song "Go Down Old Hannah," Hannah is the sun.)
	Look for ideas that may be distorted or exaggerated. Why might this be so?
	Make inferences about the lives of the workers who sang these songs.
	Discuss the mood and tone of each song. What facial expressions or gestures could be used to convey this feeling or manner?
	Consider how the rhythm contributes to the mood of each song.
	Divide the class into groups.
	Assign one of the work songs to each group. Within each group, have children prepare a dramatic interpretation of their song. Give the following suggestions: Use pantomime to tell the song's story or to illustrate the kind of work being done. Maintain rhythm by clapping, stomping, swaying, and so on.
	Allow groups about fifteen minutes preparation time.
	Have each group share their interpretation of a song while the recordings are played again.
Extension:	Have children try their hand at writing words to a song about some type of work or chore that they do.
Summary:	Reflect on the following questions: Is working with or without music more difficult? How does music affect a worker? What modern alternatives are used today in place of work songs? (radio, tape deck, walkman, and so on)
Resources:	Records:"The Hand That Holds the Bread," NW267, New World Records, 1976.
	"American Industrial Ballads," Folkways 5251.
	Folk Music in America, "Songs of Labor and Livelihood," LBC 8, Library of Congress.
	Books: *Songs of Work and Protest,* Edith Fowke, Dover Publications, Inc., 1973.
	Filmstrip: "The Mix At Work"

SIMULATIONS AND INSTRUCTIONAL GAMES

A fifth-grade class was studying the concept of *assembly-line production* in its unit on the growth of industry in the United States. In the discussion, the children contrasted assembly line production with custom-made, individually built products. The class listed the strengths and limitations of each method of production:

Assembly-Line

Strengths	Weaknesses
1. It is faster.	1. Sameness makes for an uninteresting product.
2. Every product is the same.	2. Production can be slipshod because no one person is responsible for it.
3. Can be produced at low cost.	3. The sameness of the work makes for a boring job.
4. Because of low production cost, more people can afford to buy the product.	4. A poor worker or a breakdown can stop the whole production.

Custom Built

1. "One of a kind" product.	1. Products are more expensive.
2. Higher quality because an individual worker is responsible for it.	2. Buyers cannot be sure of the product's quality because each is different.
3. Product can be made to fit the desires of the buyer.	3. Fewer people can afford to buy the product.
4. Work is less boring to the workers.	4. It takes longer for workers to become skillful in doing all the tasks needed to make the product.

The teacher pointed out to the class that each of the items they listed could serve as a hypothesis that they might be able to test. "Is it really true," she asked, "that assembly-line production is faster? Do workers on an assembly-line become bored more quickly than those who make the whole product themselves? Do workers take greater pride in their product if they do it all themselves and sign their name to it? How could we test the truth of the statements?" The teacher and the children decided they could test their hypotheses by using a simple simulation involving the manufacture of envelopes.

The class was divided into two groups: One would be assembly-line workers; the other groups would be custom workers. The teacher provided cardboard templates, or patterns, of an outline of an envelope, scissors, paste, and used ditto paper that would be needed to manufacture envelopes. After the pattern was placed on a piece of paper, its outline could be traced and could then be cut, folded, and pasted to make the finished product. The assembly-line was arranged according to a division of labor as follows:

ASSEMBLY-LINE

Pattern tracer	*Cutters*	*Folders*	*Paster*	*Stacker*
Number of workers: 1	Number of workers: 2	Number of workers: 2	Number of workers: 1	Number of workers: 1
Equipment: pattern pencil paper	Equipment: scissors	Equipment: none	Equipment: paste	Equipment: none

Total workers: 7
Supervisor: 1   SUPERVISOR

The custom workers consisted of seven individuals (the same number as on the assembly-line) and a supervisor. Each of the seven workers had his or her own pattern, paper, pencil, scissors, and paste and was required to do all the steps necessary to make an envelope. These children would be required to put their own name on each envelope they produced and were encouraged to personalize their own product.

CUSTOM CRAFTSPERSONS

Worker 1	Worker 2	Worker 3	Worker 4	Worker 5	Worker 6	Worker 7

Each worker has:
pattern
paper
pencil   SUPERVISOR
scissors
paste

All children in both groups took turns, and all participated in the activity. The supervisor from each group could make changes and substitutions as needed. Three children served as a quality control panel that would accept or reject finished products in terms of quality of workmanship.

When all preparations were completed, the teacher gave the signal to start, and both groups began manufacturing envelopes. After a half hour, the production was stopped, and the debriefing took place. Children were able to test their hypotheses in terms of the data they generated through the simulation.

We have here an example of a simple simulation. It is a strategy designed to reconstruct as closely as possible some of the essential characteristics of the real thing. Simulations and gaming strategies are enthusiastically accepted by those teachers who pursue innovative approaches to social studies teaching. The simulation may be a simple one devised by the teacher, as the one described here, or it may be one of the growing number of commercially prepared simulations and games now available.

The Nature of Simulations and Games

A *game* may be defined as an activity that involves rules, competition, and players who become winners and losers. The outcome of some games depends entirely on chance, as in the case of tossing dice. In other games, the outcome is determined less by chance and more by the decisions made by the players, as in chess or checkers. Most games involve both elements of chance and skill. It is significant that persons who are involved in a game are called "players." This suggests that games are associated with amusement—they are intended to be enjoyed. When games are used for educational purposes, they are often referred to as *instructional games* in order to avoid creating the impression that they are used only for entertainment. For this reason, too, instructional games frequently are called *simulations.* Instructional games tend to minimize chance and enjoyment aspects although most contain some elements of chance and most are enjoyed by the participants.

A simulation gives the illusion of reality but removes most of the elements that are irrelevant and those that would be dangerous to the participants. In the use of simulators in pilot training or driver training, wrong moves by the trainee do not result in disastrous crashes or collisions. Likewise, in educational simulations, errors of judgment or unwise decisions do not produce disastrous social consequences.

Experts do not agree among themselves about the distinction between games and simulations. Not all games are simulations, as, for example, such games as hopscotch, jacks, or jump rope. Similarly, not all simulations are games, as in the case of astronauts working in a simulated weightless environment. However, in education these activities often take on characteristics of both games and simulations. Consequently, they are popularly, although perhaps not altogether precisely, called *simulation games.*

Values of Simulations and Instructional Games

The values of simulations and instructional games for use with elementary and middle school-age children are not firmly established. Research evidence concerning the effects of simulations and games at the elementary and middle school levels is sparse. Nonetheless, the following points seem to be well grounded on the basis of research and practice.

1. Simulations and games are highly motivating. Children enjoy participating in these activities and do so without much urging from the teacher. The fact that learners show increased interest in the subject when they are involved in simulation games is well documented. One can assume that part of this interest is generated by the reality created by the simulation, by the competitive, gaming aspects of it, and by the fact that there are clearly defined goals to be achieved. Because of their motivating power, it is easy to get children involved in simulation games. Even children who are typically on the fringes of most class activities often become enthusiastically engaged in instructional games and simulations. These activities seem to appeal to the natural inclinations of children to be involved in imaginative play, make-believe, and role-playing.

2. Simulations and games have been used successfully for instructional purposes outside of school. They have been used in teaching military operations for many years. They are used in training programs in business and industry, in teaching management skills, in the space program, in medicine, law, political science, and many other fields. Computer science has made it possible to develop these simulations and games at a sophisticated level. Because they have proved their usefulness in instructional settings outside of school, it is fair to assume they would have value for in-school instruction as well.

3. There seems to be evidence that simulations and games are effective in dealing with learner attitudes. Wentworth and Lewis cite several studies that report positive learner response after participating in a simulation or game.[3] Many of these studies have been criticized on technical grounds, making it difficult to generalize their findings. Nevertheless, the impact of games and simulations on learner attitudes is widely reported.

4. There seems to be considerable doubt about the effects of simulations and games on cognitive gain. The research to date does not show that simulations have a clear advantage over other learning resources and procedures in promoting cognitive learning. Perhaps this is because the learners must have the prerequisite skills and must understand the

---

[3] Donald R. Wentworth and Darrell R. Lewis, ''A Review of Research on Instructional Games and Simulations in Social Studies Education,'' *Social Education,* 37 (May 1973), pp. 437–438.

basic concepts before the game is played. That is, the simulation game provides opportunities for the *application of knowledge and skills* rather than breaking new cognitive ground. This might explain, also, why researchers rather consistently report gains in the affective but not the cognitive area.

5. Almost without exception authors and researchers speak to the importance of the postgame or "debriefing" session. It is in these critiques that the major learnings can be identified and discussed. These sessions allow the participants to explore in some detail what choices were available to the players, what decisions were made, and how those decisions contributed to the outcome. In this way, the simulation or game provides the group with a common and shared experience that can be used to extend and enrich learning. From an instructional point of view, the debriefing session must be considered an integral part of the game itself.

Using Commercially Prepared Simulation Games

Presently there are many commercially prepared simulation games available for elementary school use, most being designed for the middle and upper grades. In the January 1980 issue of *Social Education,* Sharon Pray Muir provides an annotated list of eighty-eight simulation games for elementary school social studies.[4] In preparing this list, she made a thorough search of the field and included only those that are appropriate for use in grades K–6 and that deal directly with social studies concepts and processes. The list includes the title, recommended grade levels, amount of time needed to play the game, number of players, and the cost. She also indicates the social science discipline with which the simulation is associated. For example:

Economics IMPORT, grs. 4–5, 2–4 weeks, 18–35 players, $10. Simulates activities of 6 importing firms in various parts of the world. Each firm buys from several countries. To win, a firm must buy 8 products from 3 countries and sell them at a profit. Simile II; SSSS; EMI

Economics/History ROARING CAMP, grs. 4–7, five 10-minute periods, 18–35 players, $10. Players are given a $600 grubstake with which to file a mining claim and try their luck as prospectors. Each person pays $400 for initial tools, supplies, and equipment and $200 a year thereafter to keep him or her going. Chance selection of plots on which to file claims controls those who hit pay dirt and those who "lose their shirts." Simile II; EMI[5]

---

[4] Sharon Pray Muir, "Simulation Games for Elementary Social Studies," *Social Education,* 44 (January 1980), pp. 35–39+.

[5] *Ibid.,* pp. 37, 38.

A teacher may use a simulation game strictly in accordance with the instructions provided or may adapt it to suit local needs, learner abilities and interests, and instructional objectives. The teacher must be thoroughly familiar with the game before introducing it to the class. It is advisable for the teacher to play the game with friends or fellow teachers before using it as an instructional tool.

Computer Simulations

The computer can organize and manipulate data with amazing speed, and therefore it is an ideal tool for use for simulations. Once a simulation has been played, students can formulate their own hypothetical propositions in the form of "What if" questions and have the computer respond to them. This kind of creative question-asking and decision-making is useful in developing thinking skills.

Perhaps the best known of the commercially prepared social studies simulations for the elementary and middle school grades is *The Oregon Trail* developed by the Minnesota Educational Computing Consortium (MECC), 3490 Lexington Avenue North, St. Paul, Minnesota 55126. The story line is that of a wagon train party moving Westward in the 1800s. Along the way the wagon train has to deal with a number of contingencies such as foul weather, sickness, hostile Indians, and dangerous animals. As each is encountered, a decision has to be made, and a poor decision can have disastrous consequences for the entire party. The object is to get the wagon train to Oregon. This is an interesting simulation and one that is well-suited for elementary and middle school children.

A few other commercially prepared simulations that have been used with success in elementary and middle school grades are these: *The Market Place* (grades 3 – 6) produced by MECC; it is designed to develop economic concepts and relationships as the player is placed in the role of an entrepreneur. *President-Elect* (grades 8 and above), produced by Learning Arts, P.O. Box 179, Wichita, Kansas 67201, has to do with variables associated with the election of a president of the United States. *Agent USA*, produced by Scholastic, 730 Broadway, New York, New York 10003, simulates a secret agent traveling around the United States in search of a bomb as students assist in selecting best routes; it is intended to develop map-reading and geography-related skills. *Stock Market* (grades 4 – 6) and *Millionaire, The Stock Market Simulation*, both produced by Learning Arts, are designed to teach principles of the stock market. These examples illustrate the range of subject matter included in a growing list of simulations and games available for social studies education. The National Council for the Social Studies journal, *Social Education*, provides an update on new simulations and other resources for computer applications to social studies.

Preparing Your Own Game

After some knowledge of, and experience with, simulation games, some teachers have been encouraged to prepare their own games with or without a computer. This is a formidable task, and the teacher may wish to collaborate in such an effort with a colleague. Also, children themselves in the middle and upper grades can assist in creating a simulation game. In any case, the teacher may find the following questions to be of help in constructing a simulation game.

1. What instructional purpose is to be served by the game? That is, what objective or objectives are to be achieved through the use of the simulation game?
2. What real-life situations can be used to illustrate or dramatize the objectives? In most cases, this will call for the preparation of a narrative (referred to as a *scenario*) that establishes the situation and makes explicit the problem, conflict, issue, or process to be simulated.
3. What is to be the sequence of events, and how much time will be required or allowed for each?
4. What players will be involved? How many are there to be? How are they to be grouped?
5. What are the specific objectives of individual or group players? How are success or failure experiences to be recognized and recorded? What resources (votes, play money, political support, food, and so forth) will players have for trade-offs and bargaining?
6. How do individuals or groups interact in order to register wins or losses?
7. What is the role of the teacher to be?

SOCIAL PARTICIPATION

The real test of a social studies program comes in the out-of-school lives of children. If the school has provided them with new insights, improved skills, or increased awareness and sensitivity to social affairs, such learning should be apparent in their out-of-school behavior as children and later as adults. The objectives of social studies education, in other words, are tested in the way that learners apply them to social reality in and out of school. In its statement of curriculum guidelines, the National Council for the Social Studies speaks of *social participation* as one of the four essential components of social studies education.[6]

[6] National Council for the Social Studies, "Revision of the Social Studies Curriculum Guidelines," *Social Education*, 43 (April 1979), p. 266. The other three components are *knowledge*, *abilities* (skills), and *valuing*.

What could be a more appropriate experience in social participation than being involved in a ground-breaking ceremony for one's new school? Not all social participation gets as much public attention as this one, but any such involvement in civic affairs can make a valuable contribution to the citizenship education of children. (Photo by Edna Kellman, Seattle Public Schools.)

To be socially active does not mean that young children have to be concerned with the great social issues of our time. But they can and should be involved in experiences that bridge the gap between what is learned in school and the out-of-school world in which they live. They can and should practice skills and apply knowledge that prepares them for intelligent and responsible involvement in social affairs of the society of which they are a part.

Of course, children are not going to be able to be socially active without some help and encouragement from their teacher. The following are a few examples of activities that teachers have used successfully with elementary and middle school-age children.

1. Middle-graders formed a volunteer Good Neighbor Club to help elderly residents in the neighborhood with yard work, errands, and other assistance as needed.
2. A class interviewed parents, school personnel, and adult friends and neighbors to determine the ethnic background of people living in the area. They used the data to prepare an exhibit entitled "Living and Working Together — Our Ethnic Heritages" to be displayed in a local store window. This included maps, photographs, and artifacts secured from the neighborhood.
3. A group organized a food gathering campaign for the Neighbors in Need Program.
4. On a walk around the school neighborhood, a second-grade class noticed that a main sidewalk was so badly damaged that children on their way to and from school had to walk into the street to avoid it. The class wrote a letter to the City Council asking that the sidewalk be repaired. They received a letter from the president of the City Council thanking them for their concern and assuring them that it would be repaired. He also commended them for their display of civic responsibility. The sidewalk was repaired.
5. A group in a rural area organized a "Clean Up Our Hill Saturday," during which time the children picked up litter in the public areas of the neighborhood. They encouraged and assisted adult residents to do the same. Children were able to secure litterbags, decals for trash cans, litterbags for cars, antilitter bumper stickers, and antilitter literature from the local Department of Ecology. These materials were distributed by the children to the local residents.
6. A class developed a working relationship with a nearby retirement home. Residents who were able to were invited and came to school activities. The children also put on programs for the retirees at the home. As the project developed, parents of the children also became involved. Some of the parents invited residents to their homes for dinner and took them to church and for Sunday drives. The senior citizens had skills and hobbies that they shared with the children.
7. Elementary schoolchildren made tray favors for a local convalescent home for each of the major holidays during the school year.
8. Sixth-graders collected and refurbished used toys and donated them to Goodwill Industries for redistribution.
9. Children collected books in the neighborhood for the local library's used-book sale.
10. A class made a survey of their homes to look for safety hazards or fire dangers and corrected them.

11. A social studies class sponsored a bicycle safety program in the school.

12. Upper-graders volunteered to do free baby-sitting for mothers on Election Day.

DISCUSSION QUESTIONS AND SUGGESTED ACTIVITIES

1. Select a unit topic for a grade in which you have a special interest. Suggest ways that the activities discussed in this chapter could be incorporated in such a unit.

2. Criticize or defend the following statement: Social studies for young children should be more activity oriented than subject-matter centered.

3. When you visit an elementary school classroom, observe the type of construction activities underway. Are they accurate and authentic representations? What purposes was the teacher hoping to accomplish through the use of construction?

4. Demonstrate to your peers how you would proceed with a processing activity of some type (i.e., making butter, dipping candles, weaving a basket, and so forth). Indicate the concepts being developed in the activity.

5. Obtain or write an unfinished, open-ended story that could be used as a role-playing activity for children. Put the characters in a social problem situation. What alternatives are open to the major characters in the story?

6. Suggest situations that might be developed into a simulation game. With the help of two or three peers, develop a simple simulation game.

7. Develop plans for a social participation project for a grade of your choice. Have your plans critiqued by your peers.

8. The use of song lyrics was discussed in the text. What possibilities can you suggest for the use of song lyrics in learning about the period in which a song was written?

SELECTED REFERENCES

BLUMENFELD, PHYLLIS C., PAUL R. PINTRICH, JUDITH MEECE, AND KATHLEEN WESSELS. "The Formation and Role of Self-Perceptions of Ability in Elementary Classrooms." *The Elementary School Journal,* 82 (May 1982), pp. 401–420.

CHIODO, JOHN J., AND ROBERT L. KLAUSMEIER. "V.T. — The Extra Step in Classroom Roleplaying." *The Social Studies,* 75 (May–June 1984), pp. 122–123.

CRANE, LOUISE. "African Arts and the Social Studies." *Social Education,* 46 (November–December 1982), pp. 502–507.

CUNNINGHAM, JAMES. "Dancin'!" *Instructor*, 92 (February 1983), pp. 80–84.

DANIELS, ELVA S. "Great American Work Songs." *Instructor*, 92 (March 1983), pp. 55–63.

GRIFFING, PENELOPE. "Encouraging Dramatic Play in Early Childhood." *Young Children*, 38 (January 1983), pp. 13–22.

MUIR, SHARON PRAY. "Simulation Games for Elementary Social Studies." *Social Education*, 44 (January 1980), pp. 35–39.

NELLI, ELIZABETH. "Mirror of a People: Folktales and Social Studies." *Social Education*, 49 (February 1985), pp. 155–158.

RENFRO, NANCY, AND TAMARA HUNT. "Puppet Primer." *Instructor*, 92 (January 1983), pp. 37–42.

SHAFTEL, FANNIE R., AND GEORGE SHAFTEL. *Role Playing in the Classroom*, 2nd ed. Englewood Cliffs, New Jersey: Prentice-Hall, 1982.

SINGER, DOROTHY G., and JEROME L. SINGER. *Make Believe: Games and Activities to Foster Imaginative Play in Young Children*. Glenview, Illinois: Scott Foresman, 1985.

SUNAL, CYNTHIA SZYMANSKI. "Studying Another Culture Through Children's Games." *The Social Studies*, 79 (September/October 1988), pp. 232–238.

SUTRO, EDMUND, and RICHARD E. GROSS. "The Five Senses in Teaching." *The Social Studies*, 74 (May–June 1983), pp. 118–124.

TAUB, K. DEBORAH. "The Endearing, Enduring Folktale." *Instructor*, 94 (November–December 1984), pp. 61–70.

TIMBERLAKE, PAT. "15 Ways to Cultivate Creativity in Your Classroom." *Childhood Education*, 59 (September–October 1982), pp. 19–21.

TURNER, THOMAS N. "'And What Do You Think He Saw?' Using Chain Songs and Rounds." *Social Studies and the Young Learner*, 1 (September–October 1988), pp. 22–24.

WHARTON-BOYD, LINDA F. "The Significance of Black American Children's Singing Games in an Educational Setting." *The Journal of Negro Education*, 52 (Winter 1983), pp. 46–56.

14

Evaluating Achievement in Social Studies

Evaluation is an indispensable part of teaching because (1) it helps clarify objectives for learners — it helps them know what is important to learn; (2) it informs children of their progress or lack of it; (3) it informs learners if and how they are deficient so that they can improve; and (4) it helps the teacher know how well desired objectives have been achieved in order to plan subsequent instruction. Additionally, evaluation is essential in reporting the progress of children to their parents and informing the public about the effectiveness of school programs.

Assessing learning involves comparing outcomes of instruction with the anticipated or stated objectives. For this reason, the statement of objectives has to be done with a degree of precision. Unless we can define what we want children to learn and can devise ways of determining whether or not they have learned it, we really cannot make well-grounded judgments about the effectiveness of the teaching or about the

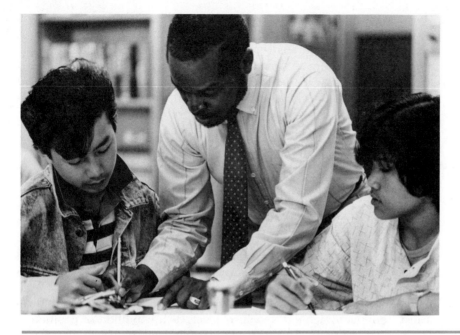

An important teaching skill is the ability to make ongoing informal assessments of the progress of students and to provide needed corrective help on the spot. We see this kind of feedback being given these middle school students by their teacher. (Photo by Kay Engelsen, Tacoma School District.)

extent to which desired learning has occurred. Assessment of achievement, therefore, always involves identifying the objectives that are sought.

Throughout this book the importance of formative evaluation as an essential part of the teaching-learning process has been stressed. Formative evaluation is done at the time the teaching takes place; thus, corrective measures can be taken immediately if children have not learned the desired material. A threefold relationship exists among objectives, teaching procedures, and evaluation; compatibility must be maintained in the relationship. It is inconsistent, for example, to state objectives dealing with the development of thinking skills, cooperative learning, and valuing and at the same time use teaching procedures that are wholly expository and evaluate only subject-matter outcomes with a paper-and-pencil test at the end of the unit. Teaching methods and evaluation procedures must be in harmony with the objectives to be achieved.

It follows logically that if varied outcomes are expected from social studies instruction, a broad basis of evaluation must be used as well. Effective evaluation depends in no small measure on the teacher's ability to select the appropriate means of appraising learner progress in accordance with the established objectives. The teacher should constantly look for evidence of improvement in the child's ability to enter into class discussion, plan, lead, answer questions, assume responsibility, show consideration for others, share, take part in group endeavors, and apply learning to everyday living. The primary goal is continuous progress and improvement in the many dimensions of human relationships for each child.

MINIMUM COMPETENCY TESTING IN THE SOCIAL STUDIES

For several years there has been a growing concern about the level of academic competence of youngsters who have completed school programs. This concern focused initially on the so-called basic skills—meaning reading, writing, and mathematics skills—but has now been extended to other areas of the curriculum, including social studies. In order to ensure that school graduates attain a level of functional competence, states and school districts have instituted testing policies that require students to achieve specified levels as a condition of promotion from one grade to the next or for graduation from high school. It is one form of holding schools accountable for what they do; it is also a measure intended to enhance the quality of education.

Whether it is intended or not, the scores children earn on competency tests reflect on the teacher's competence. Consequently, teachers, quite understandably, focus the greatest intensity of the instructional effort on those subjects and skills that are included in the competency test battery. This is clearly one reason for the diminished attention given to the arts, science, and social studies in recent years. Teachers give the greatest attention to the basic skills and, in some instances, teach directly for the test. Social studies educators, therefore, have argued for the inclusion of social studies on such competency test batteries, for they know that if social studies education is not included, it will suffer from neglect.

Competency tests can be regular standardized tests produced by commercial publishers (standardized tests are discussed later in this chapter), but more often they are tests constructed at the state or local level. Locally produced tests are sometimes hastily prepared and are wanting in technical quality. In the case of social studies, these instruments lean heavily on testing for easily measured outcomes such as social studies information and skills.

Teachers are obliged to familiarize themselves with local policies regarding competency testing and to work within those policies. But competency testing should represent only one part of the program of evaluation that a teacher uses. The day-to-day evaluation of children's work—much of it informal, much of it relying on careful observation, and much of it diagnostic — is essential if the teacher is to assess learner progress and determine whether instruction has been effective. What follows, therefore, is a discussion of evaluative techniques and procedures that can be used to provide a balanced assessment of the attainment of a broad range of outcomes that should characterize social studies instruction.

INFORMAL EVALUATION TECHNIQUES

Much of the evaluation of learning in social studies is done informally by the teacher. Many times each day the teacher observes learners and makes a judgment about the quality of their work. The teacher notices what problems individual children are encountering or what kind of help they need in order to progress. Teachers find themselves spending a considerable amount of time evaluating, diagnosing, and appraising the status of individual children and groups. The teacher then makes decisions concerning what deficiencies are apparent in children's work, whether the instruction is proceeding too rapidly or too slowly, what materials are required, how well concepts have been understood, or how proficient children are in their use of skills. Of course, formal tests have a place in this process, but most of the evaluation a teacher does involves informal methods and observation. This means that careful records must be kept if the progress of each child is to be reported accurately. Some of the more commonly used evaluative techniques and devices are described on the pages that follow.

Group Discussion

Group discussion can be used to appraise the progress of the children in terms of plans and standards that were previously established. Discussion will activate thinking along the lines of self-evaluation; it helps clarify and remind children of learning objectives; it is useful in establishing an attitude of looking forward to progress and successful achievement. It is recommended that the teacher reserve some time near the end of every social studies period for the class to discuss its progress and to make plans for the next day's work. As was noted earlier, this helps children's thinking, helps identify concepts needing further study, and reminds them of the things they are learning in social studies. In addition to the daily discussions of the progress of the class, this technique can also be used in a variety of other situations:

1. As a follow-up of a major class activity such as a field trip, a social action project, a dramatization.
2. As a method of evaluating group reports, unit projects, and creative dramatics activities.
3. As a means of improving small-group endeavors.
4. As a means of evaluating behavior of the class at a school assembly, in the lunchroom, or on the playground.
5. As a method of working out some problem of human relations within the classroom.
6. As a means of bringing to light attitudes that may be held by children.
7. As a means of verifying information obtained through individual study.

The use of discussion as a technique of evaluation necessitates the identification of standards to be attained and a knowledge of what is expected on the part of the learners. This means that in most cases the teacher and the class will have to decide on standards that apply in a given situation. For example, if a class is about to engage in an activity calling for small committees, the following standards may be agreed on:

1. Work quietly, so that others may work too.
2. Know where the materials are.
3. Arrange with other groups to borrow materials.
4. Speak quietly to other committee members.
5. Stop work as soon as the bell rings.
6. Arrange and clean up the area after work.

Specific work standards of the type just described should be posted on a chart and referred to when the work of the class is being evaluated through discussion. Verbal agreement on standards is not sufficient for young children — they forget from day to day just what the standards are. Posting the standards and discussing them without "harping" on them help remind children of their responsibilities and enhance their learning. Knowledge of progress is a strong force in the motivation of learning, and a knowledge of areas in which improvement is needed helps give direction to learning. The use of class discussion as an evaluative technique can serve both of these purposes.

Observation

Observation is among the best techniques the teacher can use in learning about children, appraising their progress, and sensing their needs for improvement. Although all teachers use this method of learner appraisal, not all teachers are skillful in its application. Much of what is called observation might properly be described as an unorganized set of impressions the teacher obtains during the course of instruction, essentially on a catch-as-catch-can basis. The teacher who makes the most of observation knows what he or she is looking for, systematizes observations, and makes an attempt to objectify the information so obtained. To this end it is suggested that the teacher

1. Spell out exactly the traits to be evaluated and state evidences of these traits in terms of child behavior. For example, if the teacher desires to observe whether or not there is evidence of progress in *consideration for others,* such things as the following would be appropriate:

   Does the child

   a. Show respect for the ideas and feelings of classmates?
   b. Abstain from causing disturbances that make it impossible for others to do their best work?
   c. Carry a fair share of the work load in a small group?
   d. Enjoy giving a classmate an "assist" when needed?
   e. Display sensitivity to injustices that may occur in the course of life in and out of the classroom?
   f. Return borrowed materials? Obtain permission to use materials that belong to others?
   g. Observe rules established by the group?
   h. Fulfill responsibilities on time? Avoid doing things that hold up the progress of the class?

2. Select certain children for intensive observation and study rather than observing "in general." This intensive observation might be limited to certain specific situations. For example, just what happens to David when he is placed on a committee to do some project in connection with a social studies unit? How can the situation be changed to help him develop more responsible habits of work in a group situation? The purpose of observations of this type is to gain insight into the child's behavior in the context of a specific set of circumstances.

3. Record observations in writing and do not depend on memory. Keep a written record of information obtained through observation, and maintain this record over a period of time to establish a definite pattern in the child's behavior. At best, observation is a highly unreliable method of evaluating learner progress, and without a record of the observations, it is of little value indeed. The written record may take the form of anecdotal accounts, a checklist, or a rating device. Information of this type is helpful to the teacher in interpreting and reporting the progress of children to their parents.

Checklists

Checklists may be constructed from previously established specific objectives and can be used either by the teacher or by the children themselves in evaluating progress. It is a good practice for classes to work out short checklists cooperatively and apply them to their work individually. The checklists may be used when children are giving reports or short talks to call attention to clarity of speaking, new information presented, use of visual material, extent of preparedness, and other responsibilities of the speaker. A similar checklist can be devised to cover the responsibilities of the audience. An example of a self-evaluation sheet developed by a teacher with a class is reproduced in part in Figure 14.1.

In addition to the checklists developed and used by the children for self-appraisal, the teacher can devise similar checklists for use in recording observations. As previously noted, this procedure adds objectivity and reliability to the teacher's observation. The specific points to be

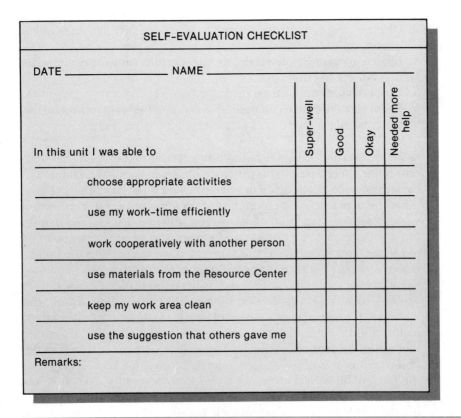

FIGURE 14.1. Student self-evaluation checklist.

checked would be the behavior characteristics that provide evidence either of the presence or absence of the trait under study. Commercially prepared behavior-rating scales may be used for this purpose.

Conferences

Conferences with children should teach them how to evaluate their own work, thereby leading to increased self-direction. The teacher-learner conference can be of help in discovering particular learning problems and difficulties that children may be having, gaining insight into their feelings about schoolwork, and becoming aware of special personal – social problems the children may be having, as well as being a method of assisting every child individually in a personal way. Teachers need to budget their time to allow ten-minute conferences with individual children on a regular basis. Children need the personal contact with their teacher that a conference can give.

A conference will be of little value if the teacher does all the talking and the child all the listening. A friendly, helpful approach is needed, one that results in greater feelings of personal worth on the part of the child along with some constructive and concrete helps for improvement. This close working relationship with children is critical to good education, especially in the social studies.

Anecdotal Records

An *anecdotal record* is a description of some incident or situation in the life of the child. A collection of such descriptions of learner behavior kept over a period of time, therefore, provides the teacher with a documentary account of changes of behavior that have occurred or are in progress. It is another way of systematically recording observations. Anecdotal records should indicate the date and time of the incident, the circumstances under which it occurred, and an objective description of the situation. If an interpretation is made of the incident, it should be kept separate from the description of the actual happening. The following are six entries in one teacher's anecdotal record on a child.

ANECDOTAL RECORD

Sara Larsen

9/24   Difficulty in getting going in independent choice work; ignored all suggestions of
          activities. . . . "It's boring."

9/26   Found a fiction book related to unit for Sara. Read during work time. Took it home today.

9/27   Finished book . . . took suggestion to make a poster showing main characters.

10/1   Asked for time to show class the poster and to tell about the story.

10/2   Showed work. Talented artist. Received lots of compliments/support from class-mates.

10/3   Sara asked for another book; suggested biography to her, plus suggested she do a map showing the area in which the person lived.

Because this is a time-consuming procedure, the teacher will want to limit its use to those particular children who seem to be exhibiting behavior that the teacher believes requires in-depth study.

Work Samples

The practice of saving samples of children's work by the teacher is similar to that of the parent who cuts notches on the inside of a closet door recording the height of a child at various ages. Both the parent and the teacher know that changes are occurring, but, because of their continuous contact with the child on a day-to-day basis, changes are imperceptible. They need, therefore, a specific example of the child's status at one point in time in order to compare it with his or her status at a subsequent time. The greater the time interval between the two samples, the greater should be the evidence of change.

Work samples that are saved for this purpose are usually written material and may include a report, a story, a classroom test, an explanation, a booklet, or a research project. The teacher might also want to save a child's map work, artwork done in connection with the social studies, or a small construction project. The tape recorder can also be used to obtain a sample of the child's oral language. For example, children find it revealing and profitable to hear reports privately that they have made to the class at various times during the school year. The same device can be used by the entire class to evaluate their progress in discussions, dramatizations, and similar speaking situations. Care must be taken, however, to ensure that such procedures do not call attention to speech disorders of specific children.

Samples of the child's work can be useful during parent conferences at the regular reporting periods during the school year. Additionally, some teachers send samples of the child's work home from time to time simply to keep the parents informed of the child's progress in school. To make sure the parent has received the material, teachers may want to use a message sheet that asks the parent to comment, sign, and return to the teacher.

Experience Summaries

Experience summaries are ordinarily constructed cooperatively by the teacher and the class and are used to record and evaluate a single or specific experience. For example, when the group returns from its trip to the airport, the children can summarize some of the important things they have learned as a result of the trip and place these on a chart. The chart may then be used to evaluate the extent to which they found out the things they set out to learn. The following is an example of an experience summary.

What We Learned at the Food Distribution Center:

1. How food is sent to grocery stores.
2. That food we eat comes from all over the world.
3. Certain foods must be kept in temperature-controlled rooms so they do not spoil.
4. It takes many people to handle the food before we see it in our stores.
5. Food is sent by railroad cars, ships, trucks, and sometimes planes before it reaches the store.
6. Grocery stores order the amounts they need each week before it is sent to them.

Diaries and Logs

Diaries and logs are similar to experience summaries except that they are kept on a continuing basis. Each day the class can summarize its progress and record it on a chart or in a notebook. This provides a running account of work in the unit and can be used to review and check on previous plans and decisions as the unit progresses. In the final phases of the unit, the class, by referring to its log, can recall many details of its work that would otherwise be overlooked or forgotten. In the primary grades, the teacher will have to assume much of the responsibility for recording the material to be placed in the log although children can and should assist in deciding *what* is to be recorded. In the middle and upper grades, individual children or committees can assume this responsibility if they are given some help and guidance by the teacher. A form such as the one on page 404 can be used to record diary or log entries.

DIARY/LOG

Date_____   Name_____

Today—

I learned a new fact: _____

I tried something new: _____

I worked with: _____

I was best at: _____

I spent most of my time: _____

TEACHER-MADE TESTS

Classroom tests constructed by the teacher usually are used to evaluate the child's progress in the more tangible information and skill outcomes of social studies instruction. Even though paper-and-pencil tests can be used successfully with primary-grade children, their value increases as the child moves into the middle and upper grades. These tests are of greater value when they test basic understandings, concepts, and knowledge rather than only the facts. Too frequently questions dealing with *who, what, when, where,* and *how many* take precedence over more reflective and penetrating items such as those that call for knowing *why, for what reason,* and *how do we know,* mainly because they are easier to construct. An important requirement of any good test is that it should enhance and encourage desirable study habits. Overemphasis on recall of minutiae and inconsequential details inevitably leads to rote memory of facts without understanding their significance or without relating them to the basic and underlying key ideas. When conventional objective-type test items such as multiple choice, alternate response, completion, recall, and matching are used, their construction should be technically correct. Many of the standard works on measurement and evaluation discuss in detail the advantages and limitations of various objective-type test items and offer suggestions for their construction.[1]

Teacher-made tests are essential in evaluating the children's achievement of social studies skills. Tests designed to measure the child's skill in

[1] See Norman E. Gronlund, *Measurement and Evaluation in Teaching,* 5th ed. (New York: Macmillan Publishing Company, 1985). Chapters 5, 6, and 7 provide excellent practical and technical information regarding the construction of objective test items for teacher-made classroom tests.

using a map—locating places, identifying map symbols, reading the legend, understanding scale, interpreting map data, recognizing landforms—are a necessary part of instruction in the use of maps. An example of this type of teacher-made test appears in Figure 14.6. Similarly, short tests can be designed to evaluate the child's ability to use reference material, to read social studies materials, to understand the vocabulary of social studies, to evaluate news stories, to distinguish between fact and opinion, and other social studies skills. Examples of teacher-made tests are provided on pages 406–414.

In constructing specific items to evaluate certain kinds of learnings, the teacher may find the suggestions of Maxine Dunfee helpful as presented in the Thirty-fifth Yearbook of the National Council for the Social Studies. A few examples of the types of items she suggests are these:

To test for *factual information* —
    Arranging in order the steps in a process
    Matching events with periods of time
    Supplying key words missing in statements of essential facts
    Matching vocabulary and definition
    Placing events or persons on a time line
To test for *understandings* —
    Matching causes and effects
    Supplying a generalization to be drawn from a given set of facts
    Stating the most important ideas learned
    Selecting a conclusion to be drawn from a chart, diagram, or graph
To obtain insights into *attitudes* —
    Responding to statements in terms of strength of belief, feeling, or opinion by indicating degree—always, sometimes, never
    Responding to statements that imply prejudice or lack of prejudice by indicating state of agreement—I agree, I disagree, I am uncertain
    Matching attitudes with likely resultant actions
    Writing endings to stories that describe problem situations
To test for *skills* —
    Interpreting an imaginary map, locating physical and cultural features and answering questions calling for interpretation of information provided
    Supplying a missing step in directions for doing something that involves a skill
    Demonstrating how to conduct a meeting, how to give a good report, and so on
    Using a table of contents or index to locate specified information[2]

---

[2] Maxine Dunfee, "Evaluating Understandings, Attitudes, Skills, and Behaviors in Elementary School Social Studies," *Evaluation in Social Studies,* 35th Yearbook, Chap. 8 (Washington, D.C.: National Council for the Social Studies, 1965), pp. 165–167.

The following are a few examples of teacher-made tests that could be used for evaluating social studies outcomes:

COMPARING HEATING FUELS

This is a test to see how well you can get information from your textbook.

Give each of the four fuels a rating of 1, 2, 3, or 4, with 1 being *best* and 4 being *poorest,* on each of the points listed. Also, write the page or pages of your text on which you found the information.

	Text page	Coal	Gas	Oil	Electricity
1. Availability					
2. Cost					
3. Cleanliness in the home					
4. Effect on environment					
5. Consumer satisfaction					
6. Reliable source					

FIGURE 14.2.

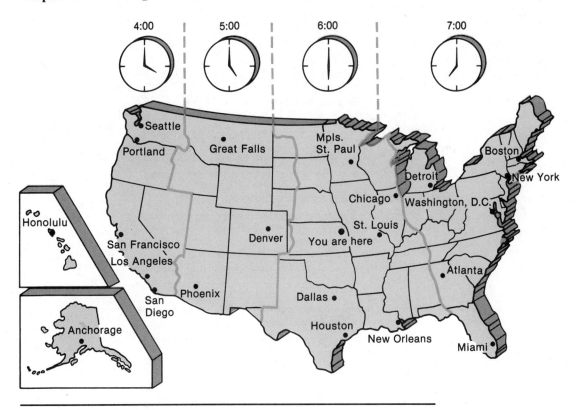

FINDING YOUR WAY AROUND

Use the map above to answer these questions.

1. If you were to go from where you are (on the map) to *Boston,* what direction would you have to travel? _____
2. If you were going to travel from where you are (on the map) to Anchorage, Alaska, what is the *last* city through which you would pass? _____
3. What large city on the map could you get to *only* by boat or airplane? _____
4. If you travel by car from where you are (on the map) to San Diego, through which large city are you likely to pass? _____
5. The map shows Washington and New York. Between those two cities are two other large cities. Place them on the map where they belong and label them. Write their names here. _____
6. You fly from where you are (on the map) to Great Falls. The flight takes exactly one hour. It is six o'clock when you leave. What time is it when you arrive in Great Falls? _____

FIGURE 14.3.

UNDERSTANDING WORD MEANINGS

One example is given for each of the terms listed. Your job is to write down *another* example.

1. Raw material

   Wood is a raw material for making furniture;
   another raw material is _____
   Used in making _____

2. Fuel

   Oil is a fuel used for heating; another fuel is _____
   Used for _____

3. Grain

   Corn is a grain used for feed; another example of a grain is _____
   Used for _____

4. Industry

   Dressmaking is an industry; another example
   of an industry is _____
   that makes _____

5. Natural resource

   Water is a natural resource necessary for life;
   another natural resource is _____
   Used for _____

6. Continent

   Africa is a continent in the Eastern Hemi-
   sphere; another continent in the Eastern
   Hemisphere is _____
   In the Western Hemisphere? _____

7. Manufactured product

   A *typewriter* is a manufactured product used
   for printing; another example of a manufactured product is _____
   Used for _____

FIGURE 14.4.

WHAT'S GOING ON HERE?

Directions: Read each paragraph carefully; then write a sentence telling what the paragraph is describing.

Situation 1. It was the first Tuesday in November. On this day the first station had the United States flag flying just outside the entrance. All day long people were going in and out of the fire station. A sign in the window said "Polling Place."

What was going on at the fire station?

_____

Situation 2. A large number of people are in the room. At the front of the room, sitting behind a large desk up on a platform is a man dressed in a black robe who seems to be in charge of things. As we watch, two men face each other in front of the man in the black robe. One man seems to be holding a Bible. He says to the other man, "Raise your right hand. Do you swear to tell the truth, the whole truth, and nothing but the truth, so help you God?"

What is going on in this room?

_____

Situation 3. A large crowd of people is in a huge room. There are signs and banners all over the place. There is much noise and confusion. People speak to the crowd, but many are not listening. The person who is now speaking has just said, "I yield five minutes to the delegate from the great State of Virginia."

What is going on here?

_____

Situation 4. People are scurrying around all over the place. Everyone seems to be in a hurry. Over the loudspeaker, a voice is saying, "The East Concourse is now open."

Where is all this taking place?

_____

FIGURE 14.5.

USING MAP SYMBOLS AND KNOWING DIRECTIONS

Use the map above to decide the correct answers. Then underline the correct answers.

1. The land north of A is (a swamp), (a desert), (mountainous).
2. The mouth of a river is located near letter (A), (B), (C).
3. The city at D is perhaps a (capital), (seaport), (mining town).
4. The river flows (from southwest to northeast), (from northeast to southwest), (from east to west).
5. An island is marked by the letter (A), (B), (F).
6. A railroad runs between (B and C), (D and B), (D and C).
7. The letter E marks (a bay), (a peninsula), (an island).
8. A peninsula is shown on this map at (B), (G), (C).
9. A delta might be found just north of (C), (A), (B).
10. The letter G is due north of (C), (A), (B).

FIGURE 14.6.

KNOWING THEIR MEANING

Directions: The phrases in the right-hand column explain the words or terms listed in the left-hand column. In the space to the left of each phrase, place the letter of the word or term that matches the description.

a. Blimp
b. Drill
c. Mohair
d. Derrick
e. Raw sugar
f. Helium
g. Gusher
h. Sulfur
i. Refinery
j. Flowing well

_____ 1. An oil well from which the oil shoots high into the air.

_____ 2. A building in which raw materials are changed into finished products.

_____ 3. The brown crystals that form when the juice of sugar cane is boiled and allowed to cool.

_____ 4. The framework that supports the machinery used to drill an oil well.

_____ 5. The tool used to bore holes into the earth.

_____ 6. An airship that floats in the air when filled with a light gas.

_____ 7. Cloth made from goat hair.

_____ 8. A very light gas.

_____ 9. A well from which a steady stream of oil flows without having to be pumped.

_____ 10. A yellow mineral.

FIGURE 14.7.

WHAT DID YOU LIKE BEST?

Directions: In the space to the left of each activity, write a letter "L" if you liked it and a "D" if you did not like it. Place a star (*) next to the two you liked best of all.

_____ 1. Making individual booklets on the unit.

_____ 2. Working in committees.

_____ 3. Dramatizing important events.

_____ 4. Writing summaries.

_____ 5. Doing map work.

_____ 6. Seeing films and filmstrips.

_____ 7. Reading different books.

_____ 8. Collecting pictures.

_____ 9. Taking the field trip.

_____ 10. Hearing the resource people.

_____ 11. Making a mural.

_____ 12. Preparing the exhibit.

_____ 13. Preparing the report.

_____ 14. Doing the simulation.

_____ 15. Working in the learning center.

FIGURE 14.8.

USING THE ENCYCLOPEDIA

Directions: Using the ten-volume *Our Own Encyclopedia* shown in this diagram, select the number of the volume in which you would find information about each of the items listed below. Write the number of the volume you select in the spaces on the left side of the sheet. Then list the volume number of *World Book* in which the same items are found in the spaces on the right side of the sheet.

Our Own   *World Book*

_____   1. Earthquakes in Guatemala   1. _____

_____   2. The French writer Crèvecoeur   2. _____

_____   3. The history of rocketry   3. _____

_____   4. The People's Republic of China   4. _____

_____   5. Russia   5. _____

_____   6. Apple-growing in Washington State   6. _____

_____   7. Jet aircraft   7. _____

_____   8. Countries that are members of the United
                                   Nations   8. _____

_____   9. Unidentified flying objects   9. _____

_____   10. The history of Czechoslovakia   10. _____

FIGURE 14.9.

TRUE OR FALSE

Directions: The following list contains some statements that are true and some that are not true. Read each one and decide whether it is or is not true. If it is true, place a "T" in the space just to the left of the statement. If it is false, place an "F" in the space, and *rewrite* the statement on the line below it to make it true.

_____ 1. Some of the dry land in Arizona and New Mexico is irrigated and produces fine crops.

_____

_____ 2. Colorado and Nevada were settled by people moving east.

_____

_____ 3. The Mormons settled at Great Salt Lake in a region then owned by California.

_____

_____ 4. Gold was discovered in the Comstock Lode in the state of Nevada.

_____

_____ 5. The large area in the Rockies that is lower than the surrounding mountains is called the Continental Divide.

_____

_____ 6. The Indian house used by the Navajos is called a hogan.

_____

_____ 7. The Plains Indians lived in villages called pueblos.

_____

_____ 8. An early mission was established in what is now the state of Arizona by Father Kino.

_____

FIGURE 14.10.

MATCHING CAUSE AND EFFECT

Directions: Each of the events listed in the first column was the cause of an event listed in the second column. In the space provided at the left, place the letter of the result that matches each cause.

_____ 1. Expanding factories needed many workers.

_____ 2. Automobiles were mass-produced at low cost.

_____ 3. Trains and trolleys were built to take people to their jobs.

_____ 4. Workers needed to live close to their jobs.

a. People with average income could buy their own cars.

b. Immigrant workers came in large numbers.

c. Laws were passed to prevent child labor.

d. Workers lived in crowded and congested conditions.

e. People could have their homes farther from where they worked.

FIGURE 14.11.

CHECKLIST FOR DISCUSSION (Middle Grades)	Always	Usually	Seldom	Rarely
1. States problems clearly				
2. Sticks to the point				
3. Shows respect for ideas of others				
4. Contributes regularly				
5. Raises questions on issues				
6. Helps in making decisions				
7. Uses evidence to back up points				
8. Helps in summarizing				

FIGURE 14.12.

CHECKLIST FOR DISCUSSION (Primary Grades)	Always	Sometimes	Not Often
1. Helps make plans			
2. Listens to what is said			
3. Takes turns			
4. Gives own ideas			
5. Considers what others have said			

FIGURE 14.13.

STANDARDIZED TESTS

Standardized tests are helpful in obtaining an objective measure of progress in the nationally recognized knowledge and skill outcomes associated with social studies. They can also be used to establish the achievement status of a class or of individuals. Standardized tests ordinarily do not evaluate many of the affective and social interaction goals of social studies instruction. Standardized tests can, however, make an important contribution to the program of evaluation in social studies.

Standardized tests are called *norm-referenced* tests. That is, a child's performance is evaluated in terms of the performance of a large sample of other children of the same age and grade, that is, the norming population. This is different from *criterion-referenced* tests, in which the child is evaluated in terms of the degree of progress toward the attainment of specific objectives. Criterion-referenced tests often are associated with the "mastery" of certain learnings, meaning that the child continues to work on the material until a certain expected level of competence *(criterion level)* has been achieved. Criterion-referenced tests have gained considerable attention in recent years because of the emphasis on individualized learning and the use of behavioral objectives.

Standardized tests provide the teacher with an objective yardstick to measure progress in learning. Furthermore, the teacher can compare the achievement of the group or of any child with other children of the same age and grade. The chief obstacle to wise use of these tests, however, is that teachers have a tendency to regard the grade norm as a standard that all must achieve if their progress is to be regarded as satisfactory. In other words, teachers believe that all children must attain a grade score on the test equal to their present grade status. *This is an erroneous approach to the use of standardized tests* because the grade norm represents an average performance. For many children this level of achievement expectation will be too low; for others it will be too high. The teacher can reasonably expect the range of achievement of groups in which children have been randomly selected to range from two to four grades below, to two to four grades above the grade norm. This range will be less in the lower grades but becomes wider as the children move into the higher grades. Just what constitutes an adequate and satisfactory performance on the test will depend on individual children. Standards or levels of achievement expectation, therefore, should properly be established in terms of the capabilities of individual children and should not be dictated by the norms of a standardized test.

Knowing the results of a standardized achievement test, the teacher may set limited achievement expectations for a child, thus producing the effect of a self-fulfilling prophecy. There is no way of overcoming this problem entirely except to sensitize teachers to it and to stress the need for data from a variety of sources before making a judgment about an appropriate level of achievement expectation for individual children. Because social studies achievement tests are so closely related to reading ability, the teacher should be especially suspicious of the validity of social studies test scores of children who are poor readers.

Published tests in the social studies differ in the extent to which they emphasize various social studies outcomes. Some are almost entirely subject-matter tests. These tests can be of value only if the content of the test and the content of the social studies curriculum are consistent. The test will lack validity to the extent that it lacks congruity with the curriculum. For example, if the teacher were administering a test that was heavily loaded with items about life in early America, the children would not do well on it unless the material had actually been taught. It would be inconsistent and improper to use such a test if the class had been studying their home state all year. It should be emphasized that decisions on the curriculum content should come first and that the selection of the test should come second although that is often difficult to do. In selecting a test, the person making the selection should ascertain that its content is compatible with the curriculum in the particular school in which it is to be used.

To sidestep the issue of building a social studies test to fit the diverse programs operating throughout the country, some test makers have placed emphasis on *skills* rather than on subject matter. Somewhat the same social studies skills should be developed in the grades irrespective of the topics studied. Children should be learning to read maps, to use basic reference materials, to read social studies material with understanding, and so on. Moreover, many of the subject-matter outcomes tend to be somewhat short-lived because the rate of forgetting factual material is high whereas mastery of the skills tends to be more longlasting. Some teachers believe that standardized tests in the social studies are most useful for the measurement of more permanent learnings such as skills and prefer to evaluate subject-matter outcomes through the use of tests they themselves construct.

The following is a partial list of standardized tests that contain sections dealing with elements of social studies or that are entirely devoted to the measurement of social studies outcomes.

1. Stanford Achievement Test, The Psychological Corporation, 757 Third Avenue, New York, New York 10017.
2. Metropolitan Achievement Tests, The Psychological Corporation, 757 Third Avenue, New York, New York 10017.
3. SRA Achievement Series, Science Research Associates, Inc., 155 North Wacker Drive, Chicago, Illinois 60606.
4. Sequential Tests of Educational Progress: Social Studies, Level 4, Grades 4 – 6, Addison-Wesley Publishing Company, Inc., 2725 Sand Hill Road, Menlo Park, California 94025.

5. Iowa Tests of Basic Skills, Riverside Publishing Company, 1919 South Highland Avenue, Lombard, Illinois 60148.
6. California Achievement Tests, CTB/McGraw-Hill, Del Monte Research Park, Monterey, California 93940.

SOCIAL STUDIES ACHIEVEMENT PROFILE

Child's Name _____ Grade _____ Reporting Period _____ Teacher _____

	Outstanding	Satisfactory	Needs improvement	Does not apply
This profile represents a comprehensive report of this child's achievement in social studies during the reporting period indicated. Teachers may wish to add items in each of the categories under the space labeled "Other." Narrative comments can be made on the reverse side of this sheet.				
Cognitive Gain				
1. Is developing a background of information related to the curriculum content of the grade.				
2. Understands social studies concepts appropriate to age and grade level.				
3. Demonstrates understanding of relationships among ideas such as cause and effect, sequence of events, predicting outcomes.				
4. Uses social studies vocabulary with understanding.				
5. Is able to cite examples of out-of-school applications of ideas studied.				
6. Applies what is learned to new (other similar) situations.				
Other:				
Skill Development				
1. Reads well enough to secure needed information.				
2. Is able to express ideas orally and in writing: Orally In writing				
3. Is able to work independently on study projects, doing assigned work.				
4. Is able to work with others on collaborative assignments and projects as a leader: As a group member				
5. Is able to gain information through attentive listening.				
6. Is able to use references (other than the textbook) to gain needed information.				

	Outstanding	Satisfactory	Needs improvement	Does not apply
7. Is able to read and use maps appropriate to age and grade level.				
8. Is able to arrange information in useable forms: take notes, make an outline, prepare a summary, keep records.				
9. Shows evidence of the ability to do critical thinking and problem solving.				
Other:				
Values and Attitudes				
1. Shows interest in social studies.				
2. Shows respect for the ideas and feelings of others.				
3. Is developing a sensitivity to the rights of others.				
4. Is developing a respect for the ideals, the heritages, and the institutions of this nation.				
5. Is developing a commitment to those common values shared by all Americans: justice, equality, responsibility, rule of law, freedom, diversity, privacy, human dignity.				
6. Is maturing in responsibility for personal behavior through increased self-direction and independence (completion of work on time, conduct in unsupervised situations, punctuality, and so on).				
Other:				
Standardized Test Score Data:				

DISCUSSION QUESTIONS AND SUGGESTED ACTIVITIES

1. Why is evaluation essential to good social studies instruction?

2. Select a unit for a grade of your choice, and write three objectives that would be appropriate for such a unit. Then prepare evaluative devices that could be used to determine how well those objectives have been achieved.

3. Do you think that it is a good idea to evaluate teacher effectiveness by the increase in achievement of children during a year? What do you see as the relationship between teacher effectiveness and learner achievement?

4. The text mentions that a teacher's knowledge of scores on achievement tests may produce the effects of a self-fulfilling prophecy. Explain how this could happen. What other teaching practices in social studies might also result in a self-fulfilling prophecy?

5. Refer to the list of major goals for the social studies on pages 6–8 in Chapter 1. Which goals lend themselves to formal evaluation through paper-and-pencil tests? Which goals require the use of other techniques? Which goals require the evaluator to observe the behavior of the learner on a firsthand basis? Which goals are most frequently evaluated? Why?

6. What advantages and disadvantages can you see in using statewide or even nationwide achievement examinations in social studies?

7. Select a child in a regular classroom, and, with the assistance of the teacher, prepare a social studies achievement profile using the form on pages 417–418 of your text.

8. Secure a basic social studies textbook for a grade in which you have a special interest, and examine the methods of evaluation it suggests and recommends. Do you regard these methods as soundly based? Why or why not? Is there a good balance in emphasis given to the evaluation of knowledge, values and attitudes, and skills objectives?

9. Suggest specific techniques you might use to evaluate each of the following:
   a. Ability to apply knowledge or a skill.
   b. Ability to generalize.
   c. Ability to detect bias in a news story.
   d. Knowing where to look for something in a reference book.
   e. Degree of acceptance of a child by other children in the class.
   f. Ability to detect sex-role or racial stereotyping.

10. What different purposes are served by diagnostic, formative, and summative evaluations?

SELECTED REFERENCES

ANASTASI, ANNE. "Educational Testing." *Psychological Testing*, 5th ed. Chapter 14, pp. 393–430. New York: Macmillan, 1982.

BROPHY, JERE E. "How Teachers Influence What Is Taught and Learned in Classrooms." *The Elementary School Journal*, 83 (September 1982), pp. 1–13.

GRONLUND, NORMAN E. *Measurement and Evaluation in Teaching*, 5th ed. New York: Macmillan, 1985.

HELPURN, MARY A. "Can Schools, Teachers, and Administrators Make a Difference? The Research Evidence." *Democratic Education in Schools and Classrooms*, Mary A. Helpurn, ed. NCSS Bulletin No. 70. Chapter 2. Washington, D.C.: National Council for the Social Studies, 1983.

LARKINS, A. GUY. "Minimum Competency Testing: A Negative View." *The Social Studies*, Howard D. Mehlinger and O. L. Davis, Jr., eds., Chapter 7, NSSE Yearbook 80, Part 2. Chicago: University of Chicago Press, 1981.

MORANTE, EDWARD A., AND ANITA ULESLY. "Assessment of Reasoning Abilities." *Educational Leadership*, 42 (September 1984), pp. 71–74.

NATIONAL COUNCIL FOR THE SOCIAL STUDIES POSITION STATEMENT. "Revision of the NCSS Social Studies Curriculum Guidelines" and "How to Use the Guidelines for Social Studies Needs Assessment." *Social Education*, 43 (April 1979), pp. 261–278.

IV

A Look Ahead

15

Social Studies and the Future: Problems and Prospects

When the public school movement developed momentum in the 1840s, the idea was to educate a citizenry that could meet the challenge of self-government. In order to enhance their economic opportunities, people were at that time moving in large numbers to the big cities and to the open lands of the West. The vastness of the country and the isolation of many areas resulted in regional dialect differences that were creating problems of communication. Communities were becoming more and more heterogeneous with respect to wealth, religion, ethnicity, and national origins. The society needed a "glue" to hold it all together, and reformers of the time saw the common school as just the vehicle to do the job. The term *common school* was used not to mean ordinary, but to mean that it was to be a school for everyone's children. One reformer of the time described *common* as "the air we breathe in common." The schools were to be free, they were to have a common curriculum, and they were to serve all the children of all the people.

The establishment of the free public school system in this country was a clear statement that the nation believed that it could not have a population of uneducated people. That is to say, education of the masses was perceived as a public good. We see many of the same kinds of concerns being expressed today. The National Commission on Excellence in Education proclaimed in 1983 that we were "a nation at risk" because the education that young Americans were receiving was not adequate for the kinds of challenges they would face as citizens in the modern world.[1] What the Commission said — and what several other study groups since then have said — is that a quality education is a requirement of citizenship in America today if the nation is to retain its position of leadership among the nations of the world.

Concerns about deficiencies in education ordinarily focus on basic literacy on the one hand, and on the highly specialized, technical knowledge and skills that are marketplace oriented on the other. But the education of free people for life in a democratic society needs to go far beyond teaching for simple literacy and developing useful job skills. This society places high value on individual decision making, on social participation, on self-determination, and on citizen participation in the determination of public policies. But how can citizens involve themselves in these processes if they are not informed about the issues and have no commitment to the society's values and principles? The question answers itself. It is social studies education that must take seriously the challenge that gave birth to public education in this nation a hundred and fifty years ago: namely, to educate citizens who are willing and able to face up to their responsibilities as a free people. No other area of the school curriculum is as specifically charged with citizenship education as is social studies. Such an education should prepare the student of today to become "an informed person, skilled in the processes of a free society, who is committed to democratic values and is able, and feels obliged to participate in social, political, and economic processes."[2]

We turn our attention now to some of the concerns and issues that seem likely to be on the agenda of those who seek to give direction to social studies education in the next decade and beyond.

DEFINING A "COMMON CORE" FOR SOCIAL STUDIES

The subject matter banquet table of the social studies curriculum is loaded with a myriad of offerings, each more tempting than the next. An entire curriculum could be built around history or any one of the social

---

[1] *A Nation at Risk: The Imperative for Educational Reform.* Report of the National Commission on Excellence in Education (Washington, D.C.: U.S. Department of Education, 1983).

[2] Walter Parker and John Jarolimek, *Citizenship and the Critical Role of the Social Studies,* NCSS Bulletin No. 72. Published jointly by Washington, D.C.: National Council for the Social Studies, and Boulder, Colorado: ERIC Clearinghouse for Social Studies/Social Science Education, Social Science Education Consortium, 1984, p. 6.

sciences. Or, an exciting curriculum could result from a focus on issues and problems that people try to resolve in ordinary living. A good social studies curriculum could be designed around the study of current affairs. And each of these approaches — and still others like them — could result in excellent programs. The question that flows from this is whether or not the young citizens of this nation are well served by such diversity in social studies offerings. Or, should there be some "common learnings" that everyone who goes to school is expected to study and to learn? Is there a "common core" of knowledge and skills for social studies?

During the decade of the 1980s, a great deal has been said about cultural literacy.[3] Developing cultural literacy has to do with identifying and learning a body of essential information needed by an individual to function in a culture. Language would be an obvious and perhaps most important example. But presumably there are other learnings that are a part of the common culture that everyone who is schooled is expected to know. Such common knowledge and skills facilitate communication between and among citizens and would solidify the society around a common body of information and values shared by all. It is argued that this is more important in the United States than in many other countries because of the diversity of cultural legacies from which this nation has derived. Many of these learnings would fall in the social studies curriculum simply because of the nature of the field and its basic concern for citizenship.

Although many may find the idea of a common core of information, values, and skills to be taught to all students mildly attractive, problems arise in identifying the specifics of such a plan. There is little agreement on what items constitute the core learnings needed for cultural literacy, nor even on who should put together such a list. The lists that have been generated by scholars and intellectuals have immediately been painted with the brush of elitism. Other lists, if developed at all, would doubtless not be found acceptable by scholars and intellectuals. The issue continues to be a matter of discussion and controversy by the profession as we enter the last decade of this century.

STUDENT INTEREST IN SOCIAL STUDIES

We know that social studies education is seriously flawed when large numbers of students find it uninteresting or even boring. Lack of student interest has been noted numerous times by observers and researchers. In an article in *Social Education,* Fred M. Newmann discusses this problem

[3] E. D. Hirsch, Jr., *Cultural Literacy: What Every American Needs to Know* (Boston: Houghton-Mifflin Co., 1987); Allan Bloom, *The Closing of the American Mind* (New York: Simon & Schuster, 1987); *Educational Leadership,* 45 (December 1987–January 1988), "Special Feature: Cultural Literacy," pp. 63–77.

as one of "student disengagement," which implies more than simply a lack of interest.[4] It suggests that the student removes herself or himself intellectually and psychologically from what is going on. It is as if the student says — and evidently many do — "I could not care less."

Student interest in social studies seems to follow a declining curve, with the most rapid drop following fourth grade. Children find the activity-oriented social studies program of the primary grades interesting and engaging. It is when social studies begins to be more abstract, more book driven, and less related to the life of the child that the students begin to drop out psychologically. Doubtless the problem could be rectified considerably by more inspired teaching. Nonetheless, the subject matter itself needs to be fashioned in ways that will help students sense its importance. As matters now stand, often the teachers themselves may not be interested in what they are teaching in social studies and are not persuaded that it is important for children to learn it. Consequently, teachers use the flimsiest of excuses to justify using social studies time to teach other subjects and skills. In classrooms where we find children highly motivated and interested in learning social studies, we find teachers who are teaching the subject with genuine enthusiasm. But whatever contributes to it, student disengagement constitutes a serious problem for social studies. It would be nearly impossible to make a case for the importance of social studies education if the students find it dull and lacking in any relevant connection to their lives.

TEACHING CRITICAL THINKING AND OTHER INTELLECTUAL SKILLS

It is safe to say that every significant curriculum document published since 1950 has something to say about the importance of including thinking skills among the major goals to be pursued in social studies education. It is on the basis of developing thinking skills and abilities that any number of innovative programs have been justified, including problem solving, inquiry, concept development, discovery learning, critical thinking, creative thinking, issue analysis, decision making, and others. Many would say that all of this is commendable. What can be more important to democratic citizenship than to teach citizens to be able to think independently?

The teaching of thinking, as well as valuing, is controversial because of what is presumed to be the ultimate source of truth and moral authority. Even though it is undoubtedly true that many — perhaps even most —

---

[4] Fred M. Newmann, "Priorities for the Future: Toward a Common Agenda," *Social Education,* 50 (April/May 1986), pp. 240–250.

public school teachers have deeply held religious convictions themselves, the public school is a secular institution. Thus, the extent to which it can teach that the affairs of human beings are somehow influenced by the hand of God is limited. Schools do not and, by law, must not promote a religious belief system. When schools engage in problem-solving or thinking activities that are based on values such as human dignity and rationality, rather than on mandates from God, they are judged to be promoting a philosophy of *secular humanism.* Certain religious groups have taken schools to task for teaching "the religion of secular humanism," claiming that this is in violation of the First Amendment. School authorities take the position that schools are simply following a well-established system of validating knowledge using the methods of modern-day science.

The procedures used by schools to teach various aspects of thinking are almost always based on an empirical problem-solving model. Although the process did not originate with the prominent American philosopher and educator, John Dewey, he popularized it and brought it to American education through his writing and teaching. This helps explain why critics of the schools even today point to Dewey as the person most responsible for bringing secular humanism to the public schools. It was out of the Dewey book, *How We Think,* that have come the five basic components of problem solving: (1) problem identification; (2) hypothesis formation; (3) data gathering; (4) testing hypotheses in terms of evidence (or data); and (5) drawing conclusions based on evidence.[5] Conclusions based on this scientific problem-solving procedure are accepted tentatively on information available at the time the investigation is made. This leaves the door open to the further refinement of explanations and conclusions — or even different explanations or conclusions — at a later time when more information may become available. This procedure stresses the *probability* of something's being true in terms of evidence rather than being true in the *absolute,* unchanging sense. This means that there are no areas closed to further investigation, obviously a point of conflict with those who embrace other ways of knowing.

Scientific problem-solving procedures are exceedingly powerful weapons in the battle against ignorance. It is no exaggeration to say that knowledge breakthroughs that have made possible modern science, technology, and medicine can be attributed to this system of thinking. But the method has also given rise to some of the most bitter conflicts between schools and parents and communities. Parents object mainly to the questioning of authority and to the idea of the tentativeness of knowledge. To put it simply, some believe that there are at least a few absolute truths that must be accepted as "givens," and that the authority supporting those truths should not be questioned, especially by children. The conflict

[5] John Dewey, *How We Think* (Boston: D. C. Heath and Company, 1933), p. 106.

becomes most severe if parents perceive the school's teaching as jeopardizing the child's belief in God as the ultimate authority.

Teachers cannot ignore the fact that a large segment of our population believes that revealed truth is a legitimate way of knowing — that is, that God revealed truth to human beings either through written accounts (such as the Bible or the Koran) or through holy persons who were especially commissioned to make these truths known to others. It does not matter in the slightest what the teacher's personal views on this matter are; the fact is that seated in the public school classrooms of this nation are hundreds of thousands, perhaps millions, of children who, to some extent, are taught the validity of revealed truth, and to fail to take this into account in school instruction is a mistake.

Where, then, does this leave the teacher who is serious about wanting to teach critical thinking and other intellectual skills to students? Does this mean that teaching for independent thinking must be done only passively or clandestinely and that it cannot be pursued affirmatively as an instructional goal? Certainly not; but the teacher needs to know that the matter remains an *issue* in education. This means that it is the context of the local school community that will govern the guidelines to be followed in teaching thinking and problem-solving procedures. The matter will continue to be discussed and debated by professionals and laypersons in the years ahead. Meanwhile, it is the responsibility of public school teachers to help children develop ways of thinking that characterize an educated and thoughtful citizenry. At the same time, teachers must be sensitive to the fact that there is so much about which we know so little; for many people, ways of knowing other than scientific problem solving appear to be more appropriate in dealing with those unknowns. The individual's right to embrace other paths to those unknowns must be respected.

HISTORY IN THE CURRICULUM

Throughout this century, the subject of history has been the jewel in the crown of the social studies curriculum. Indeed, even today to many teachers and parents alike, social studies means history. In spite of the heavy loading of history in the curriculum, the available objective evidence suggests that citizens' knowledge of events that have been significant to this nation's history is so meager as to constitute a national embarrassment.[6] When historians and other aficionadoes of history size up this situation, their prescription for a remedy, not surprisingly, is to include more history in the curriculum.

Adding more history content is not likely to produce the desired result of getting citizens to have a better grasp of historical events. More thought needs to be given to how the historical material is presented to learners, and how its importance is being perceived by them. It is a genuine thrill for students at any age to encounter a teacher who can make history come alive and seem to be more important than anything else one could want to study. But this is an experience that few learners have the good fortune of having. For untold numbers of learners, history has a reputation of being a somewhat less than engaging subject, to say the least.

Some educators have concluded that history loses its appeal to learners because of the superficial coverage of too much material. One of the chief architects of a new California State Framework for History/ Social Science, which focuses on history, thinks that the California program will help overcome some of these problems: "The new plan allows teachers to slow the pace; to introduce the rich literature, art, music, primary documents, and new social history that brings these studies alive for students; and to engage young people in thinking deeply about controversial issues and enduring ethical dilemmas that are relevant to their lives."[7]

The problems surrounding the reexamination of history in the curriculum are not likely to be easily or quickly resolved. We can be sure that the teaching of history will come under close scrutiny in the deliberations of the National Commission on Social Studies named by the National Council for the Social Studies. The National Endowment for the Humanities has funded a Center on the Teaching and Learning of History in Elementary and Secondary Schools, the purpose of which is to develop improved programs for history instruction. Additionally, the Organization of American Historians and the Organization of History Teachers continue to promote improved teaching of history and to work for a more favored place for history in the curriculum.

With increased pressure for more instructional time for history, the attention given other disciplines that have a legitimate claim to time in the social studies curriculum could be reduced. This concerns educators who represent those fields. Today geographers are making a determined effort to promote the teaching of their discipline in schools and are enjoying some success in that effort. Unless something is done to institutionalize economic education and law-related education in the social

---

[6] Arthur N. Applebee, Judith A. Langer, Ina V. S. Mullis, *Literature and U.S. History: The Instructional Experience and Factual Knowledge of High School Juniors.* The Nation's Report Card, Report No. 17-HL-01. Princeton, New Jersey: Educational Test Service, 1987; Lynne V. Cheney, *American Memory: A Report on the Humanities in the Nation's Public Schools* (Washington, D.C.: National Endowment for the Humanities, 1987); Report of the Bradley Commission on History in Schools, Educational Excellence Network, 1112 Sixteenth Street N.W., Suite 500, Washington, D.C. 20036, 1988.

[7] Charlotte Crabtree, quoted in *ASCD UPDATE* 30 (August 1988), Washington, D.C.: Association for Supervision and Curriculum Development, p. 4.

studies curriculum, these subjects are likely to continue to get short shrift. These matters have to do with the scope of the social studies curriculum and with an appropriate balance in the emphasis that is given to the various components, issues that are far from being resolved.

GLOBAL PERSPECTIVES AND GLOBAL EDUCATION

Few dispute that America's children need to know a great deal more about the world and its people than many of them know today. Anecdotal accounts as well as objective test data provide evidence that even knowledge of simple geographic place location is a glaring deficiency of many of our nation's citizens, to say nothing of understanding the cultures of the world's people.[8] Concerns that surround teaching about the world and its people have to do with the way this subject matter is to be incorporated in the social studies curriculum.

The most obvious way to build global perspectives into the curriculum is to broaden what is already included in most programs. This is what was recommended in Chapter 7 of this text. Some believe, however, that such infusion is not effective, and argue for the addition of new courses designed specifically to achieve the goals associated with global education. This idea of a new global studies course or courses is one that has received a great deal of support, and such courses have been growing rapidly in popularity. These new courses in global education, however, have themselves come under fire from critics who view them as a way of promoting one-world government and one-world religion.

The forces propelling global perspectives education are too strong to be slowed appreciably by objectors and detractors. As a nation, we *are* involved internationally in political, economic, and military networks, and that trend is irreversible. Nothing will change our continued expansion into new arenas of international collaboration because those relationships serve the best interests of our nation and our citizens. With ever increasing numbers of people coming to this country both as immigrants and as visitors, and with the vast amount of international travel by Americans for business and pleasure, we are constantly confronting human beings from cultures spread around the entire planet. Immediate images from everywhere — literally — are being piped into the homes of Americans each day. Events are shown on television the instant they oc-

[8] Salvatore J. Natoli, ed., *Strengthening Geography in the Social Studies*, NCSS Bulletin No. 81. (Washington, D.C.: National Council for the Social Studies, 1988.) Preface.

cur, or in some cases (international hijacking, for example), *while* they are happening. Global perspectives education, therefore, is likely to present some of the most exciting potentials for social studies innovation in the years immediately ahead.

RELIGION AND THE SOCIAL STUDIES

''The schools' silence on religion results in failure to tell students the whole story of human civilization,'' says a recent publication of the Association for Supervision and Curriculum Development.[9] In keeping with the mandate of the First Amendment, the schools have been diligent in their effort to maintain a separation of church and state. Some observers believe that schools have been overly zealous in removing religion from the schools. As a result, religion is treated as though it does not exist as an important force in shaping the affairs of human beings and their cultures. The First Amendment prohibition is against teaching doctrinal religious beliefs; it does not disallow the study of religion as a phenomenon of culture.

Studying religion and its impact on the lives of people is likely to become more widespread in the years ahead. Religion has had and continues to have a tremendous impact on history, human affairs, and the humanities. We need go no farther than the daily news to learn about present-day religious conflicts in Northern Ireland and in the Middle East. The challenge to teachers will be to make religion a natural part of the social studies topics studied and to deal with the subject sensitively. This means that teachers will need to become knowledgeable about the various religions of people studied, and how the lives of those people are affected by their religious beliefs. Closer to home, today's teachers will also need to know more about the diverse religions embraced by the families of the children in their classrooms.

ACCOUNTABILITY FOR SOCIAL STUDIES EDUCATION

The present state of the art in accountability seems to be arrested at a level that calls for little more than satisfactory student performance on an objective examination of subject matter and related skills. As long as

[9] *Religion in the Curriculum.* A Report from the ASCD Panel on Religion in the Curriculum. (Alexandria, Virginia: Association for Supervision and Curriculum Development, 1987), p. 27.

testing is the chief instrumentation of accountability, it is important that social studies be included. If it is not tested, social studies will simply be neglected. Perhaps testing is better than nothing at all, but it is a far cry from an accountability for those lofty social studies goals that deal with the development of thinking, problem solving, decision making, working with others, assuming responsibility, and exercising responsible citizenship.

In the years ahead, procedures will need to be developed and put in place that can provide an assessment of everything that the social studies curriculum claims to do. It may be that some of such indicators will need to be ones of long term, because much of what social studies purports to do requires years to bring to fruition. We have, as a matter of fact, some such indicators now, although they are not as precise as we would like them to be. For example, there is no doubt that numerous windows of opportunity have been opened to racial groups, the handicapped, and women in the past thirty years. During the same period, there has developed a vastly more sensitive awareness of the importance of the environment to all forms of life. Today human rights are regarded as vital concerns in international negotiations. Old movies, even the classic "Gone With the Wind," include racial slurs that today are considered objectionable. Racial discrimination *is* less pervasive today than it was in 1963 when the Reverend Dr. Martin Luther King, Jr. riveted the attention of the nation on the freedom march on Washington, D.C., with his "I Have a Dream" speech. Of course, social studies teachers cannot claim entire credit for these changes, because they are a part of the social movements of our time. But one could make a strong case in support of the idea that social studies teachers helped make these changes possible by planting the seeds of needed social reforms in the minds of their former students who are now policy makers in society. Social movements that deal with profound changes require a cross-generational effort. The teacher is, indeed, a "sower of unseen harvests"[10]—ideas that are planted in the minds of today's schoolchildren become actualized in the social changes of the next generation.

Thus, in thinking about accountability, we need to look at longer segments of time than one school year. We might, for example, identify specific variables for study over time such as equality of opportunity, evidence of racial, gender, or age discrimination, social justice, health-care, drug use, child abuse, and educational opportunity and ask whether or not we are better off, as a nation, than we were, say, twenty-five years ago. That is to say, are we making any headway in making this society and this world a better, more humane place for all creatures? Social studies programs and teachers should be concerned about such matters.

[10] H. G. Wells, *Joan and Peter, the Story of an Education* (New York: The Macmillan Company, 1918).

THE REAFFIRMATION OF SOCIAL STUDIES AS THE HALLMARK OF CIVIC EDUCATION

Even though social studies education is facing profoundly complex problems, there are some encouraging signs that indicate that there is a rising tide of interest in and expectations for the field. In the past fifteen years, this nation has celebrated its bicentennial, it has honored the centennial birthdate of the Statue of Liberty, and has paid tribute to that remarkable document of freedom, the U.S. Constitution, on the 200th anniversary of its ratification. All of these events and countless others at the state and local levels throughout the land have stirred the hearts and minds of Americans everywhere. Feelings of patriotism have never been higher in peacetime than they have been in recent years. Conditions have rarely been more favorable to channel these public attitudes toward improved civic education. And social studies education is recognized as the curriculum component most centrally concerned about civic and citizenship education.

In a great many ways, the importance of civic education, meaning particularly social studies education, is being reaffirmed. Americans care deeply about their country and its future. They want schools to have strong offerings in those subjects, skills, and values that will ensure the nation's survival. As the revision of school programs continues, it is the responsibility of social studies professionals to make the case for civic education and to see to it that those subjects that comprise the social studies are given the high priority in the curriculum that they deserve. This is not likely to be accomplished by nationally prominent educators writing reports about educational reform. Rather, it will be done by teachers and educators, in concert with parents, at the local and state levels who care deeply about the students they teach and about the future of this great nation.

The prospects and potentials for social studies in the immediate future are unlimited for the imaginative and ambitious teacher. Global perspectives education, discussed earlier, provides a mother lode of satisfying educational riches waiting to be mined. The use of computers in education, thought to hold such great promise for social studies a decade ago, is begging for creative talent. The role of social studies in helping society come to grips with the great social tragedies of our time—drug abuse, AIDS, and child abuse—has yet to be explored and program models developed. There is still much work to be done in the area of values, character, and moral education. Meanwhile, the Center for Immigration Studies has concluded that the number of legal immigrants coming to this country between 1981 and 1990 will equal or exceed the all-time record of 8.7 million recorded for the decade 1901–1910. Once again the schools are being asked to reach out and help the children of these new arrivals, with names and languages that may sound strange to us, to become a part of this nation of free people. All of these challenges and opportunities, so briefly discussed here, are really invitations to the next generation of teachers and educators to carry forward the work in what Erasmas called "the noblest of occupations."

DISCUSSION QUESTIONS AND SUGGESTED ACTIVITIES

1. What social trends do you see emerging that are likely to have an effect on the social studies programs of the future? How well do you think present-day prospective teachers are being prepared to deal with those changes?

2. What do you see as some of the "new frontiers" in intergroup education in America? How are these likely to affect the social studies curriculum?

3. What do you think of the proposal that every American school child should have a one-month guided field trip *outside* the United States before graduating from high school? How would such an experience affect the teaching of social studies at the elementary and middle school levels?

4. Think about your own K–12 social studies experience as a student in terms of how your teachers handled the role of religion in the lives of people. Would your experience validate the quote on page 431? What are *your* views on how the subject of religion should be included in social studies units?

5. What educational values are sacrificed when a school relies only on knowledge and skills test scores as a system of accountability to the public? Does it follow, therefore, that knowledge and skill test scores are not important? Discuss.

6. It is not uncommon for prospective and beginning teachers to be mildly critical of some of the things they see their older, more experienced teacher-colleagues doing in the classroom. Time passes, and five or ten years later the critics find themselves doing precisely what they were expressing disapproval of as beginning teachers! Why do you think this happens? What forces in the workplace work against change? Can these workplace conditions be modified to encourage more creative, innovative, and inspired teaching?

7. In some communities, resources and professional personnel are plentiful enough to provide parents with some choices for their children. In those instances in which parents have a choice between a highly innovative curriculum and a traditional one, parents in substantial numbers choose the more traditional program. Why do you think this happens?

8. As you think about social studies in the twenty-first century, what are five changes in social studies education you would like to see implemented in the nation's schools? Share these with other members of your class and defend your choices.

SELECTED REFERENCES

BELLAH, ROBERT N., et al. *Habits of the Heart: Individualism and Commitment in American Life*. New York: Harper & Row, 1985.

BUTTS, R. FREEMAN. *The Mortality of Democratic Citizenship: Goals for Civic Education in the Republic's Third Century*. Calabasas, California: Center for Civic Education, 1988.

GUTMANN, AMY. *Democratic Education*. Princeton, New Jersey: Princeton University Press, 1987.

HAYNES, CHARLES C. "Religious Literacy in the Social Studies." *Social Education*, 51 (November–December 1987), pp. 488–490.

KETCHAM, RALPH. *Individualism and Public Life: A Modern Dilemma*. New York: Basil Blackwell, Inc., 1987.

NAISBITT, JOHN. *Megatrends: Ten New Directions Transforming Our Lives*. New York: Warner Books, 1982.

NISBET, ROBERT. *The Present Age: Progress and Anarchy in Modern America*. New York: Harper & Row, 1988.

RASKIN, M. G., AND HERBERT J. BERNSTEIN. *New Ways of Knowing: The Sciences, Society, and Reconstructive Knowledge*. Totowa, New Jersey: Rowman and Littlefield, 1987.

SCHUG, MARK C., ROBERT J. TODD, AND R. BEERY. "Why Kids Don't Like Social Studies." *Social Education*, 48 (May 1984), pp. 382–387.

SNYDER, THOMAS D. "Trends in Education." *Principal*, 67 (September 1987), pp. 23–27.

TUCKER, JAN L. "Social Studies for the 21st Century." *Social Education*, 52 (March 1988), pp. 209–214.

WRONSKI, STANLEY P. "Looking Backward: 2035–1985." *Social Studies and Social Sciences: A Fifty-Year Perspective*. Stanley P. Wronski and Donald H. Bragaw, eds. NCSS Bulletin No. 78. Washington, D.C.: National Council for the Social Studies, 1986, pp. 189–199.

Index